ARCHILAB'S
FUTUREHOUSE

ARCHILAB'S

FUT

RADICAL EXPERIMENTS IN

URE HOUSE

LIVING SPACE

EDITED BY
MARIE-ANGE BRAYER & BÉATRICE SIMONOT

WITH OVER 600 COLOR ILLUSTRATIONS

This book is published in conjunction with the ArchiLab conference that took place in 2001 in Orléans, France. It was sponsored by the city of Orléans and organized by Marie-Ange Brayer and Béatrice Simonot.

Conception: Marie-Ange Brayer and Béatrice Simonot
General coordination: Marie-Ange Brayer and Béatrice Simonot
Contributions: Pierre Chabard, Bénédicte Grosjean, the architects and critics
English translation: Simon Pleasance, Fronza Woods, Charles Penwarden, John
    Tittensor, Gammon Sharpley, Jutta Küster, John O'Toole
Website: Paul Laurent
Graphic design: Laurent Pinon and Sébastien Morel

First published in paperback in the United States of America in 2002 by Thames & Hudson Inc., 500 Fifth Avenue, New York, New York 10110

thamesandhudsonusa.com

Library of Congress Catalog Card Number 2001096318
ISBN 0-500-28357-5

Printed and bound in Italy by Officini Grafiche De Agostini spa

ArchiLab at Orléans

Serge Grouard · *Mayor of Orléans*

Each year in May, the city of Orléans and its inhabitants join together to celebrate an event that occurred 572 years ago, the deliverance of Orléans by Joan of Arc. Yet to think that the men and women of this city are obsessed with the past is a mistake; from a long tradition of vitality, enterprise and focusing on the future, they draw a strength that makes possible all the innovations that their city's continued existence demands.

ArchiLab's international architecture convention is part of that dynamism. The aim of this gathering is to present the most innovative research in the field of architecture, and the theme selected for this year's event, habiter aujourd'hui (living today), is symbolic of that thinking about the future.

For this latest convention, the third in the series, some 90 groups of architects from around the world are presenting their designs. Thus pluralism and creativity come together in Orléans, providing each of us with the tools for reflecting on the evolution of our lifestyles and forms of shelter, the organization of both our private and public space, the links between those two types of space and their impact in their environment. We must commend the curators of this exhibition, Marie-Ange BRAYER and Béatrice SIMONOT, for their ability to bring together for ArchiLab widely varying proposals that are in some cases a prolongation of present reality, at others a break with that reality, although they are always focused on the inhabitant and his or her priorities, imagined or real, present or to come.

The desire to centre discussion on the user, that is, the resident, is a necessity, just as it is essential to place ourselves in a historical, cultural and aesthetic perspective that respects accumulated wisdom. That desire can be seen in its anchoring in local reality. Orléans, a historic city, is by no means devoid of contemporary architectural creations punctuating its urban fabric. It was logical therefore that numerous cultural institutions should be a part of this event. They include the Fonds Régional d'Art Contemporain (FRAC), whose contribution has been remarkable, the Médiathèque, the Musée des Beaux-Arts, the Institut d'Arts Visuels of Orléans, the Association des Amis des Musées, and many others.

I would also like to thank our partners, who have contributed to the quality of this event each in his or her own way: the Minister of Culture and Communication, the Région Centre and the General Council of Loiret, not forgetting those who have been preparing this event for months and notably the architects who will be in the city during May and June.

Finally, if I may express a personal wish, I hope that these periodic architectural events serve as an occasion for my fellow citizens not only to come and discover the creativity of professionals in this discipline, taking pride in the fact that they choose to express their ideas here in Orléans, but also to make this reflection on the development of their architectural environment their own. ●

contents

ARCHITECTS' PROJECTS

essays

Strategies and Tactics

Béatrice Simonot

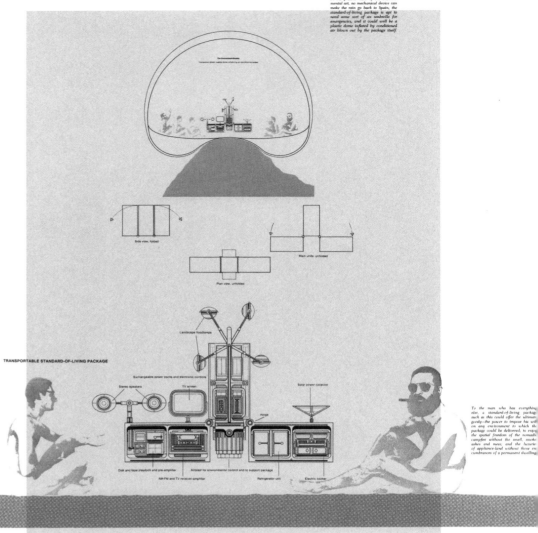

In the present state of the environmental art, no mechanical device can make the rain go back to Spain, the standard-of-living package is apt to need some sort of an umbrella for emergencies, and it could well be a plastic dome inflated by conditioned air blown out by the package itself.

TRANSPORTABLE STANDARD-OF-LIVING PACKAGE

To the man who has everything else, a standard-of-living package such as this could offer the ultimate goody—the power to impose his will on any environment to which the package could be delivered; to enjoy the spatial freedom of the nomadic campfire without the smell, smoke, ashes and mess; and the luxuries of appliance-land without those encumbrances of a permanent dwelling.

'**A** home is not a house', Reyner Banham and François Dallegret declared in 1965. And this is a stance that many a member of the present-day generation of architects has espoused. These days, we might also put it like this: home is not household, as a social group and something to be perpetuated; home is not an abode. Sedentariness and rootedness are linked with a conservative view of the world that doesn't encompass changes at work – economic and social changes, not to say the dissolution of what is called the household unit. The home is a place of strategic application in the formulation of positions with regard to problems connected with the effects of globalization. A source of democracy and a chance to open the world up to a community broadened by many different identities for some, a loss of identity and a sense of powerlessness for others, such are the political and cultural consequences resulting from this new context, which architects have to take into consideration when they construct their position vis-à-vis a new reality. Global, local and glocal are concepts that objectivize the real – at the heart of their thinking, for some, and carriers of linguistic restrictions for others. All are nevertheless agreed that the area of their activities has changed. Globalization, which we might define as the

archi media, 'i-house', 2000

François Dallegret, 'Un-house: Transportable Standard-of-Living Package/ The Environment-Bubble', 1965. One of six designs realized for Reyner Banham's essay 'A Home Is Not a House', Art in America, April 1965; Indian ink on translucid film and gelatine on transparent acetate, 76 x 76 cm.

outcome of a globalized economy giving rise to a globalization of consumerism, as a network economy embracing the dimensions of the virtual and the instant linked to the communications technology revolution, and as a market-driven system, has become the framework within which the definition of their role has to be defined. The traditional attitude, the one generally expected of architects, involves playing the part of manager, bringing order to social space. Where do architects stand in relation to the new context facing them? Is it still possible to claim that you are fashioning the world? What critical positions, what hypotheses and what action strategies are to be formulated in a system that overturns the landmarks of space and time produced by their logic of intervention? Between wanting to alter situations, to express a manifesto that tries to introduce change, and accepting the reality of the context as it is, even if at times working into it values which set up inquiry,

Santiago Cirugeda Parejo, 'The Mutant (and Silent)' Architecture, 2000

architects establish strategic patterns of behaviour. Sometimes conflicting in their wording, from resistance to pragmatism, they have less to do with form than with what we might call the flipside of form. An approach is established that includes interlocutors in the production process and involves those for whom the process is destined in the installation of form.

Refusal of the precondition of form, style, signature and expression in favour of the process of forming and constructing a situation.

Refusal of control in favour of an experience of indefiniteness and chance.

Refusal of order and the permanence of inclusion in space in favour of fragmentation, potential and communication.

Practices strive for blurredness, a diversion of procedures and tools. We are witnessing a shift of skills. Know-how and constructive habits are being challenged. Reprogramming strategies resulting from day-to-day reality take into account uses, and the way they are overlaid, to the point of proposing an architecture that has the value of make-believe and anticipation. Because the home is involved, the individual, or rather the possibilities of individualization, are overtaking 'the user', an individual included within a collective fate. Rationality is replacing desire.

Resistance, but not the grand utopia that might transform the world; bits and pieces of utopia taking different paths based on the realities encountered, micro-political interventions. No utopia and no avant-garde in search of progress, but experiments that sometimes talk in terms of innovation and, where architects are concerned, attest to their relationship to the world and the bonds they are trying to forge with a society made up of multifaceted identities.

A certain realism that means that one starts out from facts, restrictions and contradictions, from which they derive the very essence of their project.

On the basis of these strategies, tactics, which are in no way dogmatic, are introduced, connected with the different situations of dwelling. These tactics, which can be understood through the proposals formulated, sometimes have nothing innovative in what they say. The difference lies in their meaning.

Individualization is a recurrent theme, especially when projects have to do with collective housing. It's one of the tactics put forward to reply to standardization. Individualization doesn't necessarily refer to individualism, but rather to the possibility of producing an

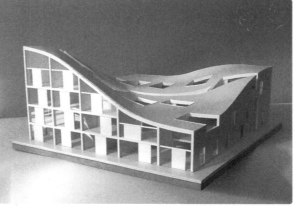

NL Architects, 'Het Funen', 2000

Kalhöfer-Korschildgen, 'do-it-yourself', 1997

identity-related space for all. This desire may even extend to a reconsideration of the boundaries between public place and private space. This is the case with Bornéo-Sporenburg, a West 8 project in Amsterdam, or the housing units designed by Périphériques in Paris (36 housing units in 5 houses).

How is it possible to avoid the proliferation of individual areas that gobble up land, and at the same time retain a certain 'unity' in terms of development (MVRDV)? How is it possible to take into account the heterogeneity of groups of people and the diversity of appropriation methods in high-density places, and deal with a wide range of functions likely to permit, not to say generate, other ways of living and working (Coop Himmelb(l)au, Kengo Kuma)?

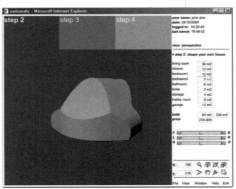

oosterhuis.nl, 'Variomatic house', 2000

Kyong Park, 'Architecture of Resistance', Detroit, 2000

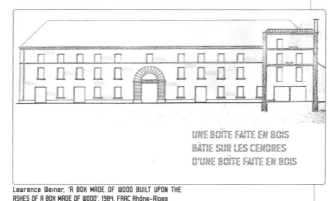

UNE BOÎTE FAITE EN BOIS
BÂTIE SUR LES CENDRES
D'UNE BOÎTE FAITE EN BOIS

Lawrence Weiner, 'A BOX MADE OF WOOD BUILT UPON THE
ASHES OF A BOX MADE OF WOOD', 1984, FRAC Rhône-Alpes

Different lifestyles have emerged, linked with changing living conditions. Taking into account these new lifestyles, which are no longer known as 'ways of life' to indicate that they cannot be reduced to mere ideas of functions or even uses, proceeds by way of reprogramming tactics. People are no longer trying to transmit values through an organization of space complying with implicit living standards (archi media); on the contrary, people are trying to take into account the day-to-day reality around them by coming up with arrangements that meet present-day needs and possible developments. Some are even complying with a declared, nomadic, deterritorialized lifestyle, turning the home or dwelling into an extension of the body, an optimized space (awg), which avoids the real landscape and reconstructs another virtual one that can be modulated as required (maO).

A different tactic from the one that revives the idea of presence in the place. Far from the 'incorporation in the site', which had architecture bogged down in sterile conformity, what is involved here is creating the landscape to reweave a strong social bond with the land and with people. Grasping the territory, incorporating the effects of time and turning them into the very substance of form. Architecture turns into landscape and becomes a unifying element between people and nature (Dominique Perrault). It is inner landscape (Actar) and creates another territory or becomes a metaphor in memory of vanished activities (S&A a).

How is it possible to dodge the normalization brought on by the 'standard plan' and put forward a diversity of development capable of meeting individual desires (NL Architects, b & k+, Wolfram Popp)?

The industrialization of building may be applied with this in mind (Diller & Scofidio), as it also may when the tactic envisaged proposes resorting to flexible solutions.

Notions of 'flexibility' and 'elasticity', already in evidence in the architecture of the 1960s in the Netherlands, Sweden and the United States, cropped up in France in the 1970s, encouraged by the administration and the Construction Plan in the name of moral values putting forward 'the primacy of the person, in the sense of the city dweller'. The flexibility being proposed these days no longer resides solely in technical possibilities offering more supple uses, but rather as the idea of an open form that can be seen as such through the ongoing arrangements it proposes (Shigeru Ban). It's the period of DIY (Kalhöfer-Korschildgen); it's also a period ushering in the formulation of unusual forms through the interplay of a combination of modular elements (su11; Jones, Partners) or through a live dialogue between architect and client (oosterhuis.nl) – a 'cooperation [in deed] with users'.

NOX, 'OfftheRoad_5speed', 1999–2000

Open subversion with Kyong Park when he rebuilds a new community in the form of a counter-utopia of the 'American Dream' on the ashes and foundations of the abandoned homes in a Detroit ghetto. A more muffled form of protest is adopted by One Architecture when they suggest, just like large construction companies, that their clients choose a home from a catalogue as a model for an extension of their villa. The one chosen was the Mies van der Rohe Farnsworth House – provocation, manipulation of signs, but respect, nevertheless, for the 'taste' of the occupants. Subverting the regulation context (Jakob & MacFarlane), experimenting with similar forms in contexts where they are accepted as either legal or illegal (Santiago Cirugeda Parejo), inventing solutions that make the notion of ownership null and void (Willy Müller), all represent so many tactical tools involving the installation of contradiction in a rigidified system and running counter to normality.

It's also at times in the actual process of creation that the social bond is sought: homology between the variability of form and the process of formation bound up with new technologies, which introduce an interplay of reciprocity between the dimensions applied and the inhabitant, of which the result cannot be foreseen (NOX); homology between the infiniteness of resulting possibilities and the great variety of social and cultural identities associated with the mixedness of population groups. Developing an architecture of the moment that incorporates the effects of time, which installs movement like a developing organism, an architecture that juggles

Riegler Riewe, photo Bas Princen, 2001

with context and territorial conflict, appropriates the day-to-day to link back up with society (François Roche).

'If architecture is finding a new relevance, it is through its involvement in a new aesthetics, which is social and not formal',[1] writes Mark Goulthorpe (dECOi), who, through open generative processes, seeks a way to find indeterminate 'malleable' products.

The renewal of architectural practices, strategies and tactics in the realm of housing is developing the idea of a collaborative production, between architect and occupant, of the space. Abandonment of the idea of power: the appropriation of situations has replaced the desire to alter the world. The composition of form has made way for the construction of arrangements and devices that include their own transformation, making it possible to develop a new link with the inhabitant. Form has opened up to future needs and future destinations. Once a demiurge, the architect now wants to be the go-between in a new relationship with the world. Permitting anyone and everyone to construct their own space. Attempts to understand appropriation phenomena are being implemented. This is the approach of Riegler Riewe and Bas Princen, when they present their work through photographs that describe places that have been revived by their occupants. The awareness that the behavioural patterns of inhabitants can't be reduced to a mere adaptation to space but that they contain a powerful symbolic component cannot be overlooked. Sociological studies have shown how the patterns of behaviour and perceptions of inhabitants with regard to their housing may be analysed in terms of strategies and tactics[2] relat-

ing back to the idea of different relations to the world linked to living conditions. Strategic differences observed in the organization and equipping (with furniture in particular) of housing, that are usually understood as the expression of tastes, reveal unconscious systems of logic, which define perceptions, representations and behavioural patterns of everyday life.[3] Alongside these strategic behavioural patterns, tactical patterns respond to specific and present situations: the form of housing may be regarded as one of those situations that offer more or less everyone the expression of their social and psychological being. Conceiving the home no longer as a closed form but as an arrangement permitting the contamination of the container by the content and the interaction between production method and product is tantamount to procuring the wherewithal to recognize the home as a symbolic asset, somewhere between use and representation. For the architect, seeing his or her role as that of go-between in a new relationship with the world, the aim of which is not the transmission of a message but rather an opening up towards possibilities and many different meanings, whose variations, depending on the settings and the times, cannot be ignored, should make it possible to avoid the danger of ethnocentricity that inevitably lies in wait for the designer. ●

Notes

[1] Mark Goulthorpe, 'Les cahiers de la recherche architecturale et urbaine', no. 5/6, Editions du Patrimoine, Paris, October 2000

[2] Béatrice Simonot, 'Espace du logement: rapports entre espace réel et espace imaginaire', thesis, Paris Sorbonne, 1981

[3] Didier Faustino's chair that scrapes the parquet floor and thus symbolically destroys form is one particularly persuasive image when you reckon that the choice of furniture and its arrangement are one of the most significant outward signs of the way in which everyone creates his or her space inside the house.

Particularities of the Minimum

Frédéric Migayrou

Martin Heidegger, photo Meller Markovicz, 23 September 1966

We will indeed have to learn how to think about the reality of our ways of dwelling by ridding ourselves once and for all of the standard model of the house. Children's drawings, primitive huts, vernacular constructions, the house would remain the universal iconic referent defining a common way of living in it. Underlying the form, the idea of the shelter, the elementary function of separation, interior, exterior, the house holds inside a more essential value, that of a territorial settlement, of a belonging that defines what is specifically dwelling, that circumscribes its peculiarity and that anchors the values of an individual identity. The house is an object of appropriation, and from behind the commercial act, the purchase of a piece of property, of a personal good, the objective of constructing an identity always emerges. But this obvious anthropological analysis of dwelling barely conceals a general phenomenon of 'de-appropriation' in which the relationship with the ground no longer conditions the forms of dwelling. The extension of networks of exchange, as much economic as transport and communication, has created a territorial unity, physical or virtual, that constitutes a new geographic unity that casts unusable domains and real and symbolic wastelands into indeterminacy. Legal modalities of installation are no longer determined by a relationship with the ground but by an involvement in a tex-

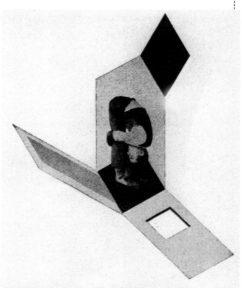

Herbert Bayer, 'Minimum habitation', 1924

ture of exchanges where space has become nothing more than a parameter in a complex cluster of considerations. Beyond natural causes, such as floods and earthquakes, massive population movements have accelerated at the pace of a universal industrialization. Unprecedented urban concentrations, local and fragmented conflicts and more simply the homogenization of transport networks have long established a pervasive vehicular culture.

The secularism of dwelling and the loss of local specificities that the industrialization of housing involves are therefore both the effect of an industrial management of territory and production as well as a necessity resulting from the secularization of thought dating from the 18th century. Autonomy of thought, 'secularism, as the end of metaphysics, or as modernism, is more than a mere dissolutive event in that it includes an aspect of emancipation that finds its full meaning in the extent to which it keeps alive the memory of its origin'.[1] The same movement of 'autonomization' accompanies the deployment of modern architecture; a growing industrialization that will lead, on the one hand, to a standardized architectural style, an 'international' style, as well as to an increased questioning of the very principles of this standardization. Architects will always be torn between a search for optimization of the logic of construction and the search for specificity, defined both by demand and by an assertion of an identity for their language, an identity for architecture. Presenting the advantages of the rationalization of construction, Walter Gropius sought to ascribe importance to the eco-

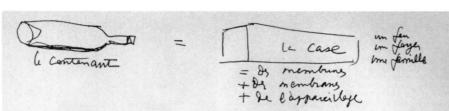

Le Corbusier, drawing designing living space according to the principle of the bottle and the pigeon-hole, 1946

Scheme of cells from the Marseilles housing development, 1947–52, inspired by the Citrohan-type houses

nomics of standardization that permit an adjustment to the needs of each individual through the diversification they offer. 'The repetition of standardized elements and the use of identical materials in different constructions offer the same possibilities of coordinating and moderating the look of our cities as those that result from the "uniformization" of our way of dressing. It authorizes a fortunate architectonic combination of maximum standardization and maximum variety'.[2] The house, having lost its ontological efficiency, which is the simple functional principle of the organization of the minimum dwelling, finds its meaning in modernism's vision as the recurring principle that defines what can still specify architecture as a discipline. The house remains a defining matrix of architectural syntax; it contains not only the idea of an architecture that organizes particularities, the rapport of identity with dwelling, but it also manifests the particularities of architecture. The house as programme bears the formal and legal certification of the unity of architecture, a sort of guarantee whereby architects would confirm the specificity, even the morality, of their language. Stanislas von Moos compares Le Corbusier to a man of the 18th century by recognizing the humanist principle of emancipation that crosses the knowledge of the engineer with the mechanization of the 'machine for living' and the profession of the architect preserving construction as a space for mediation. 'The house has a dual purpose', wrote Le Corbusier in the same vein,[3] but not thinking about the very essence of this ambivalence, not achieving it, not going beyond it, is to remain under the yolk of the identifying principles of rationalism.

Is it necessary to interpret the advent of Enlightenment thinkers as a liberation from the absolutist system of the baroque period? After the closure of the baroque period came an opening that would require man to inhabit the world on his own, a secularism that would fully herald the modern age. Then it would become necessary to abide in the world, and accordingly

to think it, to determine it as an extension, as a whole, and to define therein one's place, one's position. The concept of this infinite opening carried the utopian current of the 18th century, freeing it from classical forms of composition and, in the words of Emil Kaufman, 'establishing a new ideal of configuration according to new forms and patterns'.[4] The foundation of dwelling, of the modern form of dwelling, is thus indissociable from a new autonomy that opens up space as a domain free from any installation, as a domain that imposes wandering and mobility. Therefore, this 18th-century 'Age of Reason architecture' initiates the first questionings about the primitive establishment of human dwellings, the primitive hut, by redefining the notion of installation, while linking it to the form of a space that by its essence generates the notion of mobility. The modern notion of foundation, with the coterie of metaphors it implies when the question of dwelling is broached, remains indissociable from the loss of original roots, loss of a determining rapport with the ground. When Martin Heidegger wonders about the ontology of dwelling, he places it in a mode of disposition, the 'Gestell', the 'quadriparti', which establishes the notion of sojourning among things. This dwelling that must be built and that preserves and surrounds this sojourn must be set up, built. For the image of the house, Heidegger substitutes the construction of a bridge that, in his view, carries a more realistic metaphor of the act of dwelling as passage. 'The bridge brings together the "quadriparti" but it gathers in such a way that it gives it a place. For only what is itself a place (Ort) can provide a place . . . The place did not exist before the bridge . . . Thus, the bridge is not a place in itself but it is only from the bridge that the place originates. The bridge is a thing, it gathers together the "quadriparti", but it

Le Corbusier, Housing in Marseilles, a normalized and standardized cell, 1947–52

does so in such a way as to give it a "lieu"'.[5]

Behind this affirmation that a space is determined by a place and that there is no abstract 'space', behind this ontological definition of place, this dwelling and the house, the movement towards 'de-possession' or, more exactly, the

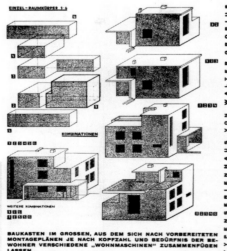

loss of particularities, directly reappears. The metaphor of the bridge, the passage, remained determinant, and Heidegger again sought to ascribe importance to this displacement that enables one to think about dwelling by evoking the housing crisis, a crisis that would not consist of a lack of housing. 'The real housing crisis resides in the fact that mortals are always seeking in the crisis the "being" of the dwelling and that they must first learn how to dwell . . . As soon as man considers pulling up roots, pulling up roots is already no longer a source of misery. Properly considered and well-remembered, it is the only call that invites mortals to dwell'.[6] Beyond the ambiguity of these permanent transfers between the real order and the ontological order, Heideggerian living is anchored in a 'de-appropriation' movement, where space is seen simultaneously as stretched, measured space, whose dimensions define an architectural order and, on the other hand, as spatiality of place, of location, that of sojourning, of 'living in the world'. Thus, according to Heideggerian analysis, there would be two possible architectures: one following the permanent 'de-appropriation' movement would in return define the particularities of dwelling; the other, identifying and conditioned by technology and industrialization, would stay on the surface of reality's objectivity. 'Building places by the gathering of their spaces', the generic construction, the primordial and founding type envisaged by Heidegger remains an allegory of the primitive house, a peasant dwelling in the Black Forest with its deeply overhanging, shingled roof, a house that 'under the same roof prefigured the imprint of the different ages of life'.

The house, an architectural object created almost empirically, is the fruit of traditional craftsmanship. It is likely to let time be as opposed to the permanence and closed presence of the industrial object. According to Heidegger, it alone would be capable of bearing a kind of ontological universality. This proximity claimed in the act of building in turn would pose the question of the beginning at the heart of built architec-

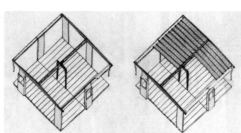

Jean Prouvé, Forms of construction for dwelling types, Montage, Brochure Studal, 1946

ture. The house more than any other architectural programme would elicit the question of a beginning for architecture. It is always the question of law that reappears, whether in the pre-architectural fables of Vitruvius or the empiricism that wrenches man from his animal nature and gathers the domestic space around a fireplace under a thatched cover that gradually moves towards an archetypal house made of stone and wood, or to the classical rationalization of Marc Antoine Laugier who, from the primitive hut, creates the first autonomous syntax for architecture. To circumscribe the origin of dwelling would therefore always be to underline a founding inadequacy, precisely the one that guided Laugier in his quest for syntactical universality, the one that pushed Claude Nicolas Ledoux to initiate forms for houses that broke with the baroque period. When Emil Kaufman linked the destiny of Ledoux with the French Revolution he positioned him as the recognized founder of a modernism that he compared with a similar rupture in the work of Le Corbusier. This process of 'autonomization' of the form defines the two boundaries of an epistemic field of modernism where architecture seems to obey only its own determinations, definitively escaping any exteriority. Emil Kaufman positioned this model of infinite extension in Kantian philosophy, which constructs, for him, this new universal and abstract legality. Beyond a typology of house forms, Ledoux anticipated the beginnings of planning and industrialization. It was thus that Hubert Damisch reframed a certain 'Rousseauism' in Ledoux: 'One will see that Ledoux tackled the question of housing in terms that anticipated the question of the phalanstery, the garden city or the common kitchen block. For all that, Kaufman insists, one cannot see the beginning of mechanized housing'.[7] With this new identity, the house negates its own essence; it gains an unprecedented objective identity. The modern house crosses Laugier's primitive effort, it originates architecture, makes it a discipline of law while negating as a matter of principle the very dynamic of dwelling.

It is this same gesture that produces modernism by stressing again the tension between purity of forms, purism and rejection of ornament, and a message of radi-

Walter Gropius, Types of series houses, 1922

Walter Gropius, Working model for the Waben system, 1922

Walter Gropius, Demonstration model showing the variations possible in the Waben system, Walter Gropius Exhibition, Bauhaus, 1922

cal emancipation, which, by advocating housing for all, develops an unprecedented morality of the body. Hygiene, sport, displacement, relationships with the ground, with light, far from the choreography of Rudolph Laban at Ascona, the modern body became the captive of function, assigned to the universality of a minimum space for a minimum existence. The open space of the open plan, behind the availability offered, springs from the presupposition of limitless 'geometrizing', the establishment of a machine for assigning, for inhabiting, uniting Taylor's universal of production with the logic of consumption and of utility. But dwelling still seems to escape; it flourishes, proliferates, becomes encrusted, disperses and does not respond to sequencing, assembly or regulating plans. It is not a matter of opposing a humanist vision to the standardization of the modernists but of wondering about the latitude taken by an architect like Hugo Häring, who worked with the urban theories of Hilberseimer and Le Corbusier, when he tried to reassert a principle of life vis-à-vis geometric order. There is a metaphysics of modern architecture, which unceasingly questions its foundations, its sources, without ever facing its own essence. Can the architect really imagine dwelling, accept this permanent expropriation that destabilizes the primary architectural fact, the foundation? Between the traditionalist game of the Sommerfeld House (1920–21) by Walter Gropius and the Mausoleum project for Professor Max (1921) by Adolf Loos, it seems as though modern architecture has always had a troubled relationship with the ground, an unacknowledged relation to the matrix, an almost unacceptable defilement because it inexorably carries the sense of destiny, a destination, an 'antinomic' finitude of modern space. The opposition and sense of completeness of the peasant and the engineer fascinated Adolf Loos (*Architecture*, 1910), who always opposed the deep truth of the earth to the superficial existence of cities. 'When, in the course of a stroll through the woods, you come upon a mound 6 feet long and 3 feet wide, in the shape of a bulky pyramid, you are seized by grave thoughts and a voice inside you murmurs: someone is buried here. That is architecture'.[8]

The intimate antinomy of the dwelling would remain unacceptable for the architect because on the one hand it imposes an essential mobility, an establishment where space is never determined; and on the other hand an assignation, an installation, an essential relation to the ground. The modern space of dwelling shows up a contradictory tension between these two poles that the architect seeks to eliminate in order only to allow the continuity of a rational quantifiable and measurable extension to appear. 'The machine has thrown us violently, with a terrible rhythm, into the most intense geometric event ever experienced'.[9] The assertion of a standard house, of a 'type' according to Le Corbusier, is articulated around a flaw where space negates the body, negates this spatial ambivalence of the body, always balancing between permanence and 'becoming', an ambivalence that incarnates the fundamental ability of the body to arrange space. To reside, inhabit, is indeed to build a dimensional order in perpetual change where the house is merely an envelope, an open place for coming together. Conversely, the modern house, the unity of the dwelling, defines a continuous order where the object of the architectural field extends from the household appliance all the way to the interior layout and the urban scale. Le Corbusier achieves the 18th-century universalist dream; he transfigures the progressive vision of the industrial world by erasing in one stroke the residual narrations of a neo-classicism that had pervaded the entire 19th century. As Alberto Sartoris emphasized, this break is not only the advent of a limitless functionalism, but rather an aesthetic change in the act of building. 'The word "functional" was not adopted to exalt a building technique but to define a profession of faith, as much aesthetic as technical. To formulate new concepts, force new materials to bend to irrational forms, functional architecture claims itself as creation'.[10]

Paradoxically, the idea of the 'unity of dwelling' imposes itself through a negation of the objective identity of the dwelling. The aesthetic break emphasized by Alberto Sartoris consists of this change in order whereby technology and industrialization of construction have created an infinite universal syntax in which rationalization allows a general translatability of processes. The apparent form of the construction conceals a set of interchangeable, standardized skills and services. Within the domestic context, the world of objects, the space of the house or

Jean Prouvé, Université de Nancy, Study model for a competition, 1949

Otto Bärtning, Prefabricated house, 1931

Walter Gropius and Konrad Wachsman, 'The package house system', 1942

M. Herlich, Case containing detachable furniture for the Rermo House, 1945

Sanitary section of a prefabricated aluminium house, 1943

the urban field, a continuum without hierarchies of scale has settled in, where standards ensure a general convertibility. The sanitary block, the house, the building, the neighbourhood and the city are no more than conventions of use that still simulate values of the grandeur of a humanism without content. If underlying all the encounters of the Congrès internationaux de l'architecture moderne was a permanent questioning about the dwelling that was then converted into a problematization of housing from *Die Wohnung für das Existenzminimum* (Frankfurt, 1929) to *L'habitation humaine* (Aix en Provence, 1953), this questioning was still according to the universalist credo of an emancipation in which architectural reason was still thought to be capable of dominating political phenomena and the logic of the market. It took the war for architects to begin doubting their position and their ability to influence reality, which was based more on the irrationality of the market than on a reasoned economy of space. The fact that the reconstruction period brought about a significant production of housing naturally achieved the total industrialization of architecture that had been anticipated by the modernists, but also definitively realized its aesthetic and theoretical assumptions. The sloganizing that proclaimed 'housing for all', 'social housing', had definitively sounded the death

knell of a unitary understanding of the house, of a spatial definition of dwelling. Architecture fully found its modern essence, that of a fundamental de-possession leading to an almost desperate quest to belong. The reiterated calls for an appropriation of dwelling, the return to more complex forms of spatial organization with Team X, a call for the participation of residents,[11] a return to vernacular forms, even those of Haussmann, of postmodern urbanism, are just the counterpart of a primordial logic of de-possession resulting from a systematic rationalization of spatial organization.

How have architects of the post-war years been able to indulge in a permanent search for identity while doggedly attempting a re-foundation or a return to hypothetical sources that should have established the legal basis for the discipline's identity? The permanent confusion of thought on dwelling and on a problematization of housing finally led to a rapid marginalization of architects faced with an industrial world little concerned with questions of identity. While architecture had established a new unity of definition of dwelling, notably with the Pavillon de l'esprit nouveau (1925), which was as valid on the syntactic as on the legal level, it remains paradoxical that one might have refused to assume the ontological consequences of such a concept. By linking the name Maison Citrohan to the field of automobile production, Le Corbusier had definitively caused a seminal break in the understanding of dwelling. The house became a true product, an object entirely organized by a system of processes, finite, circumscribed and valued in terms of cost and return on investment. The idea of a minimum dwelling directly corresponds to this translation of minimum living space into terms of economic value. The habitat is designed on the vehicular model; it is no longer defined through territorial settlement. It gains a mobility that fully raises it to the status of product, which flips it into the system of the market economy of consumption, use and wear. Moreover, the concept of 'Existenzminimum' immediately merged the functional habitat with the value of the lifestyle linked to it, thereby sanctioning the illusion of all ontological retreat, all exteriority to rational logic. The box affirms the principle of identity, universally defines the goal of separation where space is divided into so many plans, floors, walls, ceilings, into equivalent functional values, no longer provoking any discontinuity with rational space. A drawing by Herbert Bayer alone compresses this 'foreclusion' of man to a space that, for him, is in essence heterogeneous, the body

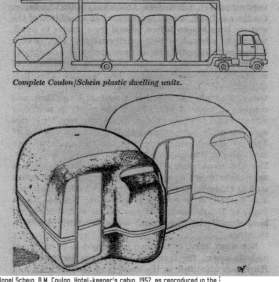

Complete Coulon/Schein plastic dwelling units.

losing all measure, bent into a box, bent to the geometry of an isometric projection (Herbert Bayer, *Minimum Habitat*, 1924).

It is indeed this heterogeneity that constitutes the sub-foundation of modern thought and it remains surprising that architects who claimed themselves to be in the modern tradition might subsequently have

Ionel Schein, R.M. Coulon, Hotel-keeper's cabin, 1957, as reproduced in the article by Reyner Banham, 'Stockating', in *Architectural Review*, January 1960. Drawings, FRAC Centre Collection

changed this logic into an identifying system in which 'geometrism' and measure constitute the autonomous and univalent domain of a new dogma. Whereas a major path had veered towards an in-depth study of the conditions of an industrialization of the habitat, another movement pushed architects to question their syntax, to make the house into an experimental object with manifest virtues, allowing the affirmation of architecture's particularities, a certain truth of architecture. A negative history of the house ought to be written and, by extension a negative history of modernism, a well-known, determinant history that would however appear minor, that of the dissemination of the house. Beyond the industrialization of manufacturing process that pervaded the 19th century, one can list a series of chronological milestones, from the Maison Domino to the Big Box of Bricks by Walter Gropius (1923), from the One Plus Two (1926) of Richard

Neutra all the way to Jean Prouvé. The manufacturing process is substituted for the unity of the constructed object, the object that vanishes behind the serial nature of production. The Wiederaufbau (1945) by Max Bill, who undertook this archaeology in the immediate post-war years, constitutes without a doubt a stage on which modernity comes into its own, shattering the ideology of particularity underlying all ques-

Carl Koch, Hudson Jack, John Callender, Acorn House, 1945

tioning on the dwelling. It would be less a matter of writing the history of mobile architecture[12] than of describing how displacement, mobility, beyond the fascination for the automobile or the aeroplane, gave birth to modernism. The two major critical currents that will attempt a re-foundation, a true new mooring of modern thought, will rely one last time on the theoretical matrix of the house in the 'Five Architects' exposition. Kenneth Frampton and Peter Eisenman undertook this last quest for source; one by a regional re-localization

of architectural vocabulary, the other by seeking to integrate the form of a de-appropriation within syntax after a reading of the Casa Giuliani Frigerio by G. Terragni. Today, the architect has only one way; he must achieve and overwhelm any metaphysics of the house, any residual humanism of dwelling, to the benefit of a genuinely operative practice. The house is nothing more than an avatar of locale; it is only a substratum made of services where duration is all that differentiates it from a hotel-keeper's reception. The notion of 'a-house' put forward by Reyner Banham in 'A home is not a house' takes on its full meaning today. It is a matter of being able at any moment to create environments provided with services necessary to a specific demand, permanently re-convertible environments. 'The functionalist slogan "the house is a machine for living" is not productive because it begins by presupposing the idea of the house'.[13] ●

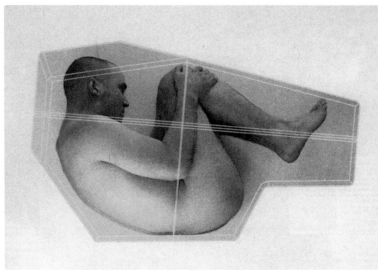

Didier Fiuza Faustino, Body in transit, 2000, MNAM-CCI Collection

Notes

[1] Gianni Vattimo, *La sécularisation de la pensée*, Du Seuil, 1988, p. 12.

[2] Walter Gropius, *The New Architecture and the Bauhaus*, Faber and Faber, p. 40.

[3] Le Corbusier, *Almanach d'architecture Moderne*, Crès, 1926, p. 67.

[4] Emil Kaufman, *L'architecture au siècle des Lumières*, Julliard, 1955, p. 157.

[5] Martin Heidegger, 'Bâtir, Habiter, penser', in *Essais et Conférences*, Gallimard, 1958, p. 182–83.

[6] Martin Heidegger, *ibid*, p. 193.

[7] Hubert Damisch, Preface to : Emil Kaufman, *De Ledoux à Le Corbusier*, L'équerre, 1981, p. 17.

[8] Adolf Loos, *Gesammelte Schriften*, Vienna, 1962, p. 317, quoted by Joseph Ryckwert, *La maison d'Adam au paradis*, Du Seuil, 1976, p. 24.

[9] Le Corbusier, *Une maison, un palais*, Crès, 1929, p. 18.

[10] Alberto Sartoris, 'The authentic dwelling in rational architecture' in *Lotus*, no. 9, February 1975, p. 212.

[11] Until 1980 the theme of participation was to fuel debate on the collective dwelling. Dan Bernfeld, Marja Mayerl, Roland Mayerl, *Architectures et urbanismes participatifs*, CCI, Georges Pompidou Centre, 1980.

[12] See Matthias Ludwig, *Mobile Architektur*, DVA, 1998, and Cherubino Gambardella, *La casa mobile*, Electa Napoli, 1995.

[13] Reyner Banham, 'Stockating', in *Architectural Review*, January 1960, p. 94.

The Diagram Debate, or the Schizoid Architect

Bart Lootsma

Over the past few years, the diagram has occupied an essential place in the debates relating to architectural design. In their introduction to a special issue of the architecture review *OASE* devoted to the diagram[1] Like Bijlsma, Wouter Deen and Udo Garritzman write, 'The diagram is a graphic representation of the evolution of a phenomenon. There are lines, a structure and a form; it works by reduction, abstraction and representation. As a medium, the diagram serves a dual function: it is a form of notation, analytical and reflexive, which sums up; but it is also a model for generative, synthesizing and productive thought.' The way architects make use of the diagram sometimes favours the former role, sometimes the latter. Most often, the diagram constitutes a practical solution that enables one to express simply an overall complexity within the framework of communicating with the client, the members of the firm or the general public. Ideally, the diagram serves as a conceptual tool through which things evolve, eventually reappearing transformed.

It is in the fundamental works of philosophers like Michel Foucault, Félix Guattari and Gilles Deleuze that one should seek the theoretical reason for the use of diagrams in design work in architecture. In the first chapter of *Capital and Schizophrenia*,[2] a text that architects have more or less forgotten or suppressed, Deleuze and Guattari write, 'Capital is indeed the body without organs of the capitalist, or rather of the capitalist being. But as such, it is not only the fluid and petrified substance of money, for it will give to the sterility of money the form whereby money produces money. It produces surplus value, just as the body without organs reproduces itself, puts forth shoots, and branches out to the farthest corners of the universe.' At the time (1972), Deleuze and Guattari could not go too far. At most, they could sketch out a parallel between wishful production and social production: 'the forms of social production, like those of wishful production, involve an unengendered non-productive attitude, an element of antiproduction coupled with the process, a full body that functions as a *socius*. This *socius* may be the body of the earth, that of the tyrant, or capital. This is the body that Marx is referring to when he says that it is not the product of labour, but rather appears as its natural or divine presupposition. In fact, it does not restrict itself merely to opposing productive forces in and of themselves. It falls back on all production, constituting a surface over which the forces and agents of production are distributed, thereby appropriating for itself all surplus production and arrogating to itself both the whole and parts of the process, which now seems to emanate from it as a quasi-cause. Forces and agents come to represent a miraculous form of its own power: it appears to work a miracle on them. In a word, the *socius* as a full body forms a surface where all production is recorded, whereupon the entire process appears to emanate from this recording surface'.[3]

Nowadays, to establish a relationship between wishful and social production no longer poses a problem: the computer takes care of it. As a sophisticated tool, the computer not only influences every particular aspect of social life, but above all it establishes a multitude of new relationships. Everything is in effect converted into a flow of data, an infinite interpolation of 0 and 1, which can be apparently exchanged and manipulated without difficulty. This flow of data has assumed and considerably expanded the role of capital. We live today in a 'space of flows', to borrow Manuel Castells's expression[4] within infinite networks, in which machines, men, desires and merchandise are linked to and converted into one another. It is a space that gives rise to altogether new relationships of power, symbolized by the new financial centres and cities that are springing up at exotic and improbable sites even today, Shenzhen, Singapore, Kuala Lumpur or Hani Rashid's virtual stockmarket. It is a space in which there is not even an immediate link between money and gold reserves. Everything simply merges in a series of metamorphoses whose beginning and end are impossible to situate. It is here that society produces it own delirium: 'Everywhere it is machines, real ones, not figurative ones: machines driving other machines, machines being driven by other machines, with all the necessary couplings and connections.'[5] Nevertheless, this situation does not resemble the stammering 'Society of the And' described by Roemer van Toorn.[6] What energy has not been spent, over the years, so that these couplings and connections take place in fluidity and silence? Since the old telephone exchanges, with their plugs and loud switches, and Hollerith's crackling perforated card machines, to the supple software programs of computers, immense progress has been accomplished. Nowadays everything has become process and the world is adapting. Data are indeed the bodies without organs of the second modernity.

For architecture and the software that has been developed for architectural design, the consequences of this evolution are obviously important. In a text recently published in conjunction with an NAi workshop,[7] Lars Spuybroek (NOX) writes, 'Maya is the most integrative tool available today. Students can combine typical data analysis from programs like Excel (Microsoft Office) with image manipulations from stills or films from Adobe PhotoShop or Premiere and the amazing surface modelling tools in Maya. The drill [that the students were given to do in the course of the workshop] emphasized time-based tools like Inverse Kinematics (skeletons with bones and joints, generally used to animate bodies such as running dinosaurs), Particle Dynamics (generally used to simulate snowstorms, fire and smoke or flocks of birds) and Soft Body Dynamics (used for complex material behaviour like fabric in the wind, rubber or jelly-like geometry interacting with other surfaces or force fields such as gravity, turbulence and vortex). One cannot overestimate the effect of this type of software on the minds of architecture stu-

dents.' Spuybroek is nevertheless one of the few to understand that these effects are 'the effects of machines, not metaphors', as Deleuze and Guattari write. 'An organ-machine is plugged into an energy-source-machine: the one produces a flow that the other interrupts. . . . Hence we are all handymen: each with our little machines. For every organ-machine, an energy-machine: all the time, flows and interruptions. Judge Schreber has sunbeams in his ass. A solar anus. And rest assured that it works: Judge Schreber feels something, produces something and is capable of explaining the process theoretically'.[8] It is in this sense that we can almost consider the famous 'schizo' as the prototype of contemporary architecture.

Yet if we interpret everything in terms of machines and the effects of machines, if everything flows and merges, how are we going to get a grip? Here the diagram plays a fundamental role. Deleuze borrows the concept from Michel Foucault, who employs the word in *Surveiller et punir* (1975) with respect to panopticism. Foucault observed that the panoptical prison had a function that went beyond that of the building itself and the penitentiary institution, exercising an influence over all of society. Stressing the function of these machines, which produced various behaviours, he discovered this coercive action in workshops, barracks, schools and hospitals, all of which are constructions whose form and function were governed by the principle of the panoptical prison. According to Foucault, the diagram 'is a working, abstracted from any obstacle . . . or friction [and which] must be detached from any specific use'.[9] The diagram is a kind of map that merges with the entire social field or, in any case, with a 'particular human multiplicity'. Deleuze thus describes the diagram as an abstract machine. 'It is defined by its informal functions and matter and in terms of form makes no distinction between content and expression, a discursive formation and a non-discursive formation. It is a machine that is almost blind and mute, even though it makes others see and speak'.[10]

Little wonder then if diagrams have over the past few years achieved an increasingly important place in architecture and town-planning debates, for these disciplines themselves have taken on more and more the appearance of a process and the (built) results influence processes. This evolution is also fostered by the fact that, in Foucault's work, the diagram presents a very clear architectural and machine-like dimension from the outset.

The analyses of the Downtown Athletic Club that Rem Koolhaas puts forward in *Delirious New York*,[11] as well as his examination of Arnhem's panoptical prison, appear to be directly inspired by Foucault.

Naturally, most architects make use of diagrams in order to obtain exactly the opposite effect of Foucault's panopticon, or the 'striated' space that Deleuze and Guattari describe in *Mille Plateaux*[12] as 'the space instituted by the state apparatus'. The two philosophers contrast that space with the nomadic, smooth space that should offer greater liberty to those living in or using it. In recent years, then, architects have used all available means to render the space of their buildings and towns as 'smooth' as possible, or at least to suggest that. The building is nothing more than a space that develops in a continuous, folding slope and which ideally is seamlessly joined to the ground. If the OMA design for the Villette park is the oldest and still the most visible example of this idea, the Jussieu library and the open floor in OMA villas, which organizes the space between the various individual living rooms, also enter this category because they impose no particular behaviour on the inhabitants. Here the rolling floor is a significant ornament, a form of architectural metaphor, a part for the whole.

Of course, it remains to be determined whether the freedom that architects imagine they are offering with this concept is a genuine freedom. In his preface to the English translation of his study *La Prise de la Concorde*,[13] Denis Hollier points out, in reaction to the theories of Bernard Tschumi and Jacques Derrida, that the liberty in question is a fictive one, because architectural spaces are, by definition, a part of the social system. The earliest texts by Tschumi were partly based on Hollier's work. To avoid any misunderstanding, the English translation is therefore entitled *Against Architecture*. Nevertheless, Hollier's critique has broader significance and is not only a response to Tschumi.

Datascapes

In the schema developed by Bijlsma and his associates, the MVRDV Datascapes tend more to analysis and representation. They are visualizations of laws, rules, norms and statistical probabilities, and as such they constitute representations of what the sociologist Anthony Giddens calls 'abstract systems',[14] that is, bureaucratic systems where the trust in the system, as well as in the people, institutions and machines that represent it, lies in one's confidence in a certain specialized expertise. In reality, these Datascapes show that the space around us is virtually shot through from the outset with the domi-

nant forces of society. In a single design, there are several abstract systems at work. These systems nevertheless indicate the maximum limits within which the architect can produce his designs. Once the different Datascapes at work have been brought to light, the design becomes the subject of a negotiation in which the architect plays the part of intermediary and director. Even if the density of legislative and regulatory norms exercises a powerful influence over the design, it is not true that it springs automatically from the accumulation and interference of different Datascapes. To borrow Deleuze and Guattari's expression, Datascapes are not abstract machines, but rather 'bodies without organs' on to which, in principle, each idea can be projected. Similarly, there are instances in which the authorities and assimilated powers impose an invisible discipline on a space. In the final design, MVRDV exhibits the greatest possible number of Datascapes, which are not mutually reconciled; when all is said and done, the approach is more of a refined form of deconstruction than a unifying technique, in which the design apparently takes shape in the margins. 'Apparently', that is, because MVRDV conserves a secret diagram somewhere that really generates the designs. And if the margins are considered a locus of freedom, Hollier's critique is applicable once again.

In the installation 'Metacity/Datatown', Datascapes seem to function as machines that generate architectural designs for cities. Metacity/Datatown shows how transformations of collective behaviours lead to a transformation of the constructed landscape. The growth in population density of this imaginary city, moreover, remains an important instrument because it reduces the margins. But clearly it is also a form of rhetoric since it refers to a disturbing future scenario in which the population increases so much that it is necessary to take rigorous steps. And the inhabitants of the Netherlands, a country that is heavily populated, fear this scenario of the future more than any other place on the globe.

Consequently, 'Metacity/Datatown' is above all a didactic tool that forces us, viewers and potential inhabitants of the city, to make political choices. These choices may eventually lead to models that have nothing in common with the models presented in the installation. In this regard, like MVRDV's earlier designs, 'Metacity/Datatown' is first and foremost a reflexive design, as Ulrich Beck and Anthony Giddens understand the term, namely, a democratic design that explicitly grants the *socius* an active role by confronting him with social risks in the form of future scenarios.

The project '3-D City', which Winy Maas recently realized with the Institut Berlage, explores the limits within which a highly dense and compact situation is possible in a series of large architectural models that examine specific commissions for the city. In this commission, however, MVRDV's secret programme is becoming increasingly clear. Suddenly, the piece is no longer a mere didactic design that forces viewers to choose. Indeed, Winy Maas openly describes it as an attempt to create a utopian city in order to anticipate the problems posed by both the increase in the world's population and the protection of the environment. The EXPO pavilion in Hannover also revealed this change since the building was designed in such a way as to pass for an isolated fragment of a large city that remained to be constructed. In this regard, it was a prototype, recalling the experiments carried out by the Japanese metabolists in the 1960s.

From the start of the presentation of Datascapes, Winy Maas consciously established a comparison with some of the famous spectacular designs in the history of architecture. At that point, the work once again amounted to a rhetorical process aiming to show that it was not absolutely necessary to draw first on imagination and individual creativity in order to realize spectacular designs. In no way was daily reality an obstacle to creativity; on the contrary, daily reality could prove sufficiently spectacular if one opened one's eyes to it.

In '3-D City', however, the intention from the start is to create a spectacular city, mixing images of Fritz Lang's Metropolis, Archizoom's Superstudio, Archigram's Fifth Element and the cities of science fiction and Hilberseimer, without Maas's seeming to worry about the intentions concealed by these images or the public's reaction. A certain ambiguity thus continues to hang over the question of whether the '3-D City' design constitutes a pragmatic solution for a spectacular problem, a radical extrapolation from an existing situation altogether in keeping with Superstudio's 'Twelve Ideal Cities', which contains the essential critical message of a utopia to be realized with pragmatic means. A large number of ideas and values associated with this utopia remain unspoken, not to mention the paranoia about what would happen if we refuse to explore '3-D City'. MVRDV's secret diagram appears increasingly like an indeterminate utopian city having an unprecedented density. But what kind of behaviour is this machine going to produce? The exploration of the physics of the constructed environment, which MVRDV inaugurated with Datascapes, seems to turn into an exploration of what Alfred Jarry called 'pataphysics', that is, the disturbing, surrealist physics of the possible. And this is precisely the physics of the schizophrenic that serves as a basis for Michel Carrouges's bachelor machines and the wishful

machines of Deleuze and Guattari. As I see it, it would be preferable to undertake a critical evaluation of the 'physics' that Datascapes temporarily provide. We might perhaps deduce the values that would be useful in the next stage. Admittedly, the debate has only just started because most architects and critics persist unduly in viewing the Datascapes design as only one of the many mini-theories that today's architects keep in reserve in order to justify their work. In that context, the '3-D City' design may be a necessary, though risky provocation, since exploration of Datascapes is in danger of getting lost in an increasingly strong demand for quantities and intensities.

The architect's dream

Ben van Berkel, Caroline Bos and UN-Studio, on the other hand, seem to take the opposite approach. In their editorial published in the special issue of the review *Any* devoted to the diagram[15] they explicitly describe the diagram as a 'loophole in global information space that allows for endlessly expansive, unpredictable, and liberating pathways for architecture': 'The end of the grand narrative does not mean that architects no longer dream their own dreams, different from anyone else's'. As they affirm in *Mille Plateaux*, Deleuze and Guattari demanded of their books, concepts and diagrams that they help to maintain a rhizomatic relationship with (parts of) reality. In other words, they had to use their roots in order to draw their nutrients forcibly from the world. With Van Berkel & Bos, this relationship is radically reversed. Like the architect's dream, the diagram is projected on to the world. Readers will note that implicitly the ideal of freedom expressed here does not concern inhabitants/users but rather the architect. Obviously, this is a polemical stand taken against the architecture of Rem Koolhaas, MVRVD, Christiaanse, Neutelings, West 8 and many others, which Van Berkel & Bos consider as 'pragmatic' architecture. In reality, the situation is more complex of course. Certain UN-Studio's designs, for example, are based on extremely detailed statistical and quantitative analyses; in other instances, ideas are integrated in an extraordinarily refined, precise manner. Nevertheless, unlike the 'pragmatics', UN-Studio favours a formal, aesthetic and metaphorical treatment of analyses: literally even, as when Van Berkel & Bos put a portrait of the 'Manimal' on the cover of their book *Move*. This computer-generated image, in which human faces and animal heads merge as in a dream, replaces the symbolic figure of a man drawn in a square and a circle, as created by Leonardo da Vinci.

Whereas da Vinci's diagram is the symbol of humanism and the central place that man, in this view, occupies at the heart of the world and the cosmos, this 'Manimal' is the symbol of a 'post-humanism' in which all possibilities merge with one another. Yet in Van Berkel & Bos's designs, as in the work of numerous contemporary American architects, this post-humanism does not in any way change the position and role of the architect. Just as the architects of the Renaissance, in the eyes of art historians, seem to have expressed symbolically a view of the world through their constructions, so Van Berkel & Bos appear to retain such a privileged role for the architect. However, if everything merges, if there is no longer either a beginning or end to discover, the architect's role is necessarily affected: how can one henceforth give symbolic form to reality here on earth and, by doing so, resolve and reconcile breaks, oppositions and conflicts? To fill that role, the architect must turn to a higher order, which remains hidden to most mortals but which he can make visible, albeit with his arse, like President Schreber attracting heavenly rays in Deleuze and Guattari's work.[16]

To that end, Van Berkel & Bos — along with many others — use diagrams that are notably borrowed from genetic technology, chaos theory, complexity theory, string theory, etc. How this theoretical physics is integrated in the design is hardly different from the way in which metaphysics was symbolically translated into past architectural designs, if we are to believe the classic interpretation proposed by historians of art and architecture. The desire to express in architecture the fundamental outlook of a period is naturally a respectable conception of the discipline. That aside, metaphysics is no longer satisfied with popes and priests: it also demands architects and artists. Moreover, chaos theory, complexity theory and string theory are extraordinarily interesting, and are studied in depth and scientifically grounded. Nevertheless, these theories have yet to teach us anything about the way we behave (or ought to behave) as individuals in everyday life. At most, chaos theory can explain the behaviour of a large population by analogy with equivalent populations. On the other hand, we still do not know what is the optimum size that those populations ought to maintain. On the purely scientific level, these theories offer no manuals for specific situations. It is improbable that they can, for example, suggest what behaviour one should adopt when an architectural design meets irreconcilable interests. The converse is that these theories offer critics no indication of how they should judge designs. If it is true, for example, as Sanford Kwinter pointed out during a lecture at the Institut Berlage,[17] that the entire world, indeed the entire cosmos, is vibrating and that these vibrations determine everything,

according to string theory, then by definition any construction obeys this determination, whether it is a building by Rem Koolhaas (as Kwinter, in this instance, would like, strange to say), Ben van Berkel, Daniel Liebeskind, Rob Krier or some talented unknown.

Of course we are fooling ourselves if we imagine that a certain type of architecture or town planning whose forms are in motion can offer greater freedom and thus contribute to preventing conflicts, the idea being that these forms adapt more naturally to certain flows. If this is the way we must interpret these designs, as certain architects inspired by Kevin Kelly, for example, believe we must, one ends up constructing a theory that in reality recalls the liberal individualism of a F. A. Hayek, based upon a belief in a 'spontaneous order', an 'invisible hand', more than the Deleuzian critique of capitalism. As the political scientist Colin Bird has remarked, 'I can believe that the state really is an organism and yet deny that it has any moral significance whatsoever. The mere fact that a jellyfish is "organic" does not elevate it to a moral status equivalent or beyond that attributed to human beings'.[18]

It is no accident if the work of UN-Studio proves a success when it comes to resolving complex questions of infrastructure, organizing, for example, Castells's 'space of flows' in the case of the Arnhem railway station. Here the different forms of infrastructure and the movements are statistical data of sorts. Indeed, it is not difficult to translate the flow of passengers into a flow of data. Theoretically, freedom is at stake here, on the individual level, since different possibilities are available for changing trains, but these possibilities are not realized at the site and, moreover, most can be ignored by the mass of people, in terms of the design. The Arnhem station is a machine that looks like the motor of a Ferrari equipped with shiny smooth manifolds. The way the diagram of the Klein Bottle in this design forms a formal thread that runs right through it once again presents a meaning that is especially symbolic and magic, so transcending the original situation that one can almost speak of an inversion. The concept of transport flows suddenly seems like the specific expression of a superior order that exercises its power over all the other parts of the design.

Involuntary (de)construction

Greg Lynn has explained on many occasions how the design for the Korean Presbyterian Church in New York was generated by means of diagrams. How in the computer different 'meta blobs' interacted according to their zones of gravitational force. How they grew and melted together into new forms until they achieved a state of equilibrium. How these meta blobs stood for different programmes, single rooms that merged into one big room with a single surface that incorporated the entire programme. How the clients loved this, because they could actually manipulate the forms themselves, making things bigger and smaller without destroying the coherence of the overall concept. Then he introduced a different strategy. A series of tubes was put on the roof of an existing building that we hadn't seen before, the old Knickerbocker Laundry. The tubes grew and developed into a rib-like structure with an inner and an outer skin. Tubes were added for access and circulation. In this phase, the smoothness of the blobs was already partly replaced by a certain degree of segmentation, but everything still seemed to be melded together. After that, there must have been a third phase in which the project was adapted to the building methods of the contractor. Constructions appeared and an industrial façade was introduced. In this phase, the project lost its initial smoothness. Today, it looks almost like a deconstruction of a blob.

What at first seemed to withdraw from language became language again; the diagrams were reappropriated by language. Today, all the materials suddenly tell a multitude of stories, about what they are, how they are made, how they are put together and how they relate to other materials. What appeared initially as a coherent form, informed by all kinds of complex systems, suddenly became a complexity again. And it goes further than that because this is a church-factory, a religion plant, which hosts services for 2,500 people. It simultaneously accommodates multiple non-sectarian programmes in 80 classrooms, a 600-seat wedding chapel, various assembly spaces, a choir rehearsal space, a cafeteria and a daycare centre. Imagine all these people here, individuals coming from different places around New York, carrying memories from Korea, moving around, doing things in different constellations, like a giant anthill.

Now, in itself this is not a problem, because as the building stands there it is in some ways maybe even more convincing than if it had been a smooth blob: that would have made a much more disturbing, science-fiction-like effect. It would have appeared as if aliens or at least something from 'out there' had just landed. Of course, Greg Lynn himself likes these references and he has referred to B-movie blobs on many occasions with a certain perverse pleasure. Because, however much disgust and queasiness they may inspire in movie audiences, they also seem to possess a higher form of intelligence. 'The term "blob" connotes a thing which is neither singular nor multiple but an intelligence that behaves as if it were singular and networked, but in its form can become virtually infinitely multiplied and distributed'.[19] This is an interesting metaphor for a building, because a building is never just one thing

and is always caught up in a constantly changing, complex web of relationships and stories. That is what makes architecture so fascinating. This process of change doesn't even stop when the building is realized, but continues forever. After it is realized, it is appropriated by the people who use it, for example. I remember a lecture by Peter Eisenman from a long time ago in which he talked about one of his early houses. When it was realized and the clients came for their first visit, the wife exclaimed, 'But I thought we were going to get a Heidi-house!'. They first moved into the basement and from day one changed the house and slowly occupied it until they felt it was their own. Eisenman appreciated that, as he had consciously built a certain resistance in the house. In some respects, the way in which the engineers and builders dealt with the original schemes for the Korean church and adapted them to construction methods with which they felt familiar is probably not so different from Eisenman's anecdote — except that it happened even before the realization.

Lynn, however, has always criticized such an approach, or at least he has criticized a deconstructivist architecture that lives on such conflicts and exploits them in geometrical conflicts. Instead of that, he proposes an architecture that is malleable, fluid and supple, to accommodate and integrate all these conflicting forces in a new whole. Complexity involves the fusion of multiple and different systems into an assemblage that behaves as a singularity while remaining irreducible to any single simple organization.[20]

The building becomes part of a larger ecology and changes accordingly, which is made possible in the design phase by the latest animation software. In the end, a form is chosen that is static — however, static like a sailing boat, which has a form that allows it to perform well in many different situations. It incorporates all these situations and the final form is mediated between them. In the case of a boat, one could make it more comfortable or faster by changing the parameters, and in the same way one could change the building according to the client's wishes.

But of course, the basic question is, what different parameters are selected to play a role in the original ecology? How complex is this ecology really? Who makes the selection of the forces and on what grounds? And, last but not least, couldn't it be that geometrical conflicts in the form of fractures and ruptures are essential to certain ecologies?

In the case of the Korean Presbyterian Church, the ecology still seems to be quite simple. That is not so strange, as it was one of Lynn's first experiments with this way of working. In the first phase of the design process, a software was chosen that allowed one to locate different parts of the programme, let's say the different chapels, the altar and the choir, into 'meta blobs', which grew together. Now their sizes and relationships could be altered, while they remained related and the overall design coherent. Then the original building was introduced and the model roughly adapted to that – roughly, because they still appear as separate entities. In later, similar attempts to introduce a new organization into an existing building, like NOX's design for the V2 Lab in Rotterdam from 1998, the relationship between the new and the existing form seems already more fluent and integrated. However, it is exactly this limited initial ecology that makes Lynn's finally realized building appear as a deconstruction of the original diagrams. These are almost completely hidden in the final construction and detailing. In that sense, in the completed Korean Presbyterian Church, Lynn comes close to the loosely layered way Ben van Berkel and Caroline Bos use diagrams in their designs as 'interactive instruments': as a kind of mission statement in the management of whole projects rather than something that should be realized literally. In an article I wrote on Van Berkel's work a few years ago, I made reference to a text on the œuvre of the Italian painter Francesco Clemente – which Van Berkel always admired – as a kind of 'diagrams in costumes'.[21] The dream of the architect is buried in the whole – that is at the same time much more interesting than the dream above.

However, Lynn seems to be more ambitious than that. Much more than Van Berkel, whose work is produced in an innovative yet traditional practice that deals with real commissions, his work springs far more from a tradition of academic and theoretical research and should be evaluated as such. In all his projects, Lynn chooses his own parameters to work with. In the House Prototype in Long Island, they are the topography, the wind and the noise from the nearby road, for example, and in the H2 House for Vienna, they are the light from the sun and the cars on the nearby highway. He also selects a particular software and recently, in his Embryologic Housing project, he opted for a production method as a starting point. As almost scientific experiments in a controlled environment, these projects are incredibly valuable and already influential among a broad group of architects. However, the question is whether that is the sole reason that Lynn allows for only a selected number of parameters in his projects. It could also be that his desire to produce a coherence in the design in the first place gets in the way of realizing this coherence in the final building, because the real ecology in which that is situated is much more complex than Lynn's selection of forces that play a role in it. 'Any object supposes the continuity of a flow, any flow, the fragmentation of the object,' write Deleuze and Guattari.[22] Fearing the fragmentation of the object in the reality of everyday life, architecture withdraws into a body without organs. Michael Speaks could be right when he says that Lynn, like his mentor Peter Eisenman, is still too much interested in the metaphysics of architecture.[23]

Machine effects

Unlike MVRDV, whose work makes use of the diagram above all as an integrating form of notation, a formal abstraction of a given complex reality, and Van Berkel & Bos and Greg Lynn, for whom the diagram is a chosen form that generates and structures the design, Lars Spuybroek alone conceives the diagram as a complete machine. 'The diagram is a very clearly lined network of relationships, but it is completely vague in its formal expression,' writes Spuybroek in 'Machining Architecture'. 'Diagrams love pulp, and they only recognize materials at their most heated and their weakest stages. The diagram is basically a conceptual input/output device which swallows matter and, while restructuring, also ejects matter. In that sense, every informational plane is always an interface between material states . . . The diagram . . . is an engine, a motor: it doesn't want to impose itself on matter, but to engage in a process of continuous formation it operates at the backside of the image, on its blind side. Diagrams are the informational nodes and codes of the world; they are stabilizing contractions in material flows – first they channel and then they relax. They are faces in a landscape, singular perceptions connecting streams of actions. They are lenses, mirroring a movement: first a contraction of matter-energy on to an organizing surface, then an expansion into many new other structures'.[24]

Contraction is the phase during which information is collected, selected, converted and graphically organized in a virtual machine. It is a process in which a three-dimensional network is converted into a two-dimensional surface. Spuybroek describes it as a movement towards quality, order and organization. Then there occurs a process of expansion in which the machine, the diagram, is put into the material, spreads throughout and gives it a shape. This is a development that enables one to shift from a two-dimensional surface to a three-dimensional structure. Spuybroek describes this as a movement towards quality, materials and structure.

Up to this point, there is nothing in this approach specifically involving a computer. In principle, an expressionist method of working, described by Vasily Kandinsky, for instance, as the chain *Emotion-Gefühl-Werk-Gefühl-Emotion*, is equally suitable.[25] A process of contraction (*Einfühlung*) and expansion

(*Expression*), which is endlessly repeated, is also at work here. In that case, individual people are themselves the machine. This process, however, can be active only insofar as it is a process that is transmittable to others, as if there existed an agreement about the nature of human beings, and all men corresponded to a humanist ideal. This is a problem if we accept that individuals are part of flow networks, in which they must endlessly make choices, and that these choices continuously modify the position, identity and therefore nature of these individuals. The process then becomes altogether subjective. In the architecture of UN-Studio and Greg Lynn, that subjectivity is not resolved because they choose diagrams that exist outside the process to generate their designs. Spuybroek's intention then is to free as much as possible the design process of the architect as well as the individual person by constructing an abstract machine that also lies outside himself and that is linked to the world rhizomatically.

As Spuybroek sees it, the computer is only a machine that reinforces communication between different diagrams. It is a diagram in and of itself, and the specific computer programs are also diagrams in and of themselves. For Spuybroek, there is no difficulty in describing as 'material computers' the dynamic models borrowed from Antoni Gaudí and Frei Otto, which he uses in certain designs to determine his buildings' form of construction. These are material diagrams because a change in one area influences the form of the overall project. The design process then comprises, in the end, a chain of different diagrams forming a design machine since they are coupled to one another and are continuously converted into one another. For this reason, Spuybroek believes that schools that teach computer-aided design should offer as well instruction in 'computer-aided conceptualization' and 'computer-aided manufacturing'.[26] Even if the computer is an expression of a tendency to make everything smoother, more fluid, Spuybroek shows that there still exist couplings and connections that harbour within them possibilities of choice. The 'space of flows' is not a fatality: we can still manipulate it in our own way.

Since then, NOX has developed this way of working in a series of designs and completed projects that include 'OfftheRoad_5speed', a housing design for Eindhoven in which the 5 speeds refer to as many diagrams; 'Wetgrid', an idea for the exhibition 'Vision Machine' held at the Musée de Nantes, or the D-Tower of Doetinchem.[27] The D-Tower design assumed a form that is, in the end, both real and virtual, for, apart from being a real object, the tower itself is also a new diagram, which continuously transforms the input of the population of Doetinchem to an Internet site.

What is interesting yet troublesome in NOX's way of working is that the result (the design and buildings that arise from that) is almost impossible to represent. It is interesting because these designs normally permit a large amount of interactivity with the future inhabitants and users of the building, or because they may play on the modification of subsidiary constraints until a relatively advanced stage; it is also troublesome because the design proves difficult to present to a client who, for example, requests that the final form be visualized before the last stage of the process. Thus, up to this point Spuybroek has relied on clients who have been able to reflect at a high level of abstraction of the design process and interpret diagrams on their own. If we wish to consider the computer as a true tool in design rather than a mere implement, if we want to know to what extent we are manipulated in the 'space of flows', it is unavoidable that we resign ourselves to this method. But then again, if Schreber was able to theorize about himself, there is no reason why we cannot do so as well. ●

Notes

[1] Like Bijlsma, Wouter Deen, Udo Garritzmann, editorial, OASE, no. 48 (1998).

[2] Gilles Deleuze, Félix Guattari, *L'Anti-Oedipe, Capitalisme et Schizophrénie* (Paris: Editions de Minuit, 1972).

[3] Deleuze, Guattari, *L'Anti-Oedipe*.

[4] Manuel Castells, *The Rise of the Network Society* (Massachusetts/Oxford: Blackwell Inc., 1996).

[5] Deleuze, Guattari, *L'Anti-Oedipe*.

[6] Roemer van Toorn, *The Society of the And*.

[7] Lars Spuybroek, 'Machining Architecture', in Lars Spuybroek (NOX) and Bob Lang (Arup), *The Weight of the Image* (Rotterdam: Nai Publishers, 2001).

[8] Deleuze, Guattari, *L'Anti-Oedipe*.

[9] Gilles Deleuze, *Foucault* (Paris: Editions de Minuit, 1986).

[10] Deleuze, *Foucault*.

[11] Rem Koolhaas, 'The Downtown Athletic Club', in *Delirious New York* (London, 1978); Rem Koolhaas, 'Revision', in *S, M, L, XL* (Rotterdam: 010 Publishers, 1995).

[12] Deleuze, Guattari, *Mille Plateaux* (Paris: Editions de Minuit, 1980).

[13] Denis Hollier, 'Bloody Sundays', in *Against Architecture. The Writings of Georges Bataille* (Cambridge, MA/London: MIT Press, 1989).

[14] Anthony Giddens, 'Living in a Post-Traditional Society', in Ultrich Beck, Anthony Giddens, Scott Lash, *Reflexive Modernization, Politics, Tradition and Aesthetics in the Modern Social Order* (Cambridge/Oxford: Polity Press, 1994).

[15] Ben van Berkel, Caroline Bos, 'Diagram Work', Any, 23 (1998).

[16] Deleuze, Guattari, *L'Anti-Oedipe*.

[17] Sanford Kwinter, lecture given at the Institut Berlage, Amsterdam.

[18] Colin Bird, *The Myth of Liberal Individualism* (Cambridge/New York/Melbourne: Cambridge University Press, 1999).

[19] Greg Lynn, 'Blob Tectonics, or Why Tectonics Is Square and Typology Is Groovy', in *Folds, Bodies and Blobs. Collected Essays* (Brussels, 1988).

[20] Greg Lynn, 'Possible Geometries', in *Collected Essays*.

[21] Bart Lootsma, 'Eindelijk echt ambidexter', *De Architect* (March 1991). See also Bart Lootsma, 'Diagrams in Costumes', *A + U*, no. 342 (March, 1999).

[22] Deleuze, Guattari, *L'Anti-Oedipe*.

[23] Greg Lynn, 'It's out there... The Formal Limits of the American Avant-Garde', *Architectural Design Profile*, no. 133 (*Hypersurface Architecture*, guest-edited by Stephen Perella, London, 1998).

[24] Lars Spuybroek, 'Machining Architecture'.

[25] Cf. I. B. Whyte, *Bruno Taut and the Architecture of Activism* (Cambridge, MA: MIT Press, 1982).

[26] Lars Spuybroek, 'Machining Architecture'.

[27] Lars Spuybroek, 'OfftheRoad_5speed', Ali Rahim, (ed.) in *Architectural Design* ('Contemporary Process in Architecture'), vol. 70, no. 3 (June, 2000); Arielle Pélenc, 'Wetgrid. Lars Spuybroek on his Exhibition Design "Vision Machine"', *ARCHIS* (August, 2000).

At the Zero Point of Housing

Andreas Ruby

To pose the question of housing today is tantamount to uncovering one of the most important topics in contemporary architecture, which, however, hardly seems to exist, being almost completely buried under other topics in the current architectural debate.

Housing somehow seems unable to shake off its trite image. It is a social requirement, a preoccupation forced upon architecture by society — how could it become its passion? Considering the fact that modern architecture established itself by the expedient of housing, just as housing was recreated thanks to modern architecture, contemporary architecture is almost forced to avoid the question of housing in its attempt to leave the shadow of its recent history behind. In a way, it's the equivalent of 'Dad's car' for contemporary architecture — something emblazoned with a red warning sign in its subconscious because it holds uncomfortably familiar memories of its own past.

This uneasiness is surely not unfounded. Since the days of modernism the dwelling has existed in a schizophrenic separation of mass housing and the private home. In tackling mass production of dwellings architecture takes on the housing problem, and thereby changes itself inevitably 'from an aesthetic to a social discipline', as formulated in his programme by Hannes Meyer, second director of the Bauhaus. To experience the suppressed aesthetic side of its personality, architecture resorts to the oasis of private residential architecture, financed by wealthy clients who are infected with the optimism of forward-looking builders. While the second CIAM congress in Frankfurt in 1929 was defining the 'Wohnung für das Existenzminimum' (housing for minimum living standards) Mies van der Rohe was constructing the 'Wohnung für das Existenzmaximum' with Haus Tugendhat at Brno, built for 20 times the price of a normal family house at the time.

This splitting of habitat into high versus low has proved to be a dead end in the situation today. Private house construction as an exclusive niche market for rich clients has turned into an architectural reservation where the project of today's avant-garde is realized only symbolically, if at all (by, for example, filling 80 per cent of the architecture magazines), but which barely has an impact on the psychological and physical landscape of the present day. What we are dealing with is housing that principally takes place outside the normal economy, or rather which founds its own economy, not unlike Georges Batailles's 'economy of waste' — architecture as a kind of potlach. At the same time the other side of modern living — mass housing — is equally inapplicable if individualization is considered the transformational impulse of the second modernity. The influence of social conditions and values during the emergence of mass housing in the industrial age is just too strong: seen as an instant solution to the housing problems of industrialized society and tailored to the needs of the nuclear family, the standard scheme of the modern small dwelling is completely unable to meet today's requirements and has increasingly become the housing form for the socially underprivileged. Anyone who can afford to moves away. This is the reason why there are presently 1 million empty prefab-panel construction apartments in the former German Democratic Republic. These buildings, barely 30 years old, are waiting to meet the same fate as the massive high-rise blocks in Pruitt Igoe near St Louis, the demolition of which in 1972 became a symbol of the failure of modernism.

Thus contemporary architecture can hardly expect to find any support in the history of modernism for its conceptualization of housing today. But then, where else to look? Peter Eisenman finds a fitting description for the dilemma when he says that we no longer have a concept for living but nonetheless continue building dwellings and living in them. In a sense Eisenman is thus picking up on Heidegger's thoughts in *Bauen, Wohnen, Denken* ('Building, Dwelling, Thinking') where he sees the real housing problem in the midst of a bombed Europe of 1951 as the fact that 'mortals never cease to search for the essence of living; they still have to learn how to dwell'. During the reign of modernism, it is well known that architecture gave itself the pedagogical authority for this *ars habitandi* and put a real propaganda machine into operation in order to distribute its new lifestyle concepts. At the outset this was restricted to instructions in book form (Max Taut's *Die Neue Wohnung* ['The New Dwelling', 1928], but soon expanded into film in order to bring modern residential culture to the grass-roots. In *Wie Wohnen Wir Gesund und Wirtschaftlich?* ('How Can We Live Healthily and Efficiently?') (Germany, 1926–27) Walter Gropius offers his city at Dessau-Törten as an exemplary location; in 1929 the Dadaist Hans Richter was commissioned by the Swiss Werkbund to make *Die Neue Wohnung* ('The New Apartment'). In 1931 Le Corbusier demonstrated the art of modern living in his short film *L'Architecture d'aujourd'hui* ('Architecture Today'; a masterpiece of architectural self-promotion), of course using his own villas – from parking in front of the house to morning exercise on the roof. Mies van der Rohe preferred to carry out this teaching function in person: He was fond of greeting accusations on the unsuitability of his houses for everyday living with the remark, 'I will teach people how to live in my houses'. Just to be sure, he would drop in unannounced on the owners of his buildings to check whether the furniture was in

MovingHouse

exactly the place he had specified in the plans (which he would have preferred to be screwed to the floor anyway).

Besides producing spaces, modernist architecture essentially fabricated lifestyles. In today's society this role has long been in the hands of an omnipresent lifestyle industry, constantly designing new models and promoting them across a broad media spectrum. Whereas the modernists organized the Weissenhof building exhibition in Stuttgart in 1927 to allow customers to try out the new lifestyle, these trials today take place at IKEA — and IKEA has certainly influenced contemporary living to a greater extent than any one architect. The same is true of the myriad interior design and lifestyle magazines, which undoubtedly define the actual culture of dwelling today more than all the architecture periodicals put together. Given these real-time lifestyle productions, architecture finds itself in a permanent state of cultural jet lag, able only to react to the innovations of everyday life without ever being able to catch up. This reactive logic extends through to the cultural institutions, which should really be supporting architecture in the foundation of a theory of contemporary living. While the 'International Style' exhibition at the MoMA in 1929 provided an important impetus in the dissemination of the modernist idea of habitat, especially throughout the USA, the 'Unprivate House' exhibition held at the same place in 1999 hardly offered more than a pale replay of developments that have long since taken place. The most unprivate house, however, was missing in the exhibition: the Big Brother House, 'built' by Endemol Studios in the Netherlands as part of the reality TV programme of the same name, which radically forced discussion on the blurring of the line between public and private in domestic life.

Exaggerated portrayals of this kind (another example would be the excessive staging of domestic life in periodicals such as *Wallpaper* or *Surface*) lead increasingly to a hybrid discourse of our artificial everyday culture. To give a direct, essentialist definition of housing, as Heidegger attempted to do, thus becomes more and more difficult for contemporary architecture. Truly qualitative statements might become possible only if one no longer investigates 'dwelling as such' but rather the conditions shaping its performance – the way we work, the type of relationship we have with one another, whether we have children, whether we set up home in the outskirts or the centre of a town or city, what leisure activities we choose, how much mobility we need and what forms of communication we use to fulfil our professional routines and organize our everyday life, etc. – to do no more than hint at a rough list of the external parameters of contemporary living. Ground-breaking research into these conditions would be a necessary prerequisite for a contemporary architectural practice of housing. This mapping of lifestyles would probably enable us to make an exact statement on where living takes place today: more or less everywhere – on the television, in the train, in the hotel, in the office – just not at home. Seen from this perspective, housing presents itself as an absent subject. The search for a concept of housing leads to the discovery of a nomadic existence, both elusive and omnipresent. In the same way that when colours are mixed together a certain colour is created only by the optical superimposition of primary colours, we may be able to define dwelling only from the superimposition of our living conditions.

This kind of ex-centric definition certainly provides access to the formative processes that lead to two fundamental transformations of contemporary dwelling – a spatio-temporal dynamization and a typological contamination.

On the former: if the dwelling of the 19th and early 20th centuries suggested a static and place-bound notion of living, the same activity today becomes increasingly spatialized and temporalized between the various poles of our existence. Given the tremendous mobility that is a part of professional normality for an ever-increasing number of people, nomadism is becoming an everyday condition. In the USA the average citizen changes job location and thus his residence every 5 years, Western Europe is slowly moving towards the same level. The flexible citizen (Richard Sennett) organizes his life primarily according to the changing demands of his professional career. The increasing trend away from long-term employment contracts and the globalization of the employment market (Europe is already a single market for employment) leads to biographies with previously inconceivable fluctuations in space and time. Dwelling thus becomes more and more subject to a culture of moving. The house/apartment leaves the realm of real estate to rematerialize itself as a mobile estate. The German architect André Poitiers therefore sees us living in transportable dwelling modules in the future, units we can take with us when we move – the house and its contents will fuse to become a transportable infrastructure of a nomadic lifestyle such that we are constantly in the process of moving house. This kind of moving will obviously change the way we dwell, too, as can be seen already, for the mobile estate is clearly subject to the logic of furniture, which has far-reaching consequences for the architectural concept of flexibility. Born in the revolution of structure in modern construction, flexibility has been turned into a trite cliché instead and prevented from acting out its performative implications. To this day, architects still understand flexibility primarily as a structural concept. The free floor plan of the Maison Domino permits the construction of a simplified load-bearing structure by replacing the walls with only a few supports. Hence it has mainly been the architect's prvilege to profit from this flexibility (because it simplifies the design process). The promise of flexible room division made to the building owner is, however, almost never kept. Given the physical inertia of walls put into place, the much-heralded transformability of the floor-plan layout is seldom more than a theoretical option. Only very recently have architects begun to understand flexibility in a performative way and to organize space such that it can actually be altered, for example by allowing previously fixed installations like kitchen units to be positioned freely in space (with electrical and water connections that move with the units, as seen in the 'do it yourself' project by Kalhöfer Korschildgen). The room is instantaneously alterable, like a traditional Japanese house with sliding walls.

This flexibility of performance is a fundamental condition for the second transformation of dwelling mentioned above: typological contamination. In the face of the differentiation of lifestyles in the age of individualization, the concept of the architectural type is becoming increasingly meaningless. A standard floor plan for a family with 1 or 2 children has become fairly pointless, if only because this family is steadily becoming less and less representative of human relationships in the urban agglomerations of the developed nations. Approximately half of all marriages end in divorce – a tempting reason to start thinking about a floor plan for a divorced family with 2 children. Conversely, single communities are gaining in importance, made up not only of young people between 20 and 35 but also older singles, i.e. retired people, who prefer forms of collective dwelling that are able to help them and who increasinly reject traditional old people's homes.

For most of these new lifestyles, adequate dwelling concepts still remain to be developed. As the needs and desires driving those lifestyles are constantly evolving, it is improbable that they will ever lead to new typologies. They might, however, stimulate prototypologies, typologies in the state of becoming that never reach completion but rather constantly react to changing situations. Just like the contemporary production techniques of rapid prototyping these prototypologies are characterized by their ability to test material structures directly in real situations and learn by adapting to external influences. In a way, they pour themselves over lifestyles, which are then in turn transformed by this materialization. The new technologies of computer-aided manufacturing with their differentiated, soft and adaptive formation methods have completely left behind the concept of the modernist standard. They provide instead the technological basis for a new correspondence between architecture and the changing organizational forms of existence within society. Thus architecture today finds itself at a similar zero point as in the beginnings of modernism. And housing, curiously enough, could once again become the research laboratory of a new architecture. ●

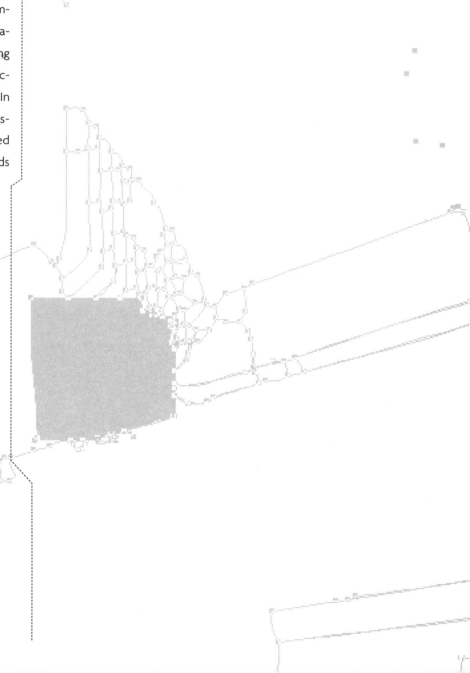

Here, Luckily, Lies the House of the Future

Christian Girard

The amazing photograph of a housing block built in Havana by the Americans in the 1950s was published in 2000 in a fashion magazine.[1] At first sight, this 30-storey 'low-rise' seems unfinished and neglected, but there's nothing to stop you thinking that it was fully occupied when the photo was snapped. Looking like something out of Sarajevo or Beirut, this block has a monumental quality, designed as it was contrary to common sense and at the same time with scrupulous respect for a functionalism taken to its limit. This apocalyptic or ruins-of-war vision seems available only for hypothetical 'shoots' of models clad in international designer clothes. This programme of housing 'for human beings', if we can so put it, is an object that is both perfectly static and statistical. As the product of a capitalist promotion, it might just as well have been built by Castro's communist government. It proposes erasing and eradicating all individuality, and putting all the residents' uniqueness behind bars and three-dimensional gates. The repeated arguments that predict the end of models, by pinpointing their obvious vacuousness, don't change a thing: such housing programmes are being built every day, here, there and everywhere, from Shanghai to what remains of the Costa Brava and the French Riviera. Yet contemporary changes are put under the heading of networks and flows, plasticity and mobility, the smooth and the nomadic, not on fixedness and changelessness.

One of the shrewdest examples of the rhetoric of flows, and one of the most extremist presentations of the world's constant state of flux — encompassing land, people, genes, languages, standards, institutions and history — has been offered by Manuel de Landa,[2] who, in an explicit Deleuze-inspired association, highlights an absolute form of evolutionism. This triumph of flow/flux-related thinking is consistent with a very special attention afforded the phenomenon of 'real time', plunging and fixing us in an eternal present from which any past and future are excluded. Thirty years after Michel Serres's 'Hermès' series, it has become almost commonplace and obligatory to envisage land and urban development from the angle of the generalized, uninterrupted and fluid movement of all things. Architecture may indeed represent, a priori, the materialization in space of projects in which men and woman can reside and live, but the gap between this definition of the discipline and a conception of the world in terms of communication, interference, expression and distribution is growing ever wider.[3]

Oddly, the geological argument developed by M. de Landa tallies with an historical period when the frequency of earthquakes and other seismic goings-on involving disasters in urban areas has become particularly marked. Land and soil give way, as does history. Those metropolises that have seen fit to turn a blind eye to the geologies upon which they have been developing are subject to fatal calls to order — or rather, disorder — while climatology has lost the few certainties still attaching to it. Housing and dwelling are not even synonymous any more with terrestrial base. The only anti-seismic features of differing forms of architecture are their physical structures, all the other components remaining at the mercy of the ever-increasing implosion of lifestyles and social practices, under the pressure of that much-

'Buena Phenix Social Club'. *Photomontage Ch. Girard*

Pragmatism has been so brandished as a banner by architects for a whole decade, starting with the Netherlands, then having conquered Spain, and lastly France, that it acts as an ideology-based ideology and a doctrine-based doctrine. After all, except when the term is used as a substitute for the crudest forms of cynicism and commercial opportunism, the pragmatic requirement has little chance of leaving the architect with the least awareness of what he is up to.[4] Designing and constructing the space of new and unknown social practices, which are being permanently reconfigured, should not, for all that, pass for a revolution. And yet all the conditions are in place to turn this architectural programme into an almost unachievable goal. We might well suppose that, these days, immersion in all manner of flow and flux is something that is and will be shared by all those involved with architecture and matters urban. The fact is, though, that the very opposite actually happens in many instances. Without even dwelling on the massive uptake of identity-related arguments, it is quite enough to see the extent to which an unaltered

talked-about phenomenon, globalization. And, as a discipline, architecture is quite close to having lost its foundations, both literally and figuratively. Because it is a matter of merging architecture into the ambient chaotic state – chaos here being intended not in the common meaning of the term – the quest for the 'right form' occurs today in relation to anything that opens up the possibility of a generalized fluid mechanics. By the yardstick of this evolutiveness/flexibility that is being sought everywhere as a panacea, three themes can be interlinked: pragmatism as a project attitude and position; adaptation complying with uses that cannot possibly be anticipated; and form understood as process.

conception of housing – the abode – may endure, not only in the most popular representations but also among the so-called economic, political, scientific, university and even artistic elites. The only thing that differs is the scale of things and costs entailed by access to those commodities called the house, the land about it and its furnishings. Resistance and the unaffected success of the 'cottage-style' residential model in the imagination of all social classes, at every latitude and in every continent, give us pause for thought. At the same time, we can see the nagging concern over 'patrimonializing' a maximum number of objects, from the smallest building to public places or what remains of them, being perversely associated with the ability to destroy the slightest trace of ordinary, invisible, common architecture.[5] As far as France is concerned, we can be sure that the building permit has now become one of the most important factors of architectural mediocrity, as aesthetic censorship pounces on architecturally loaded projects and invariably offers carte blanche to the worst horrors.[6] It is high time that the permit was reformed, even done away with altogether, if we really want there to be proper experiments worthy of this name in the realm of housing.

Representations of the famous robotized dwelling (in France, for a few years, people used the word 'domotique' [home automation] to describe the integral wiring of the abode) in the press never strayed one inch from this model. Better still, each one of these representations did its utmost to put the array of traditional home and housing codes back in proper order, the better to exacerbate the new technological components. On the rare occasions when representational tests of the 'house of the future' have striven to project an envelope of the 'future', the most hackneyed (and dated) science-fiction models have come up: from the spherical house that is still less striking than the 'Maison des gardes agricoles' designed by Etienne-Louis Ledoux in the late 18th century, to the unlikely glass bubbles, the unassumed retro-future ill conceals the absence of any criticism of the one-family residential model, whose suburban American version was so masterfully depicted by Tim Burton in *Edward Scissorhands*.[7] A painstaking collection of these projects confirms the extreme stability of this icon, made up of just a few signs (ridge roof, rectangular rooms, French-style windows, fireplace). So, flows, multiplicities, for everything one would want, but for the house it will be necessary to rely on the greatest symbolic immobility and on the greatest resistances. Too often, in places that purport to be highly experimental with regard to the redefinition of household space, we still come across certain desperate contortions that attempt to pass off as radical newness envelopes wrapping the eternal sequence 'hallway – living room – bedrooms – technical rooms' in a pseudo-mix-up quickly given away by the prosaic (or pragmatic?), easily identifiable presence of props as recognizable as a bathtub, a kitchen sink, a toilet basin. The feeling of incompleteness still prevails before the results of competitions such as 'the virtual house', which replace the programme of the late 'house of the year 2000' that has become impossible but is still included here and there in the greatest innocence.

Habitat absolutely in situ, New York, November 2000. *Photo Ch. Girard*

Undeniably, in such a context of absurd housing standardization, the projects and works of the Dutch MVRDV, in direct and clear association with OMA, represent an important stage in an eventual transformation of architectural practices and project management. In a complete change of tack, by taking it literally and pushing it to its extreme limit, the normative apparatus has been the appropriate strategy. Open to anyone to analyse their work as hyperfunctionalism, which in some respects it is, collective housing architecture would not be the same after them. The sad clones of their building with its disproportionate cantilevers in Amsterdam (The Cantilever, building for the elderly, Amsterdam-Osdorp, 1997) that are already appearing are definitely not the best lesson to be drawn from their work. On the other hand, whenever the logic of producing a building is turned into an opportunity to construct something quite different from the thing expected, a breach is opened up in the thick wall of conventions.

If the combined impulses of withdrawal into household pseudo-inwardness (the famous cocooning), on the one hand, and ceaseless roaming (journeys and trips beyond the place of residence, and surfing Internet networks), on the other, do not, in the end, produce as many contradictions as one might have imagined, this is because the physical reference of the dwelling hardly changes at all. The incorporation of the most sophisticated means of communication within the 'living environ-ment', to borrow an expression that nicely betrays its semantic clumsiness and is now happily running out of steam, does not seem to cause much upset. Only contrite aesthetes lament the acoustic and visual nuisance of the cell phone, which blends in as easily in the sourest of settings as jeans managed to do in their day.

We shall keep an even closer eye on the observations that Medhi Belhaj Kacem, author of *L'Esthétique du chaos*, makes about contemporary conditions. An expert, if ever there was one, on nomadic wanderings through the most pregnant symptoms of contemporaneousness, MBK specifically describes a future that is actually already here, where the lack of anything better to do reigns supreme: 'in the centuries to come, work will no longer be understood in the sense of laborious labour (labour is no longer that of slavery, subjugation, discipline or even control, so it is no longer that of fear, but of inactivity . . . encompassing boredom, in a word, angst: no longer of the traumatic death of war or the mar-tyrological person exploited by work, but the depressed and suicidal aspect of being at a loose end and pacification through bio-control at point-blank range'.[8] This is the kind of extra-lucid argument that architects would do well to listen to before serving up naive fictions about a kind of housing that might spare its occupants this kind of depressing situation. For what is and what will be the subject of the house? A subject entirely constructed from prosthesis whose affects themselves are downloaded from the system of networks. Trying to design the abode of such an entity will not necessarily be a very stimulating project. The research carried out by a busy minority of architects thus risks no longer finding any meaning if the prototype of the Havana building turns out, after the event, to be the horizon of the human condition. To give the lie to such a sinister vision is the task that is faced, each one in its own way, by the projects emerging in 2001. By stoutly repudiating the idea of the house of the future, we gain nowa-days the possibility of producing, in concrete terms, day by day, dwellings striving for the fulfilment of the least fantastical expectations, and thereby, paradoxically, the greatest bearers of a destabilization of architectural and social codes that are rarely questioned. ●

Notes

[1] Foxa building, press report 'Techno Vista Social Club' published in *Jalouse*, no. 35, November 2000, p. 84. Michel Figuet, photographer. There would be more material hence-forth for architects in the popular press than in the pallid publications specific to the field of architecture. At least the absence of critical and theoretical content poses less of a problem.

[2] Manuel de Landa, *A Thousand Years of Non Linear History* (New York, Swerve Editions, 2000).

[3] Michel Serres, *Hermès 1: La Communication, Hermès 2: L'Interférence, Hermès 3: La Traduction, Hermès 4: La Distribution* (Paris, Editions de Minuit, 1969, 1972, 1974, 1977).

[4] cf. conference 'Things in the Making: Contemporary Architecture and the Pragmatist Imagination' at MoMA (New York, November 2000) where we sketched out the limits of wholesale importation of the idea of 'pragmatism' into the field of architecture.

[5] cf. one of the rare texts giving pride of place to this question: 'Point de vue Image du Monde', Dominique Lyon (Paris, IFA, Carte Segrete, 1994).

[6] cf. our text 'L'Architecture offshore' in ArchiLab sup-plement of *Beaux-Arts Magazine*, no. 192, May 2000, where we considered the Parisian situation.

[7] *Edward Scissorhands* (1991).

[8] Medhi Belhaj Kacem, *Society* (Auch, Editions Tristram, 2001) p. 336, cf. also: '*Esthétique du chaos*' (Auch, Editions Tristram, 2000).

Reversible Habitat
(Other Ways of Housing)
∎
Manuel Gausa

LITTLE BOXES ON THE HILLSIDE
LITTLE BOXES MADE OF TICKY-TACKY
LITTLE BOXES, LITTLE BOXES, LITTLE BOXES
LITTLE BOXES ALL THE SAME.

(Folk song by Malvina Reynolds, popularized by Pete Seeger)

The three little pigs, this lovely, very perverse story – and at the same time so effectively instructive for kids who always have an answer for everything and are inclined to an unorthodox imagination – tells the story of how three little pigs with pretensions to be do-it-yourself architects spend their time proposing diverse solutions for build-it-yourself construction to the tedious theme of the individual habitat.

Needless to say, it is the worst of the three (that is to say, the most conventional) who ends up winning. And in keeping with logic, he is the oldest, most vitiated by routine and knocked about by life but also the most perverted by the pragmatic way of a cautious 'possibilism', incorrectly referred to, sometimes, as 'realism' . . .

And then there are the other two more rebellious and cavalier pigs that try alternative technical systems and new formulae of relations with the landscape (biological materials, light structures, dry constructions, reversible assembly, temporary occupation – understood as ephemeral – etc.).

But things just do not work.

The Hard Reality (the big bad wolf, convenient metaphor for the vast accumulation of obstacles that unceasingly stalk professionals) destroys invention: too much idealism, too much ingenuity, too many unforeseen events, too many imperfections – failure.

The consequence: seeking refuge in brick, symbol of what is tried and tested, reliable and guaranteed.

Traditional, therefore conservative...

The moral to the story: novelty, risk and innovation are punished in the end.

End of story.

The end? Perhaps not. Recent research promises new solutions, new features and, who knows, possibly another end: new techniques; new services; new possibilities; new, more precise applications; new, more exact elements; new ideas; other opportunities.

The city changes. The nature of things changes.

Stories too can change (maybe). ●

Manuel Gausa, 'Los tres cerditos convenientemente revisados'
(The three little pigs appropriately revised), in Quaderns, no. 217, 1997.

I. Topics

Three topics inevitably come to mind when one tackles the theme of the dwelling as domestic refuge – or enclosure.

• The first, this strange jumble of elements definitively incorporated into popular cultural baggage, combines, in equal parts, the double pitched roof, traditional tiles, the ramp (with balustrade), stone chimneys, French windows with cross struts and the gilded door-knockers. One could see in a Sunday edition of the paper *El País* the image of this astonishing Frankenstein illustrating the most frequent cravings of a middle class that 'would seem to have transformed its tastes into an elementary and abstract system of ideologies'[1]; X-ray – according to the statistics – of 'our dream house', 'likeness' of the most common and entrenched of our intimate tastes (rural nostalgia, caricature of well-being, conjuring up the memory of timelessness . . .).

• The second topic refers to an ambiance overloaded with 'production' and *attrezzo* [utensils, tools'] generally guarantors of the 'domestic interior': the armchair (with headrest), the lamp with shade (in parchment) and the chandelier (Venetian), the curtains (in lace) and the hangings (with flounces), the carpets (Persian) and the objects (in porcelain), the paintings (representing landscapes) all mixed in with 'old–new' electronic gadgets that have become everyday pieces of furniture (TV set, VCR, hi-fi) . . . All that composes an interchangeable decor to which must be added the wood-burning fireplace (electric), the spiral staircase (fashioned on the lathe) or the built-in bookcase and the shelving in plaster (with Ibiza-style arches) or in wood (with mouldings). A more or less Kitsch repertory that, however, would convey the 'trans-cultural', commercialized and manufactured impression of HOME.[2]

• The last topic is the 'garden dwarf'. The figurine in coloured ceramic – a gnome or a fawn – invades many flower-beds and borders around a multitude of more or less 'kidney-shaped' swimming pools. This frozen toy is the main protagonist – next to the concrete barbecue pit – of another *attrezzo*, this one outdoors, which shows, here also, the success of everything nostalgic and sentimental. It is this little extravaganza that François Roche distorted so cleverly in a little-known installation,[3] by definitively endowing one of these bearded and always grinning leprechauns with rifles and cartridge belts; little guardians of our furthest imaginations.

Beyond contexts and cultures, these topics today constitute the authentic 'fetishes' of our popular culture. In a time when the image has become an advertising spot, these 'everyday objects of desire' appear as virtual – and also deeply real – representations of the 'universal house', that most vast 'icon' of domestic space par excellence: familiar, atavistic, pleasant and, if possible, a bit infantile.

It is an everyday decor successfully depicted in a large number of recent films (from *Edward Scissorhands* to *Pleasantville*) and Georges Ritzer, in his book *La Macdonaldisation de la société*,[4] analysed so effectively by associating it with McDonald's products. Perhaps it is the Disney industry that has done the best job of following McDonald's example and taken advantage of these intuitions. But it is especially in the domain that concerns us here, that of the single family house, that the consequences have been the most crushing, the most explicit and – perhaps – the most devastating by making figurations of it that would reproduce and multiply mostly these nostalgic and 'neo-traditionalist' visions of little pseudo-popular caricatures (not far removed from the 'neo-historicist' visions inherited from postmodern revisionism) in the new housing developments favoured over the last few years by economic growth and infrastructure development.[5]

This action – and another parallel one in which the dwelling would no longer be this ritualistic and symbolic 'vera icona' but a mere 'machine', severe and functional – invades the land today. The attention given to new lifestyles or to the landscape thus gives way to the repetition of figurations or pre-established regulations, without qualitative criterion or possibility of interaction with the landscape, the programme or the user himself.

Today, however, one can detect hints of an evolution allowing one to point out new concepts in the way to approach contemporary housing: novelty in the design of the inhabited space properly speaking (the residential cell and the interior landscape that refers to it), but also in the definition of these new urban support systems (and hence, the communal decors associated with them), intended to ensure an efficient (and renovated) relation between housing, town and open spaces.

One can imagine a dwelling closer to the quality of life and the suggestive fantasy of 'leisure' and 'well-being' than the habitual 'austerity' or 'appearance' of a space designed solely as a simple social 'necessity' or 'stereotype'; a dwelling founded, in sum, on diversity and individuality more than on homogeneity and the community. A 'place' for projection and pleasure more than for simple protection or refuge, for a heterogeneous singularity produced from plurality. Following the 'casa-caja', the box-house (neutral container), is the 'casa-capa', the layer house (active envelope); following the 'distribution' dwelling, the 'landscape' dwelling or multi-faceted habitats for versatile users.

This text aims to gather these reflections on the idea of the habitat as a non-typological place, a theme that could be approached from multiple points of view: morphological heterogeneity, the relation with the city and the open systematization of everything communal. . . . We want to focus here on a new and possible relation with the landscape – a reversible relation – far from 'impositive' colonization as currently practised, as well as on a new and possible relation with the market and industry as agents involved in a new – and also possible – habitat 'format'.

II. Links and deposits

The landscape has appeared lately as the possible articulating element of a more flexible order and no longer the 'possibilist' residue of old-style planning, an order capable of opposing traditional tectonic developments of urban structures by favouring more versatile relations (not 'impositives') in tune with the dynamics triggered henceforth.

Such dynamics would suggest the ability to act with the place and with the user with a less formal attitude, more informal because unstable and mutable, open to the temporary, the ephemeral, the impermanent, and relevant to a culture of mobility and precariousness of events.

These are dynamics that, in any case, would not come from old 'beaux-arts' rules, heirs to an eminently semi-urban or 'compositive' vision, but of a fruitful complicity with a contemporary decor more receptive to plasticity, surprise and, finally, the exploration of processes based on tasks and models, on sequences and textures more reliable than axes and geometries. They would be based on 'traces' rather than on 'tracings' whose attraction would reside largely in disinterest towards the orthodoxy of language. They would be universes related to experiences arising from diverse fields of discipline and whence would flow plastic resources influenced by recycled processes, reinterpreted, as much from a pioneer 'Land Art' as from the wild and expressive nature of contemporary iconography. This would be an expressiveness in keeping with a new contemporary perception that would have, in any case, replaced the old persistence of vision founded on contemplation of another, based on a new, fleeting, fragmented, dynamic, progressively on the edge between the artificial and the natural; between the vacant and the active.

We should thus underline the implicit possibilities of this notion of evanescence as 'short-term depot', a 'reversible' presence associated with a certain idea of the inhabited lay-out, like a little enclave 'slipped into the landscape': hidden elements that nestle or thread themselves into the landscape and which would conjure up a non-aggressive occupation – of low density – of certain spaces, from a localized dispersion of little individual entities. These would be light constructions and structures only 'placed' on the landscape, without the intention of establishing geometric or volumetric deposits in places where the features of the natural space should not be altered.

The old urban dichotomy between 'urbanizable' and 'non-urbanizable' zones would then make way for diverse strategies for colonizing the landscape, varying according to the specific character of the place; such strategies could even eventually, in certain situations, put the idea of the permanent colonization of space into crisis (and, therefore, the implicit intent to underline its immanent value based on the 'stable' figuration) and replace it with other types of models based on this 'reversible' occupation, capable of receiving uses and contracts a precario. The natural landscape would appear as a scarcely modified space, not developed but adapted, by artificial 'layers', superimposed and slipped over the ground that receives them.

The 'magic boxes' drawn by Abalos-Herreros in his 'AH' project (1996) translate this idea of a generic contract with the landscape through a new idea of the habitat: machines designed as simple technical elements, 'as a tractor, a harvester or a tanker lorry might be', which would not pretend to enter into competition with the landscape but would 'translate the slightest stability and the greatest fleetingness of man's life and of the habits surrounding him'.

It is by starting from such considerations that it is fitting to comment on the work of the Actar group, their project MOAI (Modulos Optativos de Alojamiento Interurbano) – made concrete by the M'House houses and the Paraloop project – or projects such as the consultation '36 propositions for a home' led by Périphériques, the 'Amphibious living' of the Bureau Venhuizen, the 'Temporary settlements' of Cero 9 or the 'Housescapes' of IaN+, and even the 'Six Chimneys' of S&A a, among others, oriented towards a search for tactical mechanisms of residential colonization capable of fostering less aggressive, even evanescent, occupations, slipped, hidden, woven into or deposited amongst the vegetation and topography. These potentials would suggest, in any case, the capacity to act based on the mutable, the ephemeral, the random and the fleeting, an ability that is relevant to a culture open to mobility, precariousness and the rapid amortisation of objects and events.

These dismountable, adaptable, evolving architectures would allow unlimited combinations, such as the superposition of layers or superficial information messages, like messages incorporated into diverse skins intended to offer a more casual vision of the architectonic image and of its relationship with its milieu. A fragile, light, ephemeral, temporary or evanescent vision would refer to an architecture of installations more than of constructions; one of infiltrations (or of incisions) more than monumental structures; one of tattoos more than make-up.

An architecture that would refer to new lifestyles but also to new inhabited formats.

III. Kit houses – kinder houses

This necessity of interaction between current diversified demands of a certain sector of cultural sensitivity more concerned with the environment, the contemporary individual himself and the current strategic needs of industrial production today allow for offering alternatives to the 'residential article': the idea of a universal model (type) intended for a standard family has given way to the development of a line of products designed for strategic sectors of the population, clear – and not always massive – market segments.

Such products, then, would include services or more effective pledges, which would be in addition to the 'lowest cost', usually offered by the traditional prefabricated construction market, or to the strict precision – exact and 'distant' because exceptional – of those 'designer products' that would have marked the other 'slope' of historical research (from Gropius to Stark).

These 'catalogue products', new and, at the same time, 'customizable' – 'take-away houses' – meet a certain market demand oriented towards design objects, affordable and economical, and even towards quality home improvements (one has only to observe the growing importance of hypermarkets – IKEA, Aki, Habitat – targeting this segment in Europe) but also sensitive to mass-produced, seemingly customized products (Swatch watches and Smart or Twingo cars would be good examples).

In their introductory text to the international consultation '36 models for a house', the Périphériques group of architects pointed out that today we lack a new type of individual habitat, a 'close' and affordable product for a new type of consumer demand.[6] This demand refers, therefore, to the needs of a vast spectrum of populations receptive to 'another type' of products, far removed from the 'kitsch' products offered by the usual companies active in the sector; elementary, lacking imagination and not always sufficiently economical to set up, from systems still too dependent on confused archetypes (especially, paradoxically, in everything that relates to superfluous elements – the finishing – that distort techniques that were effective initially).

Facing this 'neo-traditional' implementation with unfavourable economic margins, a possible alternative route – and, over the long term, more efficient – is proposed by research and the integration of techniques, industrial materials and products, already common in other sectors with increasing development (services, heavy industry, consumer products) and underutilized up to now – if not rejected – by the traditional construction and residential sector.

Some solutions – preferably for 'dry' erection – would permit improved precision, versatility, speed and efficiency in production and construction processes and would gradually replace the traditional heavy elements with other, lighter ones made of rather 'dense', dry materials (metallic sandwich panels, multi-layered wood derivatives, possible increasing use of cement-based composites, polycarbonates and/or fibres, reactive skins and decorative patterns, etc.).

These open possibilities would allow for the organizing of new partnerships between technical design and industry. This course of action has guided several recent projects, which in any case consist of structures adaptable to multiple situations.

The 'kit house' may thus change into a 'kinder house': a place for necessity but also one for imagination and leisure.

Five recent paradigms for the industrial consumer product seem able to provide a framework for some of these solutions that have hitherto been tried based on these premises:

- The acceptance of the ICONE (referent: LEGO) would allow for the reformulation of the archetypical 'house' by setting up

– as the proposal of the Paillard-Jumeau team (Périphériques) would do – a free and contemporary version of the traditional scheme (four walls and a pitched roof) that the collective imagination would consider as absolute.

– The CAR (referent: Smart or Twingo) as 'compact abode', mass-produced, comparable in definition and type of production with the camping-car industry, although offering more varied services, would be one of the historical referents of this type of research. Among other possibilities, the 'compact multi-adherence' prototype designed by Willy Muller in 1993 would combine this interest with work on urban parasitism on these vertical 'vacant lots' of the city not yet made profitable (joint properties, interstices, etc.).

– The WATCH (referent: Swatch) as more diversified product (unique machinery, several kinds of dials and backgrounds) would guide other proposals such as the famous 'AH' houses by Iñaki Abalos and Juan Herreros, based on an integral core of services and frame panels of three different sizes that render three distinct spatial unities possible. The external aspect of this 'mechanical box' includes – as is the case for the Swatch – a vast repertory of patterns to chose from, which diversifies even further the offer and brings the product closer to the needs – and desires – of the user.

– The notion of MULTI-FURNITURE (referent: Mecalux/M3Möbel) would constitute, within this trend of assimilating the habitat to 'customizable' production systems, one step further, achieved by Actar Aquitectura in its M'House houses (1998), a menu of 'module-spaces' – floors with or without equipment – combinable (as are multi-form pieces of furniture) by juxtaposing and superimposing, in order to offer an unlimited number of spatial solutions; an 'à la carte' product, no longer just in terms of colour choice or external patterns but in the very decision of the final distribution combination (a solution relevant to each case but always on the basis of an 'immanent' system).

Beyond the final image (pure materials or added message) the quality of the project resides in the design of the operative system rather than in the organizing design: the Paraloop project – a strip adjusted according to coded spaces (landscape, space and relation, leisure, relaxation, etc., sized afterwards by the user, and which folds and unfolds, thus creating an inhabited 'pirouette' on a few framework bars) – would constitute the corollary of this course of action.

– L'INTERFACE (referent: i-Mac) as software container would finally guide proposals as emblematic as the 'Scape House' (1998) of Guallart-Muller-Ruiz. The dwelling for the 'digital user' would be a membrane – or screen – reactive, totally equipped with energy captors and 'intelligent' materials. This computerized space no longer allows for housing distributions or rooms but 'sub-equipment': functional fragments of variable forms 'programmable and re-programmable'.

Starting from any one of these strategies, the theme of the dwelling would be approached as a qualitative application of the necessary relation between industry and design intended to foster versatile systems and, in most cases, more economical, rapid and simple ones: solutions that are technically precise in their spatial configuration and even reversible in their construction, aligned with a more contemporary – and therefore more open – conception of form (and of amortization) of residential space.

IV. New challenges

We are aware that from now on the greatest crisis in housing is precisely not in the developed countries but in countries under development subject to vertiginous mutations and exponential growth, which manifests itself in destructured neighbourhoods of precarious dwellings. These are spontaneous manifestations not very far removed from those that occur in situations of unexpected civil catastrophe or emergency (earthquakes, eruptions, floods, fires, armed conflict . . .) that generate the habit of these deficient responses owing to an official machinery that is willing but often paralysed by lack of preparedness. These situations should absolutely be envisaged by civil organizations when designing effective solutions for the transfer, relocation and housing of populations in transit, resolved by alternative systems of sufficient dignity and quality to ensure new cores of habitations in more or less temporary zones of occupation.

However, it is in these 'extreme cases' that one best appreciates the possibility of working today in an 'ephemeral colonization' of the landscape associated with the capacity to design reversible systems of construction and occupation of the land. If, traditionally, the concepts of 'quality and solidity' represent the same thing (durability), it is henceforth obvious that new types of industrial production have given up this ancestral idea, which introduces the concept of planned obsolescence (with incorporated guarantee) as a supplementary component of the very quality of the object.

The architects Lacaton-Vassal displayed this type of dynamic linked to the 'rapid' amortisation (10 years) of a 'quality object but bearing an expiry date for obsolescence' in their famous Latapie house in Bordeaux and, subsequently, in their 'inhabited greenhouse' in Coutras.

This has allowed the actualization of a growing intuition that suggests a possible transformation of certain inertia connected with the utilization of the land: in the distinction between 'urbanizable' and 'non-urbanizable', between stable and temporary, but also in the revision of the classic desire for 'residential property' and of the value of land that goes with it. The strategic forecasting of certain 'areas of light colonization', low density and impact (because of temporary uses and not because of ownership) would in fact allow for the recycling of obsolete terrain, of reduced or no profitability but of high environmental value (quarries, agricultural slopes, old reused infrastructures, recovered borders, etc.) occupied according to temporary contracts *a precario*: concessions that could respond to the progressive acceptance of residential mobility associated with fluctuations in the job market and made concrete by the increase in temporary habitation − and of the work space that is associated with it − for certain dynamic communities (students, young couples, immigrants).

Or these could be concessions that might articulate effective responses in cases of catastrophe or civil emergency.

All this testifies to the existence of a debate − barely sketched out − around the will to 'preserve' our milieu, the need to 'intervene' and the subsequent interest in the forms of occupation, action on and colonization of the territory and the landscape. Which, in sum, refers to the decomposition of the old models and their replacement by new systems of relation and a new sensitivity with regard to the landscape, a sensitivity which would have substituted a new contract with nature for the old contract with the city, evanescence for presence, the fleeting flash for the durable monument. ●

Notes

[1] cf. El País Sunday supplement and other infographies on the theme in *Quaderns*, no. 221, 1998.

[2] Roemer Van Der Toorn; 'Archaïsme, Fascinisme, Réflexivité', in EUROPAN III Catalogue, Europan, Paris, 1994.

[3] The installation 'Sweety' was François Roche's response to the consultation 'A la recherche de la maison modèle', organized by the Périphériques group of architects.

[4] George Ritzer; *La McDonaldisation de la société*, Ariel, Barcelona, 1996.

[5] Adolf Stillman: 'La maison comme article', in *A+T*, no. 10, 1997.

[6] Périphériques proposed the theme of the single-family dwelling as the subject of international attention after observing the growth trend in this type of market. The sole constraint was economic: not to go over a budget of 499,900 francs, tax included.
Périphériques: *36 Modèles pour une maison*, Périphériques, Paris, 1997.

Chair, Cupboard and Carpet: Inhabiting the Household Archipelago

Marie-Ange Brayer

What is inhabiting? Are we talking about image, function, form, structure? Allegory, place? Inhabiting is being forever tugged between objects (house), functions (accommodating) and structures (private/public). But inhabiting is also subject to epistemic folds that come from the field of objects, and from the way they appear and are appropriated. These household objects turn inhabiting into an event, beyond form and beyond function. They make use of schemas, agencies of micro-environments, operators of dislocations, vectors of heterogeneous geographies, which transform inhabiting into an archipelago of cognitive and sensory territories, which are at once moving and fleeting. These household schemas are devices of de-monumentalization, they nibble away at the 'gigantic cheese' of architecture, as in Lapo Binazzi's performance (1969), and sustain us with a variation of scales and with the changeability of things. And with the precariousness of the body.

The chair, a motive for the dwelling

Radical architecture, so called by the art critic Germano Celant, developed in the late 1960s in Europe. As one of its leading theoreticians, Andrea Branzi, pointed out, it didn't involve utopia, except perhaps a 'critical utopia'; rather, it involved realism pushed to the limit.[1] For Branzi there is no such thing as research-free architecture, just as there are no scientific breakthroughs that haven't entailed research.

1. Archizoom, 'Superonda' (Superwave), Poltronova, 1966–67

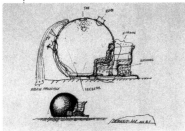

2. Walter Pichler, 'Intensive-Box', 1968

The civic, municipal dimension is the main goal of architecture. Architecture cannot develop without experimentation or without conceptual traverses. It was Hans Hollein who declared in 1965 that 'Everything is architecture'.[2] Art, design, action, performance and architecture all now engage in dialogue in the same operational vein, to wit, appropriating the present and 'discontinuous reality' in its most composite texture. The connection with the physical environment was profoundly altered, while installations and actions reactivated the dimension of the 'local'.[3] We then found ourselves up against a heterotopia of the architectural place, dealing with a crisis of the architectonic object as entity, to borrow from Tafuri discussing Piranesi.[4] The amazing proliferation of furniture created in the 1960s and 1970s was part and parcel of this busy interaction between creative modes. For these artists, designers and architects, the chair turned into a playful factor of inhabiting, with many meanings and many purposes, as can be seen in the countless postures permitted by the undulations of the 'Superonda', designed to act as bed, divan and chaise-longue, all at once (ill. 1). What could be more local than a chair? It demarcates a kind of mooring and a territory, but avoids making a permanent mark. A chair is quite capable of formulating space as a cognitive field. You sit down in it and, right away, a bubble of isolation surrounds you. In his research into the

3. Gianni Pettena, 'Wearable chairs', 1971

'Intensive Box', Walter Pichler tests this faculty of spatial condensation by the chair (ill. 2). Once a person is seated, he creates around himself an intensive field that stems from inhabiting.

In this overall refusal of the object in favour of the event, the chair helps us to explore flexible forms of inhabiting, linked with the setting and the environment. In them, the chair is neither an object nor an instrument, nor an architecture in the strict sense, but a 'motive'; it foments an intrigue and reintroduces an active relationship with living. The chair is nomadic, it has no set territory. The displacement inherent to it can be adapted to the urgency of the action and the appropriation of the moment. 'The chair has been the sole structure of inhabiting to undergo a complete, albeit separate, revolution; the house has experienced much less radical morphological modifications. We have even reached a point of defining the house or dwelling as what is "around" the chair, this latter representing a perfect minimal and thoroughly controllable structure, a sort of ideological copula of the world, site of its dynamic stasis and model for grasping what the architectural revolution signifies'.[5]

In 1971, Gianni Pettena, an architect close to the Archizoom and Superstudio groups in Florence, and one of the founders of 'Global Tools' in 1973, produced the 'Wearable Chairs' performance (ill. 3). 'It was to create architecture but with intuitive methods . . . there is no longer any need to speak of a chair or a house to describe the things you make: the things that you make you will be able to call chair or house only if we desire to speak of these things and nothing else.'[6] In so doing, Gianni Pettena posited that the important thing, in our relationship to objects, is not the nominative but the performative activity. 'How to Do Things with Words', wrote John Austin in the early 1960s; 'when saying is doing'. For Pettena, the chair is a potential performative pronouncement, to be reactivated. The real is a hydra buried within locutionary activities that are awakened by the performance. In 'Wearable Chairs', the chair has become a device, a 'link' in a syntax, involved in a sequencing of 'bodies'. Here, Pettena has reversed the relationship between person and chair: it is no longer the chair that supports the person but the person who bears the chair.

The chair has been harnessed to him like an instrument of torture. But the wearable chair enables the person to take a rest when he feels like it. As a paradox of repose and suffering, the chair is presented in its absolute adherence to the body: it sticks just when you feel like sitting down. As a miniature of the house, the 'wearable chair' recreates a way of inhabiting, without architecture, whose sole motive is the fluctuations of a body that has become erratic.

At the same time (1971–73), Riccardo Dalisi was producing papier-mâché chairs (ill. 4) with children from poor neighbourhoods in Naples. For Dalisi, architecture may or may not be constructed; it may also be just an experience of space.[7] The important thing, back then, for Dalisi, was to 'show the crisis condition of the object' and shatter our unambiguous acceptance of the object. In a period informed by 'structuralism', Dalisi opened, as though stripping off bark, objects that would thus reveal their 'floating' condition of scattered fragments – scattered in the sense of shredde; 'fields without boundaries, without quality and without future'.[8] The papier-mâché chairs speak to us about their poverty, but say nothing. They are suspended from the rugged silence of their materiality. Which is where they stop. Nothing more. Made by children, in a building game, they are an unhealed sore in the nomination of the object. Dalisi is perhaps telling us that the main thing is not the end purpose of the object, but the appropriation of it effected by the children of Naples. Once again, inhabiting is tantamount to the instant, the moment of appropriation, nor to the object itself, and not to architecture.

4. Riccardo Dalisi, 'Papier-mâché chairs', 1971–73

5. Alessandro Mendini, 'Sedia Lassù', 1974

When Alessandro Mendini got to grips with the chair in a famous performance, and had himself photographed on it before setting fire to it (ill. 5), he joined Dalisi in his wish to retain just the action of 'time', i.e. here, destroying the chair, and ironically taking its ashes like a relic, and declaring that it had shifted from the status of matter and object to that of memory. The chair, whose death was theatricalized on a pyre, was part of a sarcastic ritual involving the dismissal of icons. The performance spoke out against the rituals inherent

6. Raymund Abraham, 'Chair', 1971

in living (eating, sleeping, sitting, etc.), symbolized by the chair through its practical function and its symbolic dimension. For Mendini, the chair is a 'protoform', a type of archaic representation, which organizes the human environment as an extension of people's own spatial issues.

The chair is transformed, for Raymund Abraham, into a suffering body (ill. 6). It is irrevocably cleft, doomed to be taken apart, in two, like a sexual organ, like an irremissible ontological duality. In silent agony, the split chair supports a single, naked body. 'Architecture is essentially the conquest of a place', Abraham writes.[9] 'As finiteness of meanings and infinity of spirit', it is 'the formal manifestation of the physical absence or presence of man'. 'Constructed with elements with an archaic significance', 'architecture has been pushed back into history until time becomes space', Abraham writes elsewhere. 'Chair' (1971) tells us the tale of History, about the separation of body and mind, the perishable and the unchanging, and architecture that did not manage their reconciliation. This work, which conveys an experience of inhabiting issuing from the flesh, may also refer us to those 'two bodies of the King' that fuelled the mediaeval imagination, to that impossible overlap between the natural (mortal) body of the king and his political (eternal) body, from which the blood has drained. Architecture, here, is the body politic that has lost its legitimacy. Henceforth, only the natural body, the body of experience and suffering space, still conveys a 'sense', by referring to an architecture of the flesh. And it's in this particular body, torn, agape and mortal, that inhabiting occurs. The 'name of the king' has been emptied and hollowed out like a tomb. Richard II proclaims, 'I have no name', and 'know not now by what name to call myself'.[10] This doubt, 'which tackles the very foundations of language, a doubt that undermines the bond that links the word to the thing and the name to the being'[11] was also the doubt of architects like Abraham and Dalisi in their experiments with living, through the namelessness of architecture – formless object and felonious body.

As a graze on the floor, Didier Faustino's chair with the ironical title 'Love me Tender' (ill. 7) is perhaps also included in this fault between these two bodies, between the name and the thing, between body and architecture. Its feet do not simply rest on the floor. When it is moved by a body, the chair scratches, rips and causes suffering. Once again, the relationship to inhabiting is permeated by pain – physical pain, mental pain . . . The sharp feet, like the extremities of ravenous eagles, turn the metal chair into a prosthesis of the body. The chair-

7. Didier Fiuza Faustino, 'Love me Tender', 2001

8. Michelangelo Pistoletto, 'Casa a misura d'uomo', 1965–66

9. Archizoom Associati, 'No-Stop City. Neutral surface, habitable wardrobe', 1972

cum-body is thus capable of impairing, wearing out and exhausting its living space. This living space is no longer a royal body, unchanging in its nominal legitimacy, but a labile, natural body, which no longer refers to anything, permeable to suffering, destruction and death . . . In these experiences of inhabiting, the chair introduces a condition of 'reversion', at once temporal and spatial, which undermines the foundations of architecture. Here, the chair proceeds to the exfoliation of the unruffled body of architecture, gentle reversal of Orpheus' gesture, wrenching the satyr's skin, in a motion of baroque drapery – victory of music over matter. Is the chair, in the end, our sole condition of inhabiting?

The cupboard, the sequestered dwelling

What is the measure of the cupboard? Object or dwelling? Container or content? For those *arte povera* artists who produced household 'atmospheres' in the late 1960s, the work is endowed with a habitable dimension.[12] It refers to a phenomenal space, at once subjective and anti-rationalist. Sculptures with anthropomorphic proportions rub shoulders with items of furniture (beds, carpets, chairs) in installations presented by Calzolari, Fabro and Kounellis, blurring the boundaries between the space of the work and the living space. In 'Casa a misura d'uomo' (1965–66), Pistoletto is photographed beside the model of a house 'on his scale'. The hermetic work, refined like an archetype, is an anthropomorphic sculpture with the dimensions of a piece of furniture. You could walk into it the way you walk into a house, but one reduced to a miniaturized 'unit of habitation', or one with the proportions of a cupboard. At the same time, the works of Archizoom and Superstudio in Italy also conjure up this habitability of furniture. In 'No-Stop City' (1972), the cupboards can be lived in (ill. 9). 'Considering architecture as an intermediate category of urban organization that had to be surpassed, No-Stop City made a direct link between the metropolis and furnishing objects: the city became a series of beds, tables, chairs and cupboards; household furnishings and urban fittings overlapped completely'.[13] In the neutralized city of 'No-Stop City', the habitat or dwelling has become just another facility. The

044

house no longer tallies with any architecture and has been reduced to its minimal unit, standardized furniture. Dwelling and furniture thus have the same scale in the undifferentiated space of 'No-Stop City'. All internal space has vanished. By pushing modernism's various systems of rationalist logic to the limit, the better to make them implode, the Archizoom architects have turned the dwelling into furniture. The scaling down of these 'property units' ends up in a paratactical space, foundationless and erratic. In the absence of any spatial hierarchy, the distribution of 'habitable cupboards' in space is tantamount to an urban arrangement.

10. Ettore Sottsass, 'Container furniture', 1972

The same logic is at work in the designs for container furniture that Ettore Sottsass exhibited at the New York MoMA in 1972 (ill. 10).[14] By metonymy, the furniture (*meubles*) turned into buildings (*immeubles*), whose sole occupant was the household equipment. At once independent and interlinked, these latter appear to delimit a street, organized around a public square, itself a table surrounded by chairs. These utilitarian 'blocks', which are ergonomic but without affectation, make a mockery of municipal administration (aedileship). Unlike buildings, they are potentially movable and can be combined with one another. They function by an associative, irrational logic – a logic to do with condensing and shifting the dream . . . They are at once architecture, object, sculpture, furniture, human body, machine, cupboard and live-in cell, even though nothing can be put away in them, and you can't live in them either. Because they are actually citatory, semantic objects: their role is to 'quote' architecture, to make the city appear, and to do this their jurisdiction is furniture. They are super-referential objects, which abnormally enlarge each reference, rendering it independent while at the same time decontextualizing it. There are no inhabitants in Sottsass's drawings. Yet a human activity does seem to have taken place and then abandoned the premises, leaving the cupboards and container furniture there, like objects that have already been consumed and forgotten about in the no-man's-land of well-worn signs.

12. Joe Colombo, 'Man–Woman Container', 1964

Robert Morris stands up in 'Box for Standing' (1961) (ill. 11). The box houses and accommodates him, as cupboard and coffin alike. The body offers its dimension to the sculpture.[15] This work, which is akin to 'Box with Sound of its Own Making' (1961), gets rid of all interiority. The

subject here is just an empty agency, and the work is a frame for a minimum habitable space. As a frame between interior and exterior, body and environment, the cupboard is an extension of the ego, a prosthetic ego. The frame – agency of parergon for Kant – plays a crucial part in Robert Morris's work. It enables him to dodge representation by means of its device of 'presentification': the frame here presents a body, it is what closes and what opens, link and separation. At the same time, it has been given the depth of the object, intercessor between the physicality of the body and that of the world. The cupboard is not only that 'primary structure', that gestaltic form, of which the Minimalists were particularly fond, but it is also immanent in its domesticity, and in its being-there. It might be said of Robert Morris's work that 'A person is lying down who wants to sleep'.[16] Morris's lying–standing body, in its habitable space, is suspended. Torpor from the absence of sleep, from the absence of awakening. Like 'Murphy' swaying back and forth, day and night, in his rocking chair, at once bed and cupboard, the mind stays in a state of paradoxical wakefulness, between the world of the human and the world of things.

11. Robert Morris, 'Box for Standing', 1961

In 1964, Joe Colombo produced some multi-purpose containers, and in 1972, 'Total Furnishing Unit'. These containers are simultaneously cupboard and transportable, habitable space. When open, they define different 'private' spaces, which are detached from one another (ill. 12). These days, there are plenty of architects appropriating the cupboard, but the cupboard no longer has the critical scope of the artistic and radical experiments of the 1960s. The cupboard currently refers to a structural order. The architect makes use of it for compositive purposes: Shigeru Ban appropriates it as an item of furniture and architectonics. In 'Furniture House' (ill. 13), the cupboard is used to tidy the space that it partitions off and furnishes with elegance and discretion. It takes credit for separating the space – without dividing it – through the screen of its partitions, and keeping an open architectural form in an enclosed space. Henceforth the age is one of multi-furniture, but this no longer overtakes us with its metaphysical claims; it is the pragmatic

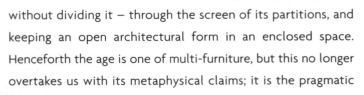
13. Shigeru Ban, 'Furniture House', 1999

instrument of our immanence, it makes sense of our horizontality to the world. Multi-furniture is operative : it can be pulled in all directions, moved, opened, closed . . . It conveys the ideology of personalization. It is the 'surrogate architecture' that makes us think that we are doing something, that we are 'active' occupants, urbanites in a hurry . . . Actar claims a 'reversible dwelling', capable of tracing 'open systems instead of closed compositions', 'a device capable of encouraging dynamic processes'. By way of a new spatial flexibility, 'new relational geographies' (M. Gausa) are introduced. Every dwelling will thus be as different as its occupants. Furniture is therefore less separation than relation; it authorizes combinations and spatial organizations. Movable equipped walls create convertible dwellings, deploying an isotropic, fluid space that can be transformed at will (M'House, 1998). Furniture is thus the conveyor of a 'reversible colonization' of the territory. The great unchanging body of architecture is thus assailed by these habitable units and this habitable furniture, which refer to the mobility of things urban and map out a 'reality of migration and communication'.[17]

The carpet, a floor in breach of the regulations
'If the modern city is uninhabitable, the deep-seated reason for this lies in the crisis of the relationship between people and the places they live in'.[18] How is it possible not to become involved in the carpet? Make the home habitable? The carpet is beyond any doubt the most perverse of household objects, because it doesn't shrink from leaving the house and invading the city and nature, covering every sort of territory, even the territory of the soul — one has only to think of the extravagant piles of carpets on Freud's 'analyst's couch', like so many shapeless layers of reminiscence (ill. 14). The carpet is the most perverse thing because it seems to partition space while contributing to its dislocation. Because it seems to guarantee us a mooring, while it projects us somewhere else.

The artistic synthesis proclaimed by the Dutch 'De Stijl' movement at the end of the 1910s developed a method of geometric spatial construction in which the predominance of the plan involved the removal of objects, which were far too irregular and expressive. Items of furniture

14. Sigmund Freud, Analyst's couch, Freud Museum, London

15. Studio of Piet Mondrian, Paris, 1925

16. Vilmos Huszar, 'Composition—space—colour', 1921

17. Bart van der Leck, 'Project for an interior', 1918

18. Lucas Samaras, 'Untitled', 1961

19. Carl Andre, '64 Steel Square', 1967

were thus neutralized and levelled; chairs, which were visually too unstable, were transformed into a dovetailing of chromatic plans in primary colours. In Piet Mondrian's studio (ill. 15), as in all neo-plasticist interiors, such as the famous Rietveld Schroeder House (1924), the furniture is dematerialized by the flat composition. Within this neo-plasticist space, the carpet is a spatial field like the painted wall and the table top. In this absence of spatial depth, the carpet already incorporates in itself the flatness of the space, and turns out to be the best pupil of this modern, synthetic and abstract order that invades furniture.

Let us take two neo-plasticist spatial experiments to do with the interior: 'Composition—space—colour' (1921) by Vilmos Huszar (ill. 16) and 'Project for an Interior' (1918) by Bart van der Leck (ill. 17). With Huszar, spatiality is reliant upon the chromatic expansion of the surface. The colour plans overlap the corners and negate the architectural boundaries of the space. The legal status of the coloured planes is identical to that of objects, subject to the same formal and chromatic reduction. In this general equivalence of homogeneous elements — object, architecture, surface, pattern — the carpet levitates beyond any mooring. Van der Leck would go further, by fragmenting space into erratic units, doing away with all spatial hierarchy and neutralizing all compositional surfaces. All the elements, squashed and compressed into the same plane, without any spatial differentiation, have the same value: the cupboard has become a carpet. In this deterritorialized space, architecture proceeds from the spatialization of coloured fields; it is intensive in relation to the non-figurativeness of the composition, where the object and the furniture are segments of colour like the rest. Living has no foundation.

The Minimalist spatial experiments of the 1960s would swell the surface of the floor or ground with a stratum stemming from the grid, partitioning space, at once a removal of the subjective order and supplementarity (ill. 18). When Carl Andre produced his floor pieces, there was no longer any spatial illusion or anthropomorphism (ill. 19). The material (metal sheets) is dissociated from the floor, and Carl Andre invites the viewer to walk over his piece, as if it were a carpet. A palimpsest of the floor, the 'carpet' is a modular grid and the basis of a generic space. Yet this tautological floor, which is supposed to refer just to itself, is neither a carpet nor a sheet: just a platitude. If we borrow from Michel Foucault, we might suggest, in this Nietzschean critique of the depth in Carl Andre, that 'there is nothing absolutely primary to be interpreted, everything is already interpretation'. In this indefatigable reference of signs to one another, and in this permanent refraction of interpretation, Carl Andre's floor pieces involve an order of resemblance, in which there is no emergence of meaning, just a floor/carpet reversion, which obliterates any origin and makes all territory fictional.

In Luciano Fabro's 'Pavimento, tautologia' (1967, ill. 20), the operation involved washing the surface of a floor, making it shiny, and then covering it with newspapers. For Fabro, tautologies are 'a way of taking note of things that are already there'. The surface has been exfoliated in heterogeneous layers of newspaper, once again consummating a loss of referent. There is no more unity, nor is there any territorial originality. Elsewhere, a sheet of lead outlines a perimeter on the floor, like a carpet, but peters out, curling at the edges, as if to make any kind of limit unlikely (ill. 21). The 'scatter piece' was frequent at that time: scattering, dispersal of scraps of rubber (Serra), rags (Pistoletto), plastic blocks (Andre, ill. 22), bits of felt, coils of copper, cotton waste (Morris, ill. 23). These works, which, in some instances, stem from shapelessness, do away with any space of representation and projection, in favour of a dimensional, random, referent-free space. On the floor they put a territory 'in ruins' back together again. Within this discontinuous space, the carpet has swelled and dwindled and, in its distensions, the architectural space is dismantled. For many of these artists, these pieces are an architecture of the non-constructed, in other words, 'negatively constructed, in the opposite sense, going from completion to incompletion'.[19] But the carpet may also refer to clothing, as with Franz Erhard Walther (ill. 24), and help to construct a spatial experience where the body is ever-moving architec-

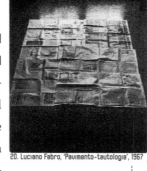

20. Luciano Fabro, 'Pavimento-tautologia', 1967

21. Richard Serra, 'Tearing Lead from 1:00 to 1:47', 1968

22. Carl Andre, 'Spill (scatter piece)', 1966

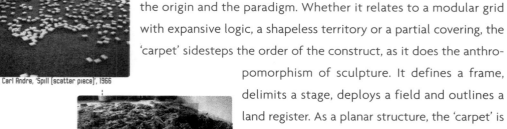

23. Robert Morris, 'Untitled (Threadwaste)', 1968

24. Franz Erhard Walther, 'Gleichzeitigkeitsstück', 1969

25. Rem Koolhaas, 'Delirious New York', 1975. 'Central Park, a synthetic Arcadian carpet, grafted on to the Grid' (plan circa 1870)

ture. In the 1970s, these carpet–clothes would become cupboards and supple boxes or caissons, with the dimensions of the body. For Gottfried Semper, the origins of architecture may reside in textiles, but the carpet is also included in this 'principle of covering', as defined by Adolf Loos, for whom the covering is something primary in architecture. So, as for Franz Erhard Walther, the carpet is also the covering or clothing of the earth.

This differential topology of the carpet, which greatly affected artistic praxis in the 1960s, questioned both the origin and the paradigm. Whether it relates to a modular grid with expansive logic, a shapeless territory or a partial covering, the 'carpet' sidesteps the order of the construct, as it does the anthropomorphism of sculpture. It defines a frame, delimits a stage, deploys a field and outlines a land register. As a planar structure, the 'carpet' is legitimate only when 'laid' on a floor, which it both reveals and conceals. Its field of induction likewise raises the question of place and habitation. As soon as you walk across Carl Andre's pieces, you are formulating a habitable space. The work doesn't represent; it depicts, in its tautological order, the territory. The carpet circumscribes a locality, which is related to the spatiality of the onlooker. It is the substratum and lever of an action. Michael Fried was probably right to define minimalism by its theatricality. These Carl Andre works are stage-like spaces, which absorb us like actors.

In 'Delirious New York', Rem Koolhaas describes Central Park as a 'carpet', in other words like an artificial nature that has colonized the Grid that underlies New York and its 'archipelago of blocks'. 'A catalogue of natural elements is taken from its original context, reconstituted and compressed into a system of nature ... Central Park is a synthetic Arcadian carpet', 'grafted on to the Grid' (ill. 25).[20] The 'quantifiable space' of the grid – that age-old dream of 'urban geometry' – contrasts with the irregular, varied, qualitative space of the 'carpet'. Here, the carpet is no longer a tautological floor, but a 'landscaped microcosm'.[21] It is typified by its 'artificial' dimension vis-à-vis the natural order. The carpet thus lies between map and territory, between representation and nature. It retains its heterogeneity in relation to the uniform organization of space by the Grid. So, for Rem Koolhaas, the carpet is a 'garden-map', at once flower-bed and geographical map.[22] In 'Caught Red-handed' (ill. 26), Koolhaas and Vriesendorp

26. Rem Koolhaas, 'Caught Red-handed'. Delirious New York', 1975. Illustration by Madelon Vriesendorp. FRAC Centre Collection, Orléans

updated this metaphor, by representing Central Park in the guise of a carpet. Within the urban archipelago, the carpet is an island-like block among the other blocks. The two anthropomorph-ized skyscrapers have freed themselves from the tabular subconscious of the Grid, lying this side of the bed, in the form of a weft or carpet. Devoid of all architecture, the Grid is empty, as if finally stripped of its architectural super-ego. Here, Central Park is, ironically, the Jamesian image in the carpet.

This carpet – 'landscape-garden', 'composite work', a mixture of nature and artifice – was already described for us by late-19th-century literature, one of the finest examples being Poe's 'Landor's Cottage'. In it the valley unfolds a ground so 'miraculously green' that it conjures up the 'velvet of the natural carpet'.[23] A cottage nestles at the head of this valley like a 'picture'. The cottage is every bit as marvellous, made with just as much art as the valley. Inside, the elegant shapes of the furniture seem, for the narrator, invented by the 'same spirit that drew the plan for the gardens'. 'The parquet floor was covered with a carpet made of dyed wool of an excellent fabric, with a white background with a repeated pattern of round, little green designs'. There is an extraordinary mirror-like aspect in the narrative between interior and exterior, with the carpet as the epicentre – a projection of the garden in the form of small repeated motifs. Within this ideal-istic merger of art and nature we find the image of the carpet, a specular reflective device between nature and architecture. For Poe, more-over, 'The carpet is the soul of the apartment. It is from the carpet that not only the colours must be deduced, but also the shapes of all the objects upon it'.[24] So it is quite easy to understand that the narrative arabesque and the dreamlike colour effects of a whole tale can also be taken from the carpet. When a nature so beautiful that it seems artificial is conjured up, it is therefore the image of the carpet that is summoned. The carpet imbues the domestic space and its natural domestic-ity with its naturalness: inside the domestic, household space, it refers to the outside – an imported fragment of greenery, a patch of

27. RsSie.D/B : L, 'Fractal City', Rotterdam, 1999

28. Lewis, Potin & Lewis, with Block, 'Tartan Lands', 2001

29. Dominique Lyon, 'Gran Horizonte', 2001

30. Actar, 'Metapolis', 1999

territory tamed by the order of representation. The carpet, as we have by now understood, is exotic, it invariably comes from somewhere else. Its ambivalence perverts inhabitance, because it is the agent of interpolation between interior and exterior.

The carpet is also a 'topomorphy', conveyor of the morphogenesis of the territory. 'Fractal City' (1998, ill. 27) by François Roche (R&Sie.D/B:L) reverses the relationship to the ground as foundation. Here it is the raised ground, become carpet, that covers and officiates as archi-tecture. For Actar, the 'fractal landscape' is an 'osmotic ground'. In this abo-lition of the figure/ground, nature/artifice polarity lies the 'carpet', 'ground on ground'. Carpet and ground now form the same 'operative land-scape', criss-crossed by strategies of camouflage and infiltration. The pur-pose of Willy Müller's 'occupative structures' is to occupy another city surface or ground, to wit, the vertical ground of advertising hoardings, by affixing a dwelling to them: don't they regard these hoardings as a kind of informative 'carpet' to be appropriated? Or, alternatively, doesn't 'Tartan Lands', the Lewis, Potin & Lewis plant habitat project, transform the habitat into a plant car-pet (ill. 28)? The tracery of the garden and the geometric sartorial motif of the tartan form the same territorial tapestry. The habitat is made up of several layers of plant sheets, on which a tartan pattern is printed in relief. These sheets have a role that is at once struc-tural and decorative, as partitions and carpets alike. In these differ-ent architectural explorations, carpet and ground are osmotic. The carpet is no longer a specific perimeter, an enclave, a discontinuous space in the landscape, be it urban or domestic. It is stripped of its status as intercessor between the ground – as material substratum – and the territory – as a mental configuration. The ground-carpet is everywhere and nowhere all at once. It is co-extensive with the architec-tural field. With it, architecture no longer has any form. In the imagi-nary subdivisions of Dominique Lyon's 'Gran Horizonte' (ill. 29), the lawn-covered roofs are carpets for household activities (playing, sunbathing, DIY, sports, etc.), and are presented in a continuous way with the landscape's skyline. How does one live in the carpet? How does one live in nature? By transforming both into household landscape. As an obsolete allegory of the introverted and middle-class 19th-century interior, as described by Benjamin, the carpet is now enjoying a comeback, the boom of its landscape expansion, while at the same time remaining a surface for household activities, as in 'Gran Horizonte'. In this way, the carpet produces a veritable chiasma, it is both within and without, substratum and territory. With Actar, similarly, outdoor activities (sunbathing, playing) are conducted not in nature but on the carpet which, though 'naturalized', continues to convey its domesticity (Ill. 30). In their development project for a public square in Barcelona (2000), they demarcated areas of greenery like so many 'carpets' in the urban space. For Actar, the carpet is a 'place of places', with ever-differentiated textures, but made of the same 'topological' matter as the territory.

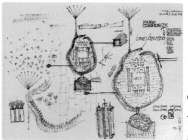

31. John Hejduk, 'The Lancaster/Hanover Mask', land development, with the Voided Centre, 1992

Living in the domestic archipelago

Chair, cupboard and carpet are all schemas that have turned the inhabitant into an actor. Through them, the inhabitant constructs his own architecture. The urban make-believe of Hejduk's 'Masks' leads to a 'topology of dwelling' that gets us to live the 'uninhabitable'.[25] Here, Hejduk pushes the bipolar logic of the subject and the object in inhabiting to its limits. In 'The Lancaster/Hanover Mask' (Ill. 31), architecture is the impossible representation of the fundamental and primitive mental space of 'dwelling', and the essence of architecture is 'merely a dead matrix which we ourselves have to animate'.[26] In Hejduk's 'uninhabitable' make-believes, the merger of object and subject tallies with the notion of 'chora', from Plato's *Timaeus*: a 'receptacle' that 'receives, in order to give them room, all the determinations but does not actually possess any'.[27] Here, there is no longer any architecture, or even any object, just a 'place of accommodation'.[28] Hejduk's 'Voided Centre' is described as a courtyard bounded by long walls; chairs are suspended in it, with access provided by corbelled planks. So you can sit in them and look at the void: 'It is almost like being on a diving board'.[29] A metaphysical fall into the void of the absence of architecture. Here the inhabitant is defined as an Observer. The items of furniture are no longer used for living in, but for examining the impossible conditions of the dwelling.

Furniture at the end of the 19th century nurtured the private experience of the household space, prompting people to sedentary projections of the dream when faced with the fear and trepidation of city and industry. In the final analysis, furniture was exotic and fantastic, and turned out to be always reflections of being, as in the writings of Kierkegaard ('Diary of a Seducer') and the short pieces by Walter Benjamin on the interior and the trace ('Paris, Capital of the 19th Century'). Fabrics, drapes, covers, cases and hangings all cast so many felted veils over the traces of inhabiting. Furniture disappeared beneath their folds, their decorative motifs invaded parquet floors, couches, tables, and lamps . . . everything was image, covering, allegory of inhabiting as a withdrawal of the urbane and confinement of the body.

The turn-of-the-century avant-gardes made furniture their prototype for experimenting with space. The piece of furniture often incorporated in it so many constructive values that it ended up evoking an architectural model. In the artistic and architectural explorations of the 1960s, furniture rid itself of its faded intimiste finery and its mimetic absorption of architecture. Furniture thus itself became a device, a cognitive tool of the real, catapulting the realm of the domestic into the realm of the city. Henceforth it outlines an archipelago of livable localities, frequented by a hasty body with uncertain outlines . . . Have the chair, the cupboard and the carpet all divulged their secrets? ●

Notes

[1] Andrea Branzi, conference on 'Radical Architecture', directed by Frédéric Migayrou, Institut d'Art Contemporain de Villeurbanne, 24 March 2001.

[2] Hans Hollein, 'Alles ist Architektur', Bau, 1/2, Vienna, 1968.

[3] Frédéric Migayrou, 'Radical Architecture', exhibition, Institut d'Art Contemporain de Villeurbanne, 12 January to 27 May 2001.

[4] Manfredo Tafuri, La sfera e il labirinto. Avanguardie e architettura da Piranesi agli anni '70, Turin, Einaudi, 1980.

[5] Andrea Branzi, Le design italien. La casa calda, Paris, L'Equerre, 1985, p. 9.

[6] Gianni Pettena, Radicals. Architettura e design 1960/75, Venice Biennale, Il Ventilabro, 1996, p. 165.

[7] Riccardo Dalisi, 'Architettura-scrittura 2', in L. Vinca Masini, Topologia e Morfogenesi, Biennale di Venezia, 1978.

[8] Ibid.

[9] Raymund Abraham, 'Spazio illimitato', Casabella, 429, 1976, in Gianni Pettena, Radicals. Architettura e design 1960/75, Venice Biennale, Il Ventilabro, 1996, p. 46.

[10] William Shakespeare, Richard II, Act IV, scene i, Paris, Gallimard/ Folio, 1998, p. 247. See also Ernst Kantorowicz, Les deux Corps du Roi. Essai sur la théologie politique au Moyen Age, Paris, Gallimard, Bibliothèque des Histoires, 1957.

[11] Margaret Jones-Davies, 'Un Roi de neige', in William Shakespeare, Richard II, Paris, Gallimard/Folio, 1998, p. 10.

[12] Carolyn Christov-Bakargiev, 'La maison dans l'arte povera', Exposé, revue d'esthétique et d'art contemporain, no. 3, 1997.

[13] Andrea Branzi, op. cit., p. 72.

[14] Italy: The New Domestic Landscape', MoMA, New York, 1972.

[15] cf. 'Robert Morris. The Mind/Body Problem', Solomon R. Guggenheim Museum, New York, 1994.

[16] Samuel Beckett, Murphy, Paris, Editions du Minuit, 1965.

[17] Manuel Gausa, Housing Nuevas alternativas nuevos sistemas, Barcelone, Actar, 1998.

[18] Andrea Branzi, op. cit., p. 148.

[19] Barry Schwabsky, 'Mel Bochner. Gravats. Représentation des premières œuvres', Exposé, revue d'esthétique et d'art contemporain, no. 2 Pertes d'inscription, Orléans, HYX, 1995, p. 143.

[20] Rem Koolhaas, Delirious New York. A Retroactive Manifesto for Manhattan, Rotterdam, 010 Publishers, 1994, p. 23.

[21] Christian Jacob, L'Empire des cartes. Approche théorique de la cartographie à travers l'histoire, Paris, Albin Michel, 1992, p. 163 ff.

[22] For a definition of 'garden-map', see Jean-Marc Besse, 'Les jardins géographiques, lieux et espaces de la mémoire', in Le Jardin, art et lieu de mémoire, Vassivière-en-Limousin, Paris, Editions de l'Imprimeur, 1995, p. 243–98.

[23] Edgar Allan Poe, Grotesque and Serious Stories, Landor Cottage.

[24] Ibid., 'The Philosophy of Furnishing'.

[25] Wim van den Bergh, 'L'Etonnement d'Icare ou la matrice des destins croisés', p. 89 in John Hejduk, The Lancaster/Hanover Mask, Architectural Association, London, Canadian Architecture Centre, Montréal, 1992.

[26] Ibid., p. 102.

[27] Jacques Derrida, 'Chora', in Jacques Derrida and Peter Eisenman, Chora L Works, ed. by Jeffrey Kipnis and Thomas Leeser, New York, The Monacelli Press, no date, p. 194.

[28] Ibid., p. 201.

[29] John Hejduk, op. cit., p. 73.

The Urban Conspiracy of Detroit (a fiction)

Kyong Park

Exactly 50 years ago, in the heart of the city, about two dozen of the most powerful men in Detroit met on. the top floor of the Penobscot building, then the city's tallest structure. The meeting was exclusive, if not clandestine. Below them, for miles and miles over the glacier-hewn plain, spread the pride of American industrialism, Henry Ford's Motor City. The destiny of Detroit, up until the last second of the second millennium, was delivered here – as an aperitif before the bounty of capitalism.

Present were executives from three of the five biggest corporations in the world, Detroit's auto companies. Across from the 'Big Three' sat a new breed of developers and real-estate magnates, who would impose a new concept of retail spaces, eventually constructed outside Detroit. The initiative was merely one segment of a residential and commercial assault upon farmlands, which later resulted in shopping malls and urban sprawl.

Invited at the last minute were city government officials who solemnly accepted the insignificance of their elected power. Facing them were the presidents and board members of Detroit's leading banking institutions, looking to privatize the 'Arsenal of Democracy', as the city was called during the Second World War, when it was the nation's leading producer of arms.

On the table lay a document titled *Would The Last One to Leave the City, Please Turn Off the Lights*. Jointly prepared by the auto industry and real-estate developers, this surprisingly brief report opened with

an introduction on the problems of centralized cities, particularly the economic inefficiency of static urban formation and the vulnerability of concentrations of population to the newly emerging intercontinental ballistic missiles armed with nuclear warheads. Sympathetic to the nation's strategic defence to decentralize its industries and population, this report recommended the regional extension of the centrifugal movement already at work, as the cities of America were expanding into metropolises.

The infrastructure that would accommodate the destined fragmentation of culture was the new interstate highway system, the largest single construction project in the history of civilization. Developed parallel to the newly created electronic communications system (initially called Arpanet, later the Internet), this high-speed vehicular network was to create irreversible movements of population and goods. Replacing traditional population centres with a matrix-based urban structure, these networks would institute the perpetual dislocation of a society and its cities and factories.

The following is a general summary of this document, a manuscript of an urban conspiracy.

Pack your bags and leave this city now

The American dream no longer lives in Detroit. The city is crowded with foreigners who do not speak our language and who are not willing to embrace the American way of life. They do not appreciate our toil and accomplishments. They are freeloaders! Besides, the city is now too polluted to raise our children, and it is too expensive to build our new, more competitive factories there.

We need to build a new city that is more open. We need bigger roads, more cars and large yards around our houses so that our children can play safely. We must demolish all tall buildings and live on the ground once again. We need to regain our frontier. For this, our people must move back into open spaces, away from the European-style high-density cities. We have space, they don't.

Turn farms into houses

Our victorious soldiers are coming home from Asia and Europe. We need to build new houses so they can start families. The old city is packed with old houses, which will cost too much to fix. We should just let them go. Don't forget: this is the new world, and we must keep on building. Besides, the materials to build new houses are cheaper than the land prices in Detroit. And we have plenty of materials. Our new highways will quickly take them wherever they want to go.

But there are better reasons why new is better than old. First, there will be tremendous economic gain in transforming farms into houses. More profits can be made from building houses than from growing corn. Second, new houses create empty spaces that must be filled. People will buy new things for their new houses. This means new refrigerators, ovens, heaters, air conditioners, furniture, bathrooms, washers, dryers, lawn mowers, swimming pools and more. The list goes on and on. As long as we make them, people will buy them.

Thanks to television, we can convince people that they can't live without our modern products. We will design and build generic houses so that everyone will fill them with the exact same things. This will make our job easy. All we have to do is design a few things and produce millions of them. We will update our products constantly, making older items obsolete. We will then build bigger, more expensive houses, farther and farther away from the city. People will buy our newer houses and fill them again, with our newer products. But more importantly, we will keep our people uneducated, so they will not criticize us. We will make consumerism a mass addiction.

From car business to house business

All industries depend on the making of American dream houses. We must first get people to buy these houses, then they will buy our cars. They will have spaces to fill, and they will need a vehicle to transport their things. We will make sure that these houses are built far away from workplaces, so that people will buy more cars and use more petrol. The fewer of our cars they buy, the more we will raise our petrol prices. The more time we force them to spend on the highway, the better our business will be. We must create traffic jams and make them commute longer and longer distances. And we will not build or fund any public transport systems. The more we make them use their cars, the sooner they will need newer ones.

We will then automate all domestic work with our modern appliances. The Detroit factories that made war machines will now make domestic machines. Before long, housewives will need to go to work too, to buy our new, more expensive products. Women will need their own cars to drive to work, and then the children will need them too. Not only will every American family need a car, but now every American person will need one. The highways will make this happen, as they stretch the population farther and farther out. The only way Americans will be able to see other Americans will be to drive cars.

That's why we, the automobile companies, must support the production of new houses. With more new houses, there will be more new cars. It's that simple. We will help build these houses, as long as they are designed with three- or four-car garages. We are certain we will also have the support of other companies that are not represented at this meeting.

Consumerism is the real peace dividend. We must spread the American way of life throughout the world, through our concept of globalization. But we will still pretend to be just a small group of car companies. We don't want people to know our real ambitions.

On ethnic cleansing

With two world wars in just 25 years, we have to believe that the rest of the world is totally unsafe. Therefore, we need more Americans to defend this great land. And we mean real Americans!

To keep America real, we must remain the majority, resisting the tide of incoming foreigners. Remember how we made this land a great place to live. We first exterminated the natives, and then beat the French, British and Spanish. From a handful of former minorities, we made ourselves the majority.

Let the Blacks and foreigners have Detroit, and we will create better places for us outside. They can have the pollution and congestion; we will breathe fresh air and have more space. We will make sure that the residents will fight and compete against each other and never unite against us. We will create mistrust in their ranks, and allow only a few of them to watch over the rest. That's how things were done with the slaves, and we should continue that practice today. Whenever we need cheap labour, we will find it in Detroit. We will make them do the work that we no longer want to do. They will work hard and long hours, thinking that the American dream will get them to the suburbs. But we will keep them locked up in the city, just as we do with the natives on reservations.

We Whites must move out and remain in constant motion. This is the idea behind our great capitalism, which relies on change and movement to generate profit. Stability is counterproductive as it is contrary to the cyclical nature of production, consumption, obsolescence and disposal. We will design our highways so that the access points to Detroit can be easily closed, to protect us from inner-city riots. Otherwise, they will burn our neighbourhoods and kill our families.

Turn the city into countryside

This is the best part of our plan. First, we will withdraw completely from the inner city, by refusing to offer any form of financial support to any property and business in Detroit. It will be impossible to build new houses and buildings there because nobody will lend money. All new houses and buildings will then be built exclusively in the suburbs. The Federal government will help us by insuring all our loans and investments. If any of our loans or developments FAIL, the government will compensate us with tax revenue. Our plan is fail-safe.

Once we start to move our big factories out of Detroit, all other businesses, stores and even petrol stations will follow. But we will not let the liquor stores leave, and they will pollute the mind and soul of Detroit. We will make sure that it's easier to get guns, drugs and sex in Detroit than it is to register for the vote, so the people there will keep killing each other. Some of us can go into the city for a little entertainment, but we will return home in perfect condition.

We will undermine Detroit's education system by pulling out funds and corrupting school officials. We will crowd the classes, pay less to teach-

Renaissance Center

Prudential Center, Southfield

Charles Terrace

Davidson / Lodge

Chene Street
Packard Plant

Packard Plant
Michigan Central Railroad Station

Brush Park
near Eastside

Near Eastside

Near Eastside

the hundreds of thousands. We will let them rot or we will burn them. We will create an extremely inhospitable and dangerous environment, which will inject an inescapable hopelessness into the whole population. More importantly, the price of land will fall lower and lower. So low, that land will be practically free when we want it.

We are moving out now, but we will be back. According to our research, it will take about 50 years completely to destroy Detroit and its population. The research also recommends that the time to take the city back is when the average price of homes drops below the average annual income of an American. By then most of the buildings and houses will have been burnt or demolished, and it won't take much more to 'clear out' the rest of them. With so many vacant lots and open spaces, the cities will begin to look more like the countryside. A tabula rasa will have been created in the old districts, ready for us to take back for almost nothing.

ers and supply no new books to the libraries. We will support only sports programmes, because we want city residents to be strong to work on assembly lines or in fast-food restaurants. This will also breed negative attitudes towards learning, causing early drop-outs. Our goal is to make the entire population of Detroit illiterate and unqualified for any professional work. We will educate only a few of them, through scholarships and religious organizations, so they can work in the fire, police and other city departments. They will control the rest of the population, under our direction and pay.

Then we can create a new city of our own, inside Detroit. The city government, so desperate for jobs and investments, will give us big tax breaks, and will build roads and parks for us. They will have no choice but to give us what we want. If not, we will go somewhere else. The corruption that we have already bred in city hall will help us. The government will let us take control of the major municipal departments, by installing us on their boards so we can deregulate or privatize them. The new city centre will be built according to our design and concept, and we will drive the existing population out. We will raise taxes, increase living costs, use the right of eminent domain and other legal and illegal means to force the residents to sell out. They should be more than happy to move to the suburbs, because they think they will be finally getting what we enjoy.

Occasionally, we will give the city some money, never much. The departments will fight among themselves for it. This will breed corruption in Detroit, and eventually no public money will ever get to the people it is supposed to serve. It will make us look compassionate, while our goal of the complete destruction of the inner city will be uninterrupted and unsuspected.

We will then abandon the suburbs, just the way we are now abandoning the city. A whole new cycle of redevelopment and abandonment will begin, instituting a perpetual sequence of built-in obsolescence. Everyone will either be moving into Detroit or out to the suburbs, buying new homes or paying higher rent for old ones. The beauty of this plan is that nobody will be aware of it: they will think that they are getting the 'American dream'. What a brilliant idea, investing by disinvesting.

When education fails and jobs move out, the inner city will become bankrupt. It will be left with the poor, old and uneducated — few people to tax. Roads, bridges, sewers, school buildings, parks and playgrounds will not be maintained. Buildings and houses will be abandoned by

Take the land by force
The best way to take the land is by force. It's the fastest and

cheapest. We have practised this for more than half a millennium, while colonizing the world through our superior intelligence and weapons.

But it is not necessary to use armed forces now. The new method is to exploit urban fears and racial hatred. Therefore we must fill every television and newspaper with scenes of urban crime, in which black faces appear. Whether they are the criminals or just bystanders doesn't matter. Through media control and manipulation, we can create an unquestioned impression that Blacks are responsible for all domestic violence and other urban ills.

We will make Detroit seem so violent that people will flee from it as if it were a war zone. Believing that their lives are in danger, city residents will sell their properties fast and low. At the same time, we can sell suburban houses high because demand will be so great. We will continue to promote ethnic and cultural differences because racial segregation is good for our business.

State-sponsored redistribution of land is not new in America. In fact, it's how we created Detroit in the first place. We took the land away from the natives, and now we will rip off the disenfranchised and uneducated Blacks.

What is at work now is neo-colonialism, operating under more deceptive and complex methods. Hidden by countless layers of economic agreements and legal procedures, it's deeply embedded and automated in the global model of capitalism. The only notable difference is that we, the corporations, are the colonizers, not the government. You could say that we help bring peace to this land, because our methods eliminate the need for wars to seize property.

The purpose of this plan is to ensure the sustainability of corporations for the next one hundred years and beyond. We are the new government of this great nation, and perhaps of the world.

The back of this report read, 'CORPORATIONS FOREVER!'

architects' projects

›

Es Pilari

| Spain |

Abalos & Herreros |

Iñaki Ábalos (1956), Juan Herreros (1958)

From their Madrid base, Iñaki Abalos and Juan Herreros have been working together since 1984, teaching in Madrid since 1988 and running the Liga Multimedia Internacional (LMI) since 1992, an organization devoted to making artistic activities more accessible and widespread. Since 1997 they have been publishing *ExitLMI, documentos de arquitectura*. They divide their activities between writing, practical architecture and teaching, as guests in particular at the Architectural Association School in London, the Ecole Polytechnique Fédérale in Lausanne and Columbia University in New York. Keen observers of contemporary architectural work and especially concerned with research on housing, they are developing the need to think about the experiences of the recent past, both modern and postmodern. Accordingly, they reject ideals that are now devoid of meaning: positivist nostalgia for the future and the exclusive values of 'memory', equally removed from a 'present time' that has yet to be investigated.

◆

Es Pilari, collective housing
Casa Mora, individual house
Projects, Spain, 2000

The tale told by the Es Pilari residential complex project shows this critical toing and froing between the influence of modernist ideas and the lament of the postmoderns, which culminates in a clear interpretation. Architects imagine local people who, in the image of their landscape, sea, mountains and sunsets, might build small houses rooted in the land, some buildings long and others high, in a narrative that itself wavers between a viewpoint 'seeking shade in the hollow of the road' and that of the modern aerial view over the 'tapestry of fields'.

The Moorish house, Casa Mora, stands in southern Spain, right by the Alcornocales nature reserve and in a protected area, but it nevertheless typifies its location in the manner of large contemporary cities, in other words in terms that are more temporal than spatial: 5 minutes from an urban centre, 20 minutes from beaches and golf courses, half an hour from Gibraltar airport, so just two hours from Paris, London and Milan. The architecture thus experiments with the possibilities of organizing a contemporary household space, referring neither to the open-plan model nor to the traditional distribution plan, while at the same time showing a well thought-out mastery in the arrangement of their themes and forms: carefully distributed functions, Mies-like interior relations, a close eye on orientation, prevailing winds and landscape views, fluent spaces hallmarked by their objects, furniture, artworks and vegetation. Likewise, it takes on

a technical complexity, the handling of climatic and visual elements, the use of solar energy, while avoiding any show of it.

The plan is based on an additive device of parallel strips, cut into successive parts of comparable size and juggling with the indoor/outdoor ambivalence: the patios worked into the lengthwise spaces create open-air rooms, while the areas that extend beyond the geometric perimeter, pond, terrace and entrance porch, moor it in the site. It forms a non-isotropic rectangle, where the strips criss-cross diagonally, through staggered doors, while they are visible lengthwise, thanks to sliding walls over the outer apertures.

The whole makes a sort of harmonious labyrinth, associated with painstaking work to create different routes, uses and room lighting, all open to many different interpretations and lifestyles. ◆

Bénédicte Grosjean

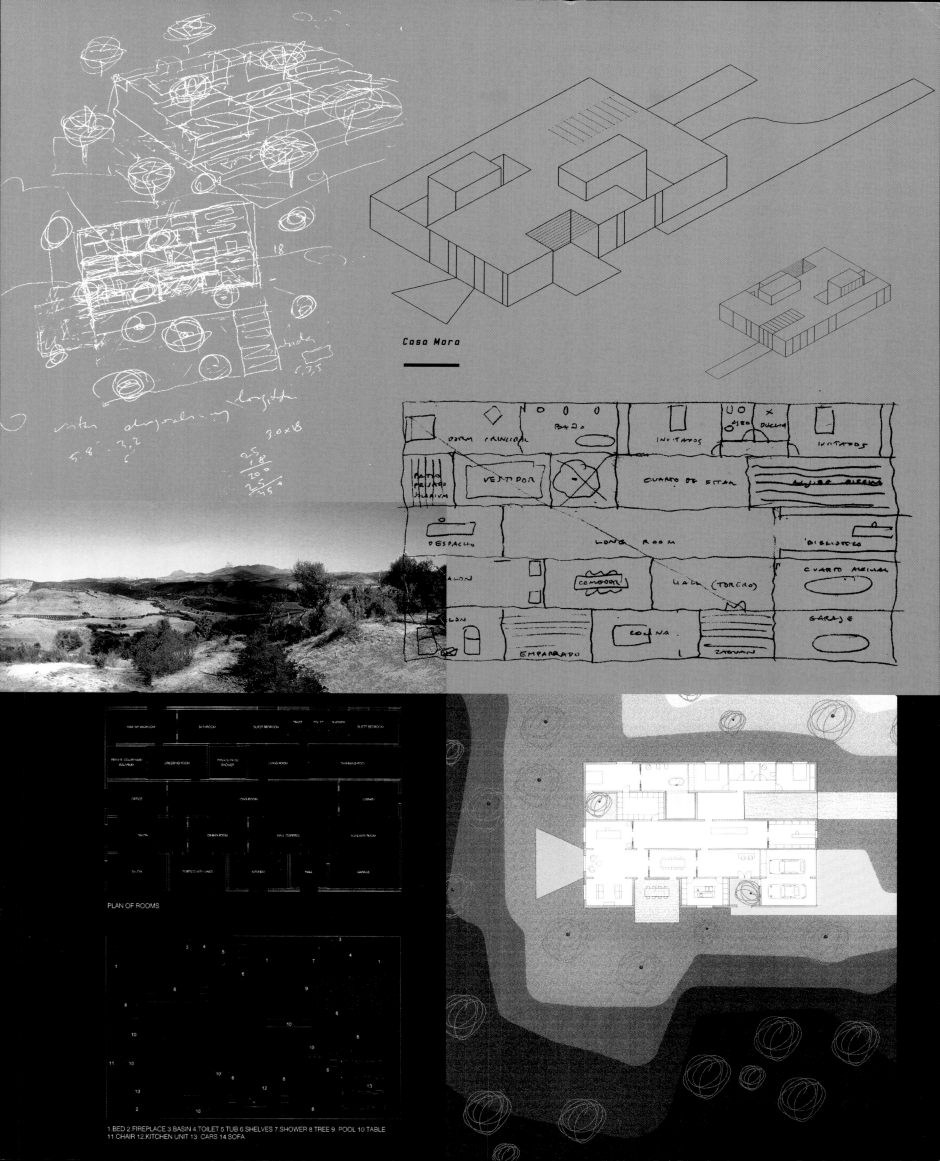

Casa Mora

PLAN OF ROOMS

1.BED 2.FIREPLACE 3.BASIN 4.TOILET 5.TUB 6.SHELVES 7.SHOWER 8.TREE 9. POOL 10.TABLE
11.CHAIR 12.KITCHEN UNIT 13. CARS 14.SOFA

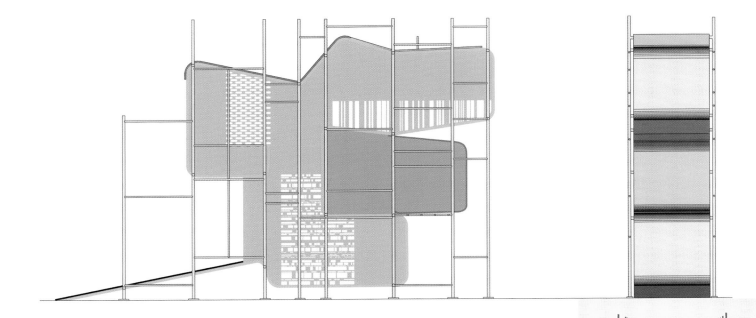

|Spain|

Actar Arquitectura|

Manuel Gausa (1959), Oleguer Gelpí (1964), Ignasi Pérez Arnal (1965), Florence Raveau (1965), Marc Aureli Santos (1960)

Founded in Barcelona in 1994, Actar Arquitectura likes to think of itself as the place where multifaceted lines of activity come together and undergo radical exploration. Producing, in no particular order, projects, buildings, books and exhibitions, the members and director of the review *Quaderns d'Arquitectura i Urbanisme*, all players on the architectural stage, are involved in a continuous and reciprocal relationship with these spheres of activity, and reject any form of division between theory and practice.

Actar projects disclaim all the various scales of the new mechanisms of linkage that are developing between society, city and territory, and are open to requests both global and local. By invariably favouring types of connection with form, Actar members seek, in their housing projects, to put appropriation strategies into practice, in other words, to leave architecture open to what still has to be formulated. ◆

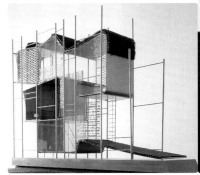

Paraloop
Prototype, Rotterdam, Netherlands, 2001

Paraloop, which was created for the Parasite Exhibition (Rotterdam, 2000), gives the impression of a fable. A man wanting a home went off every morning in search of the site of his dreams; he asked his close friends and travelled far afield, listening to elderly people and looking at children, discovering lifestyles and falling in love with landscapes. He immersed himself in languages, tastes and seasons.

On his return, these spaces took form on the basis of the intensity and recurrence of his dreams and he linked them together in a sequence of landscapes, a long one that folds and curves in a strange form: his 'landscape of landscapes', or 'place of places', the summary of his desires, where he will live happily ever after.

Actar thus pursues its quest for creative 'à la carte' housing. As in the 'M'House' (Nantes, 1997–2000), it is no longer a matter of combining modules, but rather of directly defining different 'units of satisfaction' and of assessing the desired 'quantity' of each of them. By speaking out against the typological approach to housing architecture, the Actar group also questions traditional uses, by making architecture aware of the signs and expressions of our day and age, where leisure and personal well-being predominate.

'Activity' or 'relax landscape', 'intimacy' or 'social space', 'water space', 'bodycare space' and 'parking space', all the units extend and define their materials: arti-ficial lawn and sand, rubber and plastic, wood and asphalt. Put end-to-end, the strip so formed expresses its personality, 'nomad strip' and 'ecological strip', and the architect is free to imagine the folds that will construct the diversity of the programme. Juggling with both sides and semi-transparent features, curves, slopes and reversals, the strip rights itself and coils about itself, tacking in a metal structure that can be dismantled, with many varied uses – lift, tiers of stairs and railings of the roof terrace.

Construction is thus expressed as a vector of hybridization between new pairings, inside and outside, skin and structure, place and event, while architecture presents an artificial geography, between nature and city.

To be really 'lived-in', it becomes dreamlike and 'atypical' (anti-typical), like this folded surface enveloping the multifacetedness of the programme, conjuring up new practices and sensitive to present-day cultural changes. ◆

Bénédicte Grosjean

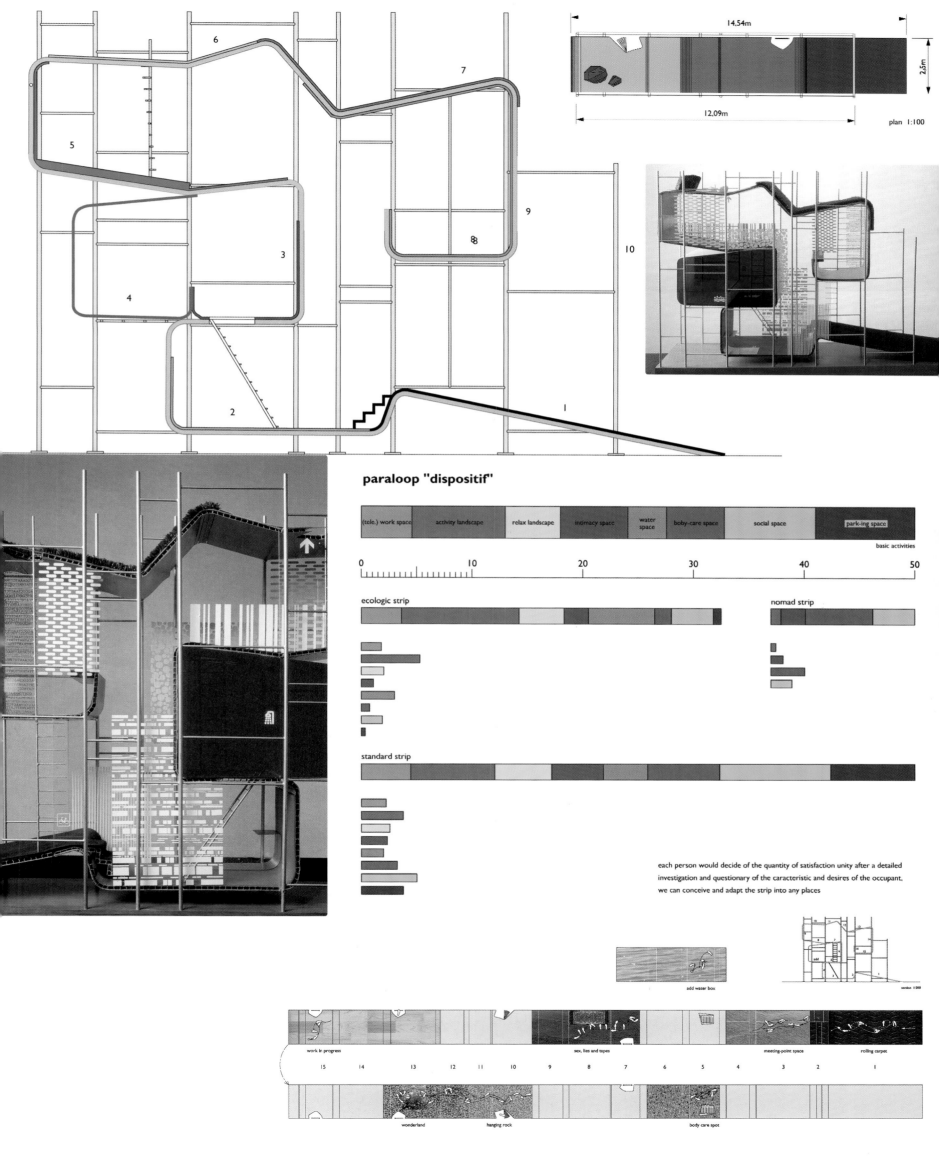

plan 1:100

14.54m
2.5m
12.09m

paraloop "dispositif"

(tele.) work space	activity landscape	relax landscape	intimacy space	water space	boby-care space	social space	park-ing space

basic activities

0   10   20   30   40   50

ecologic strip

nomad strip

standard strip

each person would decide of the quantity of satisfaction unity after a detailed investigation and questionary of the caracteristic and desires of the occupant, we can conceive and adapt the strip into any places

add water box

section 1:200

work in progress   sex, lies and tapes   meeting-point space   rolling carpet

15   14   13   12   11   10   9   8   7   6   5   4   3   2   1

wonderland   hanging rock   body care spot

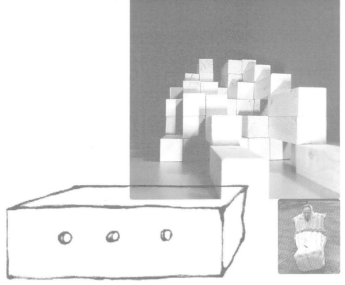

| Chile/USA |

Alejandro Aravena (Studio) |

ALEJANDRO ARAVENA (1967)

Alejandro Aravena graduated in architecture from the Santiago Catholic University in 1992. He subsequently taught the history and theory of architecture there, and in 1998, became head of that department. In addition to his architectural projects, which have won several awards, and his writing activities, contributing, in particular, to *Casabella* since the issue devoted to Chile in 1997, he was involved in the Visiting Teaching Programme of the Architectural Association, (London) in 1999, and is working as a guest teacher at Harvard from 2000 to 2003. His teaching is aimed at reducing the arbitrary factor in the production of form and conceiving the project in terms of vital relationships: his thinking focuses not on what architecture of the future should be, but rather on what it always has been.

◆

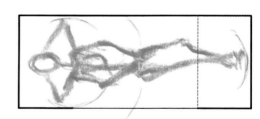

Otherwise.Ness, exercises on non-arbitrary architecture
Harvard GSD, USA. Studio, 2000

Women and Children First

04.07.99: On a site belonging to a billionaire, soccer-team owner and casino mobster, there were 200 people; 6 hours later, there were 10,000. As Pablo Allard beautifully describes it, 'starting around midnight, and before dawn, an army of 2,000 families performed the most overwhelming urban choreography in Chilean history. Every single family knew exactly where to go, what to do, how to act.' In those very first nights, architecture was reduced to an umbrella and a fire; but a rigorous geometry, the key factor for a future decent upgrading of the buildings, was already set up. The speed and urgency of this illegal seizure forced them to be very precise. Some of the precision and discipline of this subversive operation, which can also be found in emergency architecture (and its collateral effect, the 'instant city'), is what I am interested to transfer into the more conventional practice of architecture.

Otherwise.Ness

If something has characterized the modern artist, it is the hyper-awareness that his work could have been otherwise. To work with emergency architecture is to reduce the arbitrariness in the production of form, showing purely the main task of the discipline: the construction of the most accurate relationship between form and life. Yet on that winter night, despite the lack of resources, basic shelter and 'superfluous, artistic' operations were simultaneously performed (so giving rise to the question of what we call 'basic needs' and what we do not so designate).

For lack of time, the conventional execution of the project ended up giving way to the absolute present of pure reaction: emergency made it evident that the task of art is to face what has always been, to 'do always the same thing, but never in the same way' (Iommi). I like to see emergency architecture as a great source of essential, elementary, universal rules.

Beauty and Irrelevance

It seems that one is forced to choose between giving a realistic answer to emergency (risking not being able to go beyond a technical-social problem) or doing architecture (where the answer to emergency could be ineffective and inauthentic). Reality and discipline are tangent; the limit that divides them tends to be a line, i.e. there is no operational margin.

We wondered if it was possible to satisfy the need for shelter under extreme conditions and still contribute to the state of the art. To resolve the contradiction, our first decision was to replace realism with probability. The second was to try to give some thickness (consistency) to that line. The reduction that is central to emergency was thus replaced by precision. Finally, a certain slowness of pace prevailed in the studio, because, to deal with the instantaneity of emergency, we had to densify time. ◆

Alejandro Aravena

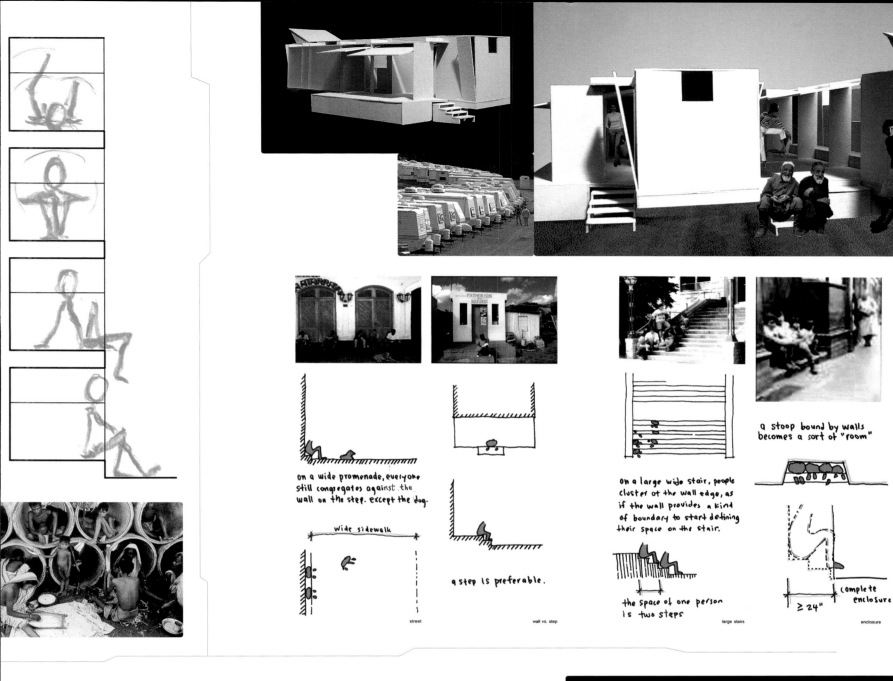

on a wide promenade, everyone still congregates against the wall on the step, except the dog.

wide sidewalk

a step is preferable.

on a large wide stair, people cluster at the wall edge, as if the wall provides a kind of boundary to start defining their space on the stair.

the space of one person is two steps

a stoop bound by walls becomes a sort of "room"

≥ 24"

complete enclosure

street   wall vs. step   large stairs   enclosure

bedroom fac   living_fac   bathroom fac   kitchen fac   screens

|France|

archi media

Fiona Meadows (1967), Frédéric Nantois (1965)

The archi media association, which was set up in 1992, started out with a two-year research project on the megalopolis in Japan. This in turn generated several architectural projects (Virtual Bauhaus, Bauhaus Academy special award) and the first architectural installations (complex(c)ity, megalovisions), expressing their interest in the use of everyday media and new technologies in the presentation of things urban. Their activities then turned to other projects, in Asia and Europe, involving new information technologies (Green and Glocal, second Europan 4 Netherlands prize, Ligne de vie, Handitech competition special prize). Their completed works, using new technologies not only on the technical level but also for what they can contribute to thinking about urban space (Drifts, the city as hypertext, Spaces of non-memory places), have secured them a place in many art events (Cities on the Move, 1st Biennale de l'image in Paris, video biennials in Bonn). ◆

Divorce House/Bo-Bo House*
Normandy, France, in progress, 2001

How is it possible to keep up a rebellious ideological position and turn a blind eye to being a fashion victim? In a perversion of models and patterns of behaviour!

BO

On an abandoned Eden site a house is being built, its typology somewhat reminiscent of early primitive huts. But the ideal of a return to roots is not part of the plan; it would be senseless in a nature whose presence is as decorative as that of a cityscape. Divorce enters into this programme, which should be understood as the application of globalized practices: the annexation of a place so as to subject it to a relocation of activities and people, the creation of a specific situation to solve the economics/use/satisfaction equation.

The divorce house doesn't belong to the place where it is situated, even though it appropriates some of the place's special features. Its materials, practical techniques and form are as much the effect of the globalization of the treatment of housing as of a compliance with local rules, whose uncertain or invented tradition is subject to regional or national directives, themselves drawn up in compliance with an overall logic. The divorce house is neither ugly and ordinary nor heroic and extraordinary: this architecture no longer seeks to express and transmit values, whatever they may be.

BO

The 'divorce house' is being developed over an area 30 metres in length and 3 metres in width, in other words, two mobile home sites. The logic underpinning its design is physically expressed by the possible division of the home into two units, both becoming satellites gravitating around a family nucleus, with a relative power of attraction. The process does not stop at this initial stage, and the break should be understood as an act of reproduction: what is involved is as much cloning as amputation. No functions are lost, because the amount of information making it possible to describe the housing project is similar in each part.

The fact of moving one half of the house to a virgin site with no other constructions on it is a form of roaming, a drift without any preordained goal, to which each participant may attach a particular significance.

The project's activity with the 'divorce house' is regarded in an extended and transversal way: it was at the root of a video triptych presented in different installations before becoming a temporary dwelling, then the prototype of a house currently under construction; and it will soon be the springboard for a mode of urban thinking: 'the divorce city'. ◆

* bo-bo: Bourgeois Bohemians

archi media

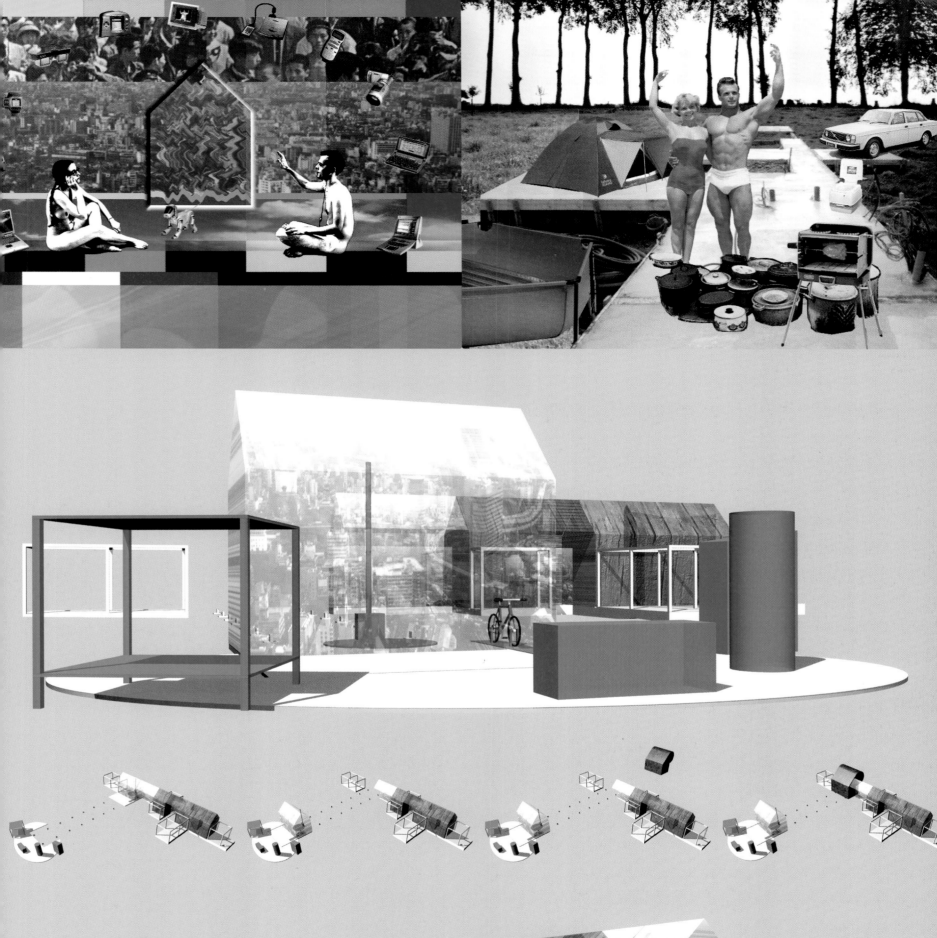

|USA|

Archi-Tectonics

WINKA DUBBELDAM (1960)

After attending the Academy of Architecture in Rotterdam, Winka Dubbeldam finished her studies in Manhattan (Columbia University) where she set up her Archi-Tectonics agency in 1994. She teaches at Columbia, in particular in the 'paperless design studios', and is keen to contribute to the development of the architect's methods and concepts — on the one hand, by incorporating the new digital technologies within the design process, on the other by making repeated cross-disciplinary detours: mathematics, philosophy. Her architectural praxis, which is based on a radical re-examination of established knowledge, goes hand in hand with a continuous programme of theorization and research. When dealing with the specific question of housing, Winka Dubbeldam develops a line of thinking about topology in both its spatial and its temporal capacity to organize complexity. By updating the idea of an organic architecture, she sees, in this investigation, a way of reconciling the many and disparate conditions of this type of programme. ◆

Gypsy Residence Trail
New York, USA, 2001

Integral Design

Industrial Innovators: the speed of innovation in industrial design technologies provides for a smoother and more inter-effective relationship between design and the life it houses. It collapses existing subject-object and interior-exterior dichotomies and hierarchies, presenting us with a set of intelligent and layered objects, surfaces and skins and a set of supple, responsive and connected subjects and interiors. With these sorts of collapses and inversions, we find ourselves in the midst of objects and subjects and exteriors and interiors, which are constantly re-tooling and optimizing each other. Gels, soft lap-tops, etc. with their mutant materials, hybrid qualities and material memories, improve the performance of the product and the relationship of the body to the product, creating greater comfort and more perfect forms. The body imprints itself on these objects, maximizing their intelligence, as these objects in turn re-contour the bodies they house. A set of unseemly interfaces is constantly under production and negotiation as the body or the private swallows its outside or its other whole, filtering and straining it through the requirements of needs and efficiency and spitting it out re-made. The object invades this same body, refining it and realigning it for optimum performance.

The house here negotiates two types: the armature, a flexible integral unit which adapts to multiple programmes and differentiated use, and the box as a wrapper, or outside protector. The armature, located in the middle, generates a zone of efficiency by which its precise shape reconfigures the geometric precision of the box. Integrated within the armature are kitchen, fireplace, heating and cooling systems, music system and bathrooms. A unit tightly connected by infrastructures of use. The box as the hard negotiation layer within the direct outside environment starts to adapt to the force of the armature and loses its rigid geometric clarity as it negotiates its 'other', fragmenting, tilting and softening.

An intelligent architecture forms an interesting example of interdependent layering, efficiency of use and negotiation of means. Here, behavioural aspects rule the state between two dynamics and architecture becomes a materially responsive expression, its intelligence promoting optimal use, high performance, smart controls and the resultant modulation of space. The human body form resembles this modulation and allows for a smooth transition between the layers. ◆

Winka Dubbeldam

SUNROOM

ENTRY

LIBRARY

ARMATURE

KITCHEN

BEDROOM

TERRACE

FLOORPL

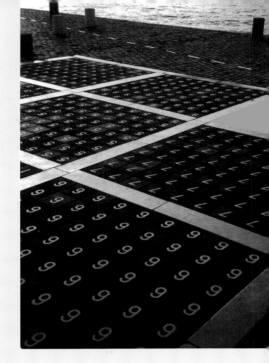

| GERMANY |

Architekturbüro Bolles + Wilson

PETER WILSON (1950) JULIA BOLLES-WILSON (1948)

The Architekturbüro Bolles & Wilson has been based in Münster since 1988. It is run by Peter Wilson and Julia Bolles-Wilson. Peter first studied in his native city, at Melbourne University, before joining the Architectural Association in London in 1972, where he was Unit Master for ten years from 1978, the year that Julia Bolles studied there, after graduating in 1976 from Karlsruhe University. They started the Wilson Partnerships in London in 1980 and the Architekturbüro Bolles & Wilson in 1987, before setting up shop in Germany. Their designs include a 'garden folly' for the International Garden and Greenery Exposition at Osaka, the WLV office building at Münster and the Kop van Zuid at Rotterdam. In housing, we should note their work on the Suzuki House, Tokyo (1993), where the narrowness of the urban building plot gave rise to a modest project cleverly mixing lightness and materiality and already signalling their fascination with urban zones of confrontation and intermediacy, with the interior-exterior reciprocity of the gaze. ◆

Bridgewatcher's House + Quay Landscape
Kop van Zuid, Rotterdam, Netherlands, 1997

The Bridgewatcher's House in Rotterdam is equipped with a high-quality music system and is occupied 24 hours of the day. It is a dwelling in which the residents are engaged in a never-ending relay, a new form of collective dwelling where domestic and professional lives blend together. The subject of the Bridgewatcher's House is vigilance. Occupants are elevated to a ship's captain's eye-level; they nevertheless turn their backs on their spectacular panoramic view, preferring a digital/radar relationship with their subjects. The bridgewatchers process the complex data of maritime trajectories and instigate momentary strategic interventions or open bridges. It is a system-penetrating and subversive strategy in relation to parallel urban circulation networks.

The territory on which the Bridgewatcher's House stands is neither appropriated nor remodelled; it is an invented context, a constructed field, over which are strewn Electronic Rocks (used by Rotterdammers for wedding photos) and inlaid stainless-steel digital fallout. The granite of the quay is itself code carrier (Garden of Constant Numbers). Height above sea level (all-important in Holland) and the abandoned numbers of this decommissioned (shipless) quay are strewn as stainless-steel inlays between Fountain, Fisherman's Seats and a Number Puzzle (answer 15).

A basalt ramp negotiates carpet-like the 1.5-metre drop from street to quay level. Standing crane-like on this carpet is a 70-metre-long steel beam (two `U´ sections with elevated walkway between). Up high, a perspective over the town offers visitors a privileged panoramic advantage. The quay is a sequence of such stations, constructed views, connections over distance (to the skyline of Rotterdam) and intimate encounters. Conical forms like the expanding end of the colonnade are perspectival machines, traversable but ultimately rejecting the singular conclusion of classical focus.

On the far side of the Erasmus Bridge is an electronic answer to the Garden of Constant Numbers – the Tower of Moving Numbers signals across the Maas (5 LED boxes caged like cyber birds). Useful and useless numbers. Time. '0'. Temperature. A Random Cube. World population (burning at one end like a cigarette). ◆

Bolles & Wilson

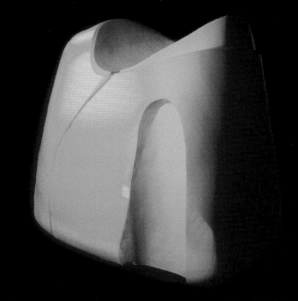

| USA |

Asymptote

Lise-Anne Couture (1959), Hani Rashid (1958)

Lise-Anne Couture, from Canada, and Hani Rashid, from Egypt, founded Asymptote in New York in 1989. The aim of this transdisciplinary organization, in which the two architects call on the know-how of computer experts, engineers and various kinds of scientists (entomologists, biophysicists, etc.), is to be a forum of genuinely technological thinking about architecture. The need for some kind of interpolation between the physical space and the visual and technical world opened up by the new electronic media is a bedrock conviction for both Rashid and Couture. For the past ten years, in their virtual projects, urban and architectural alike, their multimedia installations and the research and teaching programmes that they run (in particular at Columbia University and at the Guggenheim Museum), they have been exploring the reciprocal architectural implications of these two continents of the real. Asymptote is famous for having designed a virtual market hall for the New York Stock Exchange (3DTF), where the data and economic movement are visualized in 3D and 'spatialized' in real time. ◆

The FluxSpace Projects
FluxSpace 1.0, San Francisco [CCAC Institute], 2000
FluxSpace 2.0, Venice Biennale, 2000

The two projects are full-scale built works utilizing digital technologies in both their design and manifestation. The aim of FluxSpace is to blur the distinction between virtual and actual through an exploration of digitally augmented architectural constructs. FluxSpace 1.0, an installation whose size lies somewhere between that of a large model and a small building was modelled in the computer and constructed using full-size computer-generated templates. The computer's ability to create a model with a high degree of accuracy and the ability to output to exacting specifications afforded the opportunity to create both a virtual object and a one-to-one scale constructed counterpart. An augmentation of the 'architectural reality' of the installation was created by the manipulation of the wireframe assemblies and the projection of these transformations on to the constructed objects in the gallery. These 'images' were then triggered by surface embedded sensors, sensitive to movement and proximity, which created the effect of a structure in a constant state of mutation and distortion in real time and real space. If one approached this built artifact or passed a hand over its surface the object would immediately respond by means of its electronic counterpart. An audio soundtrack derived from the same algorithmic structures that were being deployed to manipulate the form accompanied each physical transformation to complete the multi-dimensional experience.

FluxSpace 2.0 sought to move the experiment in another direction, that of architecture as intermediary to an online or Web-based spatial experience. The project was somewhat larger than the San Francisco project, measuring 30 metres in length and standing over two storeys high on the grounds of the Venice Biennale. A computer-generated steel framework that dictated the configuration of the interior cavity supported an air-filled pneumatic envelope. Inside the structure two large discs incorporating one-way mirrors measuring 2.4 metres in diameter and pivoting about the vertical axis, were located at two 'focal' points at opposite ends of the space. At the centre of each semi-reflective, semi-transparent mirror a 360-degree camera was housed to capture the ever-changing interior space and relay that information to the Internet. As these cameras were able to record the interior condition of FluxSpace 2.0 at 30-second intervals for the duration of the 5-month installation in Venice, over 1.6 million different spatial configurations could be viewed and virtually occupied on the Web. What was experienced on the Web and in the actual space was a continually mutating spatiality; this double occupancy provokes a new understanding of architecture in a state of simultaneous virtuality and augmented reality. ◆

Asymptote

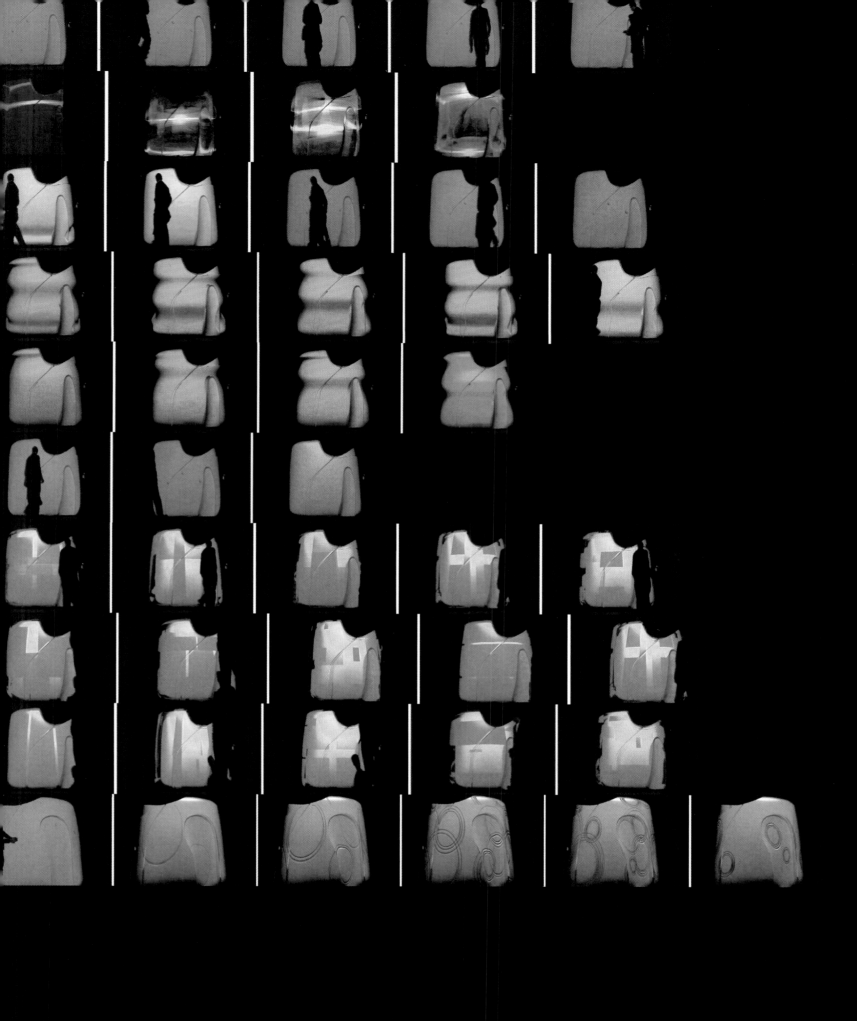

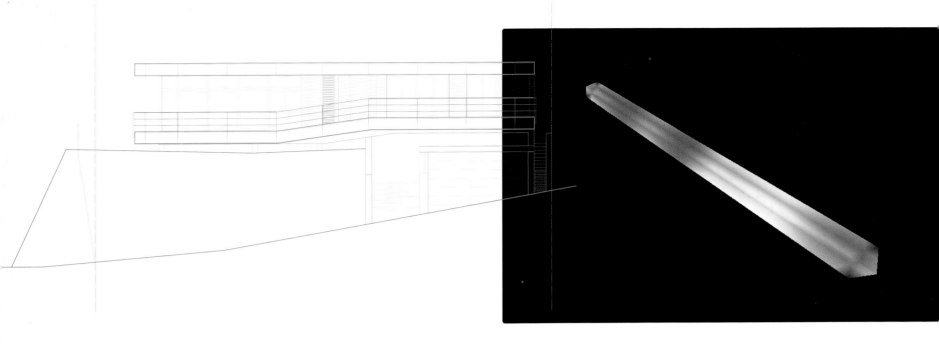

| JAPAN |
|Atelier Hitoshi Abe|

HITOSHI ABE (1962)

Hitoshi Abe obtained an MA in architecture from the Southern California Institute of Architecture in 1989. From 1988 to 1992 he worked in the Los Angeles office of Coop Himmelb(l)au. In 1992 he was awarded a doctorate in architecture from Tohoku University and founded the Atelier Hitoshi Abe at Sendai, where he was born. Since 1994 he has also been director of the Architecture Laboratory at the Tohoku Institute of Technology. Certainly one of the most transculturally active architects of his generation, Abe alternates between public programmes (Miyagi stadium, 2000), houses (N-House, 2000; M-House, 1999) and installations ('Search for Paradise', 2000, 'The Ichibancho Arcade'). His resolutely experimental approach is constantly probing at the limits and contradictions of architecture. Inserting a building in the landscape, designing for the masses and conceiving everyday spaces for the use of others all imply a responsibility, which Abe confronts through the permanent application of doubt, the unquiet search for 'paradise'. ◆

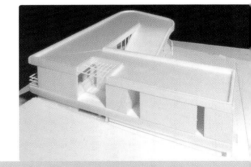

i-house
Sendai, Japan, 2000—01

This project is part of a more general meditation on the theme of dwelling that Abe is pursuing through his various projects, one that questions the limits of the roles of the architect and of architecture in the elaboration of a habitat. He has described this problem as follows: 'It is obvious that "a home" is never created until people occupy the building as a receptacle. It is never created until the site and the life of people physically encounter each other. Originally, it was not something created by designers. Our role is neither to define nor to explain "the ideal life, the ideal home", but to precisely describe the life (a conglomeration of activities with specific tendencies) of people which is about to begin on the site (a kind of field or environment with various visible/invisible information). In the design process, I consciously try to index on to a new form of a field the events that happen when a specific site condition and a specific life interact with each other. It is a question of indexing onto a building through a form as a medium various characters and relationships of events that happen during the design process. . . . We are experimenting with the method of diagramming life as a geometrical environment and with observing and indexing the transformation that happens when it is installed into the site, which is also diagrammed as a geometrical environment.'

The geometrical diagram that subtends the i-house is an ascending spiral, a fluid and continuous helicoid that runs through the entire space of the building. It begins at the entrance and then takes us, successively, into the living room, the dining room, the kitchen and, finally, going back above the entrance, into the area given over to the bedrooms. From there, as we come out of the house, we can, in the same movement, continue the ascent up to the terrace roof. As the linear organizing principle of the programme, the spiral also resolves the relation between the architecture and its site. Located on the edge of a steep slope, the house is accessible from the lower level but spreads out on the upper level, where it can take advantage of the garden. The spiral form is precisely what makes it possible to resolve this clean topographical break while making the most of its architectural possibilities. When distributed along the helix, the difference in height of about 3 metres, which might otherwise have seemed insurmountable, becomes a way of defining the house's different spaces. The architecture gives way to the occupants, leaving them free to construct their own personal relation to their surroundings. ◆

Pierre Chabard

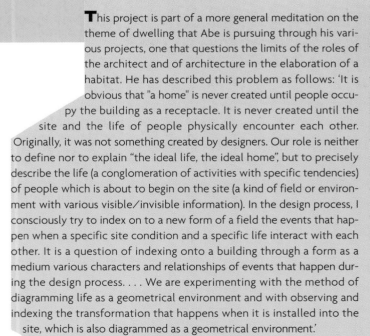

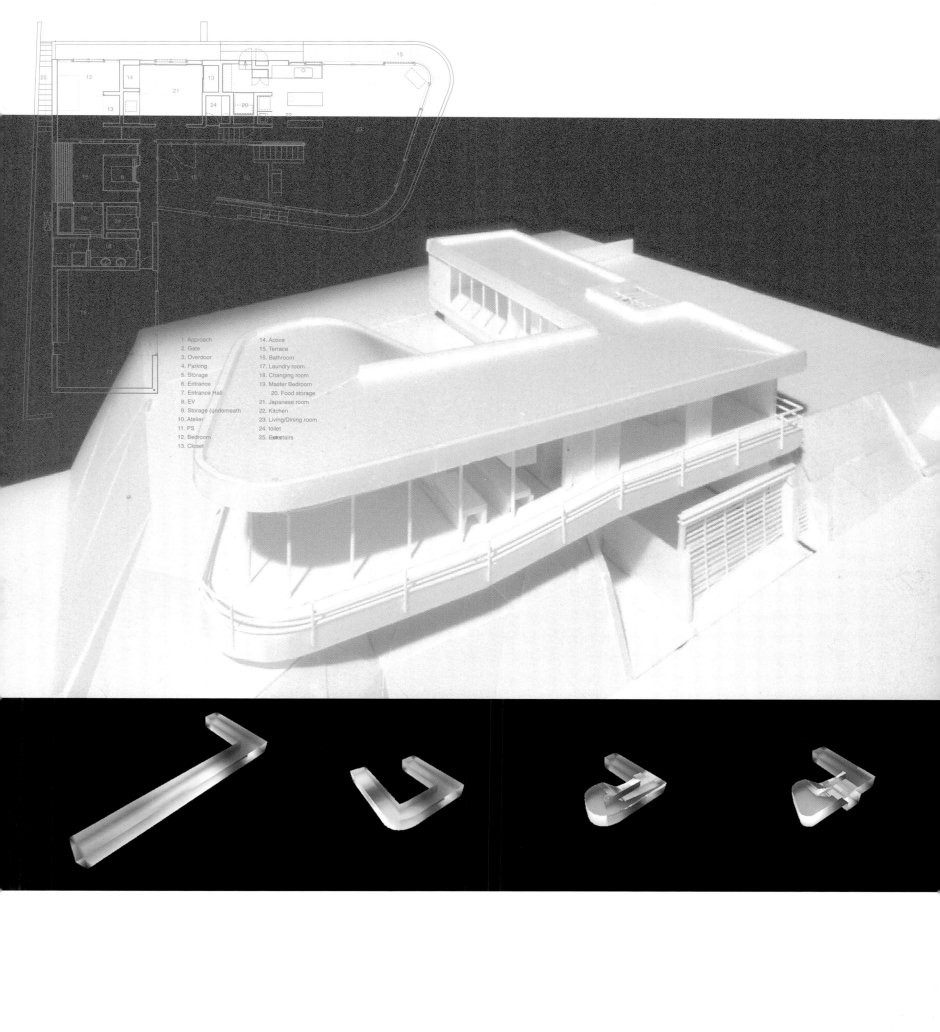

1. Approach
2. Gate
3. Overdoor
4. Parking
5. Storage
6. Entrance
7. Entrance Hall
8. EV
9. Storage (underneath)
10. Atelier
11. PS
12. Bedroom
13. Closet
14. Acove
15. Terrace
16. Bathroom
17. Laundry room
18. Changing room
19. Master Bedroom
20. Food storage
21. Japanese room
22. Kitchen
23. Living/Dining room
24. toilet
25. Exit stairs

| NETHERLANDS |

Atelier van Lieshout

JOEP VAN LIESHOUT (1963)

Joep van Lieshout is a graduate of the Rotterdam Art School. Since 1995, his artistic practice has developed collectively within the Atelier van Lieshout, based in the industrial outskirts of Rotterdam. The work produced by the Atelier, heir to the most radical counter-culture of the 1960s and 1970s, has been exhibited on many occasions in solo and in group shows; it is also represented in several collections. Joep van Lieshout oversteps all cultural and social bounds and occupies real space, using tools that do not belong to art, and blurring the boundaries between art – in its symbolic dimension – and life. Above all else, the work produced by the Atelier van Lieshout fiercely challenges the contemporary issue of independence and the autonomy of self-determination. For several years now, as players in their own works and authors of their own fictional biographies, the Atelier's members have been formulating the material conditions for a self-sufficient, communal form of housing and habitat. This project, currently under construction in Rotterdam, stems both from a form of subversion and a representation of the real. ◆

AVL-Ville
Rotterdam, Netherlands, 1998 (ongoing)

Freestate

For some time Atelier van Lieshout (AVL) has been devoting its energies to realizing AVL-Ville. With AVL-Ville, Atelier van Lieshout wants to create its own village, a free state where the people from AVL can live and work. AVL-Ville contains artworks that can be used to live a more or less self-sufficient life. Most of the artworks that AVL has been producing for the past few years are made ultimately to function in AVL-Ville, for instance, a central power plant, living and working units, agricultural equipment, a canteen and even an emergency hospital. The village can be regarded both as an open-air museum and a permanent exhibition of work of Atelier van Lieshout and as an artwork in itself, a 'Gesamtkunstwerk'. Another important part of AVL-Ville is the 'Pioneer set'. This is a prefab farm that can be assembled and disassembled when necessary. It consists of a farmhouse and accommodation for the animals such as chicken coop, rabbit hutches and pig sties. There will also be agricultural development in AVL-Ville.

Shipping containers

A lot of the artworks are made from refurbished ship's containers, such as the 'AVL Canteen', a fully equipped large kitchen and a dining room. The 'AVL Hospital' is a simple field hospital where the sick and injured can be nursed. The hospital contains several beds and even an operating room with all the necessary instruments. The 'Arsenal' is a workshop for terrorists and in the the 'Alcohol and Medicines Workshop' is a distillery and laboratory.

Location

For AVL-Ville there are two locations. One is next to the AVL studio on Keilestraat; this is AVL-Ville 1. In AVL-Ville 1 there will be the workshop, office, restaurant and party area, several mobile homes and artworks. There will also be several infrastructural devices such as a water-purifying system, compost toilets and AVL city-heating system. Visitors can come and tour the grounds and use the bar and the restaurant. AVL-Ville 2 is located near AVL-Ville 1 on Vierhavenstraat. It is a bigger piece of land and is partly covered with grass. The Pioneer set is located here and will be home to a farmer.

AVL-Transport

Another important part of AVL-Ville is AVL transport. which is of the agricultural type: a horse and carriage and a tractor with a farmer's cart. The carts ride around in the centre of the city as well as along the cultural axis. There are several fixed stops, but the carts can also simply be stopped along the way. A couple of times a day they go to AVL-Ville 1 and 2. The transport is free, but drinks are obligatory. ◆

Atelier van Lieshout

EXTEND

| Austria |

awg_AllesWirdGut|

Ingrid Hora (1976), Friedrich Passler (1969), Christian Waldner (1971), Andreas Marth (1969), Herwig Spiegl (1973)

This young team (their average age is 28.48 years old!) is made up of five Viennese architects who all attended different international architecture schools (Vienna, London, Montreal and Ann Arbor (USA)). They have been working closely together since 1997 and set up awg_AllesWirdGut in Vienna in 1999. Their projects, several of which are currently under construction, describe a very sweeping field of action and research, ranging from the urban scale to design. They are determinedly pragmatic, and seek to make use of all the possibilities inherent in each and every situation. In AllesWirdGut projects, technical, programmatic and administrative restrictions are systematically 'overestimated', just as the most unfavourable urban situations are intensified in their quest for new uses and new ways of living: motorway infrastructures (VIE, z.B.BZ or vimp projects), carparks (pIN project), and shopping centres (WW$ project) all thus reveal unsuspected and undreamed-of conditions. ◆

turnOn – urban. sushi
Visionary housing experiment prototype, 2000

1. Motives

With the continuous advances in the car industry, 'science-fiction' has more than once become reality. By developing cutting-edge technologies and using prefabrication and mass-production, the enterprises managed to reach a level of sophistication hitherto unknown to housing engineers. Housing still conforms to the same parameters as it did a thousand years ago. We still live on plane floors, limited by corners. The rigid configuration of these parameters restricts our individuality – our desire to express ourselves is imprisoned within austere white walls and norms that confine the spirit.

AllesWirdGut presents the enterprise for this millennium: urban. sushi – a virtual society for subreal urbanism. Our goal was to combine the various advantages of both industries – housing and automobile – and create a new experimental lifestyle: the turnOn.

2. Living space reduced to the maximum

A series of revolving modules – like giant hamster wheels – contain all the living programmes. There is no longer any distinction between wall, floor or ceiling: just one transitional space, all in one, all at the same time! While one is cooking, the couch becomes the ceiling, the dining table a wall. Living all around: the easiest way to shift furniture. The interior space changes constantly with the endless positions of each ring: a new flat every day; a maximum of flexibility and space-experience on a minimal surface. Anything is possible: whether sleeping, working, having a party or jogging in an integrated landscape. Consult our catalogue and design your own home simply by adding as many modules as you want.

3. The catalogue

The AllesWirdGut catalogue designed for the project is based on a typical car catalogue: starting with some nice sketches, giving technical information and showing different types of segments; it offers an endless number of different rings and infinite possibilities for combining them. It also includes colour and texture samples and an order form.

4. Facts about the 'turnOn' prototype

Diameter: 3 metres. Depth: 1 metre. Weight: about 300 kilograms. Material: insulation roofing core; wooden superstructure; fibreglass skin with non-flammable 'plaster resin'; steel base. The turnOn prototype consists of three single pieces (each approx. 3 x 1 x 1 metres) plus a steel base (2 x 1 x 0.25 metres). ◆

awg_AllesWirdGut

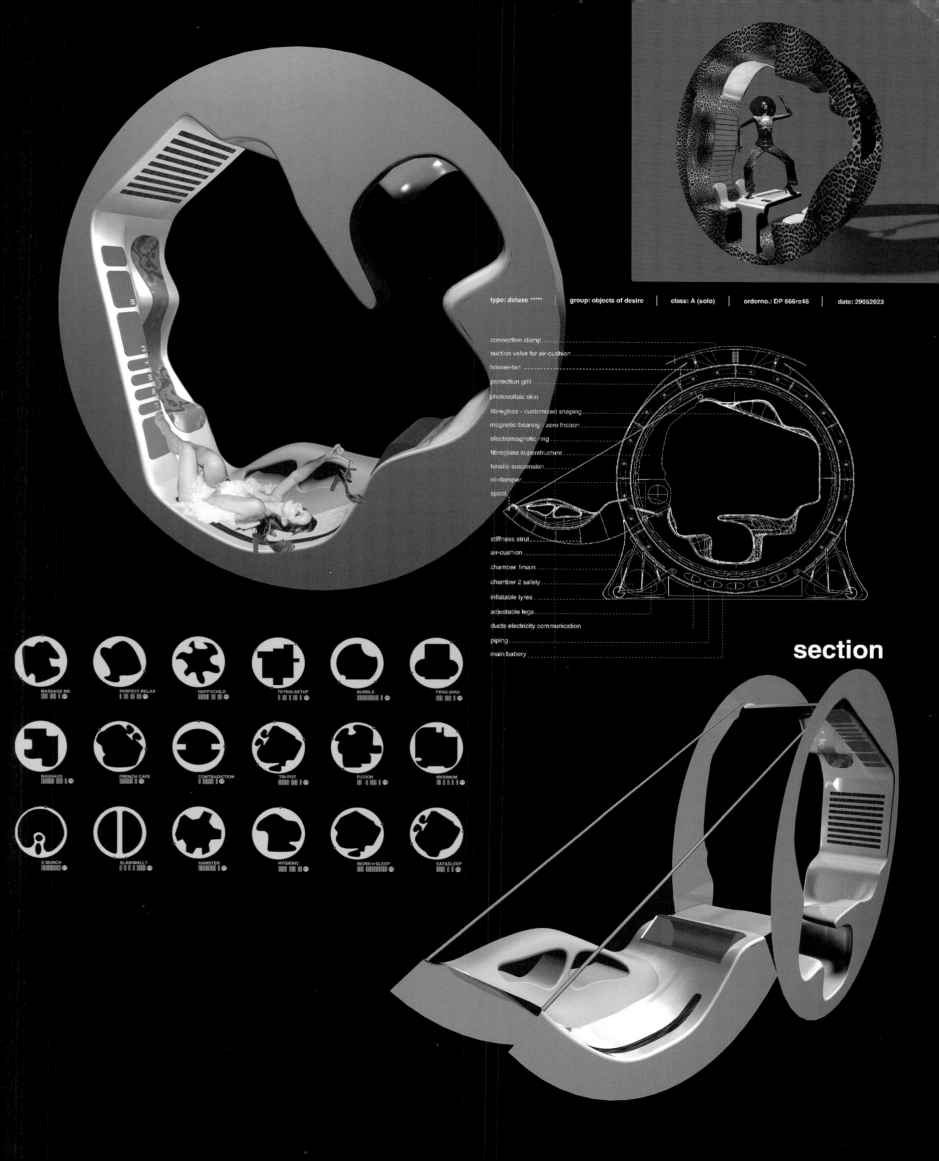

type: deluxe ★★★★★ | group: objects of desire | class: A (solo) | orderno.: DP 666re46 | date: 29052023

connection clamp
suction valve for air-cushion
hoover-fan
protection grill
photovoltaic skin
fibreglass - customized shaping
magnetic bearing - zero friction
electromagnetic ring
fibreglass superstructure
tensile suspension
oil-damper
spool

stiffness strut
air-cushion
chamber 1 main
chamber 2 safety
inflatable tyres
adjustable legs
ducts electricity communication
piping
main battery

section

MASSAGE ME
PERFECT RELAX
HAPPYCHILD
TETRIS-SETUP
BUBBLE
FENG-SHUI

BAUHAUE
FRENCH CAFE
CONTRADICTION
TRI-POT
P.COOK
MAXIMUM

E.MUNCH
SLAB/WALL?
HAMSTER
HYGIENIC
WORK<>SLEEP
EAT&SLEEP

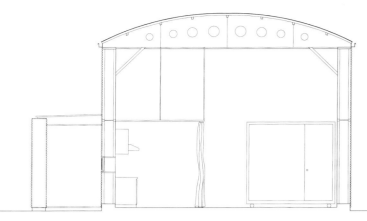

| JAPAN |

Shigeru Ban

SHIGERU BAN (1957)

Shigeru Ban was born in Tokyo in 1957 and graduated from the Cooper Union School in 1984. He worked as an assistant to Arata Isozaki for a year, and then set up his own agency in Tokyo in 1985. In tandem with his architectural practice, he has been teaching since 1993. He is currently teaching at Columbia University, where, over and above the theoretical aspect, he strives to introduce reflection on the reality of praxis. Most of his works are based on new construction techniques and methods, such as the use of cardboard tubes as load-bearing structures, which are both recyclable and cheap, in emergency housing projects, developed in Rwanda, then in Kobe. In these works, however, we often find inspiration drawn from Japanese tradition: walls that are rarely load-bearing or even non-existent (Wall-less House, 1997), sliding walls that adapt the space to its purpose, and the filtered light produced by the transparency of paper. The overall plan — single space with no partitions dividing it — is still one of his major concerns. ◆

Naked House, Case study 10
Tokyo, Japan, realized, 2000

It always takes some time of careful thinking before I accept a private residential project. I often wonder if what I want to achieve as a designer, in a project, meets the client's needs and desires for his home, without either of us having to compromise our own beliefs.

Having met the client only once, I was again considering what to do about the project of this house, when the client sent me a facsimile making precise requests. The budget for the project was about 25,000,000 yen. The family members were his mother, aged 75, the client and his wife, both in their late thirties, their nine-year-old son and seven-year-old daughter, and a dog. What he wanted was described as a house that 'provides the least privacy so that the family members are not secluded from one another, a house that gives everyone the freedom to have individual activities in a shared atmosphere, in the midst of a united family'. After reading his fax, I knew that I should take up this challenge.

The site of the house is by a river and is surrounded by fields with greenhouses here and there. The external walls made of two sheets of corrugated fibre-reinforced plastics and the inner walls made of a nylon fabric are both mounted on wooden stud frames and sit in parallel. In between are attached clear plastic bags, carefully stuffed with strings of foamed polyeth-

ylene for insulation purposes. Through these bags a soft diffused light fills the interior of the house.

The house consists of one large space 2 storeys high in which 4 personal rooms on casters can be moved freely. To reduce weight and optimize mobility, these rooms are not very large and hold a minimum of belongings and fittings. They can be moved according to need. Placed against the walls of the house, in front of the heating or air-conditioning units, they allow warm air or a cooling breeze to flow in. They can also be put side by side to create a larger room when their sliding doors are removed. They can be taken outside on to the terrace, to free up the space inside. They can also work as a supplementary floor for the children to play on.

This house is, indeed, a result of my vision of pleasant and flexible space, which evolved from the client's own vision of accommodation and family life. ◆

Shigeru Ban

| Austria |

Bitter/Weber

Sabine Bitter (1960), Helmut Weber (1957)

Since 1993, Vienna-based artists Sabine Bitter and Helmut Weber have cooperated on projects related to urban geographies, architectural representations, cultural shifts and related visual politics. Educated in art in an experimental class by architect Laurids Ortner at the University of Art and Design, Linz, they have focused on emergent sites and overlaps of architecture, urban developments, communications systems and modes of artistic and cultural production as they are mediated through photography, video and new media technologies. The recent project 'CITYalias' – in collaboration with the Canadian writer Jeff Derksen – engages with specific moments and sites of globalization, as well as the culture-ideology of globalization, as they are materialized in architecture. With projects dealing with migrancy and communication, architecture and repetition, the aesthetics of social housing blocks, and architecture as a frame for spatial meaning, Bitter/Weber work at the interface of architecture, new media technologies and systems of representation. ◆

Z_orb
video N/B, 1998–2000 [sound: Peter Rantasa]

Inspired by the leisure sport of 'zorbing' down alpine meadows, the Z_orb video shows a clear inflatable orb, with a person encapsulated within, rolling in a black space and then receding into the dark distance. Oscillating between recognition and defamiliarization, Z_orb plays out the tension of banalization with the utopian potential of inflatable structures. The slightly sci-fi, temporary and transparent inflatable structures of the 1960s and 1970s (such as Haus-Ruckers Co. Oase No. 7, 1972, and Ballon für Zwei, 1967) held the promise of new architectural and social meanings through a flexible relationship of the body to built space. With the alpine landscape masked out and the background reduced to a uniform black surface, the Z_orb shifts between a possible architectural space with futuristic references and its own real status as a device for sport and relaxation. Yet, uncannily, through this decontextualizing, the Z_orb is debanalized and returned to its architectural reference. This not only shows how architectural meanings are altered through unpredictable uses in other fields, but raises the original social and aesthetic questions about the potential of such inflatable and flexible structures.

instead of pixels) image. source joins architectural and textual representation. However, unlike ASCII imagery, which randomly substitutes characters for pixels to make a representative image, image. source embeds (via a specifically written perl script) an intact and readable text into the ASCII based image.

Conflating the poetic problem of form and content, image. source puts architecture and text, and architectural meanings and social meanings into a dialogue relationship, eschewing representational strategies of architecture that produce gorgeous images of built spaces hovering outside of a web of determinants. Instead, aesthetic and social logics are semantically embedded into these images through text excerpts by Saskia Sassen, Rem Koolhaas, Mike Davis and Walter Gropius.

This combination of low-tech/high-tech mediation of architectural imagery puts the accent on the social mediation of architecture by the parallel emphasis on technological alteration of the image. With this critical mediation, and by using the near-iconic example of the Bijlmer, image. source recontextualizes and reactivates the debate on housing. ◆

Bitter/Weber

image. source
Digital print on vinyl, 2000.
By reproducing aerial images of the Bijlmer housing project in Amsterdam through ASCII characters (these standard characters constitute the image

       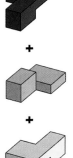

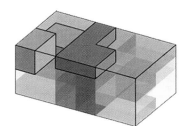

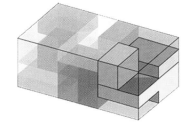

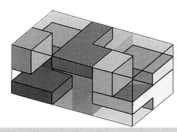

| Germany |

b & k+ |

Arno Hans Brandlhuber (1964), Bernd Georg Kniess (1961).

Since it was set up in Cologne in 1996, b & k+ has been working regularly with artists, composers and scientists, who are accommodated 'in residence' in their agency, thus opening themselves up to different disciplinary fields, but who are also incorporated as actual partners in their projects. For b & k +, architects are no longer those great general practitioners, but rather 'positive dilettantes' who, through their own capacity for incorporation, work at offering greater freedom of action. The cautious reservations of investors towards innovative architectural propositions has prompted them to split their projects into two versions, one. com (commercial with dictated budgets and constructive details), and other. org, an independent project and conceptual exercise where inventiveness and interdiscipli-narity are at their most fertile – the Liquid Sky group, for example, has produced a CD with the music of project. org of the Hanover hydroelectric power sta-tion. Brandlhuber and Kniess, who have designed several award-winning housing units in Cologne, are also associate professors at Wuppertal University. ◆

New Loft/Am Kölner Brett
Cologne, Germany, realized, 2000

By its layout, the New Loft building challenges new phenomena of metropolization, urban density and ideas of proximity and distance. You come upon it in an urban development zone in Cologne, at once close to the city centre and 'on the outskirts', as a result of its scattered volumes, the heterogeneity of the buildings and an industrial past engraved in the land. In this setting, their pro-ject maximizes the use of the plot and marks the corners of the streets with a shiny green box, offering huge flexible spaces, deliberate-ly 'nowhere' but above all 'interwoven', connected and reticulated.

By mixing programmes of housing, workshops and offices, archi-tects intend also to make an issue of the diminishing role of the tradi-tional house and the loss of boundaries between private space and public place. The model for safeguarding family life is here turned into sequences of juxtaposition and overlay, in this critical and experimental architecture, which is enhanced by new applications and extensions proposed by the users themselves.

The project has recourse to an L-shaped basic model, where one of the branches, i.e., one-third of the surface, is of double height. This ele-ment turns vertically, horizontally or mirror-like, and is then dovetailed and creates inner configurations that are invariably different. This building kit-like box creates a 'modern' building, whose neutrality enables it to be 'informed' by the occu-pants about their needs: the dentist supplies his surgery, the photographer his laboratory and the inhabitants choose their bathrooms; mezzanine floors may be added; an 'apartment hand-book' provides explanations for the various options. It is also the 'art of omission' that prevails, the architects' choice to refrain, which may make the whole thing financially accessible and spatially approachable. The better to imagine subsequent hybridizations in the building, the circula-tion system is external, as if independent of the building and even structurally detached from the ground, acting as a counter-balance. This communication area is also one for leisure and recreation; bal-conies and terraces are added and the roof is covered with lawn and hedges. The green-yellow colour is the same as the translucid plastic coating that covers the concrete walls of the façades, which are still illuminated by the gilded metal window frames. The way the vegetation and synthetic materials are handled turns them into elements creating new 'reservoirs of nature' and systems of ephemeral housing in urban regions. ◆

Bénédicte Grosjean

MISS SARGFABRIK   0 1 2 3 4 5   10   LEVEL 9

MISS SARGFABRIK   0 1 2 3 4 5   10   LEVEL 7

MISS SARGFABRIK   0 1 2 3 4 5   10   LEVEL 5

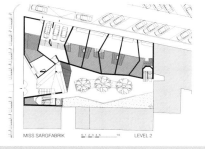

MISS SARGFABRIK   0 1 2 3 4 5   10   LEVEL 2

| AUSTRIA |

BKK-3 ZT |

JOHANN WINTER (1949), FRANZ SUMNITSCH (1961) WITH REGINA GSCHWENDTNER AND CHRISTOPH MÖRKL

The name BKK-3 first of all contains traces of a story. In 1984, Johann Winter was part of the group of Viennese artists and architects who founded the BaukünstlerKollektiv, around a shared space and in the same spirit. Ten years later, this very open-ended structure turned into BKK-2, which was more akin to the organization of an architectural agency. Today, with Franz Sumnitsch, Johann Winter runs the BKK-3 agency, which has retained from the BaukünstlerKollektiv that same critical stance towards the institutional and professional identity of the architect in Austria. The architecture of BKK-3, structured around a radical programmatic line of thought, explores every type of formal and functional interweave, combination and interpolation. Looking for an intensification and densification of the real (which they call the 'bonus effect'), BKK-3 is keen to resolve, through architecture, the complex programmatic equations that they themselves formulated. Their concept of the habitat resides in the extension of this quest for mixedness and complexity, as existential qualities. ◆

MISS Sargfabrik
Vienna, Austria, realized, 1998–2001

In several respects, the 'MISS Sargfabrik' residential complex comes across like a product of 'evolutionary' architecture. First and foremost, this project is the evolutionary extension of an idea and a building formulated 10 years ago by the same project developer (Verein für Intergrative Lebensgestaltung) and the same architects (Johann Winter with BKK-2). This earlier operation, the 'Sargfabrik' (1992), derived its name from the place where it stood, a plot of land with an early-20th-century factory on it. What was involved here was an attempt at community living, which experimented with the programmatic connections between individual space and collective space, between places of privacy and places of sociability. The first 'Sargfabrik' mixed the housing units with a cafe, seminar rooms, a day nursery, public baths, a swimming pool and a garden. It also proposed making certain functions shared by all — kitchen, laundry room, heating (heated façade).

Carrying on from this initial and successful experiment, BKK-3 built 'MISS Sargfabrik' in 2000. This operation, which was incorporated within the standards for social housing, consists of 39 apartments that are all different. BKK-3, which opposes the idea of repeating the same model of minimum, ideal housing, favoured the diversity and multiplicity of spaces and forms, in order to meet the wide variety of current lifestyles. The building

thus presents an interweave of heterogeneous typologies — some housing units are equipped for the disabled, others may be adapted for students and teenagers. As in the first Sargfabrik, the living areas are accompanied by many collective areas and facilities — kitchen, refectory, library, multimedia room, laundry room, offices (for working at home), etc. All these areas of community interaction are located in the heart of the building; they form its nucleus. They also enhance each housing unit with possible extensions into the collective sphere, offering easy alternatives to private life.

'MISS Sargfabrik' stands at the crossroads of two contrasting systems of logic: individualization and specification of each housing unit, community orientation and collectivization of the entire housing complex. This paradoxical condition, which forms the conceptual nub of the project, offers an architectural solution that is both complex and unifying. Far from reducing the basic heterogeneity of this programmatic hybridization, BKK-3 puts forward a synthesis that reveals all its possibilities. ◆

Pierre Chabard

| ITALY |

Andrea Branzi

Andrea Branzi (1938)

Designer, critic, theoretician, teacher of design, architecture and city planning, all rolled into one, Andrea Branzi, the Florentine of Milan, is a whole continent of the recent history of all these disciplines. Between 1966 and 1973, in the avant-garde group Archizoom, which he set up with Corretti, Deganello and Morozzi, he was involved in critical and cynical thinking about the post-industrial age, claiming the need to reach a crisis point of 'positivism' in both architecture and city planning. This militant and iconoclastic approach was part of the 'radical architecture' movement. In those years, Branzi contributed, in particular, to the exhibition 'Italy: the New Domestic Landscape' (MoMA, 1972). Associated with experimental industrial design studios (Alchimia then Memphis) at the end of the 1960s, as well as with major publishers (Cassina, Zanotta, etc.), he threw himself into research, design, spreading the word about design (the reviews Modo, Domus, exhibitions, publications), looking for new relationships between people and objects. ◆

Eindhoven, a model of gentle urbanization
Notes for a master plan
Eindhoven, Netherlands, 2000

Through his project for converting the Philips industrial site in Eindhoven, A. Branzi describes the crisis afflicting all definitive forward-looking programmes – the crisis of powerful modernist certainties – and develops a 'defunctionalized' attitude to architecture and housing.

For this research group, resulting from seminars organized by the city of Eindhoven, our day and age is made up of continuous experimentation, stable uncertainties and temporary balances. Just as the 'low' current that drives electronics is replacing the mechanical energy of industry, so systems of scientific logic are moving away from the absolute aspect of mathematics and looking into the indeterminate, and politics are dispensing with once-and-for-all solutions in favour of a system of permanent reform. This complex world is striving to survive itself, giving itself a level of user flexibility, guaranteeing itself a reversibility of choices and bristling at the intrinsic rigidity of functions.

The city is accordingly becoming a system of 'micro-structures', both of services and relations, derived only to a small extent from traditional, metaphorical and compositional architecture, and for the most part from diffuse and low-level forward-looking attitudes, capable of dealing with urban competitiveness but incapable of coming down on one side or the other.

The programming of the site – the Philips Strijp – thus involves a network of routes for pedestri-

ans, cyclists and trams; a kind of large, tartan-like plan, with weak, intersecting penetration, which reconstructs a total permeability of the former industrial area. A series of strata is overlaid on it in a completely independent way – services, housing, gardens, lighting, shops, all separately designed and criss-crossed by an extended system of windmills supplying natural power. The 'marketing' of this huge zone envisages putting it on the European market as a place for new businesses in the post-industrial economy. Unlike old industrial zoning, this emergent entrepreneurial generation needs a relational space that is busy with juxtapositions – an informational setting such as only the 'urban market' can offer.

Because the city is a 'system of objects', architecture is individualized. Unaffected by urban form, and leaving the space of meaning open-ended, it is the time of objects, and the praxis of design is extending to the scale of metropolitan territory. 'Cityless architecture' is shifting from the industrial reference to the agricultural reference: a more flexible model, open to self-regulation, incorporating natural power. The building itself will be executed like a diffuse system of light, transformable prefabrication, which can be dismantled and has reversible uses: as housing or something else. ◆

Bénédicte Grosjean

| Netherlands |

Bureau Venhuizen |

Hans Venhuizen (1961)

Hans Venhuizen is a visual artist, but he also had a background in town planning at the University of Nijmegen (Netherlands), in architectural design/monumental art, at the school of fine arts, Arnhem (Netherlands) and in urban design at the school of fine arts in Berlin (Germany). Mankind's continual need to find places to settle and resettle is the theme of Hans Venhuizen's works: the irrational and intuitive aspects, the creativity and the vision required to extend the consciousness of the city's residents beyond their own backyard. That Venhuizen does this as an artist is not strange: his art gives him a more independent position. Visual art has increasingly become a discipline that does not so much yield products for sale as try to intervene in the ever-changing discourse that is culture. In visual art, making has become less and less important in comparison with developing a position on culture in the broadest sense of the word, a cultural concept. Everyday culture must be taken seriously and it is crucial that in this search for the potentialities of urban culture different disciplines be employed, for urban culture expresses itself in many different ways. ◆

Amphibious Living
Barendrecht, Netherlands, competition, 2000

Amphibious Living concept

(Bureau Venhuizen) The Amphibious Living project started early 2000 with a competition. From the more than 150 original and innovative designs and solutions in the fields of architecture, urban planning and physical planning for amphibious locations, a number of ideas were selected for further elaboration by professional implementation teams.

Amphibious Living appeals to us to abandon our compulsive control of water and to accept climatic influences, tides and seasons in the living environment. It is a plea for a new concept of living. Controlling natural conditions does not begin with imposing one's own will on the landscape, but through taking full advantage of the qualities of a dynamic relationship between land and water. At the same time, this means that the living conditions cannot be predicted. Living in harmony with nature also entails living in a legal no-man's-land and demands an adventurous mentality and a high level of self-sufficiency.

Amphibious Living in Barendrecht

Lucas Verweij; Schie 2.0 and Dennis Moet; Bureau Park, in cooperation with: MG Architecten (Rotterdam), Future Lifestyle Innovators (London), Martijn Schoots (Gouda) and Van Velzen La Feber Bonneur Architecten (Schiedam).

The task given to the workshop was to produce a plan for an amphibious environment in which there would be a place for various functions (such as housing and nature). The core of the workshop's plan is literally and figuratively an 'amphibious zone' in which the wet character of the area is not opposed but taken instead as the starting point for a new and exciting landscape in which to live and find recreation.

The new amphibious landscape of the Zuidpolder makes new natural values possible, with a rich vegetation that differs according to the water level: the diversity of the flora and fauna will increase. The essence of the approach is timescaping: evolving with time and exploiting natural processes and dynamics, changing with the seasons – and the years. So no static end-result can be described.

The residents can have a dwelling designed for them or choose from a catalogue. The land will not be sold, but permits for moorings will be issued, so the residents enjoy great freedom: they choose their own spot, alone or in a group. The conditions dwellings must meet will relate mainly to their durability. The dwellings and life inside them must be largely self-sufficient and autonomous, and they must be in equilibrium with the amphibious landscape (autarkic living). ◆

Hans Verhuizen

16.00HRS 22ND NOVEMBER 2015

16.00HRS 8TH SEPTEMBER 2010

16.00HRS 13TH JUNE 2000

NON-BUILD AREAS   AMPHIBIOUS HOUSING AREAS   DRY HOUSING AREAS   TREE HOUSING AREAS

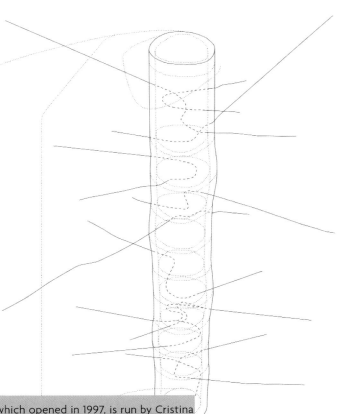

| SPAIN |

|Cero 9|

CRISTINA DÍAZ MORENO (1971), EFRÉN GARCIA GRINDA (1966)

The Madrid-based Cero9 agency, which opened in 1997, is run by Cristina Díaz Moreno and Efrén Garcia Grinda, both graduates of the Escuela Técnica Superior de Arquitectura of Madrid, while the latter also attended the Bartlett School. The works of these two young architects, which have come to notice in a large number of international competitions and have often been published and exhibited (Venice Biennale, 2000), illustrate a major interest in the issue of housing and the urban habitat, and are conspicuous for their originality and their radicalness. Both architects are well aware of current issues and, above all, of the changes happening in the architectural profession, so they deliberately organized Cero9 around an open and cross-disciplinary praxis, capable of envisaging its references beyond the strict framework of architecture and introducing specific multidisciplinary cooperative projects. By regarding architecture as basically inseparable from its environment, in the broad sense of the word, they attempt, in their projects, to develop and intensify relations (spatial, temporal, ecological, etc.) between one project and the next.

◆

Temporary Settlements in PRS
Madrid, Spain, project, 1997

In a Regional Park to the southeast of Madrid, in a two-dimensional landscape with no precise boundaries and no apparent perceptible form, Cero9 proposes housing designed for temporary visits, encouraging contact with nature, horse riding and cycling, and observation of the physical environment with its wildlife and flora.

Slender constructions, grouped together in the meanders of the river Jarama, rise up like thin columns of smoke, seeking close relations between them and offering a territorial readability of the park, in the form of specific places marked by programmatic intensity, discontinuity and local instability.

This is neither emphatic verticality of places in the landscape nor any quest for visual control, but a specific and dispersed topological organization, a set of fleeting and retrievable actions. The materials are actually chosen to be put together dry and screwed to a tubular steel structure – a technical system that permits complete reversibility.

The maximum slenderness of the buildings helps to minimize both the use of the land and the impact on the environment and the water table, while their eclectic and random configurations vary in accordance with the site, exposure to the sun and the prevailing winds; and the horizontal section is altered in accordance with the lines of force of the best viewing angles over the quarries, marshes and hills. The interior is designed like a stratified overlay of housing units, each with minimal kitchen and bathroom, and sharing common services, thus adapting to the changing ways in which things are used and the social groupings of the occupants.

A thick and porous skin forms the envelope of the towers, and there is an intermediary space, which thermically regulates and ventilates the interiors in summer while it captures and accumulates heat in winter. Through its hollow spaces air circulates as a result of different pressures, with minimum energy consumption: the towers work like chimneys and give form to the wind. In this in-between area there is also a spiral stairway, which becomes gradually wider as it passes and differentiates the housing areas. Each floor is thus deformed and polarized on the basis of the position of the stairway and the preferential viewing angles.

The outer envelope is made of transparent cellular plastic, whose colour reflects the variable hue of the sky. The overlaying of these skins distorts our perception of the silhouette; it is blurred and sketchy, reflecting the ephemeral and transitory purpose of the project.

◆

Bénédicte Grosjean

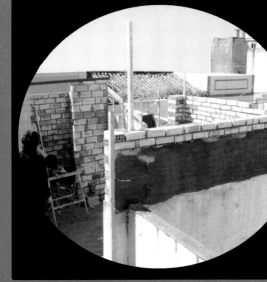

| Spain |

Santiago Cirugeda Parejo |

Santiago Cirugeda Parejo (1971)

Spanish artist, theoretician and 'activist' Santiago Cirugeda lives and works in Seville. His main areas of investigation are present-day housing and the present-day city, and private space and public place. He teaches at the School of Scenography in Seville and at the ESARQ in Barcelona, where he is involved in the postgraduate course: 'Habitat: contemporary housing and environments'. His many urban exhibitions, installations and performances are based on the view that the administrative and planning organization that governs architecture and construction in cities is basically incapable of encompassing 'the complexity of human reality', which is the very condition of living somewhere. Santiago Cirugeda suggests literally throwing off this strait-jacket from within. Distortion, contamination, unauthorized and illegal installations, non-official contractual arrangements: he formulates realistic and empirical strategies to push the law to its limits and find pockets of non-law in which to develop a possible habitat. ◆

'The Mutant (and Silent) Architecture' |
Seville, Spain, 2000

How are urban refuges to be built, how is the street to be taken back and how are reserves of urban land to be created? First, ask the city planning department for a permit for 'minor works' requiring scaffolding (3,000 pesetas tax), like, for example, repainting the façade next to which you wish to install yourself: some graffiti will suffice, if necessary, to justify this. Second, get a friendly architect to approve the scaffolding project and its safety standards, a straightforward procedure that is easily copied. Next, register the project with the Order of Architects (4,000 pesetas tax) without filling in the box 'length of work' (sic). Last, construct your own urban refuge with the materials and stylistic features that you want: the committee for monuments and sites in the old city centre will not be able to do anything during the few months when you want to live in it.

As a practical 'tricks of the trade' handbook for use by one and all, part of Santiago Cirugeda's work consists in carefully examining what the law fails to define, so as to think up urban occupation strategies in its loopholes: how to be legal, in spite of everything. When different owners in a residential complex wish to set up communications between several spaces on different floors, a project shared between architects and lawyers is embarked upon, dealing with the status of the inner patio and the legal provisions for subletting square footage between neighbours, to work out a structure of external circulation that can be dismantled.

Other highly instructive propositions envisage, instead, how to be illegal: the 'double hidden projects' reflect the fairly common temptation to dodge the plan drawn up for the building permit, while providing for movable and/or cardboard elements for site inspection visits. Last, by assuming an 'absolute illegality', projects such as an inhabitable 'prosthesis' on a roof, in a zone where there is a ban on raising building heights, teach us how to hoist up materials without using cranes and without making any noise, getting rid of rubble by truck at night and camouflaging scaffolding.

Why this 'civil disobedience'? 'There are as many reasons for taking back the street and constructing an urban refuge for yourself as there are people daring to do so.' Spatial needs, be they functional or intellectual, individual or collective, the day-to-day development of certain forms of civil disobedience, like so many liberating impulses and critical parodies of administrative structures, all at least cast doubt on what is 'legitimate', in view of the use people wish to make of things.

◆

Bénédicte Grosjean

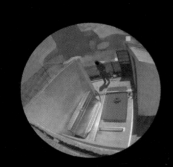

SEM-ILEGAL
(To stick)
House on scaffolding
3 Months (1997)
Taking the street
SOCIAL
Student - Ineffective person?

LEGAL
(To lean)
Capsule for institutions
(11 Months (1988-9)
To Expand the limited functioning
CULTURE
Artist - Important person

ILLEGAL
(To inlay)
Prothesis in nowhere
Underlined: to modify your
PERSONALITY
City - anonymous person

SEVILLA
Amplía su casa con un andamio
Múltiple intoxicación alimentaria en una residencia de estudiantes

Perfil
Santiago Cirugeda: «La ciudad es algo vivo que se debe de adaptar a las necesidades humanas»

Ejemplo de desobediencia civil

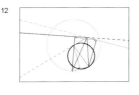

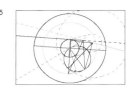

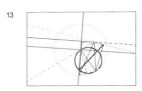

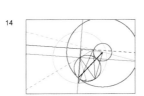

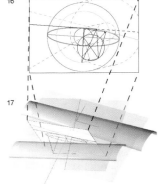

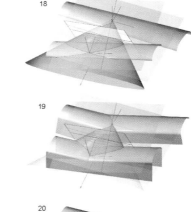

| USA |

Preston Scott Cohen |

PRESTON SCOTT COHEN (1961)

Having graduated from the Rhode Island School of Design and the Harvard Graduate School of Architecture in Cambridge, MA, Preston Scott Cohen taught at Princeton University, Ohio State University and Rome, and is currently associate professor of architecture at Harvard, where he teaches projective geometry and coordinates the first year of architectural instruction.

He is the author of theoretical writings (*Contested Symmetries and Other Predicaments in Architecture*, Princeton Architectural Press, 2001, and *Permutations of Descriptive Geometry*, 2002) in which he puts forward the idea of combining the conflicting techniques of perspective and orthographic projection in a descriptive geometry which he calls 'Stereotomic Permutations'. The outcome of this is a set of geometric procedures, which Preston Scott Cohen would like to develop as techniques of formal transgression capable of informing the paradoxes of architectural form. ◆

Wu House
Burson, California, 2000–present

In Wu House, geometric primitives – elliptical cylinders and cones – are positioned and intersected in such a way as to create sinuous lines derived from topological surface geometry.

In the history of classical architecture, intersections of cylinders have almost exclusively followed two different types. The first, created by congruent perpendicular barrel vaults, produces a groin vault. The intersection line is an X in plan representing four individual surfaces contiguous along cusped borders. A variant of this type is the case in which one of two crossing vaults extends no further than the apex, thereby creating a half X or V, a single cusp. The other type involves two vaults whose ridges are set at different levels and therefore are not tangent. This produces one or two curvilinear intersections.

Usually a V cusp is prolonged by two lines or none. In Wu House, a third surface passing through the point of tangency between the two previous tangent surfaces creates a Y intersection and a fourth surface – a wall – is tangent with both one of the original two and the third. This causes the Y to close and to become a loop or lasso.

The main body of the house is composed of three 'saddles' – three pairs of intersecting vaults. Cones pass between and intersect the saddles to produce joined lassos that create what appear to be broken figure 8s. At the outer limits of the two peripheral vaults, two lassos are the product of smaller elliptical cylinders that act as termini for the trio of saddles otherwise linked by cones. From the outer limits of the two peripheral saddles, the cylinders pierce back towards the central saddle as if to terminate the repetitive pattern of vaulted spaces.

The central saddle contains the focus of activity in the house: the kitchen and dining areas. It leans slightly towards the neighbouring living room saddle, with a conical connection between these two saddles that plays the role of an oculus in the kitchen. In the living room, the same cone appears as an extremely compressed domical figure and the oculus like the ring of a distorted lantern.

The third saddle, containing the study, is most evidently an independent entity. Its primary entry is from the courtyard. Yet, two passages link the study to the other two saddles. The first is a cone, which joins it to the kitchen. It is too high for viewing and serves only for the passage of sound. The second passage is a corridor lined with books, which, like a periscope, bypasses the kitchen and connects the study directly to the living room. The corridor cuts through and lies below the kitchen level. The central saddle is as if divided by a moat that defines two separate occupiable areas that are spatially continuous with one another. The occupant is required to navigate the gap by moving between the saddles. Passages for movement act as counterpoints for the conical and cylindrical passages for light, listening and viewing. ◆

Preston Scott Cohen

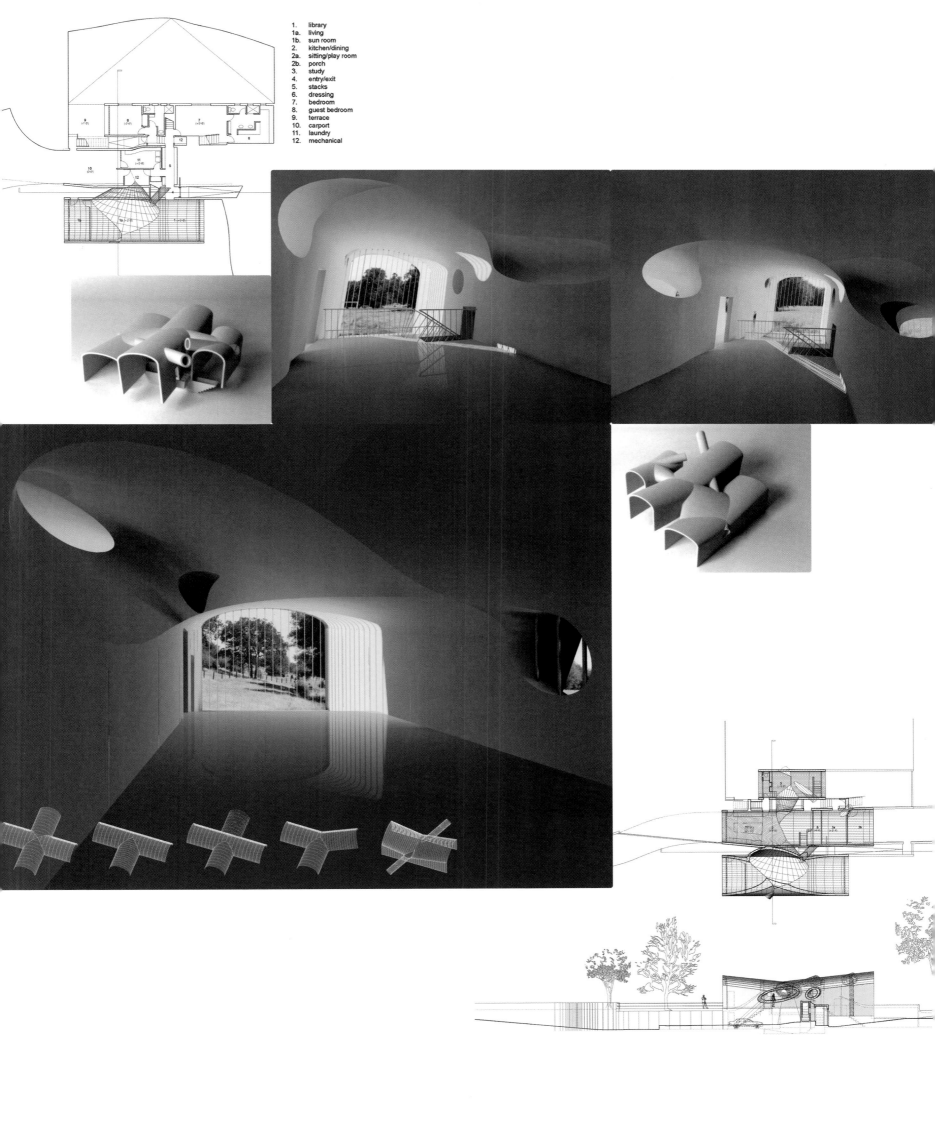

1. library
1a. living
1b. sun room
2. kitchen/dining
2a. sitting/play room
2b. porch
3. study
4. entry/exit
5. stacks
6. dressing
7. bedroom
8. guest bedroom
9. terrace
10. carport
11. laundry
12. mechanical

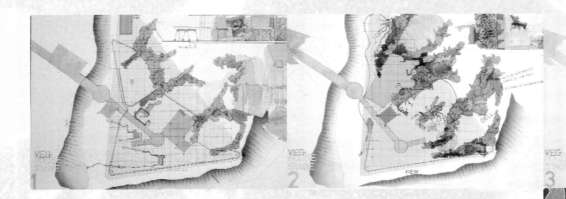

|UK|

Peter Cook

PETER COOK (1961)

Peter Cook graduated from the Architectural Association in the late 1950s, and was a student of Peter Smithson and James Gowan, among others. In 1961, with David Greene, he published the first issue of the magazine *Archigram*, a springboard for one of the most significant architectural and urban counter-utopias of the latter half of the 20th century. Between 1962 and 1976, together with Ron Herron, Warren Chalk, Dennis Crompton and Michael Webb, and accompanied by the theoretician and critic Reyner Banham, Peter Cook co-produced, in the name of *Archigram*, a very large number of projects challenging the relationships between architecture, the city and Western civilization consisting of leisure, media and mass consumerism. These spectacular projects, at once critical and enthusiastic, saw, in nomadism, ephemerality and obsolescence, new ways of living for human communities and new ways of living in the world. Since 1976, Peter Cook has been associated with Christine Hawley, and is still developing radical and theoretical projects involving, in particular, contemporary technological and territorial changes. He is also head of Bartlett School in London and a regular contributor to the *Architectural Review*. ◆

The Veg. House

The final form is hairy. Almost a barnacled wreck. An architecture that celebrates vegetation, The Veg. House sits on a shelf of hillside overlooking a river. A triangular table is set up, held on the three corners. The table serves as cover and service space. You approach by one of the longer sides. The space is tall enough for two floor heights. A power point is established near the corner. That's it. Very straightforward.

On closer observation, there is nearby vegetation waiting to be invited into the triangular space. There are some modest series of 'trainer' wires within. Inevitably, the vegetation will follow them. The scheme is described in four phases. At the first, some fairly tranquil infilling is made. The double height is exploited by platforms. A glazed skin envelops the triangular shape. A trickle of planting moves slowly along trainers. In the second phase the vegetation begins to infiltrate further. It also begins the process of weaving spaces out of that vegetation. The arrangement of 'rooms' has shifted. The skin begins to deflect. Odd bedfellows such as kitchen appliances and bushes are encouraged to mix together. We realize that this is no longer a 'house' or 'garden', nor a house stretching into the garden. The next stages seem to accelerate the process, so that sound devices, heating devices, virtual reality devices join into the plantation. And it is this notion of plantation that is the clue to the whole project. In the past we have clung to our comfortable definitions of primary and secondary element, of substance and surface, of appliances, devices, services, appendages, the 'natural', the 'artificial'. By implanting the most contrived and artificial (and quizzical) of contemporary gismos into the most wayward and relaxed substances (the bushes and vines), one is positing a free-origin web of sound, smell and comfort.

An urbanism of a sort had to come out of all this. After a few months' reflection I set up a small piece of hillside as a proposition. With covered patches (no longer just triangles, but a variety of fairly useful shapes). Paths winding in the most efficient way. Also, on closer inspection, a gridded system of service outlet points. The patches encourage enclosure and plantation as before. As time goes by, the covers and the rest increase in density.

Something else is happening as well; the development of patches that cannot really be inhabited or enclosed but are undeniably imploded. Some have definite linear structuring, some seem just to absorb everything around them. I had realized that to just repeat the formula of covered plantation and paths was to fall into the old 'house-and-patches' trap. If this is to be a 'Veg-Village' it must welcome the wayward infestation of all conditions of ground. The Veg. City is yet to emerge. ◆

Peter Cook

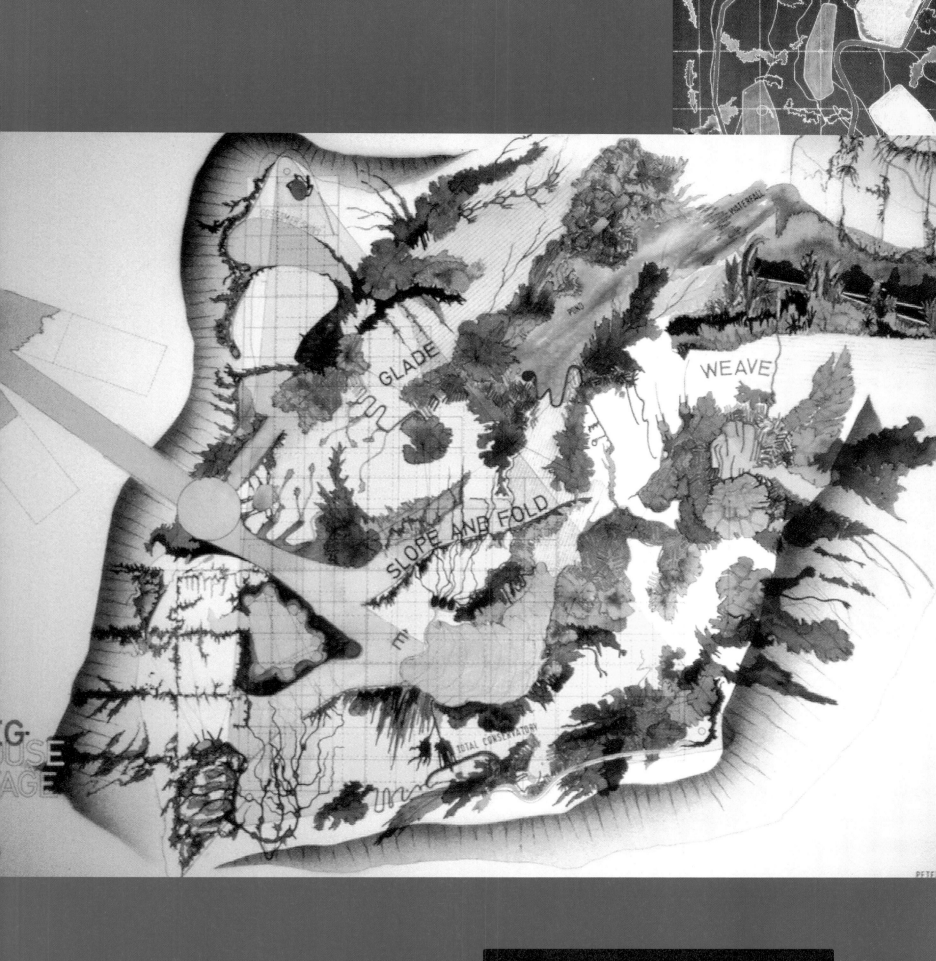

GLADE

WEAVE

SLOPE AND FOLD

TOTAL CONSERVATORY

| Austria |

Coop Himmelb(l)au |

WOLF PRIX (1942), HELMUT SWICZINSKY (1944)

Wolf Prix and Helmut Swiczinsky founded Coop Himmelb(l)au in 1968, being acutely aware of the crisis shaking Western culture, and as a radical and violent reaction to the specific context of postmodern Vienna. For more than 30 years now, Coop Himmelb(l)au has been situated in the uttermost, critical reaches of architecture, on the borderline of conceptual art, scenography, design and city planning, the better to 'liberate' architecture and open it up to itself. Despite certain attempts to deal with assignments (Deconstructivist Architecture, 1988), the work of Coop Himmelb(l)au, where constructed works form just the visible part, is unusual and defies pigeon-holing, by being endlessly self-doubting, lying somewhere between violence and indeterminacy. W. Prix and H. Swiczinsky have declared that they are keen to 'make an architecture that floats and changes like clouds' – an architecture that wriggles out of the restrictions imposed upon it, that becomes elusive for the flows and movements permeating it and that breaks away from the reasoning and argument of its designer. It is an architecture that is uniquely subject to the mysterious and instantaneous emergence of the idea, which is as lightning-fast as an accident. ◆

Gasometer B
Vienna, Austria, 1995–present

The four historical Gasometers originally housed the tanks for the gas supply of Vienna. After the closure of these Gasometers the interior elements were dismantled, leaving the classical façades. Because of the specific location of these Gasometers within an industrial site as well as the unusual character of the resulting spaces, the Gasometers were often used for diverse cultural activities.

The location of the project presents a special opportunity to develop the urban fabric of Vienna by means of various alterations of the transport system, such as the extension of the U3 subway and the construction of the Northeast Highway. In addition to Coop Himmel(b)lau three other architectural teams are working out new living opportunities to be realized in the remaining Gasometers. An Entertainment Centre and Shopping Mall will also be integrated into the complex, making it into a new city centre.

The concept of the Coop Himmel(b)lau Gasometer B adds three new volumes to the existing façade: the cylinder inside the Gasometer, the striking addition of the shield that is visible from outside and the multifunctional Event Hall situated in the base of the Gasometer.

Inside the cylinder and the shield are apartments and offices. The lighting for these inside spaces is provided by the conical inner court, and that for the outside through the old Gasometer wall. The lighting for the shield is provided through a spacious, north-oriented, glass facade with loggias. The 360 apartments offer differentiated living forms, ranging from 3-room maisonette apartments and loft apartments to student apartments. The combination of offices and apartments is expected to give rise to new ways of working and living.

The Gasometer – with different entrances for residents and for visitors – can be accessed either from the outside via Guglgasse or directly from the subway station through the connecting shopping mall. The mall connects all Gasometers at ground level. Inside Gasometer B a spatial and functional buffer between the Event Hall and the apartment/office wing is created. Internal communication is thereby intensified. The 'Sky Lobby' on the 6th floor creates a social space for the residents. Other remaining spaces can be used as common areas.

The foyer of the Event Hall is connected with the subway both by means of the 'Night Mall' of Gasometer A and directly through an entrance in Guglgasse. The 'Night Mall' also hosts common spaces, thus becoming a transit area for people arriving or leaving the Event Hall. ◆

Coop Himmelb[l]au

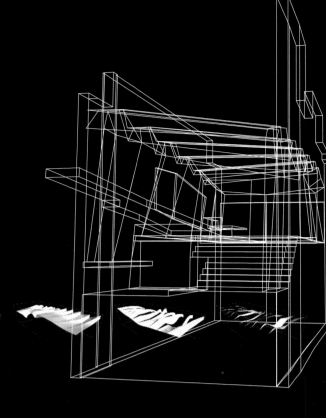

|dECOi|

| FRANCE |

MARK GOULTHORPE (1963)

dECOi, which was founded in Paris in 1991, describes itself as a research group encouraging project cooperation between architects and specialists from disciplines outside architecture. Nowadays, dECOi is operating at an international-al level in the form of an enlarged network within which mathematicians, computer programmers and engineers all take part in the same type of formal research. In addition to exhibitions, such as the Venice Biennale and more recently at the FRAC Centre in Orléans, Mark Goulthorpe is currently teaching at the Ecole Spéciale d'Architecture in Paris, as well as at Llubljana University in Slovenia. The year 2001 will see the installation, on the façade of the Birmingham Theatre, of 'Aegis Hyposurface', a reactive architectural surface with metal facets which will be deformed by stimulae caused by the environment. For dECOi, new design and production procedures have radically altered architecture. The extension of the Dietrich-Richardson House thus makes the most of all the creative possibilities of generative processes. ◆

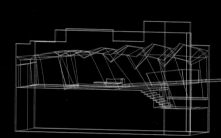

Dietrich-Richardson House
Extension, London, 1999–2002
Concept: Mark Goulthorpe, Gabriele Evangelisti, Greg More
Engineers: David Glover & Ed Clark of Group IV Ove Arup & Partners, London

The Dietrich-Richardson House is an extension to an existing London townhouse, where we have proposed to infill the dark and narrow walled garden with a top-lit living/dining space. The client, an architectural publisher, encouraged us to advance our research into the formal possibilities offered by new modelling techniques.

Making good use of the Bremner House experience and the building of his greenhouse, we study now possibilities provided by parametrical modelling, using the computer in order to generate, not a finished model but a set of relationships between 'elastic' variants.

The project marks an attempt to produce a highly rationalized diagram that nonetheless results in a complex geometrical form. Beginning from a pure rectangular space, defined parametrically, we have deformed the building envelope to allow for drainage, ducted air and storage space, producing a series of warped trapezoidal frames in the margins of which such functions are accommodated. Such 'elastic' process, sampled successively, has given birth to a crystalline form of faceted white surfaces (plastic and plasterboard). The serial deformation shifts the interior volume differentially, creating an animate interior volume of folding planar surfaces, bathed in natural light. The project, which follows on from the parametric studies of the earlier Luschwitz House, demonstrates the opportunity for an enriched formal vocabulary within a highly constrained budget.

The creative process is indeterminate in its open-ended possibility, yet precise in its result. This shift we characterize as a move from auto-plastic to alloplastic tendency, which describes not a formal condition, but a basic creative psychology and practice. In this form, whilst highly articulate, it is inexpressive, precisely indeterminate, resting on significations that occur in the generation of an animate potential or latency.

Ideally all surfaces would be not only cut by CNC machine, the templates derived automatically from the generative software, but would be lightly incised with a secondary graphic that would catch the light obliquely, floating the surfaces as a suspension of delicate motifs. This spatial suspension, coupled with the slight shifts in the angle of the surfaces, intends to offer a proprioceptive swell that further opens the luminous space. ◆

dECOi

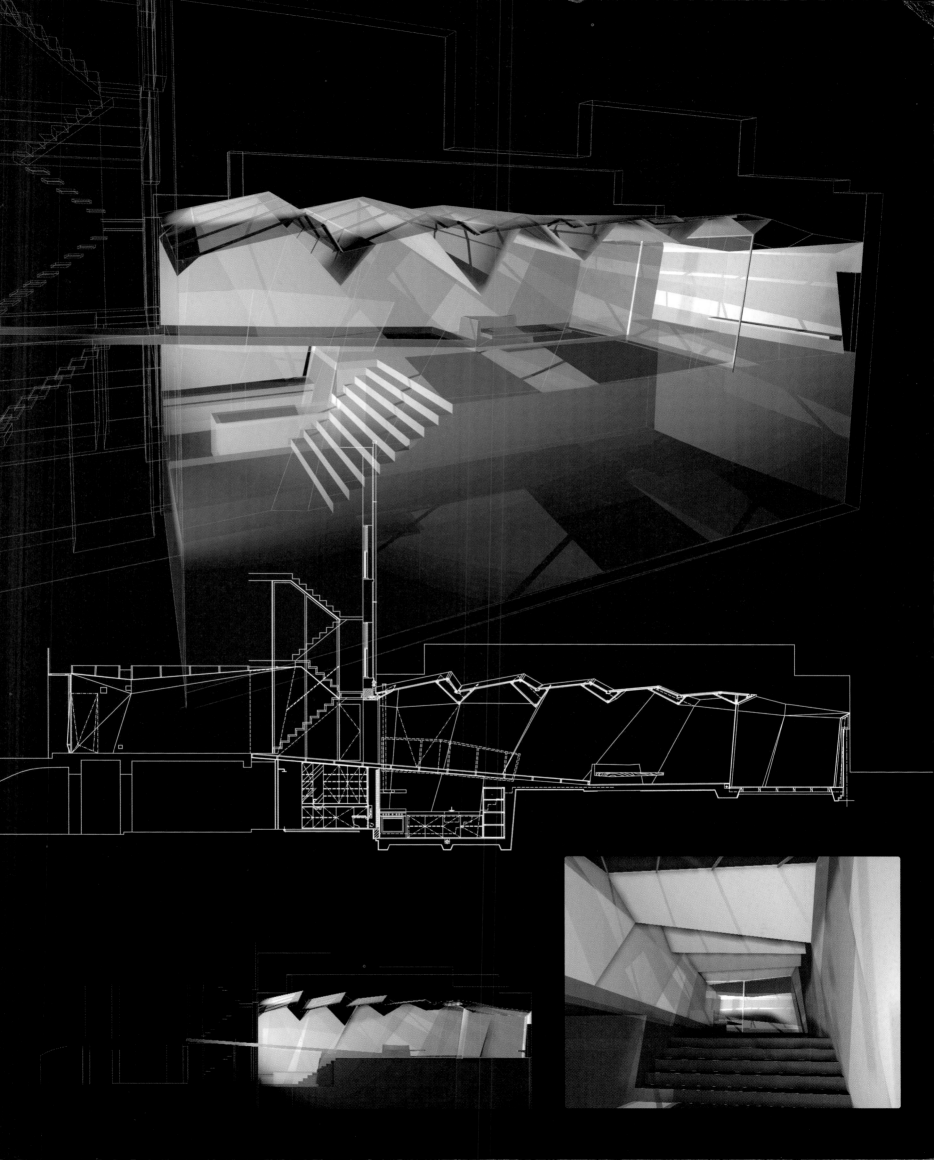

Diller + Scofidio

ELISABETH DILLER (1954) RICARDO SCOFIDIO (1935)

What the work of New York architects Elisabeth Diller and Ricardo Scofidio, who have been associates since 1979, primarily does is question all the changes occurring in Western civilization in the age of mass communications and the media. Their praxis goes well beyond the strict field of architecture and borrows from the visual arts, performance, installation, scenography, writing and multimedia art, along with their respective methods and spaces. They also teach – Elisabeth Diller at Princeton since the early 1990s and Ricardo Scofidio at Cooper Union since 1965. Their many different works attempt to highlight the new norms and the new relationships between the body and space and time introduced by information and image technologies, through their daily and generalized use: the 'real time' issue, the mediate/immediate link, the matter of speed, etc. Several of their installations have been to do with the issue of the home and living in it, in the face of these new space-time conditions ('The Withdrawing Room', 1987, 'The Slow House', 1991, etc.). ◆

'Slither' Housing
Gifu, Japan, realized, 2000

The 'liberating' potential of standardization that promised 'variety' in mass housing was one of the myths introduced by European modernism in the early 20th century. Unfortunately, this promise produced anonymity and thus doubt in the progressive ideals of the modern movement. The economic constraints that unavoidably produce the repetition of standardization in social housing, however, need not lead to the erasure of the individual dwelling.

The reptilian 'Slither' building is made up of 105 housing units. After we designed the unit, we performed three small disturbances in plan and section as a modest resistance to the inevitable anonymity of mass housing:

1. Seven units are assembled vertically into a stack. Each stack interlocks with the next stack, wedging an increment of 1.5 degrees at the joint. The accumulation of this slight angle along the building's 15 stacks results in a shallow curve, convex to the street and concave to the communal courtyard. The long elevations are faced with diaphanous overlapping 'scales' of perforated metal screening, which modulate the degree of privacy at the circulation corridor and the balconies.

2. Each unit slips 1.4 metres in plan from the next unit, thus freeing every entry door to be approached on axis. On the north side of the building, each front door is metaphorically a private façade. The slippage also produces a private balcony on the south side.

3. The floor slab of each unit is offset 200 millemetres vertically from the next unit. The circulation system of shallow continuous ramps strings together all the units, creating a subtle artificial topography in which no two units share the same elevation. As the lowest unit at the west end of the building and the highest unit at the east are offset by the dimension of one full floor, the building appears to rise from the ground. ◆

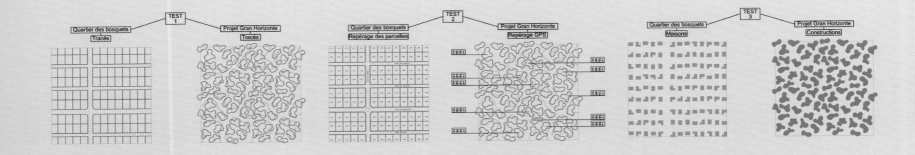

| FRANCE |

Pierre du Besset & Dominique Lyon

PIERRE DU BESSET (1949) DOMINIQUE LYON (1954)

Du Besset & Lyon established their own agency in Paris in 1987, after training in the offices of Jean Nouvel and, in D. Lyon's case, Frank Gehry, . Du Besset & Lyon have constructed several critically acclaimed buildings: in 1990, the building for the newspaper *Le Monde* in Paris; in 1994, the Médiathèque (Multimedia Library) in Orléans, and forthcoming, the Library in Troyes and the Médiathèque in Lisieux. Dominique Lyon is also the author of some significant books (*Les Avatars de l'architecture Ordinaire* ['Variations of an Architecture of the Ordinary'] and *Le Corbusier vivant* ['Living Le Corbusier']), as well as critical writings. By challenging their own architectural praxis, du Besset & Lyon develop fluid and relational spaces. The graphic aspect of the serial patterns and the chromatic transparencies at Troyes and the principle of varying colours and materials in Orléans mean that architecture evolves between its surface and its depth, its inscription and its mobility, in quest of a pleasure in architecture that is shared by its users. ◆

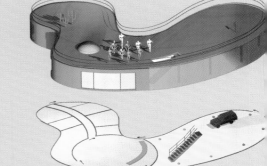

Gran Horizonte
Project, 2001

For decades now identical estates of individual urban houses have been spreading over the land. This urban landscape is built as if by reflex. Nothing is questioned. Obviously, the success of these estates is not due to a perfect conjunction of supply and demand: there is no clear, stable demand in this area. No, their formidable effectiveness comes from the fact that they offer a direct, unselfconscious and imposing representation of modern boredom. They are to urbanism what the soap opera is to cinema: a form of slackening. Their dismaying triviality becomes an advantage once they start openly boasting about smoothing over conflicts, ignoring contradictions and formatting the imagination while imposing false appearances. Therein lies their power of seduction.

Their great feat is to have managed to pass off as an ideal a house that is cramped and no bigger nor more varied than a flat. A house that blocks off a garden surrounded by hedges. Hedges that fail to keep the neighbours at a distance in a regularly constructed space. A built-up space forming a landscape whose natural dimension is limited to a succession of small playlets with plants. TV is the end of the line. Let us turn the situation around and rediscover a little ambition, if not idealism.

How to live in a bigger dimension and dwell in the infinity of the landscape? How to amortize the 4WD and get the most out of our GPS? How to fill our ever more intrusive free time and fill up its boredom? Where to do the

DIY, play ping-pong, pump iron, organize a party? Where to find a garage to start up a business?

Simple. Get rid of hierarchies, ignore false appearances, resolve contradictions and go for performance. Build the Gran Horizonte project.

Programme :
- The construction is small: build on the whole plot.
- The plot is cluttered, the garden cramped: plant on the whole plot.
- The fences limit the space without distancing the neighbours: do without the fencing and distance the neighbours.
- The car has trouble getting into the garage, which has trouble getting into the house: build the garage identical to the house.
- The houses clutter up the landscape: make the landscape with the houses.
- Driving along the roads on the estate is depressing: drive through varied scenery that is full of surprises.
- The houses spoil the view and hide the horizon: climb on to the houses to recover the horizon, a bigger dimension, the setting sun. ◆

Dominique Lyon

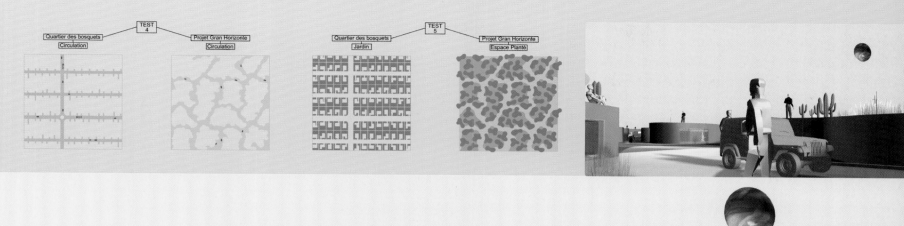

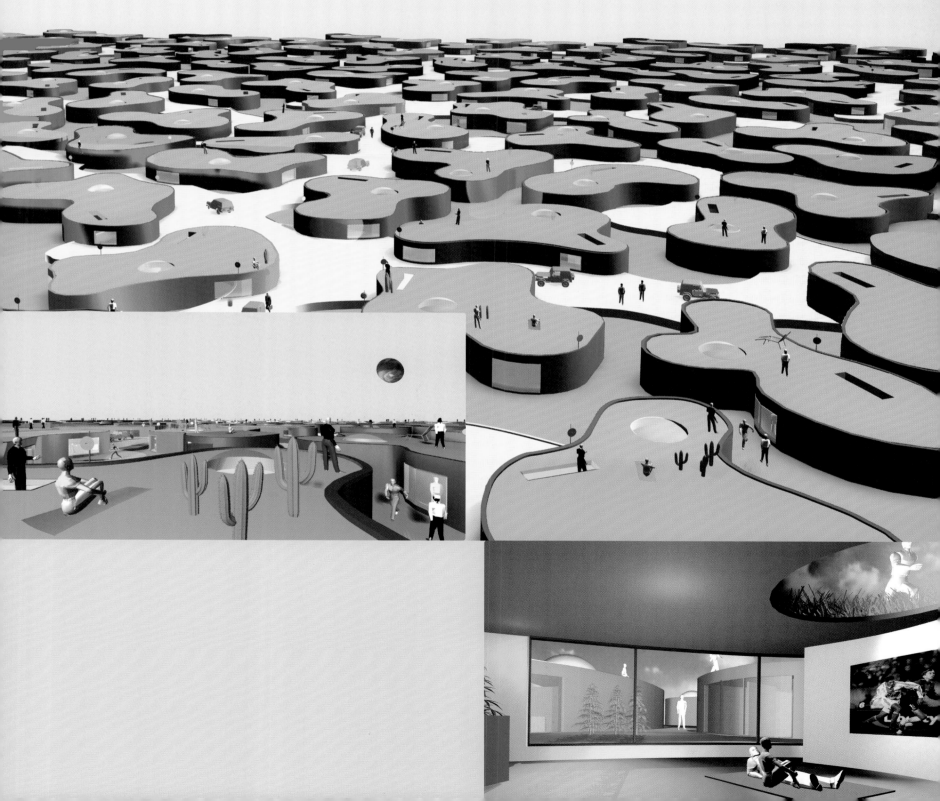

| China |

EDGE (HK) |

Gary Chang (1962)

Architect and designer Gary Chang, who graduated from Hong Kong University in 1987, went into association with Michael Chan (Edge) in 1994, and then set up his own agency in 1998: Edge (HK) Ltd. Edge symbolizes that porous rim, to do with interface, that Gary Chang intends to establish between all the different scales of our contemporary environments. Between the object, the 'interior space' of architecture and the urban territory, he refuses to recognize intellectual and methodological breaks and attempts, on the contrary, to intensify exchanges and relations – relations that are, in his view, already tangible in the labyrinthine morphology of the Hong Kong megalopolis, which he describes as a 'liquid city'. The complexity that Gary Chang looks for in his projects is not endogenous; it is imported from one scale to another, and it is deterritorialized; from city to architecture (cineplex, Chongqing, 1998) and from object to house ('Suitcase House', Shui Guan, 2000), etc. Chang's constructed work, which is rare and sophisticated, is the outcome of this rigorous approach to research and experimentation, which undermines accepted practices. ◆

Suitcase House
Communal house near the Great Wall, China 2000

Stuitcase: stiff, flat-sided case for carrying one's personal items, etc., when one is travelling; a building esp. one constructed as a home for a family – unfolding the mechanics of domestic (p)leisure.

Placing a question mark over the proverbial image of the house, this scheme attempts to rethink the nature of intimacy, privacy, spontaneity and flexibility. It is a simple demonstration of the desire for ultimate adaptability, in pursuit of a proscenium for infinite scenarios, a plane of sensual (p)leisure.

The dwelling represents a stacking of strata. The bottom stratum acts as a container for domestic fittings and equipment and services and living quarters for domestic staff. It also fulfils the requirements for storage. Compartments are concealed by a landscape of floor panels, which, when raised, give access to the world below. The top stratum houses a series of blinds that may be raised or lowered to subdivide the space. Similarly, the building envelope is a stratification of vertical layers. The outer skin is a wrap of full-height double-glazed folding doors while the inner layer is composed of a series of screens forming a matrix of openings. The abstract façade pattern is thereby rooted in its user-oriented operational logic. Together, these strata give form to the zone in between.

The middle stratum embodies a reincarnated piano nobile, ideally suited to habitation, activity and flow. Adapting a non-hierarchical layout with the help of folding and sliding mobile elements provided by the envelope, it transforms itself readily according to personal preferences for degrees of enclosure and privacy. At any point in time, only the essential elements required will have a spatial presence. It is a metamorphic volume. The floor panels evoke unmistakable associations with the interior of a luxury cruise ship. They are pneumatically assisted for ease and convenience. When opened they reveal an interior that corresponds to the programme contained. As mid-level compartments fulfil most requirements little furniture is required.

The house is located at the head of the Nangou Valley near the Great Wall at Badaling, north of Beijing. The site, which slopes steeply towards the north, is relatively exposed. To maximize views to the prominent Great Wall and solar exposure in the continental temperate climate, a north-south orientation is adopted. It will be possible to see the Great Wall from all major spaces within the dwelling whilst seated. The dwelling is provided with multiple entrances, all with equal status, while each room is differentiated by the provision of unique amenities, as one of the essential components of luxury is choice. ◆

Gary Chang

| USA |

EMERGENT Design |

Tom Wiscombe (1970)

Tom Wiscombe collaborated with Coop Himmelb(l)au in Vienna and Los Angeles for 8 years. He was project architect for the critically acclaimed Dresden UFA Cinema Palace project (1998). In 1999, he founded EMERGENT Design, a network of designers dedicated to researching issues of globalism, technology and materiality through built form. This year, EMERGENT, in partnership with Coop Himmelb(l)au in Los Angeles, led the design team that produced the winning scheme for the Lyon Science Museum Competition, due to open in 2005.

Their work is concerned with the dissolution of critical practice and idealism in the formulation of architectural proposals in favour of locating and exploiting opportunities indigenous to a dynamic, globalized society. Their approach is informed by contemporary models of biology and business, particularly because both are flexible and tactical. Those qualities, which result in the evolution of more intelligent and resilient species and technologies, produce an architecture of incorporation, where buildings take on multiple identities. ◆

Micro-Multiple House |
Los Angeles, USA, 2001

Not 'a home', this house avoids Heideggerian notions of being and origin in favour of Deleuzian becoming and multiplicity. Contrary to the German idea of 'Heimat', denoting intimacy and warmth as well as homeland or 'coming home', the Micro-Multiple House serves as a station, a travelling through, an orifice with no body.

This project is both a landscape and a network. It spreads out intelligently, channelling and re-routing multiple flows of information, vehicles, liquids and particles, reacting opportunistically to various contingencies. It is deployed as a sequence of flexible steel strands, which twist and bend to perform like roadways, ramps, rivers, balconies, entrances and windows. Strands do not operate independently from adjacent strands; inflections are not violent deformations but rather local affiliations mapping on to a global system.

A new species of house emerges: one giant 'living room' with qualities of interior and exterior, urban and suburban, geographical and technological. Unexpected spatial experiences unfold from this interchange — driving through a subterranean lake to get to the garage, picnicking in an interior leisure garden, seeing the carving out of reflections of water glimmering on video displays, meandering endlessly from home to office without ever stepping outside.

The construction principle, rather than defaulting to a reductionist stick-built system, is consequently based on the flexible repetitive unit. Strand segments are sized according to the maximum width and length of delivery trucks and engineered as universally jointed trusses. On site, they can be set out flat, twisted, locked into position and panellized. Geometrical changes and new information can therefore readily be incorporated into this system during construction.

Ecological rather than 'machinic', the Micro-Multiple House behaves like a living system, flourishing by incorporating differences, negotiating win-win synergies and pursuing multiple goals. This house becomes a scalar multiplicity, at the junction between a spreading in of micro-intensities and a spreading out of a mega-organization. The result is a space that will not stand still, fluctuating between building and landscape, one and many, part and whole. ◆

Tom Wiscombe

|Shuhei Endo Architect Institute|

SHUHEI ENDO (1960)

Based in Osaka since 1998, Shuhei Endo belongs to that generation of architects who, in the early 1990s, sought to go beyond the contradictions of postmodernism. As the most blatant, not to say the most literal, example of 'Folding Architecture' (cf. *Architectural Design*, March 1993), Shuhei Endo's work aims, first and foremost, at rethinking the legacy of the modern movement in this day and age. Endo's architecture thus sees itself as para-modern, and no longer breaking with, but rather linking up with a critical dialogue with the modernist doxy. From this, Endo takes on the expressive mode, the effectiveness and the phenomenological significance, but he rejects its analytical penchant for segregating formal features (post, beam, wall, roof, etc.). For Endo, the fold — a form that is at once complex and synthetic, smooth and knotted, and freed from the restrictions of Euclidian space — represents the preferred way of perceiving, in an ongoing way, the ever more numerous and contradictory elements of contemporary architecture. He has made corrugated steel sheet, which combines flexibility, water-/air-tightness and an auto-load-bearing capacity, the basic material for this folding architecture. ◆

Rooftecture M
Tokyo, Japan, project, 1999

This project is part of a series. 'Rooftecture' is the generic title given to a number of Endo's projects (Rooftectures T, N, O, Y, H or W). Other projects form series called the 'Springtectures' or the 'Halftectures'. These different families of architecture constitute so many parallel lines of research in Endo's work. What differentiates them is not the scale or size of the operations (as in Koolhaas's *SMLXL*, say) or the programme itself (Rooftecture W is a project for the Geneva headquarters of a global organization whereas Rooftecture M is a house). The classification of Endo's projects is in fact genetic and conceptual. It identifies different problems or strategies concerning the use of the fold in architecture. In the Rooftectures, the 'folding' concerns mainly the roof, as a unitary and synthesizing element. In the case of this particular house, located in a residential district of Tokyo, the folding of the roof was initially a response to the context. The plot of land is a long, narrow strip running from north to south, surrounded by other houses. Only the small northern side of the plot offers access from the street. Endo's response to this sensation of the pressure exerted on the plot by its surroundings is simple and obvious. At once cuirass and container, the smooth metal surface of the Rooftecture counters the presence of its neighbours with its compact, convex form, like the membrane of an organ trying to adapt to the hollow of a body. Folded along the lengthways axis of the plot, the roof leaves the smaller side very much open to the light and generously accessible from outside. As an architectural response to the urban context, the Rooftecture also solves the question of the house's interiority. Like an arc or an arch, the Rooftecture spans and at the same time invents the domestic space: it effects a programmatic synthesis of it.

Echoing the organic reference adumbrated by the city itself, the interior of the house is broken up according to its main functions, which are treated as so many specific but interdependent organs: bathrooms, bedrooms, living room, tatami, artist's studio, dining room, kitchen. Endo assembles these units both functionally and topologically, giving rise to an efficient and formally undefined programmatic complex that is unified by the enveloping Rooftecture. ◆

Pierre Chabard

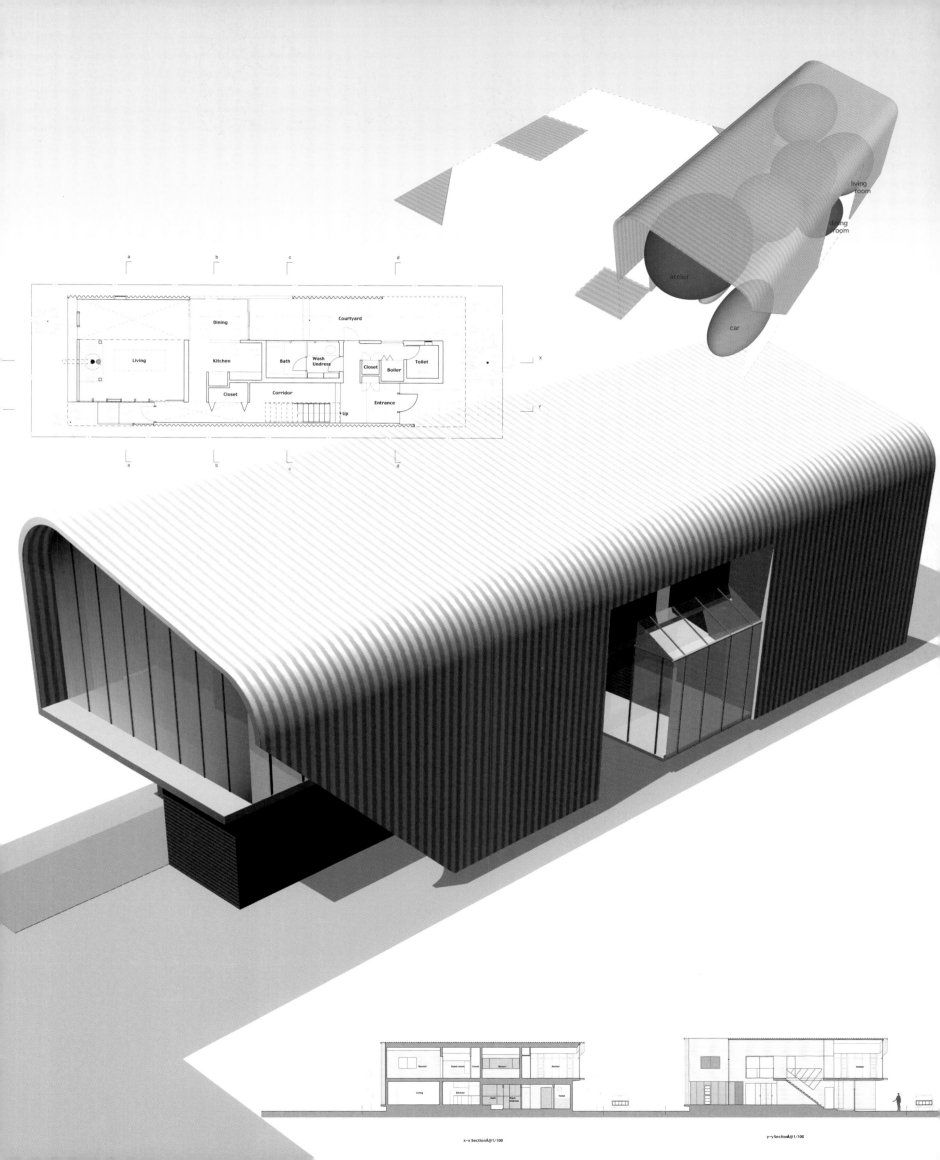

a   b   c   d

Dining   Courtyard

Living   Kitchen   Bath   Wash
Undress   Closet Boiler   Toilet

Closet   Corridor

Entrance

Up   X

Y

a   b   c   d

living
room

dining
room

atelier

car

x–x SectionA@1/100   y–ySectionA@1/100

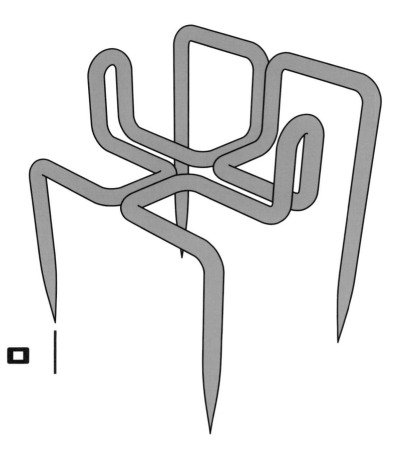

| FRANCE/PORTUGAL |

Didier Fiuza Faustino |

DIDIER FIUZA FAUSTINO (1968)

Commuting between Lisbon and Paris, Didier Faustino develops the multi-faceted activities of an architect, artist and magazine editor. Performances, videos challenging the relationship of the body to space, exhibitions and texts are all combined in his architectural research. As a co-founder of the LAPS (Laboratory of Performance Architecture and Sabotages) in 1996, and of the Fauteuil Vert agency, in Paris, in 1997, he has also been running the Portuguese aesthetics magazine *NumeroMagazine* since 1998. At the last Venice Architecture Biennale, he exhibited a suitcase designed for transporting an illegal immigrant by air ('Body in transit'), its form moulded and clinging to the folded body, made specially for this function. Faustino produced a critical project, stigmatizing the forced nomadism of whole groups of people, condemned to exile, and 'sharpening our awareness of reality'. Housing is the same thing. For ArchiLab, Didier Faustino is showing a new prototype, designed as the extension of a typical home, which changes as different residents pass through it. ◆

Love me tender |
Prototype, 2000 |

In the space encompassing our body's abode,

four sharp feet signal weightlessness.

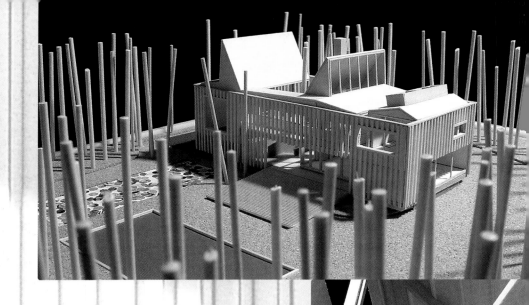

| USA |

Field Operations

STAN ALLEN (1956), JAMES CORNER (1961)

Stan Allen graduated from Cooper Union and Princeton University, and currently teaches architecture at the Graduate School of Architecture at Columbia University. Since 1999, he has been associated with the city planner and landscape designer James Corner, within the Field Operations organization, in New York and Philadelphia, offering strategic approaches to the design of cities, buildings and landscapes. Field Operations marks a shift from the one to the many, from static to dynamic, from narrative to performance, from object to field.

Field Operations implies not only the arrangement of forms in space, but also the orchestration of the various forces (ecological, cultural, economic, political, legislative, etc.) that shape cities, buildings or landscapes over time. It is this concern for the structuring of dynamic, relational geographies rather than creation of autonomous objects that distinguishes our practice.

Through close attention to the logistics of implementation, Field Operations can be responsive to a wide range of spatial, temporal and cultural variables while remaining open to the uncertainties of future development. ◆

'Domestic Landscapes' Weekend House
Sagaponac, New York, prototype, 2000–01

Avoiding the traps of esoteric formalism, literary and personal narratives, or 'critical' interrogations of domesticity, this project looks for new opportunities in the dispersed fields of consumer desire and mass media. Instead of designing hypothetical objects for imaginary clients, we examine the material operations and procedures required to produce multiple houses for as yet undefined clients. The site is described as a series of generic conditions: wooded or open, flat or sloping, rather than mythologized as a generator of meaning or place. The results are intended to be evocative and formally nuanced. We examine multiple sensibilities and take seriously questions of image, allusion and popular taste.

Programme: One of the primary characteristics of networked systems is that individual parts or machines are less important than the overall system, and the paths of information flow within that system. Using the various technologies of the house as a starting point, it is possible to think of the flow of activities, energy and information as a loose programmatic scaffold. This allows us to look at the house as a whole, through the filter of an abstract, diagrammatic schema. We can move beyond the current obsession with private or public space, and look at the house as a potential field of information exchange and energy flow.

Site: We see our work as part of an alternative tradition, which plays close attention to the construction of the site itself, and views the house and site as a unified field.

Plans: No matter how radical the proposition, plans will have to be drawn, discussed and submitted to regulating agencies, and will form the primary basis for construction.

Details: Details mark transitions and articulate material differences. Details mediate inside and outside, acting variously as barriers, filters or passages, and they often mark the point of contact between the body and the building. As such, details can trigger larger readings as the eye or hand parses the architecture.

Surfaces and skins: Surfaces work primarily in two dimensions, implicating pattern, texture, scale and colour. If the surface is primarily a problem of two dimensions, it is also true that the problem of the surface always implies a question of depth as well. Issues of transparency and translucency suggest thinking of the surface in relation to interface: a membrane-like character, in which the surface is an active space-defining element rather than a static divider of space. ◆

Stan Allen

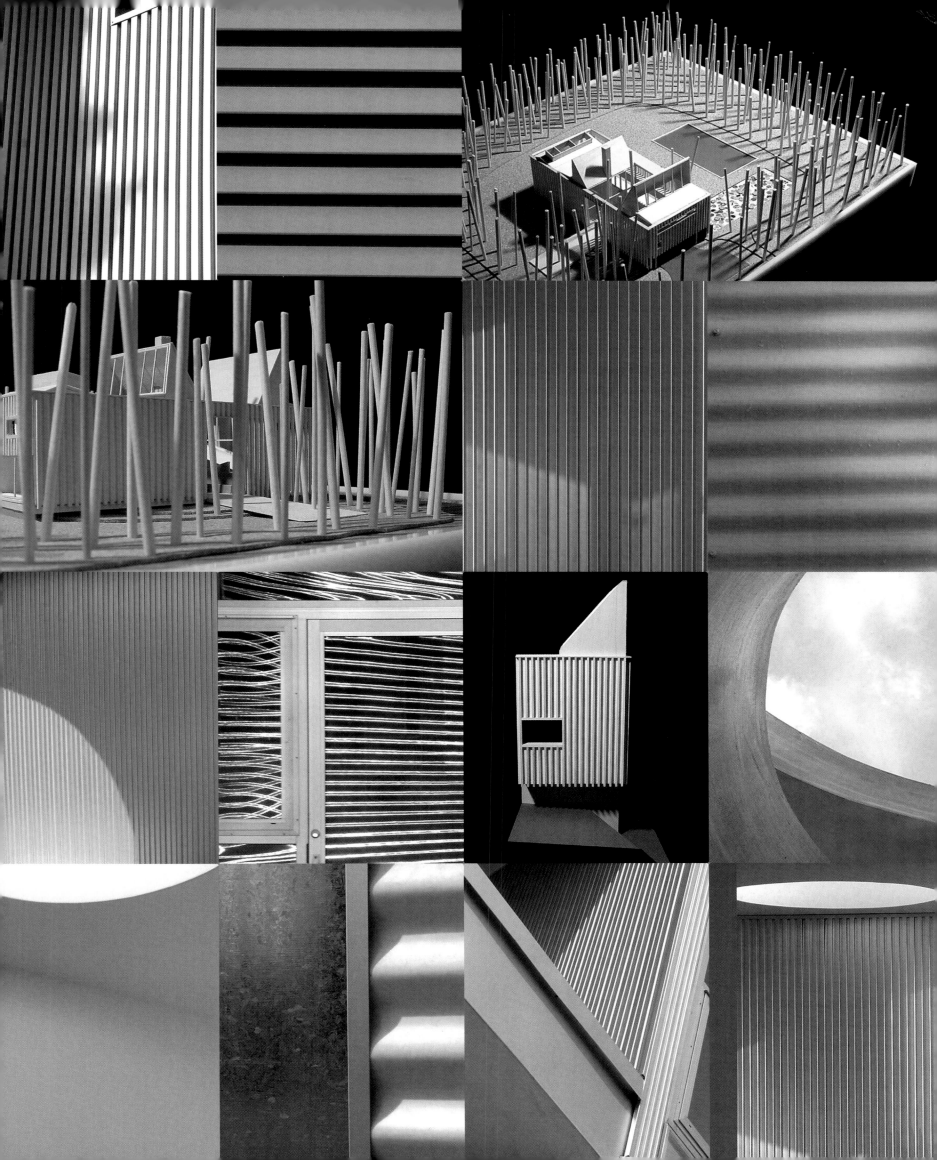

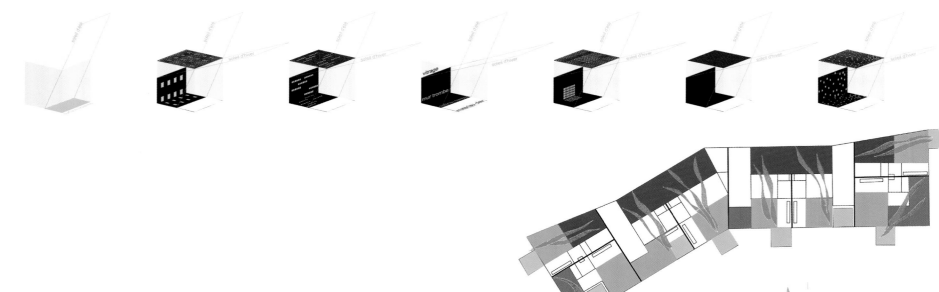

| France |

Manuelle Gautrand Architectes

Manuelle Gautrand (1961)

Manuelle Gautrand set up her agency in Lyon in 1991. She won the Albums de la jeune architecture prize in 1992, and opened her own business in Paris the following year. As an experienced builder of a large number of tertiary units and buildings, she was selected for the Monitor prize for a first work in 1994, and for the international Dupont Benedictus prize in 1999. Last year she was awarded the AMO 2000 'architecture and workplaces' prize. In addition to her architectural work, Manuelle Gautrand teaches at the Ecole Spéciale d'Architecture and at the Paris-la-Seine school. As a realistic, pragmatic and expert architect, Manuelle Gautrand expects to bring about some changes in architecture through technology and constructive innovation. She is well removed from high-tech formalism, which, above all, saw an aesthetic end purpose in technology. She herself sees in it a pragmatic way of associating architecture with the programmatic and cultural restrictions of the day. ◆

110 dwellings H.Q.E.
Rennes, France, project, 2001

This project, developed on behalf of a private developer (the property developer Espacil), is part and parcel of the forward-looking policy of the city of Rennes, promoting the construction of H.Q.E. buildings. These housing units are not to be experimental, merely exemplary, so as to be potentially reproducible. The goal is to undertake an H.Q.E. project that is financially and technically realistic, in order to inspire future operations.

This operation is based on a 'theoretical' study conducted in partnership with the electricity company (EDF), which specified a series of ecological criteria for 'green' collective housing: incorporation in the landscape, the environmental passivity of the building (minimization of energy, water and other forms of consumption; waste sorting of the site, and then of households), flexibility of use, etc.

The 110 housing units are divided into three linear buildings, facing north–south to make the most of long, fully south-facing façades. Between each building and the next there is a dense, deciduous strip of vegetation, shady in summer and permeable in winter. The south façades and the roofs are optimally placed to catch the warmth of the sun. All the apartments are of the through type, and all the warmth captured on the south side can thus be channelled through to the north-facing rooms. To the south, this solar capture is achieved by means of a very simple device: a cubic glass veranda, closed in winter and open in summer, and fitted with a black concrete veil acting like a modern 'cascade wall'. These verandas run along the south façade and are attached in an irregular way to each apartment, either at an angle or embedded. Based on their position in relation to the classic plan, the housing unit becomes a three- or four-room apartment and the relations between the various rooms differ, offering many typological configurations.

The roof and the south façade are experimental areas where constructive, typological and architectural research are combined, all geared towards a real household ecology. The materials and the technical devices (photovoltaic cells, 'cascade wall', etc) are regarded, over and above their environmental qualities, as potential supports or back-up materials for new uses, as well as means of a real architectural expression. The intent of this project, lastly, is to demonstrate that the very cumbersome H.Q.E. constraints can, without huge cost overruns, be adapted to a flexible, open and appropriable home, whose receptive and reactive architecture must fit in with its environment. ◆

Pierre Chabard

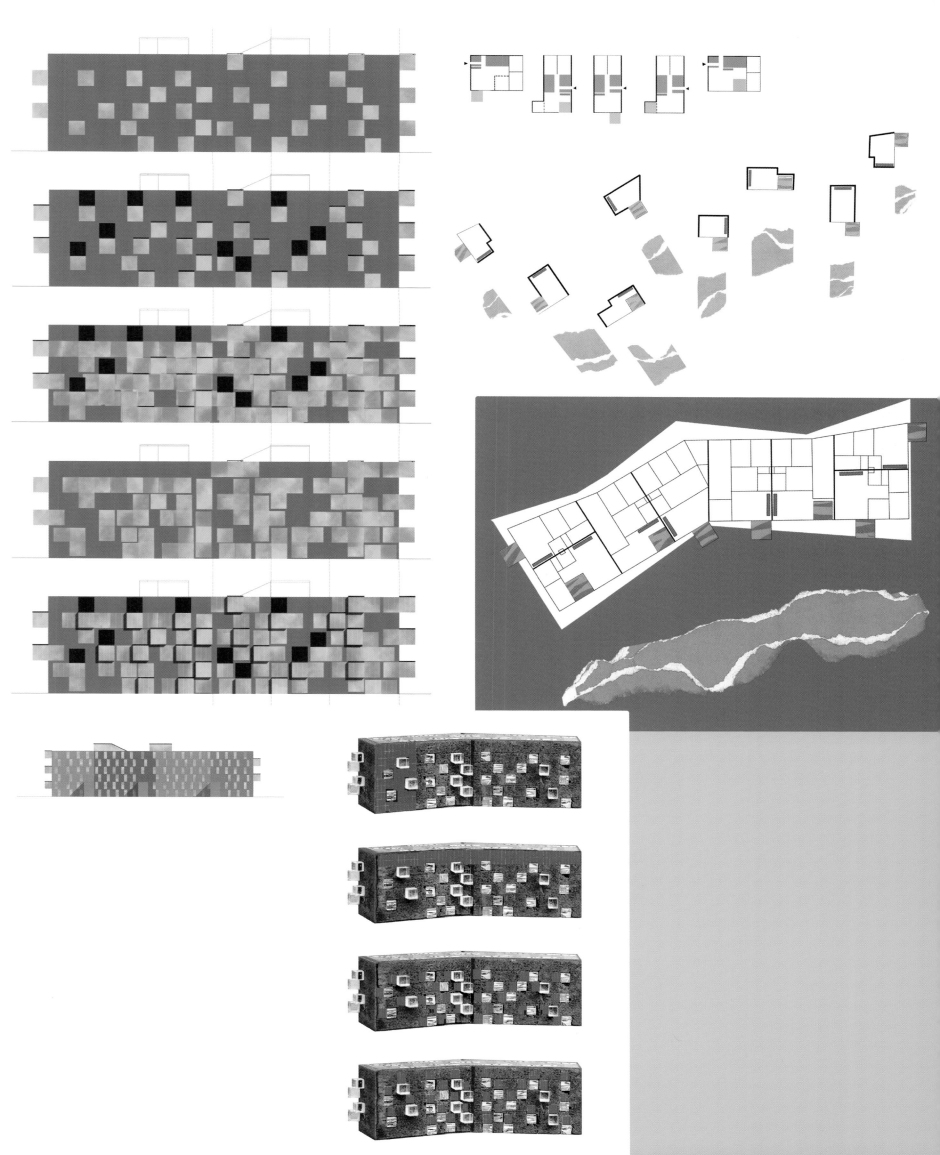

$y=f(x)$

$y=cx$

$y=c$

$y=0$

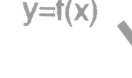

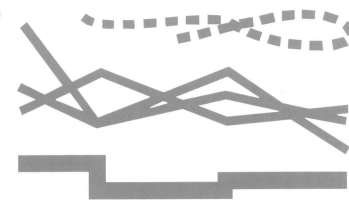

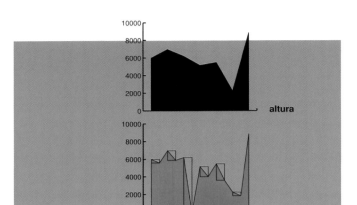

altura

altura+tiempo(bajada)

altura/0

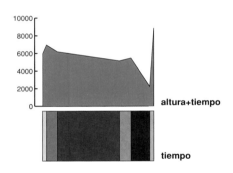

altura+tiempo

tiempo

| Spain |

Vicente Guallart |

Vicente Guallart (1963)

The architect Vicente Guallart has been based in Barcelona (where he founded his own agency in 1992) since 1988, and divides his time between teaching and research (Polytechnic University of Barcelona), multimedia production (RA CD-ROM collection for NEWMedia Productions) and organizing exhibitions (Metapolis). His architectural projects involve a dual extrapolation – both from the landscape and geographical scale and from the digital world of new information technologies. In his quest for a possible habitat, Vicente Guallart actually sees in architecture a means of continually rethinking current changes, be they territorial or technological. Over and above the real/virtual split, Guallart explores the potential of the natural/artificial dialectic in his projects. On the one hand, objects of nature (trees, rocks, etc.), and geographical forms (islands, mountains) are conjured up as possible urban and architectural forms. On the other hand, the new media, considered as a new 'nature', introduce us to an artificial ecology capable of guiding the conception of physical spaces. ◆

The House of Seven Summits
La Puebla de Vallbona, Valencia, Spain, 1998
[Vicente Guallart, Max San Jullian, structure: David García]

The primary theme of this house is a biographical one. The 'seven summits' evoke a sporting feat achieved by its owner in 1999. That was when Enrique Guallart took up a titanic challenge: to climb the highest mountain on each continent. Commissioned to design a house for the mountaineer and his wife, Vicente Guallart developed an idea that he had already explored in other houses (e.g., the house at Lliria), a domestic architecture that extends and reveals the lives of its occupants. Their personality – especially when it is so powerfully and spectacularly expressed – constitutes a real programmatic factor, the basic premise of an architectural fiction. To build a house like a biography is to reformulate through architecture the uniqueness of the inhabitant. Conceived in the same way as one develops a story or edits a film, the house is differentiated, altered, 'personalized'. Built on an old playground, the house is set in a district of Valencia that is typical of 1960s urbanization. Contrasting with this context, it comes across as a kind of life-size maquette. The biographical and architectural fiction put together by Guallart is manifest above all in the use of height, in a vertical sequence. Conceived as a series of superposed strata, the house asserts the idea of 'ascent' as its favoured course. As one continues the upward progression through the house, the geometry of the strata gains in complexity while the building loses density. The floors pile up horizontally, striating and punctuating this main sequence and expressing the programme through their geometrical metamorphoses. The lower level is determined by the folds of the level that comes immediately afterwards. The space is thus differentiated: the main functions find their own space with reference to each other (living area, bedrooms, kitchen), the service areas fall into place (stairs, etc.). Likewise, the upper level draws its logic from what is above it – the roof, which lets in the light through the play of its openings and folds. The system of terraces is the site of an encounter between this virtual geography depicted by Guallart in his house of the 'seven peaks' and the impalpable and changing form of the sky itself, which may be seen through a fold or reached by one last architectural climb. As the intimate refuge of a mountaineer, recalling a universal 'race', this house is, according to Guallart, 'like a representation of the world on the scale of 1:1,000'. ◆

Pierre Chabard

architecture > < landscape   architecture > < landscape   architecture > < landscape

interference 01   interference 02   interference 03

118

| ITALY |

|IaN+|

Carmelo Baglivo (1964), Luca Galofaro (1965), Stefania Manna (1969)

IaN+ was set up in Rome in 1997 as a multidisciplinary team combining theory and practice. IaN+ is also involved in teaching in seminars and workshops at the European Institute of Design and Rome University, as well as in publishing and organizing exhibitions, such as 'American Architecture @ The Edge of the Millennium' in Rome, then in Los Angeles. IaN+ attended ArchiLab in 2000, followed by the Venice Architecture Biennale, and is currently working on several projects including a residential complex and a square on the outskirts of Rome, which challenge contemporary urban conditions and extreme situations. For IaN+, architecture is not a fixed object, but rather a permanent system of links and exchanges. IaN+ rethinks the programme using topological diagrams, which map the various activities going on in a given building. Here, just like the body, architecture will be an unchanged structure, but with inner configurations that are varying all the time. ◆

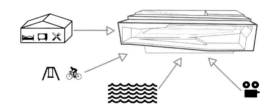

Housescape
Project, 2000

The city doesn't have boundaries and roots any more, nor does it have central places or ethical bonds: vacuums and disorder are the new areas that interest the members of IaN+. If the vacuum is perceived of as a place of unresolved confrontations of the forces involved, and if its edges give rise to relational fields, then between nature and artifice, the architecture of IaN+ has a role to play — looking for the smooth within the grooved, and on each occasion further singling out a space in the complex grid in which it is enmeshed; opening up an interference between landscape and body, and becoming the lived-in landscape, or 'livingscape'.

Precisely where functionalism sought the *existens minimum*, a project constructed like a straitjacket around a static body, restricting the connections to places to a series of preconceived and repeated gestures, IaN+ proposes, in its residential unit, an *existens maximum*, by working not on the form, but on the life system of the people in question, producing freedom of movement, circulation and activity, and paying heed to the content more than to the container. In this tendency of functions to colonize the household space without lending it any form, thus comparable to the sprawl of urban development in the internal space, the loft has remained an enclosed space, isolated from the territory. The 'livingscape', on the other hand, is an action on the vacuum between architecture and landscape, an action causing interference: if the smooth can organize the grooved, the city vanishes in the landscape and all landscape becomes city.

So, like a Möbius strip, the housescape involves inner and outer spaces, above and below, in an architecture of itinerary and continuity of surfaces, from the land of cars to the sky of trees. The occupants are free to redraw the rules for living and create lifestyles in new relations to the oblique function. The homes find various sites in the landscape and each architecture becomes a fragment of the natural complexity.

Housescape attempts a hybridization thought up simultaneously in the uses of social modes and spatial sensibility, to meet the requirements of the project's new data: being aware of randomness, when order and disorder have the same value and when one organization can spring from another; sensitive to the setting and the influence of the place, unlike those city-planning tools that are abstracted from it; sensitive to the overall data and the reciprocal relations of the parties involved. In order to be this interface, architecture must be toned down; it must be the vacuum that will be configured from the tension between the need to inhabit and landscape. ◆

Bénédicte Grosjean

architecture > < landscape

continuing space

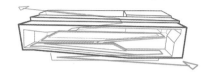

architecture > < landscape

continuing space

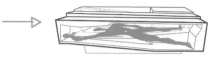

existence maximum

housescape

| JAPAN |

Osamu Ishiyama Lab. |

OSAMU ISHIYAMA (1944)

■samu Ishiyama set up his architecture 'laboratory' in Tokyo in 1968, the year he graduated from Waseda University. His time is divided between the very open-ended activities of his agency (architecture, town planning, design, marketing and multimedia) and his active teaching and research role (since 1988) supervising the Waseda Bauhaus School workshops for architects, tradesmen and children at Saga. His own work is distinguished by its radically experimental and anticonformist character. From his first projects, he began using highly unusual materials such as corrugated iron (the Gin-an House) and sheets of riveted aluminium used in the aeronautical industry (Rias Ark Museum). Ishiyama's aim is to create architecture that is suggestive – perhaps even provocative – and popular, and whose forms have maximum public impact. His constructions have won a number of prizes, including the 1985 Isoya Yoshida prize and the prize of the Japan Architectural Institute in 1995. ◆

Setagaya Village
Tokyo, Japan, 1996–present

Setagaya Village is Ishiyama's own house. It is being built in Setagaya-ku, a labyrinthine residential district of houses and gardens that is a 15-minute train ride out of Tokyo. In a number of ways, this house-cum-studio-cum-gallery is a real manifesto for Ishiyama's approach, and a real act of experimentation. First of all, Setagaya Village represents a radical alternative to the dominant modes of Japanese housing production. In this project, Ishiyama has set out to prove that there is nothing inevitable about the soaring inflation of building costs, and that it is possible and indeed quite realistic to pursue different and perfectly effective strategies by acting on a number of parameters: DIY building, phasing and organization of the work, type of materials, etc. All the secondary work here is being done by Ishiyama and his collaborators. The only part of this house to have been subcontracted to specialists is the structure, which is a sweeping metal armature whose long beams straddle the small traditional house originally built on this site. Although it will eventually be demolished, this small detached residence is also part of the general organization because it is serving as a home for Ishiyama and his family during the work. This idea of independence and autonomy with regard to the building timetable is an essential part of Ishiyama's strategy. It is an extension of the general concept underlying the project and running through every aspect thereof: flexibility. Instead of the rigidity of the dominant system, the Setagaya Village construction site embodies an open organization, an 'open technology' that is accessible to all. The house counters the threat of seismic activity in the region with the strength but flexibility of its metal structure. Going against rigid and definitive typologies, it makes the most of a free and luminous plan that can be configured to meet the occupant's needs. The same flexibility and lightness also characterize its relation to the environment. For example, in this house Ishiyama experiments with autonomous energy systems (solar batteries, tiny wind generators). The construction even treats the idea of completeness with irony and detachment. A resolutely open structure combining autonomy and flexibility, the house seems to be a kind of ongoing building site accompanying the lives of its inhabitants. ◆

Pierre Chabard

CE DOSSIER EST A LIRE ATTENTIVEMENT

| France |

Jakob + MacFarlane |

Dominique Jakob (1966), Brendan MacFarlane (1961)

Dominique Jakob, a graduate of the Paris-Villemin School of Architecture, and Brendan MacFarlane, graduate of the SCI-Arc (Los Angeles) and Harvard, set up their agency in Paris in 1992. As members of the Périphériques association from 1995 to 1997, they took part, in particular, in the competition '36 Models for a House' (1996) and in the Savigny Café-Musique group project. As the brains behind both the recent conversion of the Georges restaurant on the fifth floor of the Georges Pompidou Centre, in Paris, and the restructuring of the Maxim Gorky Theatre at Le Petit-Quevilly, Dominique Jakob and Brendan MacFarlane readily admit to the steadfast interest they have in the sites where they conceive their projects. Their architecture is a constant attempt at critical reinterpretation and diverted expression. In declining a vocabulary of continuity and folds, it is developed and enveloped as the programme and the setting dictate. Like a kaleidoscope, which distorts and intensifies all at once, it increases the identity of its surrounding context, seeking a renewed relationship with it. ◆

Air House
Athis Mons, France, 2001—present

This project may be seen both as a concrete proposition, adapting to a real and specific set of problems, and as a critical reflection on an archetype of the residential home: the small house designed for a typical family made up of two parents and two children. One of the main strands of Jakob and MacFarlane's thinking for this project has to do with its administrative context. The small plot of the Air House is actually a place of concentration and overlaps of various forms of city legislation. The rules of withdrawal and prospect typical of this residential suburban landscape come into play first, as well as the rules specific to this urban zone. For example, the proximity of Orly Airport puts the plot under the aegis of norm CU 91 02798P4, which very precisely draws up the 'list of constraints and encumbrances affecting the use of the land: clearance easement *non altius tollendi*, radio-electric easement against obstacles'. On the other hand, the proximity of the river puts it under the aegis of prescriptions and provisions peculiar to the floodplains of the Seine Valley. This complex administrative context, relating to the plot, determines a constructible virtual volumetry. From an angle that is both pragmatic and critical, Jakob and MacFarlane decided that the form of the house would use this maximum gauge as an absolute factor. Dealt with in all its abstractness, this volume borrows the archetypal form of the primitive home: rectangular plan, ridge roof. Jakob + MacFarlane's architecture thus comes across as reflection on the surface of this volume. This surface, whose geometry, as we have seen, is the result of a very complicated city negotiation, will become the preferred formula of the house's architectural style. On the borderline between urban restrictions and the domestic programme, it is like a continuous skin, which identically covers all the sides and walls of the volume. This generalized façade is intended as an active interface, a place of exchange between social and family-related projections and representations. Like a mirror, by day, it refers their own identity back to the context and the city. The vertical surfaces replicate the image of the surroundings, drawing the suburban identity into a mirror-like vortex. The horizontal surfaces are dematerialized in the reflection of the sky, enlivened by the ceaseless passage of aircraft. By night, the house is reversed and becomes a huge active screen, which both hides and publicizes the family's identity and privacy. ◆

Pierre Chabard

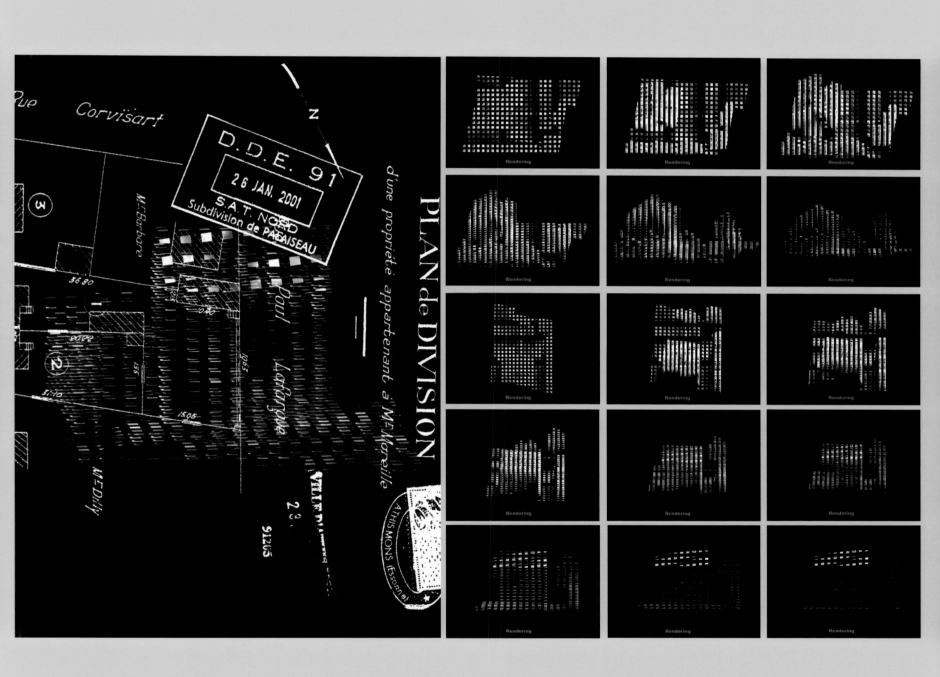

| USA |

Jones, Partners: Architecture

WES JONES (1958)

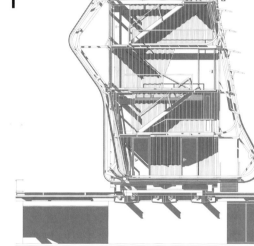

Since the mid-1980s, Wes Jones has been exploring the paths of 'machine-architecture', in search of a connection between the body and its technological world, and a vernacular expression of mechanistic forms and industrial objects. The work produced by Jones Partners: Architecture (founded in 1993 in San Francisco, and then in Los Angeles), intends – through this assertion of the technical/logical quintessence of architecture – to sidestep the tyrannies of form and 'signature'. By deliberately limiting the size of the agency and the scope of its activities, Jones, Partners: Architecture become fully involved in a project only if it calls for experimentation and the formulation of prototypes that can be made potentially widespread. As a firmly convinced heir to the modernist tradition, Wes Jones rejects the idea that 'modernity' is just an historical style. On the contrary, without losing a subtle sense of humour, he asserts that, as a stance, it can still be active and operative today. ◆

Pro/Con Package Housing System
Project, 2000
J, P: A (Wes Jones, George Tolosa, Aryan Omar, Doug Jackson, Jim Rhee)
and UCLA (Dora Epstein, Robert Ley, Kevin Gotsch, Matt Gillis, Franco Rosetti, Allesandra Gotsch)

From the Pro/Con Package Home website, a consumer chooses among different corporate-specific activity-oriented pro(gramme) con(tainers), or 'packages' – loosely organized along the lines of traditional architectural programme divisions, but also departing from the coarseness of that grid as new markets are sensed and new niches are filled. He can relax and listen to music in the Bose sound system package, cook a meal in a package by SubZero or enjoy countless activities in packages from Soloflex, Quake, the NBA, even Playboy. Once ordered through the website and detailed by the individual companies, Pro/Con Packages are consolidated and distributed using the intermodel transport infrastructure of shipping containers. The website serves as a clearinghouse for all phases of the home procurement and delivery process, from the initial uncommitted shopping experience to the ultimate financing and infill construction subcontracts. Because each package can be either leased (leaving open the possibility to upgrade) or owned (allowing for second-hand economies), traditional concepts of home ownership are rejected in favour of technological adaptability and affordable affluent mobility. Because each container wears a corporate logo, publicity of the interior becomes a matter of community discourse. And, because each container behaves as a fully realized appliance–environment, the space in between, left idle and without programme, deploys a range of exteriorities and interiorities, and exchanges the performance of affect for the signification of effects.

As apotheosis, as customization without affect, the Pro/Con Package Home produces fulfilment as it produces authorial dissatisfaction. Although assembled from standard 6-metre shipping containers, the perfect generic of multinational conglomeration, each Pro/Con Package Home is tailored according to individual consumer choices and budgets. Although linked to a global infrastructure of assembly, shop fabrication and transportability, each Pro/Con Package Home is continuously setting out its relation to the street and the neighbourhood anew as new containers are added, upgraded or discarded. And, although bricked together orthogonally, each Pro/Con Package Home is composed of both programmatic micro-environments and non-programmatic but active spaces, postulating an architecture of multiple spatial and cultural fluidities. A Pro/Con Package Home is open-ended precisely because of its specificity. Production-line concatenation, prodigal consolidation, ready satisfaction – the Pro/Con Package Home is radically present. ◆

Dora Epstein & Wes Jones

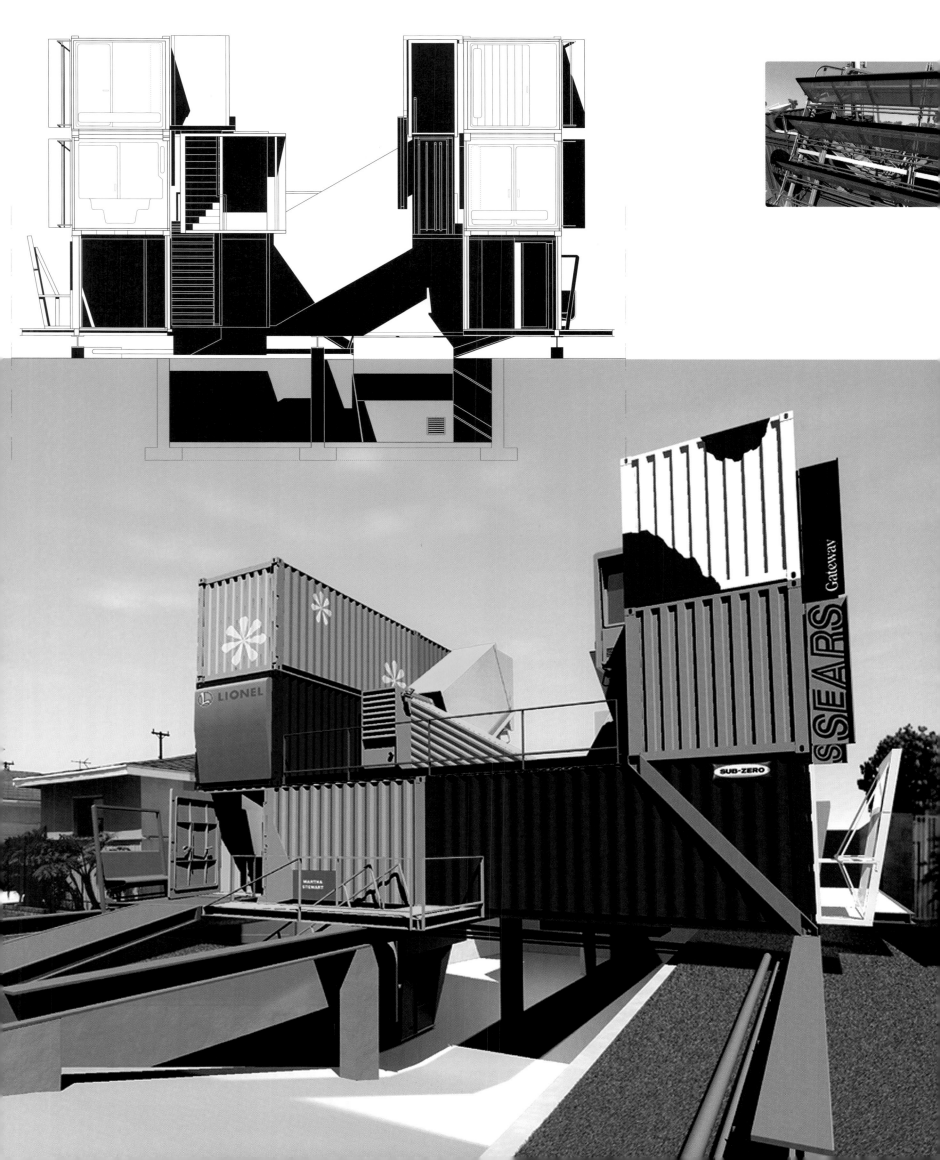

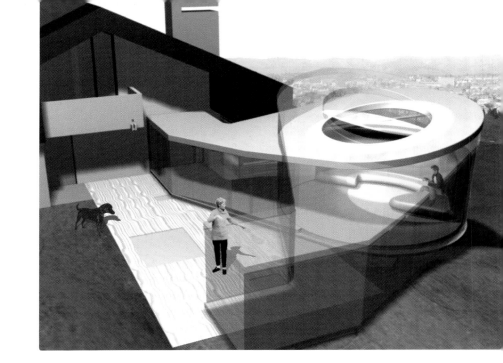

| GERMANY |

Kalhöfer-Korschildgen|

GERHARD KALHÖFER (1962), STEFAN KORSHILDGEN (1962)

'Cheese and Dessert' – Optional architecture

The Kalhöfer-Korschildgen office deals in 'transformable' architecture. It produces mobile architecture for changing states. Its constructions are modular spaces that can be rearranged by their users over and over again. This interactive process makes the user's relation to the architecture immediate and natural, giving the fact of use a sensual quality: it is not only functional but also provides a certain amount of pleasure. As Vilém Flusser puts it, 'The sedentary own, nomads live'. The projects by this office are a first step towards metamorphosing structures, structures that are open to interpretation. A more complex spatial concept results from the simultaneous availability of several spaces that can grow up in one and the same spot. The frontiers of classic space, with its fixed forms and uses, are erased. What counts is not form but process. ◆

Tourne...sol
Mobile extension, Arnsberg, 2001–present
Collaboration: Sabine Beuscher, Guido Meier, Claudia Weikert
Images: Ulli Wallner, Franck Skupin
Research: Thomas Jürges, Director: Kosch Jürges

Conflicting requirements

Conflicting requirements and uncertainty about the exact position of the extension constituted the starting point of this study. Rather than rule out some solutions right from the start, the architects listened to the complex desiderata of the client, analysed them and synthesized them in the form of a new building. The objective was not a building that went in a single direction, balancing these legitimate demands, but a construction that transcended and reconciled them in the play of metamorphoses.

Change of typology

The result is a nomadic, polymorphous construction with different orientations and organizations of space. The user is now sole master of his structure. By rotating the building, he transforms the winter garden into a house, turning an additional construction into an autonomous building and thus dissolving the fixed link between space and function. The relation between the existing building and the new construction is played out on several different levels: as a winter garden directly linked with the living room, the new construction brings about a new perspective, a new orientation that moves away from the usual principle of the orthogonal living room. As a house, it constitutes the other border of the terrace, along with the patio.

A room full of light

To the north, the house has an unrestricted view over the valley but no opening towards the mountain – that is to say, towards nature and sun. The mission was not to dilate a space but to give that space extra quality: to make up the deficit of the internal rooms by extending them towards the south and the sun. The project creates a space that turns around the sun, that makes the user aware of the phenomena of solar light (hence the punning name of 'tournesol': sunflower/turnfloor). The light shaft in the roof concentrates the light and makes it more apparent. Like a sundial, it gives information about the position of the sun.

Interior space

The interior of the new construction is conceived as a rotating floor that the user can move in accordance with the sunlight. The sofa/wall constitutes the mobile back of this rotating floor. It determines whether it opens on to nature or the city, and the degree of luminosity in the glazed room. To transform this room, one simply moves the sofa/wall.

Construction

It is a metal construction. The two distinct rotating movements are obtained economically using the same kinds of discs that are fitted to the front axle of vehicles. In order to dematerialize the frontier between exterior and interior, and to ensure the fluidity of the gaze, the glass façade is load-bearing. ◆

Kalhöfer-Korschildgen

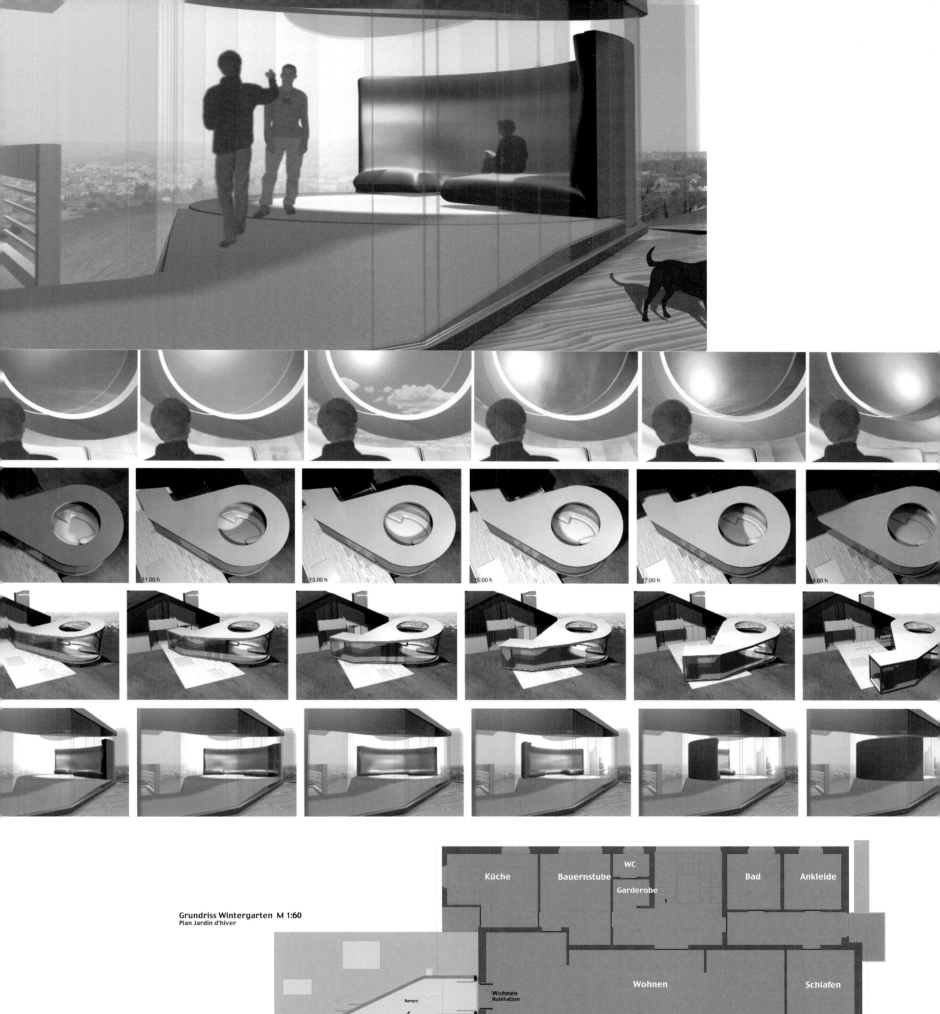

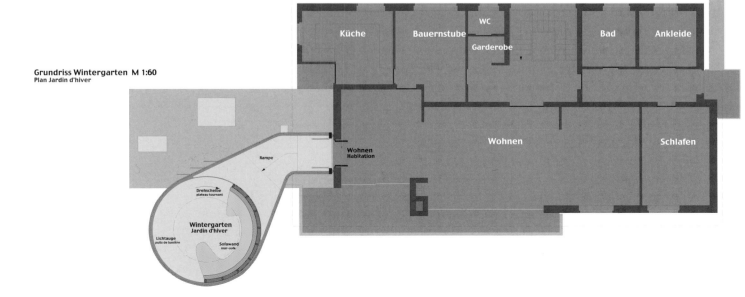

Grundriss Wintergarten M 1:60
Plan Jardin d'hiver

Küche

Bauernstube

WC

Garderobe

Bad

Ankleide

Wohnen

Wohnen
Habitation

Schlafen

Rampe

Drehscheibe
plateau tournant

Wintergarten
Jardin d'hiver

Lichtauge
puits de lumière

Sofawand
mur-sofa

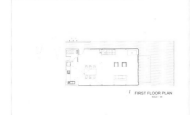

SECOND FLOOR PLAN

FIRST FLOOR PLAN

ROOF PLAN

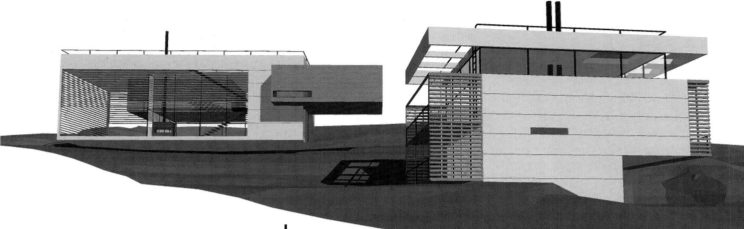

| Chile |

Mathias Klotz

Mathias Klotz (1965)

As the heir to a lengthy tradition involving the import and vernacular adaptation of modern architectural paradigms, the work of Mathias Klotz weaves its way between references to the 20th century avant-gardes and an assertion of the Chilean cultural and geographical context. For him, architecture has a duty to be clear. By favouring simple figures and rough, unfinished materials, Klotz strives to find answers, which, in the most readable way possible, balance site restrictions and programme data. Mathias Klotz bases the specific nature of each of his projects within this equilibrium. Having graduated in 1991 from the Catholic University of Chile in Santiago, he teaches in the Architectural Workshop at Federico Santa María University in Valparaíso, and at the Santiago Central University. His impressive body of work, including private houses, apartments and small facilities, exhibits an architecture involving piles, cantilevers and tensions between geometric abstraction and brutalist materials, between bareness of volumes and nature's luxuriance. ◆

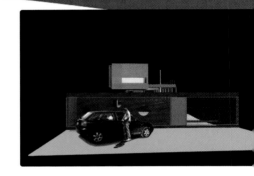

Casa Ponce, Buenos Aires, Argentina, 2000—01

Casa 75, Casa Ponce, Casas Vejle
Cantagua (Chile), Buenos Aires (Argentina), Vejle (Denmark), 2000—01

If one of these houses on its own is enough to evoke his perception of the site and its uses, then when two or more dialogue or react to one another their rich specificity is expressed and a sensuous image of dwelling begins to take shape.

The first two houses to echo one another are at Vejle, Denmark, where they are built on the same piece of land. Visually, first of all, there are the two main volumes in concrete, on to which are grafted smaller, lighter and more closed structures in wood. Subjected to the same climate, their main spaces look out towards the sea, to the northeast, and have large openings to the southern sun. However, there is a subtle contrast in the ways they are implanted on their sites: whereas the taller building stretches to two levels, parallel with the horizon, the one on the lower-lying land is more compact and rises up in a turret, laid out in half-levels. Thus the dialogue begins with volumetrics. With the footbridge access to one and the top floor with 360-degree windows on the other, and with numerous terraces and tall chimneys, the image of the ocean liner soon comes to mind.

Standing on the opposite side of the Andes, the Ponce House in Buenos Aires and the house in Cantagua also enter into a dialogue. Rising up from the ground, floating on thin piles or transparent walls, disappearing from the landscape and letting the garden seep under or in – all this signifies both presence and absence. The land of the former, very elongated and surround-ed with plants, goes down to the Rio de la Plata, like a clearing in a forest. Since it would have been inadmissible for the house to block this long vista, the bedrooms of this rather hermetic, elongated box are built over copiously glazed rooms flanked by an external gangway. And as the volume here runs parallel to the slope, all the rooms, which are in a linked row, have sweeping views over the ocean. At the garden level, there is just the access ramp: it is visible by day and lit up by night. The basement houses the ancillary services and the 'machine room'.

Each of these 'marine' houses reflects a very particular kind of family use, topographic context and programmatic organization. In the north, they huddle into their land and observe the sea from a distance; overlooking the Pacific, the view is wide open; and, at the Rio de la Plata, one seeks the fluidity of air and outlook. However, talking to one another across the oceans and rooting themselves on their sites the way a ship drops anchor may be the way these houses have of evoking contemporary mobility, flexibility and 'globality'. ◆

Bénédicte Grosjean

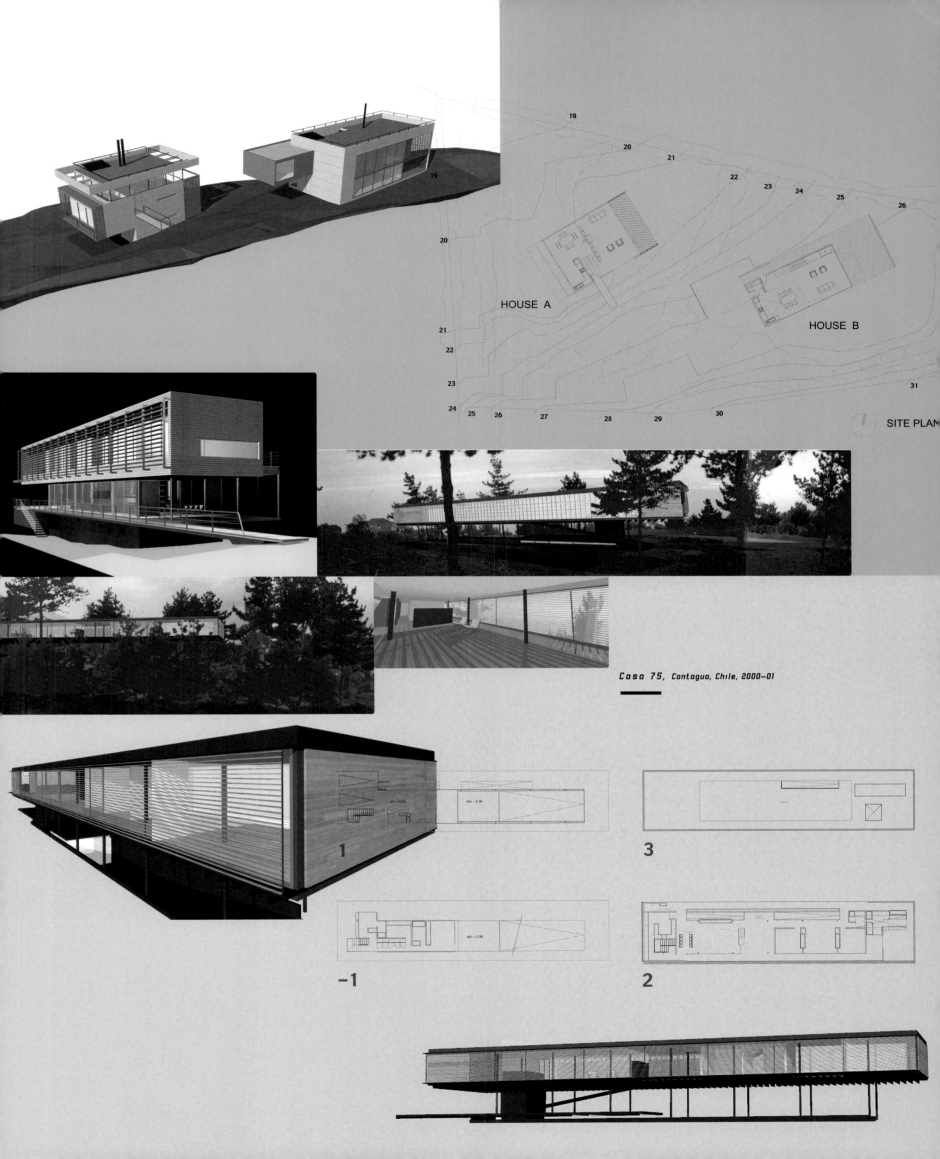

HOUSE A

HOUSE B

SITE PLAN

Casa 75, Cantagua, Chile, 2000–01

1

3

−1

2

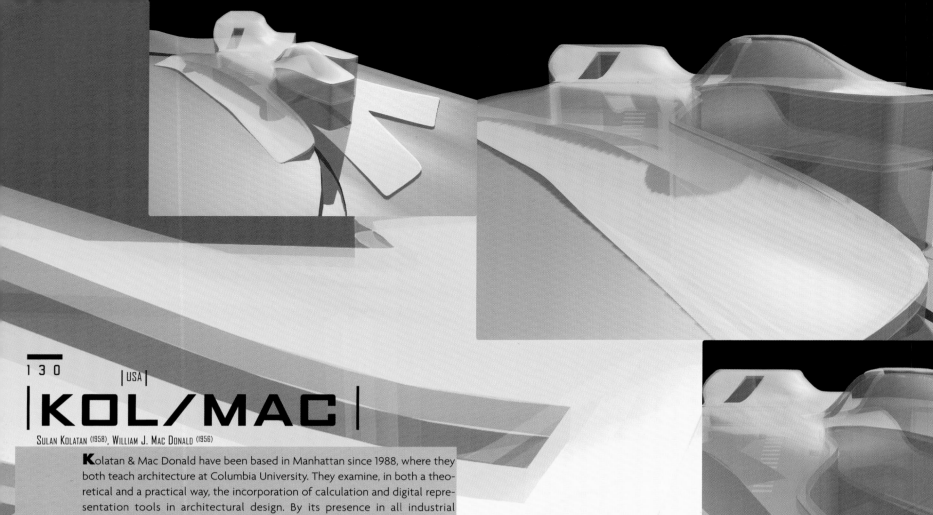

| USA |

KOL/MAC |

Sulan Kolatan (1958), William J. Mac Donald (1956)

Kolatan & Mac Donald have been based in Manhattan since 1988, where they both teach architecture at Columbia University. They examine, in both a theoretical and a practical way, the incorporation of calculation and digital representation tools in architectural design. By its presence in all industrial processes, the computer tool represents for Kolatan and Mac Donald a chance to bring about some change in architectural methods of design and building towards an adaptable and 'non-standard' architecture. Their work is focused around a flexible and inventive method – 'co-citation mapping'. The most diverse factors and features of a project, transformed into computerized data, are subjected to a systematic combinatorial analysis, making it possible to conjure up conceptual affinities between the different categories. This systematic mapping of possibles opens the way to endless hybridizations of forms and uses. ◆

Ost/Kuttner Estouteville 2.0 House |
Charlottesville, USA, project, 2001

Meta-HOM
The meta-HOM project is a house conceived from the elements and particularities of a domestic programme. It investigates the construction of 'House & Home' as a distributed dynamic system. Attributes, relationships and hierarchies of this dynamic system are provided by a number of co-citation maps charted for the project and evolved throughout the design process.

Co-citation maps
Co-citation maps consist of thematically or categorically organized clusters with cross-thematic or cross-categorical connections where co-citation occurs. For example, one of the maps has the following co-citation clusters: Thomas Jefferson, O/K Apartment, ecology, topology, black and white, looming and loft. On this map, 'hollow column' is a co-citation between ecology (ecology–water–recycling–drainage–pipe) and topology (topology–cylinder). Another map, shown below, is constructed to find existing co-citations in the given programme. On this map, 'bedroom' is co-cited in 7 clusters (parent, child 1, 2 and 3, visitor and long- and short-term guest).

Micro-HOMzones
The design strategy uses information from both these maps to construct hollow columnar topologies charged as autonomous programme clusters. Development of upper and lower planes in the not yet further qualified cylindrical topologies produces a number of structurally self-sufficient micro-HOMzones. Each micro-HOMzone is then further qualified in three ways. First, with high-performance specificity as in a codified domestic programme. Second, with low-performance specificity codified as 'living'. And third, with high-performance specificity codified as 'storage'. Micro-HOMzones thus have their own programmatic and morphological identity. Multiple micro-HOMzones aggregate to form hierarchical clusters. And multiple cluster-aggregates merge into structurally organic meta-clusters with mixed identities. The meta-HOM operates as a chimerical über-brand of multiple individually branded micro-HOMzones. The 'living' programme here is not a separate entity but a combined surplus of particularized zones. ◆

Sulan Kolatan &
William Mac Donald

| Australia |

Tom Kovac |

Tom Kovac (1958)

Kovac's projects, which are neither sculpted nor modelled, define a 'third term', to borrow Leon Van Schaik's phrase, where the architect works not only the construction material, but also the empty space, the cavity, trying to regard the formalization of space as the real meaning of architecture. For this architect, hailing from Slovenia and based in Melbourne, Australia, since 1970, the surface thus becomes the preferred instrument of this spatiality, which has an outstanding plastic quality. It also becomes the at times highly technological matter of an intentionally deep architecture where we find a combination of concern for light and a renewed concern for fluidity, in a spirit of deliberate levity. Tom Kovac founded the Kovac Architecture Agency in 1990 in Melbourne, where he also founded the Curve Architecture Gallery in 1994. He is a graduate of the Royal Melbourne Institute of Technology, and obtained his MA in Architecture in 1997. ◆

C 01
Melbourne, Australia, project, 2001

The question of housing is one of ubiquity. It is something we are already part of, a process, a spatial re-formulation and a response to lifestyle systems that are prevalent in this new 'bandwidth'. It may be the digestion of the new and moving of the old, a dialogue with mass function, a development of methods that befits this entirely new set of circumstances.

The new form is located at the urban periphery and is a catalyst for urbanization, that is, an interminable urbanized area with no coherent form; a phenomenon that manifests itself in other locations – Los Angeles, Tokyo, Hong Kong, Shanghai. There is no singular or clear outline for its articulation. It is a kind of extrovert/introvert habitat for the new economy, which is shaped between zones of constant overlaps. It is a blending of media flows, a filtration of merging data bits that shape our progressive geometric world, a Deleuzian/Guattarian metamorphosis of shifting scapes. A transparent product devoid of artistic pretension or distinguishing marks, it is a formal neutrality. It automatically prioritizes direct arousal of experience, the sensory experience of space, material and light. It exists outside assumed contextuality derived of dogmas and moralisms of the urbane but elicits a laconic response from visual, spatial and tactile sensation; it is a new 'phenomenological' use of digital tools to create precise imprecisions. An architectural resistance that is most evident in the processes of globalization.

The form is deployed outside of traditional context and gives no hint of accommodation or categorization. . . . a fusion of Maya, Rhino 3d max and CATIA into a heterogeneic human desire where the global becomes the new recognizable freezing. It is the reconfiguration of a new intimacy and a source of emotional meaning through decomposition of the old and re-emergence of the new by distortion of the digital 'tools'. It is the translation of the culture through the software into three-dimensional form that reinvents techniques and procedures that previously shaped our manufactured world. This new materiality is formed by processes that paralyse the inert state of architecture and comfortable predictability. The explosion of the exponentials and technological convergences have the capacity to absorb the technological transformations that are shaping our time. It can be categorized as a phase transition or a shift between two stable states when perhaps we cannot imagine the future. It accommodates the switch in our understanding of time and space, which in turn redirects our understanding of architecture and its role within the new global condition. ◆

Tom Kovac

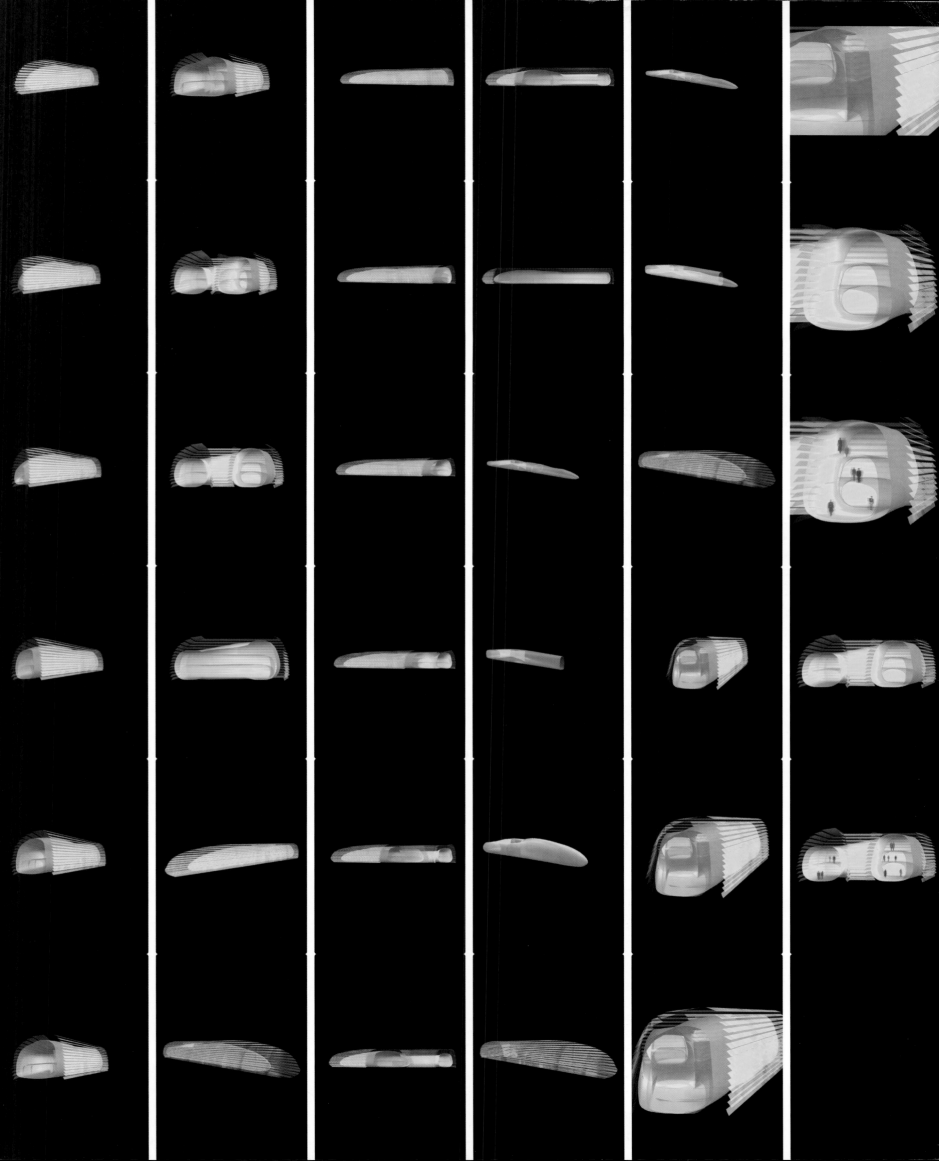

| JAPAN |

Kengo Kuma & Associates

KENGO KUMA (1954)

After studying at Tokyo University and spending a year at Columbia University, where he was a resident researcher in 1985–86, Kengo Kuma founded his agency in 1990. 'Doing away with architecture', making it vanish, is the goal he then intended to pursue. The m2 building (1989–91) made a postmodernist attempt to be blurred as an object in the miscellany of the Japanese city. Another radical approach consists in no longer being seen: the Kikatami Canal Museum (1999) is buried and becomes part of the continuity of a road that is hewn out, interpreting the ambiguity of the canal, where the artificial goes inseparably hand in hand with the natural. His most recent subtle architectural propositions tend to disappear as they appear: whether a material, to create the Bamboo House (2000), simply 'positioned' and (almost) thus by chance, like the stones and pebbles in a Japanese garden; or an application, the application of stones in the porous wall of the Stone Museum (1998), which creates 'particles' from the light; or alternatively the landscape, in the Hiroshige Museum (2000), whose blades of wood filter the fluctuating effect of nature. ◆

Shinonome Project, The Multi-faceted, Three-dimensional City
Tokyo, Japan, 2001–present

Returning to the city, with its chaos, density and overvalued square footage, the architect tells us, ' I wanted to make a street, not a building', in other words, a hollow, not an object. And if Kengo Kuma's new project wants again to disappear into the background by offering something else up for view, it is obviously the sky, with its changing hue and scudding clouds, that the beautiful geometric documents reflect in the long, glassed-in surfaces. And the white passageways also run towards the sky, just as the footbridges stand out etched against it, and it's the sky that enters the building via the inner street that runs through it from all directions.

It is Kengo Kuma's intent to reinterpret the concept of Le Corbusier's Unité d'Habitation, or living unit. While 20th-century public housing was limited just to the residential function, the architect tries to inject a functional and hands-on quality of life, by means of the multi-purpose nature of the construction. But far from being a lush and verdant utopian context, it is a matter for Kengo Kuma of taking hold of the 'random chaos of the street' and erecting it emphatically as a total three-dimensional structure. And rather than being separated from the ground as a compact block, the small, slender buildings are on a base, with broad steps firmly anchored in the street network running down it, and are so arranged as to open up many different angles and perspec-

tives, themselves pierced by 'notional' large-scale windows, apertures between the passageways, again turned towards the sky.

The multi-purpose aspect is conveyed in the programme, which combines homes, offices (SOHO: Small Offices, Homes Offices), commercial and public amenities and facilities, but also through a flexibility in the use of the housing units. The whole construct proposes, scattered around atria, basic 60-square-metre/650-square-foot units and adjoining 25-square-metre/270-square-foot units. These latter may be used as an extra bedroom, studio, offices, shops, and the range of combined uses, sizes and sites forms the three-dimensional structure of 'the street'. Each individual family can occupy several units, distributed on several floors or on either side of the atrium, creating, along with these housing units in 'meshed networks', an alternative to the conventional type of 'inhabiting' typical of the 20th century, for extended family modes.

It is probably the footbridges, passageways and stairs, crossing in the sky of the atrium, that best express the great variety of itineraries, the diversity of the passers-by and the multi-purpose nature of the spaces, which will be the urban sense of this building, as it offers its own presence in silence. ◆

Bénédicte Grosjean

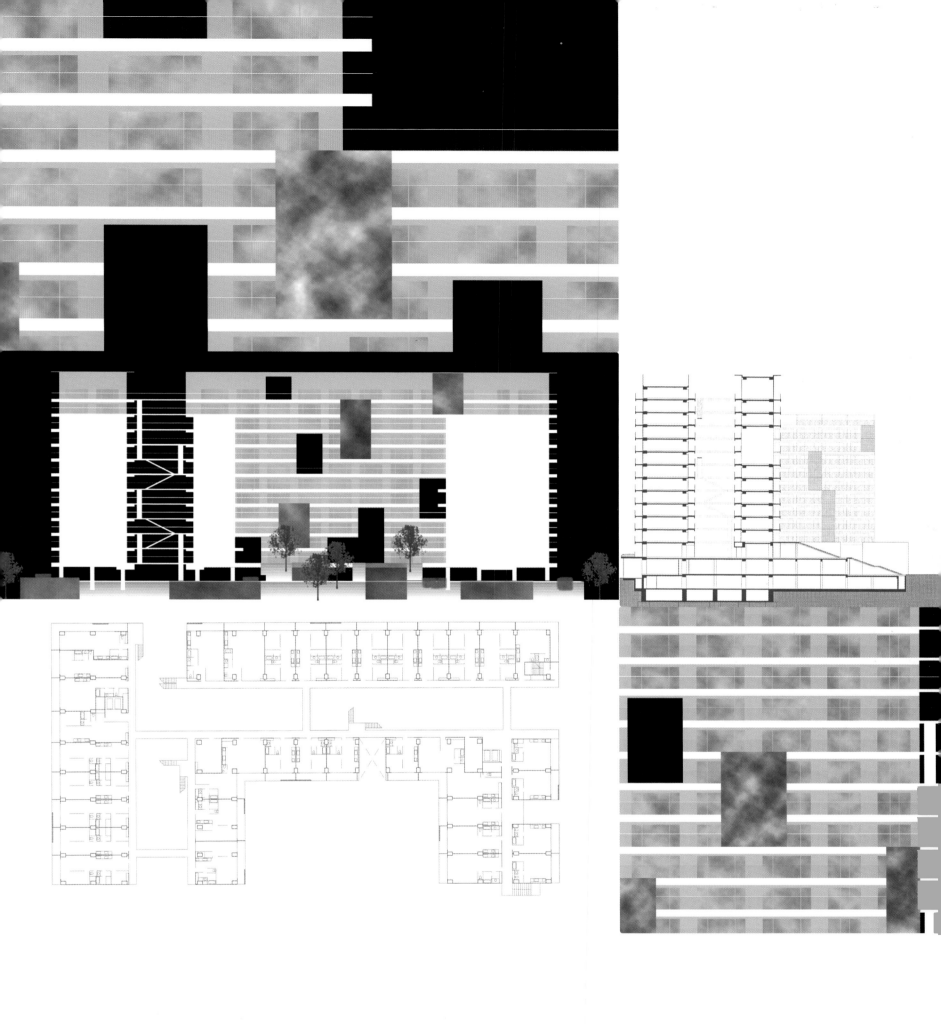

| FRANCE |

Lacaton & Vassal |

ANNE LACATON (1955), JEAN-PHILIPPE VASSAL (1954)

The work of Anne Lacaton and Jean-Philippe Vassal, which is in essence the outcome of thought and research on the economics of architecture, focuses on projects that cost as little as possible, so as to be able to renew the dialogue with the developer. Mindful of the flexibility of uses and of their development by a precise installation in the surrounding environment, they make use of a wide range of techniques, often chosen from outside the usual construction arena. Their projects and works, which have been recently shown at the Guggenheim Museum SoHo in New York, in the Taisei Gallery in Tokyo, and at the Architectur Zentrum in Vienna, thus cover a huge programmatic field – collective housing and individual, detached homes, cafes, offices and hotels, the Archaeology Museum in Saintes (France), and an extension to Grenoble University. They also impart their desire for new spatial and constructive designs through lectures, from Bangkok to Rome, London and Oslo, and they teach at the Bordeaux Architecture School. ◆

House at Coutras
Coutras, France, 2000

'We are lacking in extraordinary architecture because we are a bit too comfortable. New ways of living and life. The House: invent something else; get rid of foundations, mobility, nomadism. The box, the parallelepiped, what else? The Farnsworth House, and then?' So what these architects are after – lightness of materials, very delicate installation, a certain obviousness of forms – is expressed in a very pure way in their latest work at Coutras. Situated in the countryside, 50 kilometres/30 miles west of Bordeaux, the plot of land is very elongated, running parallel to the local road, and opens out on to a very broad perception of the landscape: scattered homes, cultivated farmland, copses and shrubs, market-gardening greenhouses, low density and low hills, dominated by the sky. The building will be put up, or rather assembled, at the end of the plot, well removed from the road and neighbouring buildings, on the edge of a no-construction zone. The architects actually envisaged using an industrial material that was also traditional in the farming landscape, horticultural greenhouses, mass-prefabricated, with metal structures and transparent rigid cladding, which are fitted with the automatic equipment needed to control the climate.

The house, set squarely, is made up of two identical adjoining greenhouses. While the one on the west houses the living rooms, the other, to the east, is a huge winter garden. We thus find the idea of the extendable house that changes with the seasons, in relation to the use and openness of the successive areas – the evolving nature of the Latapie House (ArchiLab 99).

But the choice of these basic elements cannot be made without a detailed technical study that looks at the adjustment and control of the climatic data. It is based here on the double-skin principle: the living rooms are contained within a plywood parallelepiped, pierced by aluminium frames, itself contained within the volume of the greenhouse, and between which there is a blade of air. In addition, the ridge of the roof opens automatically along its entire length, to get rid of the accumulated heat, and the whole rim of the façades is made up of sliding panels, which means that half their surface can be open.

The innovative use of an industrialized and technically well-developed material allows these large live-in volumes to mesh with efficient economic conditions (around 1700 French francs per square metre), and a refined, readable and rigorous architectural proposition of carefully studied simplicity. ◆

Bénédicte Grosjean

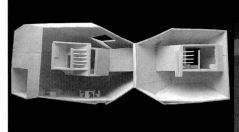

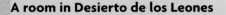
Suro House

| Mexico |

LCM (Laboratorio de la Ciudad de México) |

Fernando Romero (1971)

After working with Enric Miralles (1996), Jean Nouvel (1997) and, above all, Rem Koolhaas (1997–2000), the young Mexican architect Fernando Romero founded the LCM (Laboratorio de la Ciudad de México) in 1998, a multidisciplinary organization, akin to the OMA (Office for Metropolitan Architecture), bringing together architects, artists, designers, city planners and researchers.

As a forum for a renewal of Mexican architecture, the LCM is structured around a three-part programme: studies and research projects; design (architectural and urban); and cultural and publishing projects (PCCM., Programme for the Dissemination of Contemporary Culture in Mexico City). The LCM is involved in observing and analysing urban phenomena, and in May 2000 published ZMVM, a study about changes in the metropolitan area of Mexico City. The architecture produced by Romero and the LCM, which is fuelled by all the other activities of the group, is markedly collective and experimental: each project is the topic of a specific strategy and a different process, which leads to a one-off result that cannot be reproduced, thus dispensing with the concept of an author.

A room in Desierto de los Leones

The experiment here resides both in the conceptual process and in constructive research. The client's request was for an annex to his house, to accommodate a children's room and a playroom. The existing building, from the 1950s, is modernist – a structure with an orthogonal post-and-beam 'open plan'. Romero sees his approach as the confrontation of two times, two periods, and perceives his annex as one of the potential developments of the initial building. He imagines a skin, a continuous material, which coils around itself to define a honeycombed inner space, abuts one side of the existing façade and ends smoothly with a slide-like ramp leading to the garden. The structure of this form is in steel, covered with expanded polyurethane and lined with fibreglass outside.

Suro House

The Suro House project, which pays just as much attention to the morphogenesis of the volume, but is somewhat crystalline, is designed for a young collector of contemporary art, who wants a programme that will clearly separate private and public areas. This time, the architectural research is not focused on a fluid continuity of the spaces, but on their paroxysmal juxtaposition: the private areas literally cross the main public area, 'floating' in the large room where the artworks are displayed, letting just what they need in terms of light filter through. The architecture thus explores a powerful spatial paradox, between a vast, wrapped, internalized place, which nevertheless contains open areas within it, in direct contact with the outside.

House for the artist Gabriel Orozco

Here, once again, the architect unhesitatingly confronts his models and manipulates – even slightly 'tortures' – them. The point of departure of the design process is the Mies van der Rohe Farnsworth House (1943), 'symbol of modernity'. For this family home requested by the artist, in a small valley outside Mexico City, Romero develops a system already tried and tested by the OMA agency to unify different geometries and create an evolving envelope, while doing his utmost to stay away from conventional household parameters. And the evidence that this architect does the exact opposite is plentiful: an ovoidal shape, folded in upon itself, smooth and centripetal, with a circular plan that opens out in every direction, and a whirling, centrifugal interior layout.

What emerges from these complex and complete objects, which come to rest here, are 'fastened' elsewhere and at times, independent and futuristic, might almost take off, is a fervent desire to challenge and determinedly confront both ruts and paradoxes. ◆

Bénédicte Grosjean

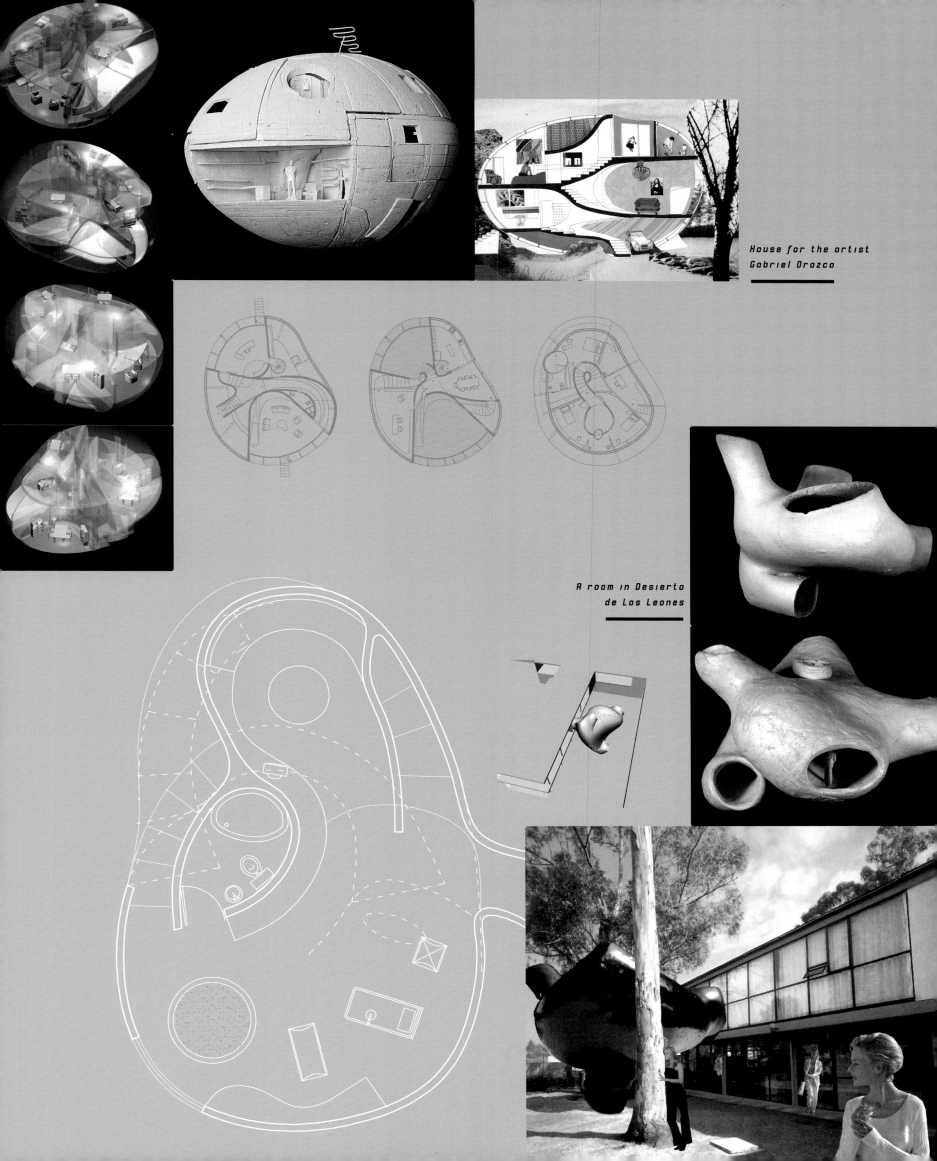

House for the artist
Gabriel Orozco

A room in Desierto
de Los Leones

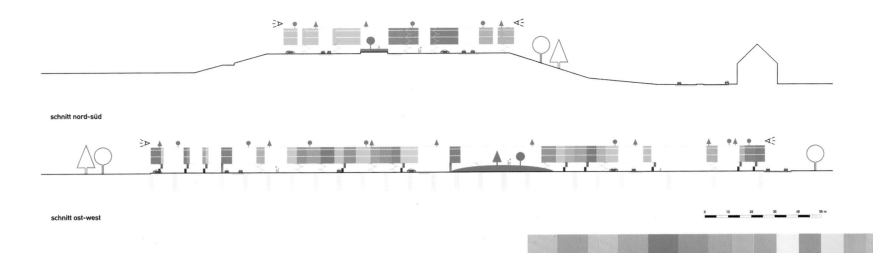

schnitt nord-süd

schnitt ost-west

|USA|

Leeser Architecture

Thomas Leeser (1952), Jörg Leeser (1967)

After training in Europe and the United States, and, in particular, ten years spent working with Peter Eisenman, Thomas Leeser in New York and Jörg Leeser in Cologne are working together on precise projects. The former established Leeser Architecture in New York in 1969, with a huge team of architects – an experienced agency dealing with both public works projects and residential and urban schemes.

They encourage close contact between clients and designers, and strive to express the complex cultural and socio-economic trends that engulf them, including a form of eclecticism and the commonplace, which they actually explore as such, through broad teaching activities (Columbia University, Illinois Institute of Technology in Chicago, Princeton University, to name but a few) and for example 'Quaint and Queasy, Architectures of the Banal', which they developed with students at the Rensselaer Polytechnic Institute in New York. Not without irony, they do their utmost to catalogue the 'successful' items of a domestic landscape – golf course, shopping mall, two-garage homes – and tackle the possibility of imagining a new urban typology. ◆

Urban Garden Villa for 200 families
Bochum, Germany, competition, 1998

In this 'garden city' project for 200 families, the urban strategy, applied to new residential forms, has been constructed on the industrial model of the old Krupp steelworks, which used to occupy the site – a three-floor block structure, where the floors are staggered or locally linked with each other, densely takes over the site and demarcates its edges. The whole can be read like one and the same construction, set on piles, with traffic passing beneath it, while its flat roofs are covered with private gardens, a continuous, expansive space for vegetation, which spills down over the façades.

The possibilities of appropriation by the occupants are many and varied, but in each instance they are conceived not to alter an overall perception of the architecture or disturb the community life of a neighbourhood. The areas on the ground, not counting the ground-floor gardens, are shared and multi-purpose, earmarked for various activities and protected from the rain by the building itself, without any imposed hierarchy. The huge blank paved area is available equally for bicycles and skateboards, car traffic and parking.

The gardens on the top floor form a levelled skyline of plants, an open, sweeping view, visible to all, because of a rectangular inset planned for each roof to accommodate garden furniture, where applicable.

The façades also have to be created by the occupants: wall coverings, windows, lighting, everything has to be chosen from a proposed range, then applied by computer-designed pre-fabricated panels, thus lending the whole a typological homogeneity in its variety. This system even makes it possible to adapt the housing to the tastes of new occupants and to new whims and wishes.

Even the interiors are full of possibilities in terms of expansion and shaping, to stay as close as possible to the contemporary needs of family life: divisions, sharing and combinations of areas are easily introduced, without altering the constructed edifice, and the allocation of functions to specific rooms is reduced to a minimum.

An inventive and richly complex arrangement, the project espouses the shared demands of the occupants, as well as their economic and ecological desires and their demand for community life, which the density thus established can deal with: minimizing the space required for traffic and maximizing the percentage of parks and gardens proper, juggling with the great variety of uses of the ground areas, it proposes a flexible overlay of choices, intended to be as close as possible to an ordinary and 'real' life. ◆

Bénédicte Grosjean

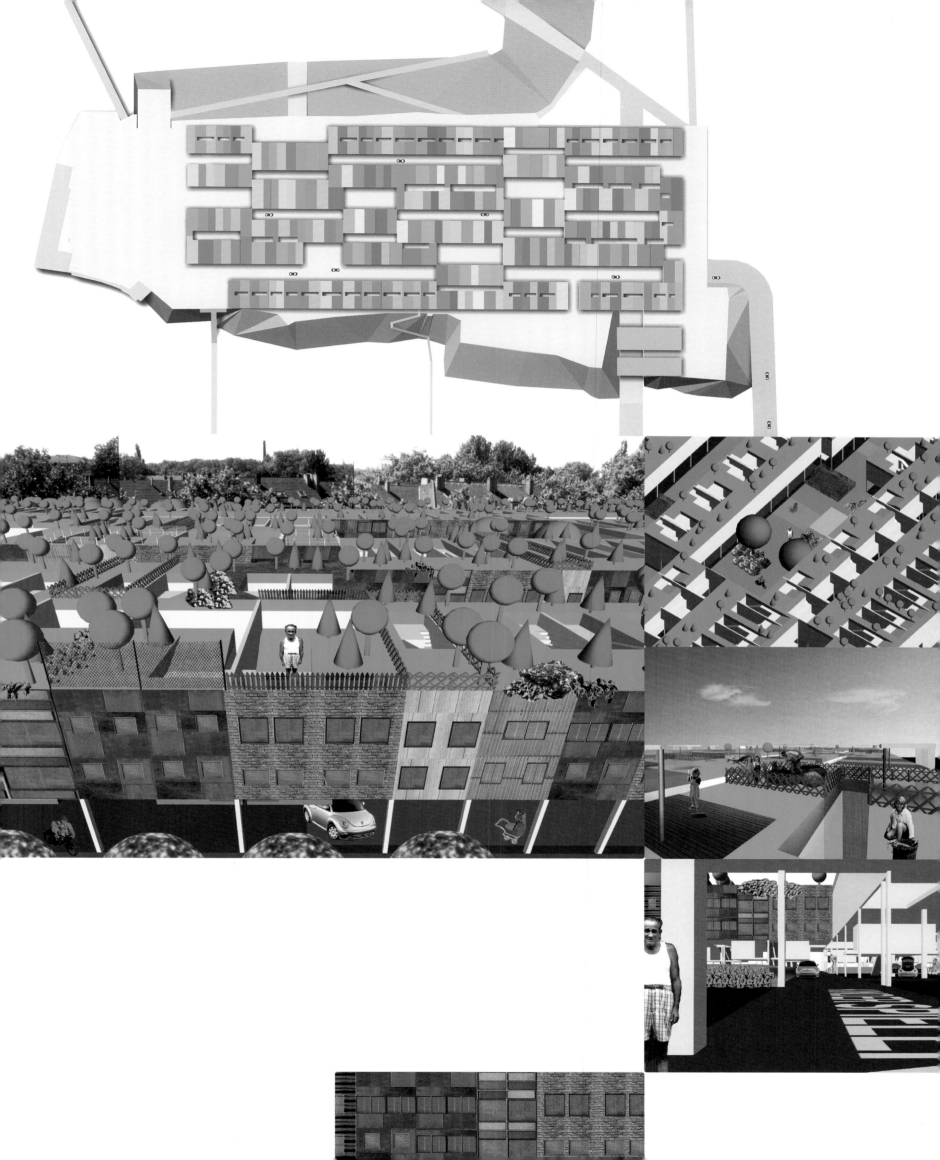

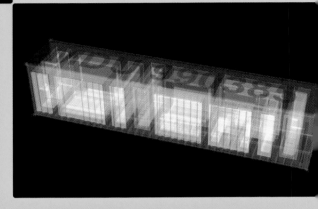

| USA |

|LOT/EK |

Ada Tolla (1964), Giuseppe Lignano (1963)

LOT/EK (a homophonic allusion to 'low tech') is a design and architecture office set up by Ada Tolla and Giuseppe Lignano, two Italians who graduated from the Faculty of Architecture in Naples (1989) and Columbia University (1991). Based in New York, they divide their time between architectural and design projects, art installations, and sets and scenographic works. Drawing their inspiration from the artistic avant-gardes – from Marcel Duchamp to Arte Povera – in their projects, Ada Tolla and Giuseppe Lignano develop a line of thinking about the re-use, transformation and processing of technological and industrial products, regarded as raw material. Toying with an ingenuousness coming from the frontier between learned ('highbrow') culture and popular ('lowbrow') culture, they design environments of found objects and post-industrial rejects, introducing novel pragmatic and aesthetic interactions with the subject, in search of a home and a habitat that are freed from the functionalist grip of technology. ◆

Mobile Dwelling Unit
Project, 2001

In the logical sequence of their critical thinking about the diversion of industrial and technological products, Lot/Ek proposes, with the Mobile Dwelling Unit (MDU) project, an exploration of the primitive form of the transport container, symbol of 20th-century industrial culture. As an extreme extrapolation of the Corbusier-like housing module, which a giant hand slides, like a drawer, into a 'Cité Radieuse' structure, this experimental project consists in turning a standard container into a mobile dwelling unit, for use by travellers and nomadic citizens in the globalized world. By applying their original logic, Ada Tolla and Giuseppe Lignano see, first and foremost, in the container a receptacle, a storage volume, whose capacity specifies the maximum gauge that cannot be exceeded of the furnishings, arrangement and accessories of the Mobile Dwelling Unit. So the container is thus regarded, first, as an absolute solid. In the displacement or travel phase, it is just a dark mass of cluttered objects, lending its ideal volumetry to every manner of manipulation and every kind of standardized international transport process. Making the container livable is tantamount, for Ada Tolla and Giuseppe Lignano, to hewing out from its interior 'sub-volumes' and getting them to slide out, like drawers, thus freeing up the entire inner area for the occupant. The container's metal sides undergo selected cuts, forming so many doors and filters for the extrusion of the 'subsidiary volumes'. Each of these extruded volumes, by turns, inert storage space and active equipment, encloses and then unfurls a part of the programme and functions of the MDU. When it is in a livable position, the container turns inside out and this time offers its smooth surface to the interior. The occupant is thus swathed in this active inner façade, made of fibreglass, opening on to all the programmed 'boxes'. At each halt, the MDU is hooked up to a vertical 'port', available in the world's major metropolitan areas. These MDU towers will be equipped with lifts and all possible systems (information, electricity, water, sewage, waste processing). Each MDU is run by a central computer, which controls the ventilation, heating and lighting. At the port, it is possible to connect the MDU, heavily equipped with monitors, microphones and loudspeakers, to every communication network, thus at any given moment incorporating its nomadic occupant within the globalized space of information. ◆

Pierre Chabard

MDU 990385

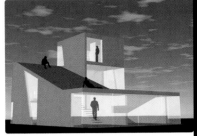

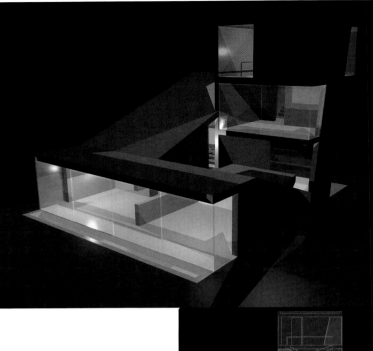

| ITALY |

Mantiastudio |

GIUSEPPE MANTIA (1964)

The Mantiastudio agency, which was set up in Rome in 1999, bases its praxis on two interwoven challenges, programmatic and urbanistic. According to Giuseppe Mantia, who attended the UAV (Venice) and the Berlage Institute (Amsterdam), this twofold research is the condition of a truly experimental form of architecture. His projects are invariably structured around complex programmatic diagrams, which identify the possible interferences, dovetailings and hybridizations of spaces and time frames. Mantia uses this programmatic strategy as a way of thinking about present-day metropolitan territories. An advocate for re-assessing of the notion of urban dispersal, he formulates new methods for analysing and reading the contemporary city ('Interference. The Everyday Landscape', research, 1996). A critical analysis, mixed with the administrative, programmatic, social and cultural context, can, according to Mantia, bring forth new architectural opportunities that reveal lifestyles at work. ◆

Carpethouse
Project, Italy, 2001

Carpethouse is a project that manipulates the regulations for the building of housing in the countryside of northern Italy. For this reason I developed a house concept through a diagram that put the roof in relation with the ground. This new type is based on the continuity of spaces and of the organizational system of movement. The grass ground becomes pitched roof and vice versa. The preservation of the agricultural environment in Italy, theorized in the latest 20 years by the mainstream architectural cultural debate, has imposed banal forms on the individual family house. In the so-called 'E-Zones' houses have to be built according to building techniques derived from history. The final shape, which a preservation committee will check, is thus subject to a strict code. There is no need to question the organizational system, the modification of lifestyles, the shift that the car and a different relation between work, leisure and the contemporary environment are provoking in the life of the population of the countryside. The project tries to question the possibility of this landscape and of the people living in it. In the countryside we have particularly strict regulations for roofs. On the typical slope of 30% imposed by the regulations, we have built a continuous landscape. In this way the green architectural ground is transformed into a continuous artificial ramp, a private open space where different domestic open-air activities can take place. The car enters the basement via a ramp. Here the owner can gain

access to the workrooms underground. A staircase leads to the ground floor where a kitchen connected to the dining room looks out on the garden of lawns and tree plantings. On the other side are the living room with sofa and television. Another staircase leads to a second door, which opens on to the roof garden or the mezzanine studio. Here we enter the night zone with two beds and two bathrooms. The latter has a door to the roof. In this way the structure constitutes a continuity between the upper and lower levels. The sequence of programmes and the possibility of circulation are the key elements of the project, which is evidence of an attempt to determine programme and form through the experimental manipulation and negotiation of the everyday problems that face architects. ◆

Giuseppe Mantia

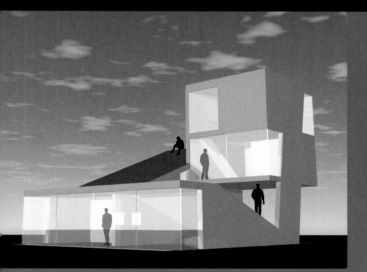

REGULATIONS MANIPULATION

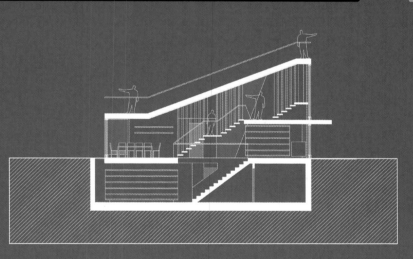

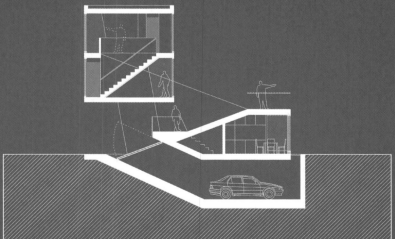

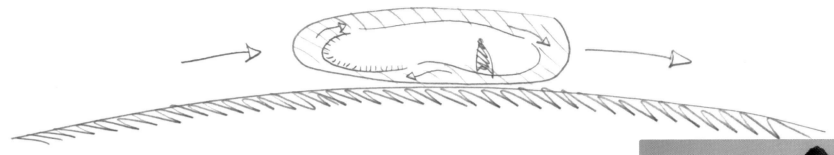

|Italy|

maO/emmeazero studio d'architettura

Tommaso Avellino (1966), Frederico Cavalli (1966), Massimo Ciuffini (1966), Ketty Di Tardo (1968), Alberto Iacovoni (1966), Luca La Torre (1964)

maO/emmeazero was formed in 1996 around the project of densifying a low-rent housing complex in the suburbs of Rome. Based on experimental programmatic thinking, this project proposed sustainable, ecological strategies for land use. From this early project on, the members of maO were involved in a paradoxical approach, in which architecture is always conceived and formulated beyond itself, in the bonds it forges with its externality (the city, territory, geography, virtual space, etc.). This desire to construct, beyond architecture, relational environments recurs in the numerous works undertaken by maO: research, competitions, projects involving architecture, landscape and city planning, multimedia installations, exhibition sets. maO also works very often with the Stalker urban art laboratory, also Rome-based, for which it acts as an operational base. ◆

h-Ouse
Project, 2001

h-Ouse is an experimental project which presents as an architectural interpretation of the phenomena of globalization and the new space—time conditions they bring about: the local and the global, the polluted and the sustainable, the near and the far, the material and the immaterial, etc. h-Ouse is a house made for living in this world of widespread deterritorialization. One of the major themes tackled by maO, in this project, is that of sustainability. Given the global ecological imbalances at work, building a house can no longer claim to be a neutral and innocent act, but calls for an actual strategy of land development and use. As an always unpredictable place of articulation between the local and the global, the house, for maO, must also be a place with very great flexibility of use, so as to be able to keep up with ever faster changes, and meet the varying needs of the occupants. In a period when movements and journeys (professional, political, tourist, etc.) are increasing exponentially, the subject is actually confronted with increasingly complicated situations, where housing, habitat, identity and culture all become staggered and off-centre spheres. Lastly, the members of maO intend, with the h-Ouse project, to reflect upon the changes in our consumer society and the land areas left empty by material goods in favour of new virtual objects of desire: all the multimedia products. To this threefold questioning (ecology, flexibility, virtuality), the h-Ouse contrasts an elusive form permeated by many and

endless metamorphoses, an inner landscape that is forever changing and whose component parts (floors, walls, ceilings, etc.) are regarded a priori as habitable surfaces. All the vertical and horizontal walls and surfaces are resolved in a single continuous surface, where the covering alone differentiates between the specific areas. This surface, a kind of womb-like membrane, twists, adapts and is deformed in relation to the life of the occupants of the house. As an active interface between the household universe, the physical world and the sphere of the virtual, this skin has also been designed like an immense medium, accommodating every kind of information flow. As the sole counterpart to this total flexibility, a 'technical box' contains all the house's amenities: kitchen, bathrooms, toilets, multimedia accessories, etc. The h-Ouse, which is halfway between housing and clothing, aims to be a tool for exploring the world, and a creator of endless landscapes. ◆

Pierre Chabard

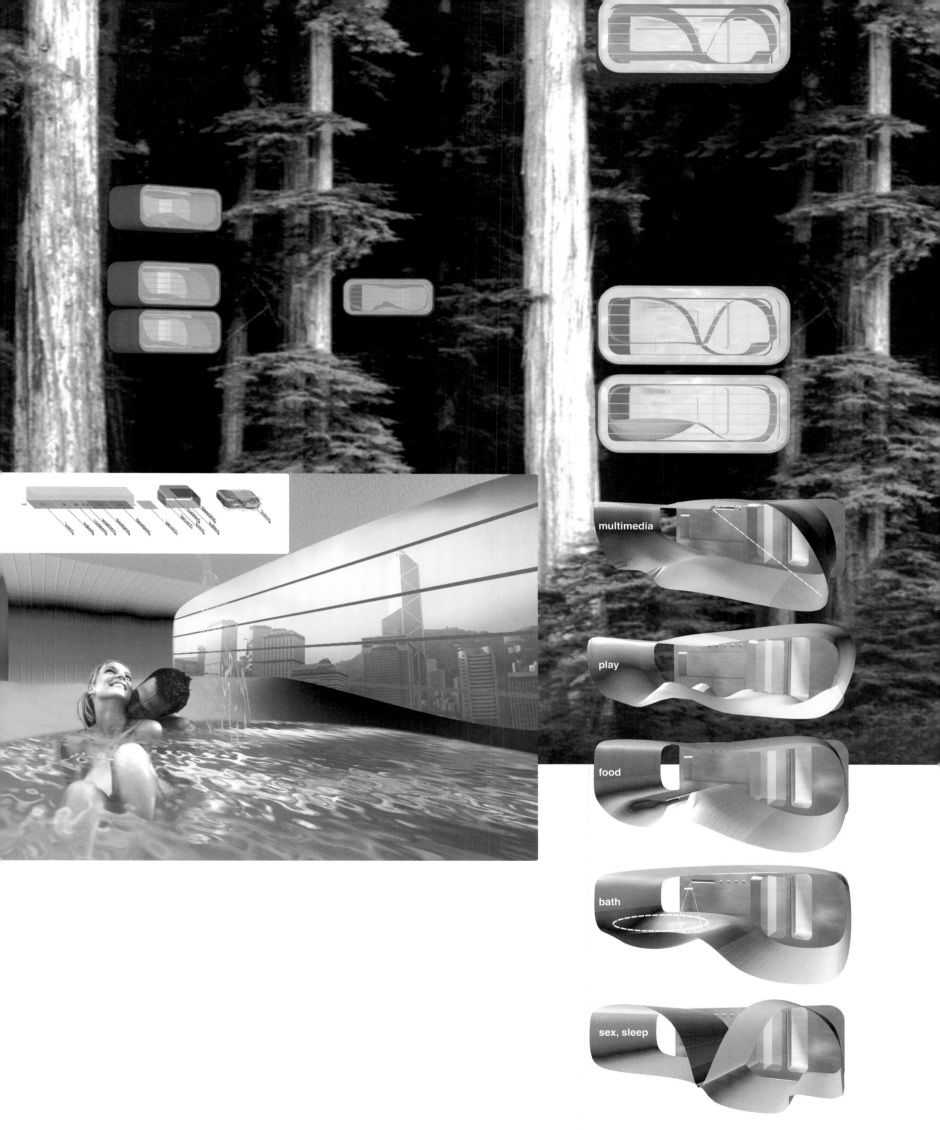

multimedia

play

food

bath

sex, sleep

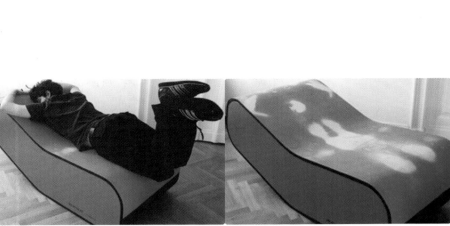

Heat Seats, installation, 2001

| GERMANY |

J. Mayer H. Architekten |

JÜRGEN MAYER HERMANN (1965)

Jürgen Mayer H. practises cross-disciplinary design research related to architecture, communication design and new media. In 1996, after studying at Stuttgart Universtity, Cooper Union in New York and Princeton University, he established his studio in Berlin and is currently teaching at the University of Arts in Berlin and at the Graduate School of Design at Harvard University. In his work, architecture is instrumentalized as an interacting surface, animated by climatic conditions that blur architectural conventions. Applied to an urban scale, the Ascona Lakefront project uses seasonal changes, like global tourism and local climatic conditions, to choreograph programmatic and spatial permutations. Beyond unmediated weather effects on architecture, new smart materials extend the interaction of the macroclimatic into the microclimatic field. Realized examples are thermosensitive surfaces that react to body temperature and computer-controlled leaking roofs, as built in the town hall project for Ostfildern (Germany). ◆

The Weather House
Princeton, USA, project, 1994

The Weather House is a study project that Jürgen Mayer H. worked on at Princeton University. Inspired by an observation made by Walter Benjamin on the obsession with time, which he sees as a symbolic expression of boredom, this project was aimed at 'rethinking comfort in the domestic pocket of air stagnation or inside the weather channel'. This subtitle, added like a programme, announced Jürgen Mayer H.'s desire to design a house that would challenge the 'dogma' of the absolute isolation and protection of the household space from outside conditions. In his view, the 19th century, with its technical positivism and its obsession with control, triggered this climatic break between the interior and exterior of the home. Household architecture could be conceived, only in these conditions, on the basis of a sequence of impenetrable dualities: inside and outside, the unforeseeable and the controlled, the natural and the artificial. The ideal of comfort that resulted from this, consisting in the artificial upkeep, regardless of outside metamorphoses, of a constant atmosphere within the home, ran right through the 20th century. For Jürgen Mayer H., however, this binary distribution of the real is no longer valid. The matter of climate, as reformulated by the turn of the century, goes beyond and neutralizes all these categorizations. The great ecological imbalances due to globalized human activity, make the very idea of any kind of ideal climate null and void. The watershed between the controlled and the uncontrolled no longer overlaps with the watertight boundaries of the house and home. This latter, according to Jürgen Mayer H., must thus be able to open out to the uncontrolled. Oriented towards the prevailing winds, the interior of the Weather House is a kind of seasonal filter for the fluid and changing conditions of the world outside. The programmatic organization is determined by this architectured crossing of the climatic flows: the house isn't divided into functional areas (kitchen, living room, bedroom), but distributes differentiated climatic zones (the area where you are normally or lightly dressed, where you are naked, etc.). Like a calendar, the architecture of the house transforms on the basis of the seasons, selecting for each of them the desired aspects and thus translating the climate into a complex indoor landscape, but one that is changing and controlled. Rain, floods, heat, humidity, snowdrifts, condensation, all are part and parcel of the interior architecture of the Weather House, as actual spatial and programmatic categories. ◆

Pierre Chabard

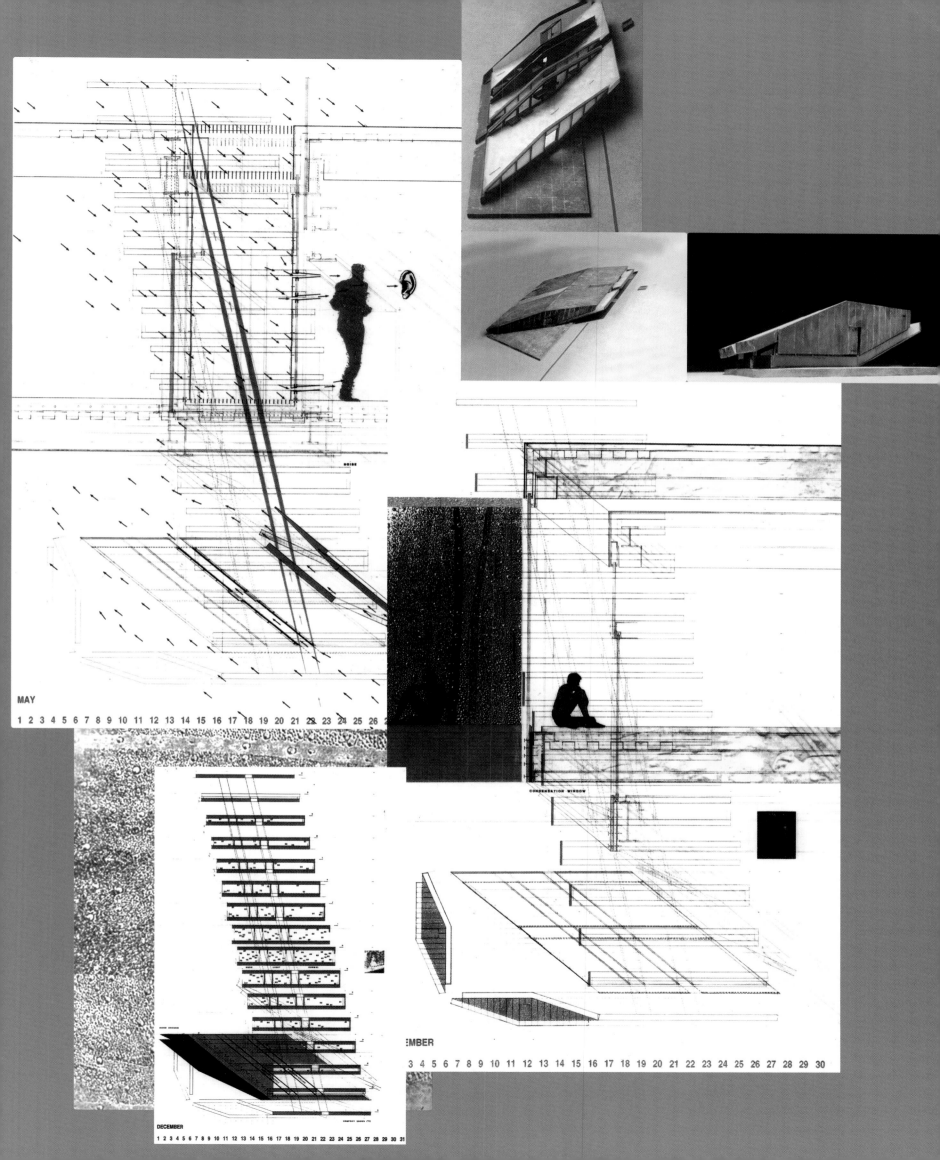

MAY
1 2 3 4 5 6 7 8 9 10 11 12 13 14 15 16 17 18 19 20 21 22 23 24 25 26 2

DECEMBER
1 2 3 4 5 6 7 8 9 10 11 12 13 14 15 16 17 18 19 20 21 22 23 24 25 26 27 28 29 30 31

EMBER
3 4 5 6 7 8 9 10 11 12 13 14 15 16 17 18 19 20 21 22 23 24 25 26 27 28 29 30

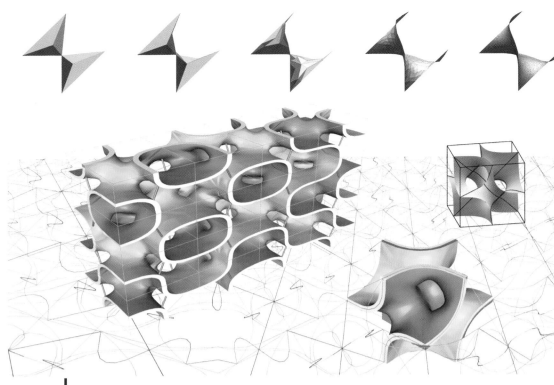

| Australia |

Minifie Nixon |

Paul Minifie (1965), Fiona Nixon (1968)

After stints teaching at RMIT and then working for renowned design offices in Melbourne and Singapore, Paul Minifie and Fiona Nixon set up their own agency in 2000. They are developing an approach that uses CAD to extrapolate the implications of spatial configurations. The system they are working on makes it possible to consider a variety of formal solutions for any given set of parameters. Already in 1993, the 'Queen Victoria' project used a topological description as its point of departure for revisiting the geometrical paradigms that underpin architecture. The idea was to represent a mathematical form in three dimensions — the surface of a side — in order to verify its architectural validity. For the recent project to extend the 'Marina Line' subway line in Singapore, they used sculpted forms derived from digital networks in three dimensions. In residential programmes, too, the plan is conceived flexibly as part of an expanding mesh that can be locally modified by means of insertions and modulations. ◆

Harbour Study, Corner Study |
Melbourne, Australia, 2001

These projects — Harbour Study and Corner Study — inhabit a type of minimal space, one of zero mean curvature. They investigate a class of surfaces where each element is of least area, held in an equipoise of tensions. The surfaces are evolved by continually subdividing a precursor, whilst sliding down the gradient to their lowest energy configurations. Yet they retain their ability to proliferate, to link and extend continuously. A topologic project might be seen as establishing the extents of a domain. Here we are sampling these terrains, finding instances that may be interpreted as a kind of habitation in our realm.

The familiar slab block can be seen as the datum plane rotated horizontal to vertical, thickened and inhabited. Architects manage the limitations of this intention, determining length, height, thickness, the legibility of edges. Decisions are made about the relationship between formal intent and the constitution of the inhabitants.

'Harbour Study — Schoen's unnamed 12' proposes a similar kind of thickening, but constrained by the threshold beyond which continual projections reduce to a self-intersect. Each building is a different vesicular instance of the virtual proliferation of the surface. The presence of sides is maintained, one side defined by the tracking of access and perforations in the structure, the other inhabited. An apartment is located, like a particle, in the two-dimensional space of the surface. Unlike what happens in the plane, not only does the location in three-dimsensional space vary in all three dimensions, but so does the orientation of the normal. Each apartment is part of the whole not as a tile or brick but as a sequin or bristle.

'Corner Study — pseudo batwing surface' investigates another variant of this surface type. This surface permits the partitioning of space into two continuous interlocking crystalline structures. Each is continuously traversable and discrete. The building is a kind of aerated foam, expanding into the site. One of the partitioned spaces is inhabited and private. Here apartments are linked spaces connected on the diagonal. The other is public space enfolded into the building. It forms a continuous grotto interlaced with the inhabited spaces, a series of plateaux ascending through the structure. ◆

Paul Minifie

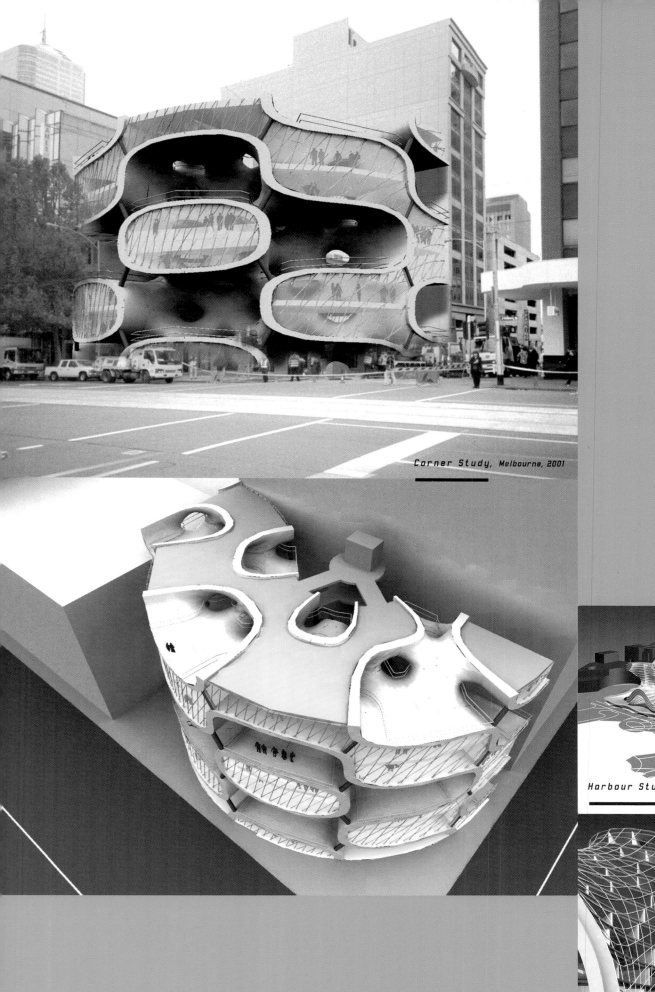
Corner Study, Melbourne, 2001

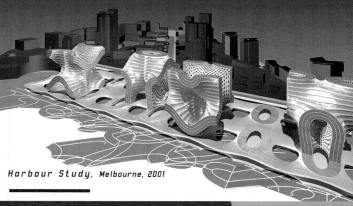
Harbour Study, Melbourne, 2001

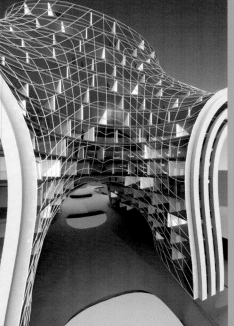

Tribal Clusters, Krielerstrasse, Cologne, 2000

| GERMANY |

Pablo Molestina, Gruppe MDK Architekten

PABLO MOLESTINA (1955)

Born in Ecuador, educated in the United States and finally practising architecture in Germany, Pablo Molestina started to work with Hassan Fathy in Egypt to study and experiment with the logic of vernacular architecture, an experience that was to influence his later work in terms of an interest in unconventional building techniques and the architectural materiality of local conditions. Ever since he set up his practice in Germany with partner Michael Kraus in 1991, he has been exploring the transforming condition of habitation through a series of built projects ranging from private residences to multi-party housing to temporary homes for elderly people. One of his concerns is how specific social parameters affect the definition of living, in both its performative and its typological dimension. Along these lines Molestina is searching for new types of habitation that are adapting to ever-changing contemporary urban lifestyles, trying to define typologies that relate to life rather than to usage. ◆

LivingROOM
Video, 2001

The idea is to present three architectural projects that deal with the theme of dwelling, but to do so in such a way that a familiar, living room-like atmosphere develops for the viewer in the presentation of the projects. The main exhibit, the actual exhibition box, resembles a living room cupboard, wherein some architectural models are incorporated, like typical decorative objects. The projects in the cupboard are presented through a 'home' video film. The film not only explains the idea of dwelling in the architectural projects but also offers the viewer the experience and the feel of dwelling, which has a home-made quality.

I. A child comes to the camera and announces that there is a meeting taking place between an investor and an architect to discuss a new idea (the motel project). The child will provide structure to the short film by announcing the action that is about to take place and occasionally commenting upon it (mini chorus). The scene takes place between cars in a parking lot. The architect has found a way to bring cars into the very floors of a building, so that the difference between spaces for cars and living spaces is obliterated. The investor is interested. His wife, who is also present, is not convinced by anything in the project and continually interrupts the discussion with objections and critical remarks. In the end, the investor leaves the scene, arguing with his increasingly vociferous wife, but appears to have been convinced to invest some money into this idea.

II. The child reappears in front of the camera and now announces that a different scene is commencing, one involving a student, a house and its owner. The house has caught the interest of the student, and he knocks on the door to ask for a tour. The owner, a rich and somewhat spoilt young woman, is glad to oblige and proceeds to show him the whole house with evident pride. The student is impressed and is pleased to have seen the project.

III. The scene changes to a street in a nice part of the city. While driving with his wife, the investor is intrigued by a nicely renovated building. Looking closely at the building, they discover that there is a whole complex behind it, which contains several very modern single buildings. They wander into the courtyard, which is an unfinished building site, and proceed to knock on a door to have a peek into one of the buildings. They are shown around, and in the process one obtains a detailed explanation of the project.

IV. The child comments on the events in the film and presents the views of the actors on which project has been of interest to them. An invisible interviewer gets the child to give his reactions to the different architectural pieces he has experienced; this is another way to approach the projects. ◆

Pablo Molestina

Mobile Living, Baulücke Project, Cologne, 2001

Wooden House: appropriate technology, Beyers house, Cologne, 2000

| France |

Moussafir Architectes Associés

JACQUES MOUSSAFIR (1957)

Having completed a degree in art history and collaborated for 10 years with various architects (Kohn, Hauvette, Gaudin, Perrault, Soler, etc.), Jacques Moussafir founded his own office in Paris in 1992. Jacques Moussafir, who is now an experienced builder, is well aware that most of the alternative solutions to stereotyped conventional housing arise from criteria of mobility, precariousness and urgency, flexibility and sociability. As such, he is most enthusiastic about the type of housing that he defines, over and above the mere fact of having a roof over one's head, as a way of being. With his abiding interest in cultural and metaphysical factors relating back to the human condition, time and the cosmos, Jacques Moussafir tries above all else in his projects to make space for a void – a kind of metaphysical argument – conditional on the formation of interiorities, which he often means in a paradoxical way. ◆

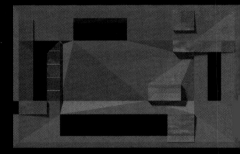

The House of Adam in Paradise
Montreuil, France, project, 2001
[Jacques Moussafir with Aldric Beckmann, Florent Biais, Laëtitia de Lubac, Rémi Schnebelin, Christiana Floris and Gilles Poirée]

The uniformization of the public and private spheres and the profusion of information, images and signs are making us increasingly inclined to conceive of housing as a refuge, a time of silence in the procession of urban sequences. The home must enable each person to withdraw from the urban and experience his or her own interiority. The interior is where we are; the external is elsewhere. It is thus perfectly possibly to feel that we are on the interior when we are outside. Interiority is a not a quality of being inside. It can take many different forms, but in any case it requires that a space become a place.

It was from this perspective that we approached our study for a house in the heart of the old village of Montreuil. The land, a market garden plot running north–south along an old wall for peach vines and delimited on the three other sides by fencing backed up by vegetation, is like an inlay of plants in a mineral urban fabric. It forms an enclosure that delimits a zone of silence and light defined by the movement of the sun – an interiority conducive to dwelling.

This project develops the idea of a dual temporality of housing: the nomadic and the sedentary. These are synthesized by two symbolic elements, the roof and the walls, two terms that are not mutually exclusive but cast light on each other. Total rootedness is the grave and a total absence of bearings leads to the dissolution of being. Dwelling is neither one nor the other, and yet it partakes of both. Here it is summed up in a sheet of Indaten steel cut out and folded, which houses various technical functions and rests on a masonrywork base composed of walls housing the sanitary facilities, cupboards and pipes for liquids. The house can be seen only on the horizontal plane, in a face to face with the sky.

More than a fifth façade, the roof is the house's only façade, substituting the horizontal dialogue with the town for the vertical one with natural elements. This roof with its considerable overhang catches the rainwater in the grooves of its folds, then stores it in two built-in reservoirs. This water is used for sanitary purposes and for watering the garden. There are also sun panels with holes in to allow the light through and affording a vision of the foliage of the trees. Hanging from the roof, sliding, foldaway partitions can be fully drawn aside along the patio so as to fully open the domestic space to the outside. The roof is both a technical element ensuring viability and the symbolic interface between earth and sky which makes it possible to 'dwell' in the sense that signifies not only protection from outside aggression but, above all, 'the way mortals are on earth' (Heidegger) – in that it designates what it is that makes 'man, insofar as he dwells, liberate the earth, welcome the sky and await the divine'. ◆

Jacques Moussafir

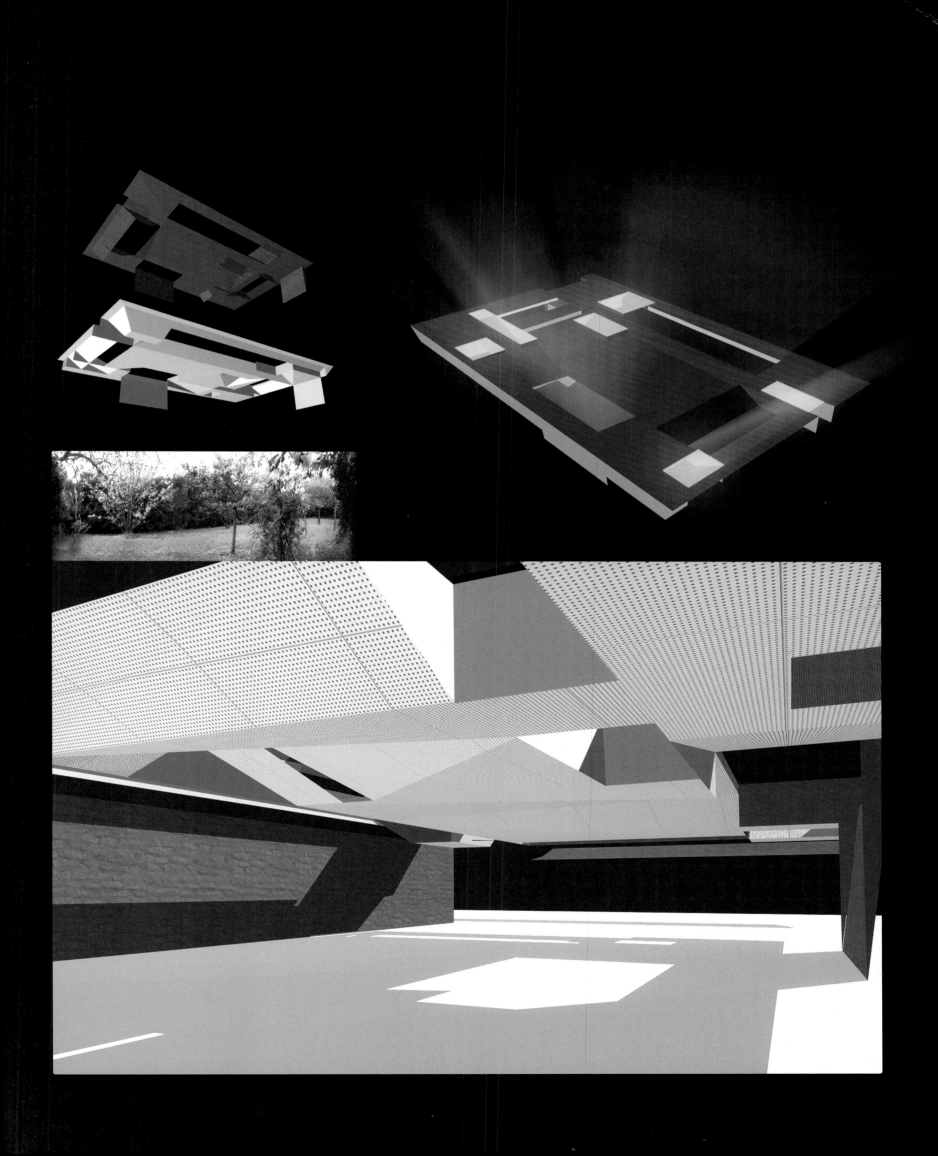

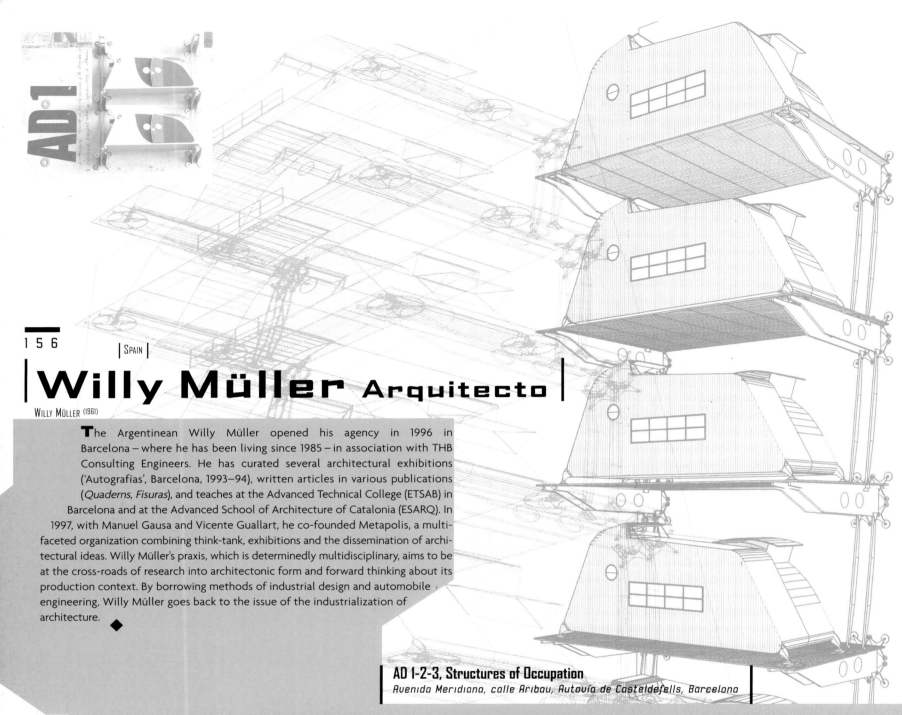

| Spain |

Willy Müller Arquitecto

WILLY MÜLLER (1961)

The Argentinean Willy Müller opened his agency in 1996 in Barcelona – where he has been living since 1985 – in association with THB Consulting Engineers. He has curated several architectural exhibitions ('Autografías', Barcelona, 1993–94), written articles in various publications (*Quaderns, Fisuras*), and teaches at the Advanced Technical College (ETSAB) in Barcelona and at the Advanced School of Architecture of Catalonia (ESARQ). In 1997, with Manuel Gausa and Vicente Guallart, he co-founded Metapolis, a multi-faceted organization combining think-tank, exhibitions and the dissemination of architectural ideas. Willy Müller's praxis, which is determinedly multidisciplinary, aims to be at the cross-roads of research into architectonic form and forward thinking about its production context. By borrowing methods of industrial design and automobile engineering, Willy Müller goes back to the issue of the industrialization of architecture. ◆

AD 1-2-3, Structures of Occupation
Avenida Meridiana, calle Aribau, Autovía de Casteldefells, Barcelona

AD is a way of exploring projects in occupation or tenancy architecture. Structures are adapted or adhered – AD-arch – to the empty spaces or surfaces in the city, with the aim of reintroducing architecture to the place that has appropriated its absence: advertising. These AD-arch cells work as regenerators of the town's lacerated urban tissue, a 'post-it' architecture, that is, adhesive, informative, mnemonic, introductory, temporary. Such structures introduce thickness to advertising surfaces, occupying another kind of space, the vertical floor of the city. This X or Y coordinate creates a new advertising concept, which embodies a tridimensional product.

Open spaces empty of roads, spaces not yet built on, urban ruins have become big urban screens, surfaces for writing present events, speeches, images, slogans and social references, as essential as traffic signals or monuments. One cannot envision a city suddenly stripped of all its advertising banners. The city is like a huge tattooed body, breeding an interchange of plural and personal ambitions, as well as commercial or political ones, that forces us to intensify perception and rationalization in order to interpret, select or forget things.

These temporary works – which are becoming daily more and more permanent – are covering the urban surface by a legal form of occupation: payment for temporary use. This advertising strategy, which does not require ownership of the land, opens up our thinking on future new possibilities in architecture, and architecture without the need for ownership.

AD-arch structures are different models of architectural intervention in an urban landscape full of advertising. These bracket- or shelf-structures, designed to be hung from or fixed to vertical surfaces, support all kinds of containers, sensors, cameras or other gadgets intended to test the quality and quantity of urban phenomena.

From serigraphed laboratory containers – AD-lab – used for environmental control, to sponsored experimental abodes – AD-hab, from mechanized arms that orient advertisements according to the direction of traffic on the roads, to new suspended public spaces (transgenic gardens, urban gym, birdcages . . . these structures introduce movement and volume to the advertising.

The mutant urban landscape in these meta-cities could thus become the antithesis to pollution: it is a question of instigating a debate between managers, entrepeneurs and creators.

◆

Willy Müller

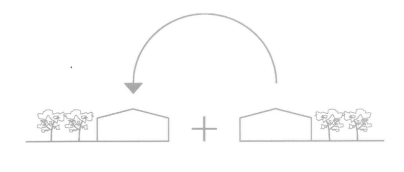

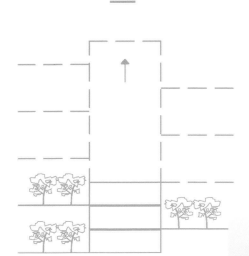

| Netherlands |

MVRDV |

Winy Maas (1959), Jacob Van Rijs (1964), Nathalie De Vries (1965)

MVRDV is the abbreviation of the names of its three founders, Winy Maas, Jacob Van Rijs and Nathalie De Vries, who have been associated and based in Rotterdam since 1991. Their activities lie at the confluence of several disciplines – architecture, city planning and design – and pay no heed to the boundaries of the various areas of activity. What typifies their approach is probably the pragmatism they display, combined with a manipulation of programme parameters, pushed to the limit. They emphasize a determination to take on the programmes and the sometimes conflicting viewpoints of the parties in question – commissioning bodies, users, spectators – and they turn these tensions into the actual matter of their architecture. Far from culminating in a synthesis, their architecture appears rather as an experiment with extremes. Notable examples are: 'WoZoCo's', dwellings for elderly people in Amsterdam (1999), the Netherlands pavilion for the Hanover exhibition in 2000 and 'VPRO Public Broadcasting Company', at Hilversum (1999). ◆

3D Garden, design for offices and 29 apartments
Hengelo, Netherlands, project, 2000

Like their main publications, *FARMAX* (1998) and *Datascape* (1999), the work currently being done by MVRDV is concerned with the extensive, total and continuous urbanization that is rampant in the Netherlands (and elsewhere). Their response is to work on planning 'in three dimensions' and to come up with inventive solutions for ultra-high-density development. They decry an illusory 'filling' of the territory and the way huge tracts of countryside are being transformed into an ocean of planned 'mediocracy', a suburban mixture of detached houses and simple warehouses without content or point. Refusing to accept this reality, they aim to deploy a whole network of parallel strategies between economy and ecology, using densification as a way of reducing infrastructure and preserving 'natural' spaces. They plead the case of contrast against uniformity.

We can include among these investigations their new housing project, entitled '3D-Tuin' (3D Garden), at Hengelo. The edifice proposes two programmes. On the ground floor, a set of services, offices and shops have their windows overlooking Weemenstraat. Then there are ten storeys of flats: nine floors with three apartments each and two 'penthouses' on the top floor.

Going to extreme lengths with the overhang principle developed for the WoZoCo's project, 3D Garden takes up the challenge of providing each flat with a vertiginous terrace. The proposal is impressive both for its area and its overhang, and seductive because of the huge tree planted on each terrace, which seems to be hanging in the void.

In fact, the whole building imitates the structure of a tree, because of the superposition of its flats and corbelled gardens. This 'tree tower' with its 'branch-terraces' may eventually grow to a height of 42 metres. And, on the ground, the implantation of the building overlaps an entrance to the adjacent car park, seeming to swerve aside to spare an old tree, standing in majestic counterpoint to their architectural metaphor.

For MVRDV this tree project, unlike any other in the Netherlands, is a new and surprising addition to the history that began with the hanging gardens of Babylon. It materializes a new way of 'living in the countryside' in a vertical structure, within a dense urban network that runs counter to the rampant suburbanization. ◆

Bénédicte Grosjean

Client:	Assen Projekten BV, Borne
Location:	Oldenzaalsestraat, Hengelo
Design:	MVRDV with Duzan Doepel
Structure:	Pieters Bouwtechniek, Delft

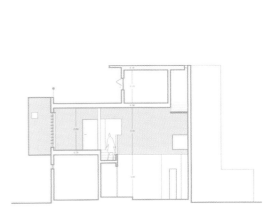

COUPE TRANSVERSALE aa

| France/Senegal |

Ibrahima N'Doye |

IBRAHIMA N'DOYE (1973)

Ibrahima N'Doye graduated from the Paris-Villemin School of Architecture in 1999 and lives in Paris, where he is pursuing graduate studies in architectural theory. Spotted during a EuropanDOM 1 competition, this young Franco-Senegalese architect is currently working on several projects in the metropolitan area of Dakar: urban redevelopment of the commune of Yoff (construction of a market and renovation of public places) and construction of private homes (Seck 1 House, Seck 2 House). The architecture of these houses stems from a rigorous project-oriented approach combining mimesis and differentiation (a situation that reflects Ibrahima N'Doye's cultural duality). The simultaneously physical, social and cultural context in which his projects are incorporated is systematically examined, in order to bring out the local, spatial and domestic paradigms. Once identified, these arrangements are included in a project logic within which they are at once transgressed and updated – a logic that is akin to a proper process of abstraction. The resulting objects, which are at once alien and familiar, open the way to a possible habitat. ◆

Seck 1 and Seck 2 House
Dakar, Senegal, 2000–present

The Seck 1 and Seck 2 houses are located at Yoff in the suburbs of greater Dakar, Senegal. In this dense and architecturally heterogeneous urban setting, these two prisms with their simple, concise forms are strange, silent presences amidst the everyday cacophony all around. My approach to the project is defined by an oscillation between difference and mimesis. The mimetic tendency is based on an approach that consists in observing particular aspects of the context and local customs and translates into the definition of domestic spaces. This attitude is then superseded by another, more paradoxical one whose role is to transgress, to free itself from the pre-established rule of context by shifting it towards the quest for a logic of a self-referential object: difference. This dichotomy is where the project questions itself and is structured. Without really expecting an answer, the project opens up a possibility.

Seck 1
Built on and wholly occupying a trapezoid of 150 square metres, it is like a porous monolith. The domestic object counters the opacity of the outer membrane with the complete porosity and fluidity of its inner spaces (double height, terraces and passages) with a view to accentuating depth through playing on the dynamic afforded by the walls and the angles of the trapezoid.

Seck 2
This house built on the seafront is, from a spatial viewpoint, similar to a loft. Compared with the first, it might be said to constitute a kind of 'variation on the theme', except that this one opts for a completely modular spatiality because of its system of flexible walls that work by the play of rotation and translation around a kernel, which makes it possible to free up a large part of the space. The folding back of the partitions against the walls allows the part of the living room on the mezzanine to develop beyond a ramp, which crosses the empty space on the upper floor. The house deliberately mimes the depth imaged by the marine horizon, which it tirelessly contemplates. ◆

Ibrahima N'Doye

plan du niveau 1

plan du rez-de-chaussée

plan du rez-de-chaussée

plan du niveau 1

Naito Architects & Associates

| JAPAN |

HIROSHI NAITO (1950)

Hiroshi Naito graduated from Waseda University in Tokyo in 1974 and won the Murano Award for his degree project. He then continued his studies under the supervision of Professor Takamasa Yoshizada. From 1976 to 1978 he worked in the Fernando Higueras agency as project director, then in the Kiyonori Kikutake agency in Tokyo until 1981, when he opened Naito Architects and Associates, also in Tokyo. Since 1986 he has been teaching, first at Waseda University, then at Tokyo University. The important thing, for him, is to communicate with the public. He makes reference to the nostalgic, romantic music of Piazzola, and readily compares his position on architecture with it. He is eager to build 'for everyone'. He makes use of computer technology, but only for the purposes of presenting his work. Computers enable him to imagine and execute everything required on the structural level, but they do not help him to solve the problem of the link with nature, or to find a way to deal with natural forces. It is the adaptation to the context and surroundings that dominates the way Hiroshi Naito conceives of form; it is also often the use of one of his preferred materials, wood. For him, architecture must be 'noiseless'. And this is an ironical way of saying that it must speak for itself, and sidestep discourse. ◆

House no. 21
Setagaya, Japan, 1997

For Hiroshi Naito, building a house is a primitive, essential act that harks back to the very origins of architectonic art. As it happens, the limited budgets and various restrictions that usually characterize this kind of construction often oblige architects to concentrate on the essential, to radicalize their choices. For Naito, this rigorous and difficult exercise represents a special opportunity to strip architecture of everything useless and, beyond that, to reconcile structural rationalism and vernacular simplicity, tradition and modernity. Since House no. 1, which he built at Kamakura in 1984, he has designed a score of houses of which several have been built. In 1993 he completed House no. 14, conceived for a couple of artists in a wooded natural setting at Tsukuba. Organized around a centred plan, it evokes both the nine-section Palladian villa and traditional Japanese houses. Four wooden posts hold up an ample roof whose four parts cover the domestic space. House no. 18, completed in 1995 at Ito, also fits into a natural landscape, standing on a woody mountainside on the Izu peninsula. On this occasion Naito designed a linear, longitudinal house, a long nave crossed by wooden frames supporting the two parts of the roof. Here again, it is above all the roofing that constitutes the house. The architecture is basically determined by the design of the frame. The house's other features – the quality of the light, the relationship to the site, uses, etc. – flow from the inception of this particular tectonic order. In this series of houses, House no. 21 occupies what is in several ways an extreme position. First of all, it is located in a very restrictive urban context. Flanked on both sides by adjoining houses, it fits into a long, deep plot that is barely 3 metres wide. This house is also notable for its small size (52 square metres of living space) and, as the architect sees it, its 'almost non-existent' budget. Once again, Naito surmounts these many constraints by means of a strong structural theme. Built out of inexpensive pieces of timber generally used for the framework of tunnels, the house is a longitudinal series of cross-frames built in close succession. The recesses formed between these porticoes can be used for storage or as apertures for natural light. Each gable is wholly glazed. At the southern end, the light is filtered by the flight of stairs. The geometry of the steeply sloping roof contributes to the house's natural ventilation. ◆

Pierre Chabard

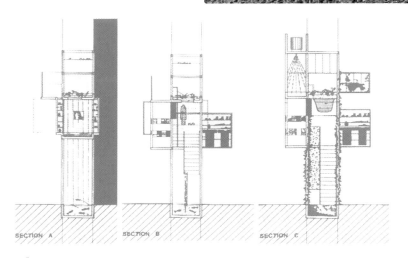

| USA |

Taeg Nishimoto & Allied Architects

Taeg Nishimoto (1955)

After studying architecture in Japan and the United States (Cornell University and Columbia University, New York), Taeg Nishimoto set up his own agency in New York in 1989. He also teaches at the Pratt Institute and Columbia University. In 1995 he was chosen for inclusion in the publication *40 Under 40* and in 1995 he won a prize from the New York Foundation of the Arts. Nishimoto's work is punctuated by various theoretical and experimental productions (Plot Houses, RE-f®action), which constitute the conceptual roots of his architecture. In the installation RE-f(r)action (1993, 1995) he used minimal structures (a few arcs made of bent wood, stretched and hung from invisible threads in an empty room) to bring into existence a tectonic space simply from the tension created out of these modest components. Nishimoto has prolonged and developed this phenomenological approach to spatiality in his buildings. His architecture is thus developed as a relational and phenomenal field in which the material and the immaterial, the formal and the functional and the spatial and the temporal interweave and collapse into one another. ◆

SECTION A   SECTION B   SECTION C

PLOT House(s)
3 Projects, 1992–2000

PLOT House: The house is conceived as a direct response to the manner in which the physical objects of contemporary living are perceived in certain instances, such as the piling up of junk mail or the presence of a fax machine. Space in this house, therefore, is not understood as a volume but as a dimension expanded from these objects and of particular relationships between each object. In that sense, the programme is directly derived from these objects and related specific activities. Each probable object is put into a certain situation, which works as an independent plot within the whole narrative to be read completely simultaneously.

Within and directly outside of the 1.5-metre-wide structural frame, these plots occur both sequentially and elliptically along the connecting circulation link. According to the choice of objects and situations, the design of the house can modify itself with no conclusive formalization.

PLOT House(s): The two protagonists in this living structure never meet in reality, i.e., never occupy the same space, although they are confined in the X-shaped structure that conspicuously provides each individual spatial configuration. Instead, they look at each other through electronic images on the monitors, taken by video cameras. They can feel the presence of the other through these real-time images, while at the same time they are given the ability to manipulate the dimension of time by playing recorded images from the past. The spatial articulation of the living situa-

tion is therefore turned into the articulation of time, in terms of the manipulation of remembered time in each image. The physical presence of the monitors in the living space, cameras outside the transparent walls and the liquid crystal glass to manipulate the availability of the images to the other person are the building components that respond to this descriptive programme.

PLOT(ted) House: The circulation device, i.e., stairs in this case, makes daily life possible based on the cooperation of the other inhabitants. While the structure has four floors, each resident occupies a part of three different floors programmatically articulated into living space, bathroom and kitchen/dining. In order for them to be able to move among these articulated spaces, they have to get another resident's cooperation to use the stairs. They communicate with each other through the intercoms, which are located within each space.

The instability and the dynamics of the domestic situation created by the momentary interaction among the residents are the enigmatic condition of this programme (like a game). ◆

Taeg Nishimoto

refuse

mind

body

functional zones   light scheme   supplies

| CROATIA |

Njiric & Njiric Arhitekti |

HELENA NJIRIC (1963), HRVOJE NJIRIC (1960)

Helena and Hrvoje Njiric graduated from Zagreb University in the late 1980s and set up their agency in the Croatian capital in 1996. Njiric & Njiric, who have come to notice in various major international competitions ('Yokohama Port Terminal', 1995, etc.), are currently managing several major projects in Zagreb and Maribor. The 'Baumaxx Hypermarket', a shopping centre that was completed in 1998 in the Slovenian capital and overturns every convention for the genre, is a good example of the mixture of pragmatism and inventiveness that are a hallmark of their architecture. Where habitat and housing are concerned, Njiric & Njiric have participated in various competitions (Europan 4, 1996; Viskovo Urban Planning, 1996) and come up with several experimental projects.

Here everything is built out of the juxtaposition and declension of concepts, used as interactive and generative matrixes: classification by colour, networks of multiple itineraries, changing façades of signage, the progress of the seasons, variations on motifs of density or land use, typologies of empty sites, etc. ◆

A House with Three Courts ©
Malmö, Sweden, Parasite Exhibition, 2000 |

'Read the text as you desire'*: A parasite house experiencing reality through the set of accessories, designed to meet the needs of a contemporary urban nomad, a deliberate combination of the modernist legacy and updated standards.

'Participate without belonging'*: Changed ratio of dwelling areas leads to a different syntax of functional zones: spaces for mind, body and refuse seem to share an equal percentage of living space.

'Reformatting'*: A House with Three Courts by Mies van der Rohe: The interactive, outer layer is about the exchange of goods and waste, a sort of infrastructural court; the central, sky-lit zone is a virtual court and provides general information about the outer world through a cube of light, but is otherwise to be accessed by the non-physical networks. This e-court is a mind zone, a silent retreat of the house; the third court is a common one - an extension of the body zone, an area for exploring different kinds of physicality. It could even embrace the existing nature as a part of the internal open-air space.

'Make room for absence'*: The House has no windows. A façade is a billboard – a surface ready to be completely covered with jumbo posters, or eventually with prismavision® – movable bars with alternating messages.

'Be wherever, whenever'*: The House fits into any of the sites offered, but preferably into the dense one, to demonstrate its resistant nature and 'profitable' character.

'Downsize'*: The curvature of the envelope highlights the rigour of the plan and reduces the visual impact of the volume in its immediate surrounding.

'Misread'*: A House is, according to the brief, designed for a couple, but its typological neutrality keeps it open for other purposes as well: an office, a gallery, a veterinary surgery, a kindergarten...

'Rework what others have exhausted'*: We propose a simple timber-frame structure of prefab elements – eight equal wall elements, segmented roof and floor panels – all measured to fit into a container.

'Refine your noise-to-signal ratio'*: An efficient set of services should provide an 'ideal standard'. Low-tech solutions for heating. Natural ventilation is generated by the section of the house. Three 'climatic' zones are related to the function of the three bands.

'Saturate'*: An all-white interior is saturated with diverse accessories, offering a fully autonomous retreat. The exposed timber beams of the roof panels provide a solution for indirect lighting – different shades of white with different colour temperatures throughout the House.

'Present yourself as a flexible, highly skilled, short-term commodity'*: A parasite house is unlikely to predict whether one buys or rents it, or how long or how frequently one is going to stay. A parasite – 'just there'. ◆

Njiric & Njiric
* quotes from: Andrew Boyd, *Life's Little Deconstruction Book, Self-help for the Post-hip*, Penguin Books, London, 1999

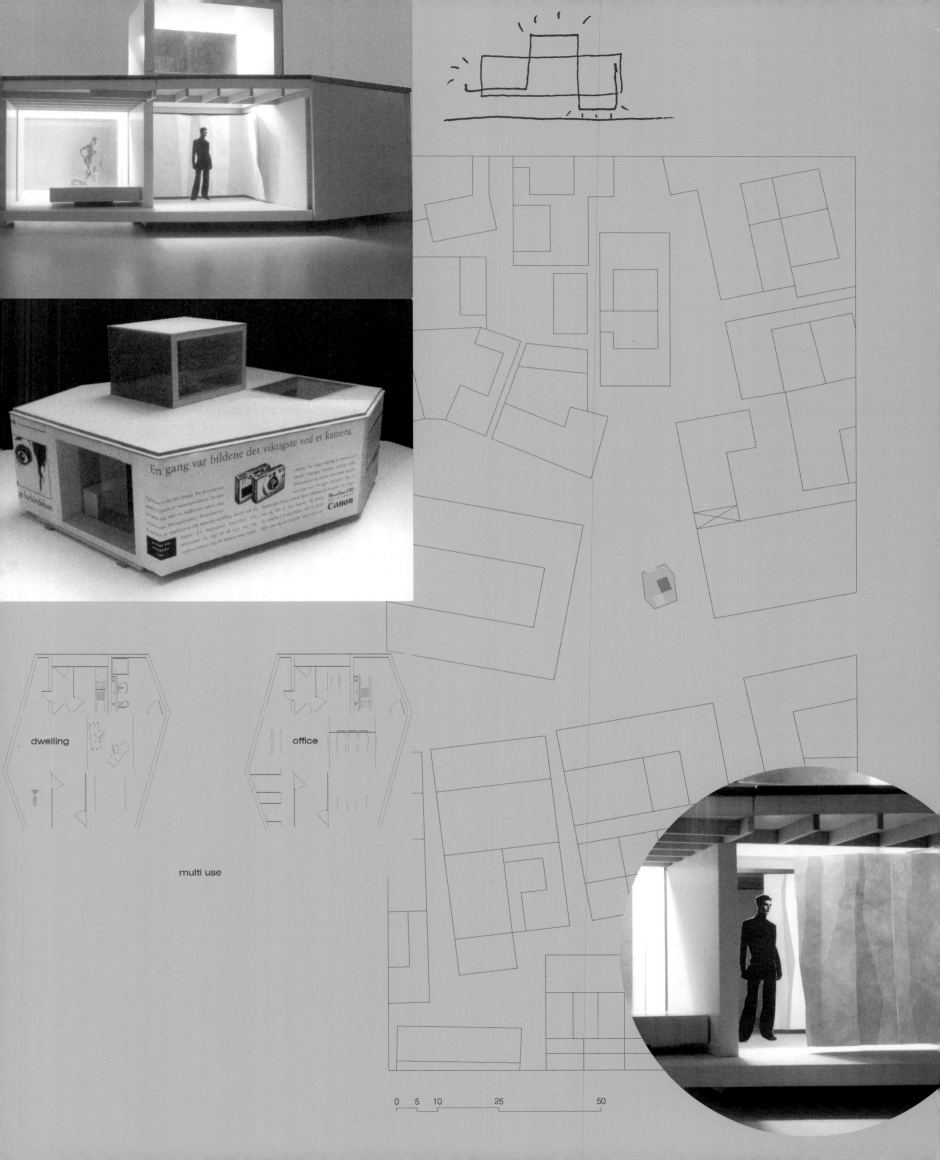

En gang var bildene det viktigste ved et kamera.

dwelling

office

multi use

0 5 10   25   50

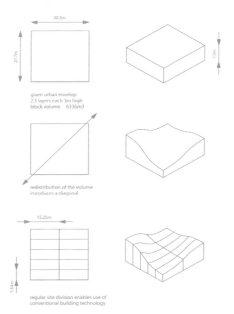

given urban envelop
2.5 layers each 3m high
block volume 6336m3

introduction of interior street rids
façades of ducting and obligatory
storage

redistribution of the volume
introduces a diagonal

interior street offers views on open
outdoor spaces

regular site division enables use of
conventional building technology

internal redistribution of volume
over dwellings
all dwellings equal exactly 633.6m3

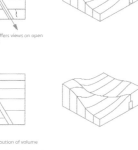

| NETHERLANDS |

NL Architects

PIETER BANNENBERG (1959), WALTER VAN DIJK (1962), KAMIEL KLAASSE (1967), MARK LINNEMANN (1962)

Pieter Bannenberg, Walter Van Dijk, Kamiel Klaasse and Mark Linnemann founded NL Architects in 1997, in Amsterdam, but their collaborative work dates back to the early 1990s, when they were all students together at the Technical University in Delft. Radically critical of the present-day metropolitan and suburban condition, NL projects are typified by an extreme sensibility on all the issues, scales and processes that are encountered. It is in order to deal with the most commonplace aspects of the real and the most prosaic practices that they develop the most innovative solutions, to get the most out of the unexplored potential of the things all around us: a car park, a shopping centre, a highway, a house, etc. Through its capacity to articulate paradoxical conditions, architecture is, for them, the preferred tool for synthesizing new types of buildings, programmatic hybrid structures. This decidedly realistic and pragmatic dimension of NL production cannot be separated from a markedly critical, ironical and forward-looking stance. ◆

Het Funen
Amsterdam, Netherlands, 2001–present

These 10 houses are part of a master plan, Het Funen, by the Architecten Cie. The site is located close to the historic centre of Amsterdam. The overall layout could be considered as a new development in the typology of the semi-open building block. The entanglement of the responsibilities and interests of the department of public works and the private developer resulted in a gradual transition of private outdoor spaces and a public park: a new merging of the public and private realm. Along the east side and the south side of the plan a wall containing a little over 300 apartments and some office spaces shields the site from the noise of the adjacent railway. Inside this semi-open block a loose grid is set up, containing 16 smaller housing blocks designed by 8 other architectural offices. These 'Hidden Delights' vary in height from 2½ to 6 floors. All have their front doors in the park.

The envelope of the NL Block measures 30.5 metres by 27.7 metres and is 2½ floors in height. The houses are accessed from a central 'isle' in the middle of the block. This 'alley' rids the façades of the obligatory storage spaces and technical facilities by placing them centrally in the apartments, thus opening the façades up to the light. The block is situated in the middle of the plan area. The east side faces the protective wall. Three other building volumes with slightly smaller footprint, but considerably higher (18 metres), are right next to the other three façades. This proximity makes it difficult to provide any private outdoor space. Also the fifth façade, the roof, does not offer any real privacy. By interpreting the given 2½ floors (see the movie 'Being John Malkovich') as 2 + ½, the block offers a new perspective on existing ideas about floor-to-floor heights. To create space inside the master plan the volume is deformed and redistributed over the envelope, pushed away as much as possible from the adjacent volumes. Within the orthogonal grid, a diagonal view now opens up. Internally this operation becomes possible by rotating the alley, orienting it to the vent out to open spaces between the blocks. Point of reference is the given 633.6 square metres per dwelling. While all houses are at the same time stretched and compressed, either in height or in length, they still maintain this original volume and their typology. The amplitude of the building varies from 5 to 15 metres, but overall the average is still 2½ floors. In the process the standard building bay, conceived as an organizational tool of dwelling, becomes obsolete. ◆

NL Architects

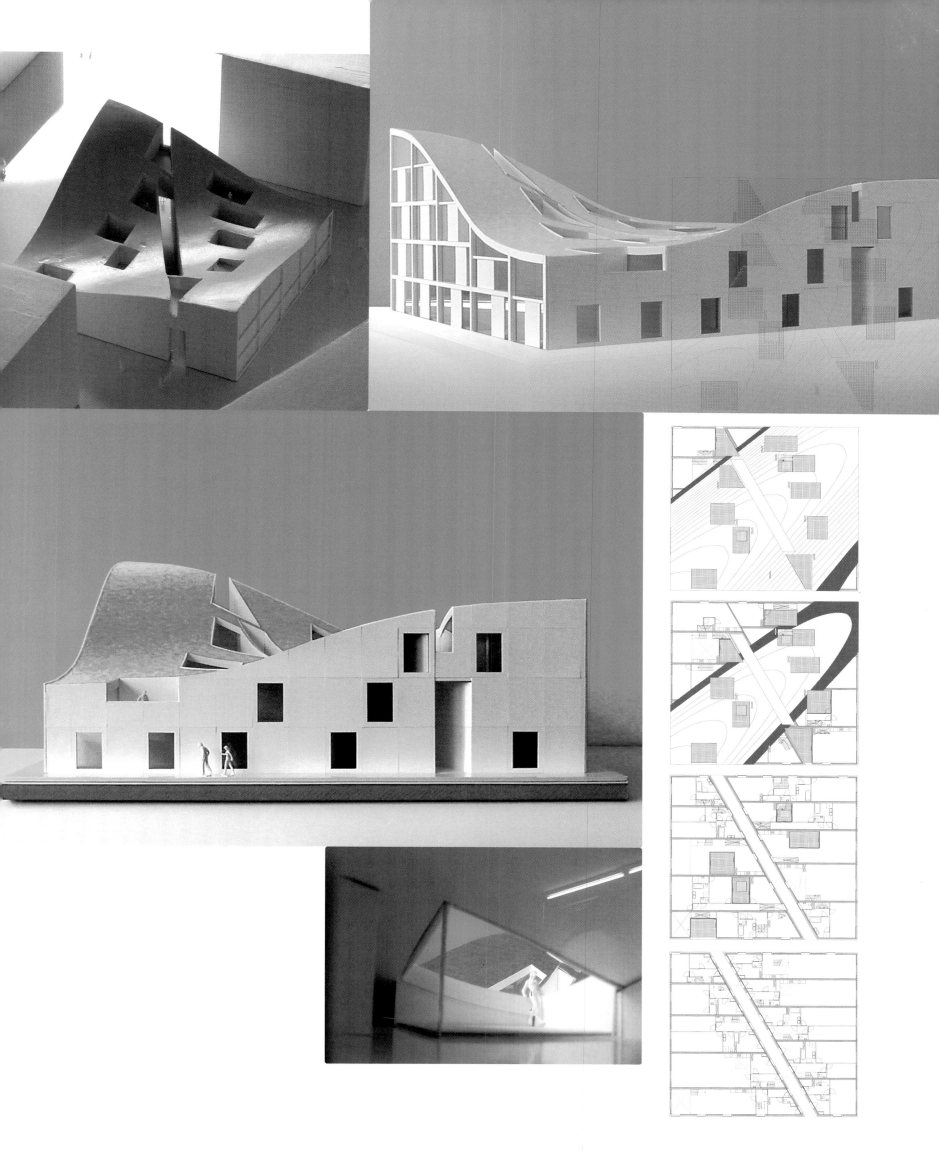

| USA |

NMDA (Neil M. Denari Architects)

NEIL M. DENARI (1957)

As director of the prestigious Los Angeles School of Architecture SCI-Arc since 1997, Neil Denari has been developing areas of research since the mid-1980s, which bring together the varying potential of the technological and industrial world with the world of architecture. Neil Denari is an architect, teacher and author of books, which have been acclaimed for the felicitous combination of their content and their graphics (*Interrupted Projections*, *Gyroscopic Horizons*), and which simultaneously explore the visual and informational world of advertising, the media and technology. After building the experimental space of the MA Gallery in Tokyo, Denari is currently at work building the Arlington Museum of Art in Texas, as well as renovating housing in Los Angeles. The technicity of the world is the basic reference of his modular and flexible architecture, with its folding of supple, smooth surfaces, like those of a car. The house appears like a factual body, at once mobile and independent. The inhabitant is the 'passenger', permeated by the ebb and flow of globalization. He is in transit in his home, with which he interacts as if with a machine. ◆

Corrugated Duct House
Palm Springs, USA, project, 1998

Neil Denari conceives of the house as bio-technological interface between man and his globalized environment. For him, 'dwelling' goes well beyond domestic frontiers and concerns our broader relation to the world. This relation is mediated by a number of technical objects of which the house is one, just slightly more complex than the others. This familiarity and intimacy, the organic relation one has with the machines of everyday life (car, computer, phone, television, air conditioning) is the model that Denari seeks to apply to the relation between the occupant and the machine/house that he designs for him or her. This problem of domestic architecture is particularly manifest in the Corrugated Duct House, because of the extreme climatic conditions of its site. As Denari says: 'The desert mountain ranges in the Coachella Valley and the dramatic heat and sunshine of Palm Springs, California, form the context for this experimental house. Its concept is derived from the position that since air conditioning is unavoidable in this area, then environmental micro-conditions, as expressed in spatial and material conditions, can drive the organization and techniques of construction and air conditioning. Programmatically, the house is 2,800 square feet (260 square metres) of conditioned space with a flexible interior. Three bedrooms and two baths are required for the private spaces, while the kitchen and living spaces merge in and between the structure/plenum system. Parking for two cars fits below the roof. The scheme is oriented around a large, white-painted steel roof. Constructed from $\frac{1}{8}$-inch (0.3-centimetre) steel sheet, the roof section is a series of supersized corrugations mirrored top and bottom to form structural depth and air-conditioning plenums. The double-skin cavity roof system reflects heat so that cool air and water can flow through the plenums to the interior of the house. Air-handling units are attached to the roof edges. While the corrugations mainly form the roof, they also twist and turn to form specific columns/grooves/shafts as well as exterior wall fragments, internal partitions and built-in furniture. Cool air flows through the entire system, with small vents and registers placed in precise ways to cool the body inside the house. Micro-environments are formed also through humidity control and misting systems. A concrete floor and aluminum and glass curtain walls complete the material conditions of the house. ◆

Pierre Chabard/Neil Denari

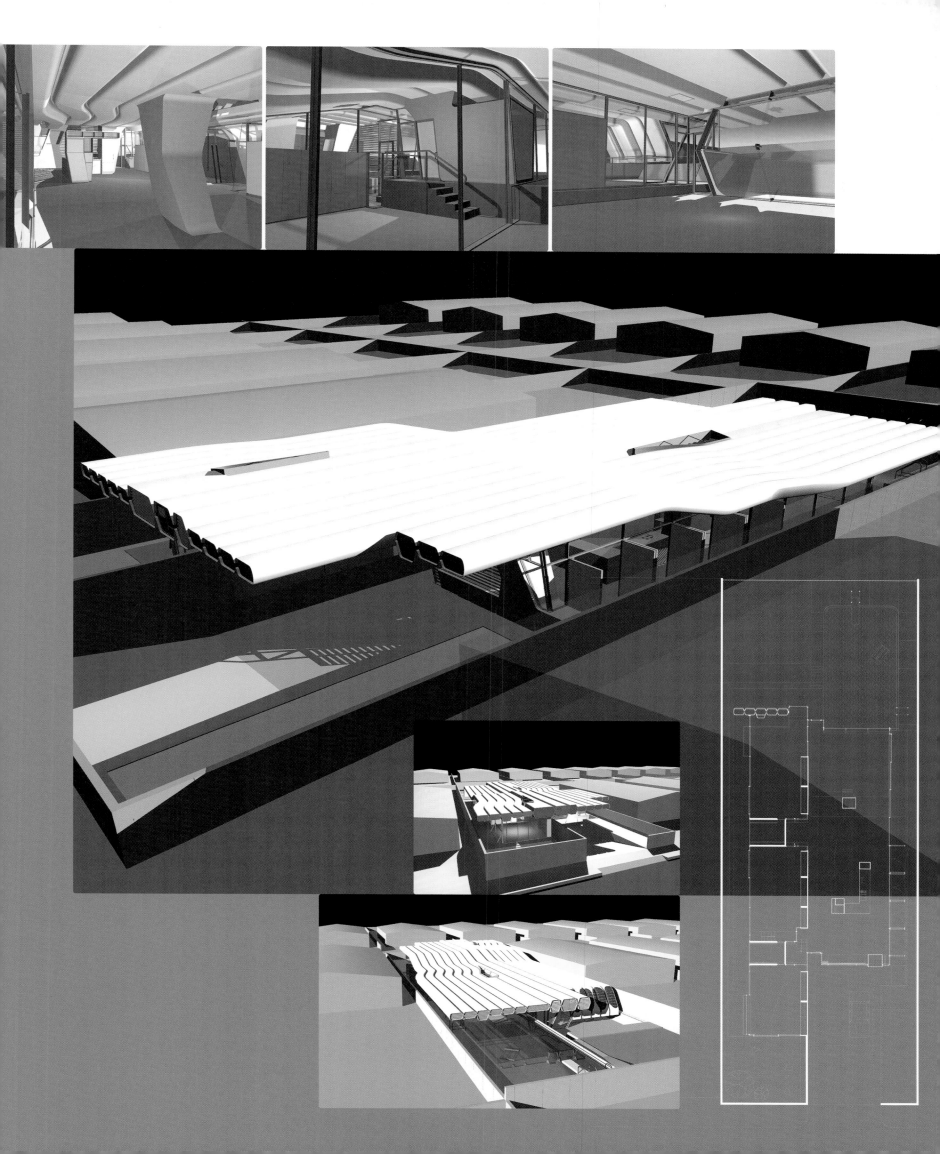

PROCESO DE HIBRIDACION 001
area Galindo

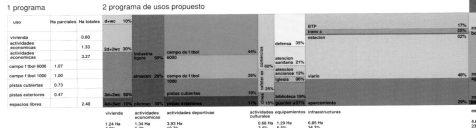

1 programa			2 programa de usos propuesto												ocupacion total en planta 20.00 Ha	
uso	Ha parciales	Ha totales	d+wc	10%										BTP	17%	zonas verdes:	20%
														tranv a	05%	bosque	
vivienda		0.60	2d+2wc	30%	industria ligera	50%	campo f tbol 6000	44%	defensa	35%			estacion	02%		
actividades economicas		1.33							atencion sanitaria	21%						
actividades economicas		3.27							atencion ancianos	12%	viario	48%	zonas verdes: c sped	50%
campo f tbol 6000	1.07				almacen	20%	campo f tbol 1000	26%	iglesia	06%			agua	05%		
campo f tbol 1000	1.00		3d+2wc	50%			pistas cubiertas	19%	biblioteca	19%			zonas duras peatonales	20%		
pistas cubiertas	0.73				oficinas	30%	pistas exteriores	11%	guarder a	07%	aparcamiento	29%	juegos ni os	05%		
pistas exteriores	0.47		4d+3wc	10%													
espacios libres		2.40															

	vivienda	actividades economicas	actividades deportivas	actividades culturales	equipamientos	infraestructuras		espacios libres	
	1.24 Ha 6.2%	1.34 Ha 6.7%	3.93 Ha 19.7%	0.68 Ha 3.4%	1.29 Ha 6.5%	6.85 Ha 34.3%		4.67 Ha 23.2%	ocupacion en planta % sobre 20.00 Ha

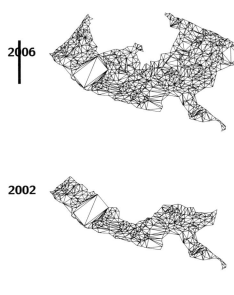

2010

2006

2002

1999

| Spain |

NO.MAD. Arquitectura

Eduardo Arroyo (1964)

Eduardo Arroyo graduated in 1988 from the Escuela Tecnica Superior de Arquitectura of Madrid, where he lives, works and teaches (ETSAM since 1996). His work, in his NO.MAD. Arquitectura agency, is mainly focused on city planning and the planning and architecture of urban structures (residential areas, university, sporting and administrative complexes, etc.). He worked with the Office for Metropolitan Architecture (OMA) in the very early 1990s (Kunsthal Congrexpo), but does not actually conceive of architecture outside an overall reflection not only about the city but, beyond it, about the territory itself, on a geographical scale. The distinctive feature of the NO.MAD. Arquitectura approach lies in the project-based methods Arroyo is gradually introducing and putting into practice in order to connect all these spatial scales together and convey their logic and their respective complexity. ◆

Hybridization Process PH001
Galindo-Barakaldo, Spain, competition, 1998

A landscape hybridization process, which liberates town planning from traditional urban design duties. An urban transformation system made of correlative steps and three final products: a hybridized landscape, urban hybrids and domestic hybridization.

The first stage in the process is to create an objective and homogeneous distribution of each function to be inserted into the territory. Out of these proportions, a series of patterns appears in relation to the overall surface and determines a variety of densities of use. A second analysis of the existing urban elements in the area shows their possibilities of remaining or disappearing in the future and they are considered as vectorial realities. The interaction between the densities of use and the vectorial realities gives rise to forces of repulsion and attraction, which transform the initial patterns by a mutation of densities. This process will only stop once the equilibrium point has been reached, determining their final position inside the territory.

The process continues by the recognition and grouping of the different building data. This procedure links to the configuration of the urban hybrids. Once this clear identification has taken place, the whole landscape is qualified by a gradually different density of hybridization, which constructs a statistical landscape of occupational possibilities.

The first final product is recognized as a landscape hybridization, a simple system of constructing possibilities intended to create a more human city, where distances between dwellings and workplaces are diminished physically, not by means of vehicles or sophisticated communications.

The next step in the process is to read the information contained in each hybrid file, in which each use has a participating percentage in the configuration of the constructed section.

A simple calculation of surfaces and the superimposition of different uses make the original volume appear. Afterwards, this virtual volume is transformed by border conditions, which give a new shape to the primary volume according to the existing landscape and also by the predetermined heights of each usage. As a result, the generic section of the building is built and characterized by all the information related to the functions and also amongst them and their structural volumes.

Considering the multiplicity of characters and the hedonism of contemporary man, his increasingly atypical characteristics of mobility and communication, living units are designed to relieve architecture of its rigid organizational function and allow a mere supporting role for all kinds of vital possibilities with a maximal absorption of cultural multiplicity. ◆

Eduardo Arroyo

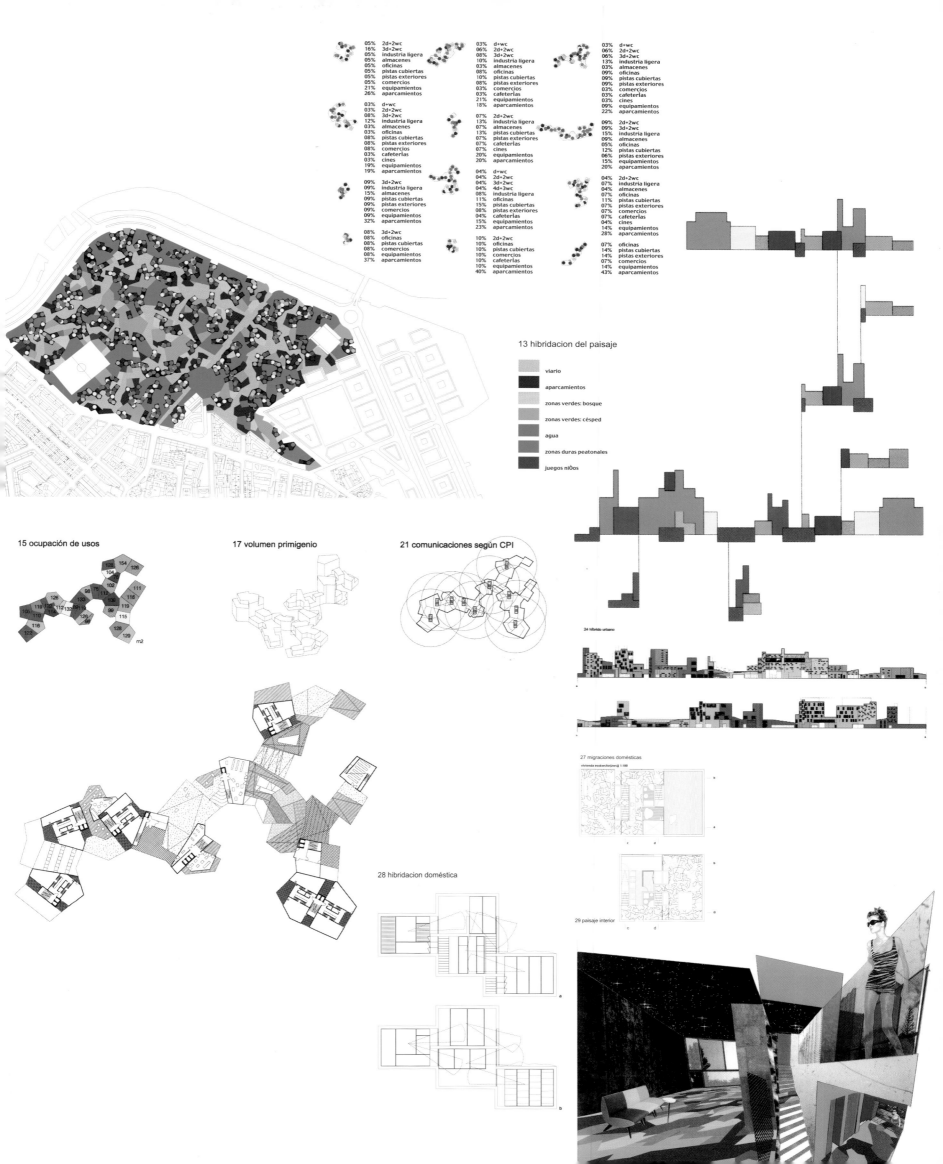

05% 2d+2wc
16% 3d+2wc
05% industria ligera
05% almacenes
05% oficinas
05% pistas cubiertas
10% pistas exteriores
05% comercios
21% equipamientos
26% aparcamientos

03% d+wc
03% 2d+2wc
08% 3d+2wc
12% industria ligera
03% almacenes
03% oficinas
08% pistas cubiertas
08% pistas exteriores
08% comercios
03% cafeterías
03% cines
19% equipamientos
19% aparcamientos

09% 3d+2wc
09% industria ligera
15% almacenes
09% pistas cubiertas
09% pistas exteriores
09% comercios
09% equipamientos
32% aparcamientos

08% 3d+2wc
08% oficinas
08% pistas cubiertas
08% comercios
08% equipamientos
37% aparcamientos

03% d+wc
06% 2d+2wc
08% 3d+2wc
10% industria ligera
03% almacenes
08% oficinas
10% pistas cubiertas
08% pistas exteriores
03% comercios
03% cafeterías
21% equipamientos
18% aparcamientos

07% 2d+2wc
13% industria ligera
07% almacenes
13% pistas cubiertas
07% pistas exteriores
07% cines
20% equipamientos
20% aparcamientos

04% d+wc
04% 2d+2wc
04% 3d+2wc
04% 4d+3wc
08% industria ligera
11% oficinas
15% pistas cubiertas
08% pistas exteriores
04% cafeterías
15% equipamientos
23% aparcamientos

10% 2d+2wc
10% pistas cubiertas
10% comercios
10% cafeterías
10% equipamientos
40% aparcamientos

03% d+wc
06% 2d+2wc
06% 3d+2wc
13% industria ligera
03% almacenes
09% oficinas
09% pistas cubiertas
09% pistas exteriores
03% comercios
03% cafeterías
03% cines
09% equipamientos
22% aparcamientos

09% 2d+2wc
09% 3d+2wc
15% industria ligera
09% almacenes
05% oficinas
12% pistas cubiertas
06% pistas exteriores
15% equipamientos
20% aparcamientos

04% 2d+2wc
07% industria ligera
04% almacenes
07% oficinas
07% pistas cubiertas
07% pistas exteriores
07% comercios
07% cafeterías
04% cines
14% equipamientos
28% aparcamientos

07% oficinas
14% pistas cubiertas
14% pistas exteriores
07% comercios
14% equipamientos
43% aparcamientos

13 hibridacion del paisaje

viario
aparcamientos
zonas verdes: bosque
zonas verdes: césped
agua
zonas duras peatonales
juegos niños

15 ocupación de usos

17 volumen primigenio

21 comunicaciones según CPI

24 híbrido urbano

27 migraciones domésticas

28 hibridacion doméstica

29 paisaje interior

NOX is not an architectural agency in the traditional sense of the term. Lars Spuybroek is just as busy producing videos, books, magazines, websites and multimedia installations. In his view, the technological revolution ushered in by computers no longer allows people to stay within the boundaries of a single discipline. The computer is not so much a simple representational tool as an instrument that blazes trails to another world; by cultivating linkage, superposition and interaction in data systems that it would have been impossible to put together before, NOX escapes from the usual logical systems of architecture. It makes use of every kind of technique and technology and applies them both in the creative process and in the final product, which are inseparable. He focuses on the idea that information should not intervene at a particular moment of the design, but rather that it is part of a process that is permanently structuring the forces in question, within an interactive system. ◆

OfftheRoad_5speed
Prefabricrated, non-standard housing along the A58 motorway, Eindhoven, Netherlands, project, 1999–2000
[Lars Spuybroek with Joan Almekinders, Remco Wilcke and Gemma Koppen]

OfftheRoad_5speed is a commission from a builder of single-family houses, the TRUDO Housing Corporation, which had noticed a widening gap between a standardized supply of housing and a steadily expanding and diversifying demand. The way it responds to the dual need for mass production and broad typological variety makes OfftheRoad_5speed more than a mere architectural project: what it proposes is a complete system for production of non-standard, prefabricated housing on a massive scale. Designed as an actual process, the project is intended to react to and incorporate every phase and aspect of the question: town planning, architectural, technical and so on. Lars Spuybroek himself compares OfftheRoad_5speed to a house-producing machine, capable of functioning at different, interconnected levels and of adapting to each shift in perception of the problem, just as a car's gearbox adapts to the speed of the vehicle. Each of its phases is characterized by an individual 'sphere of action' of which the project must integrate, 'absorb' the specific forces. '1st gear', the first of OfftheRoad_5speed's five stages, is entitled 'interference (level of urbanism)' and consists of defining the pattern – or rather the disposition – of the houses. Rejecting the rigidity of a right-angle grid, NOX offers a moiré pattern generated by interference from a series of 100 parametric lines running perpendicular to the motorway. The project's '2nd gear', termed 'bending (level of typology)', is the point at which the imprint of the houses on the ground and their setting on the site is formalized. The basic 23 x 6–metre rectangular module allotted to each is going to be deformed by contact with the force field generated by the first phase, thus giving rise to an infinite series of variations. As it moves into the '3rd gear', called 'tunnelling (level of programme)', typologies have to be developed. Each bent module is separated out into three separate lines of force, three 'deepenings' of the programme corresponding to three different programmatic aspects of the house: the collective, the private and the intimate. Developing not so much a programme as 'the potential for a programme', this phase generates in all 3,600 different configurations. With the '4th gear', or 'panelling (level of manufacturing)', the phase of computer-assisted production of the prefabricated panels is begun. Lastly, the '5th gear' – 'lifestyling (level of living)' – will consist of kitting out the inside of the houses. According to NOX, the production of domestic accessories can be approached in the same non-standard spirit as the house itself. ◆

Pierre Chabard

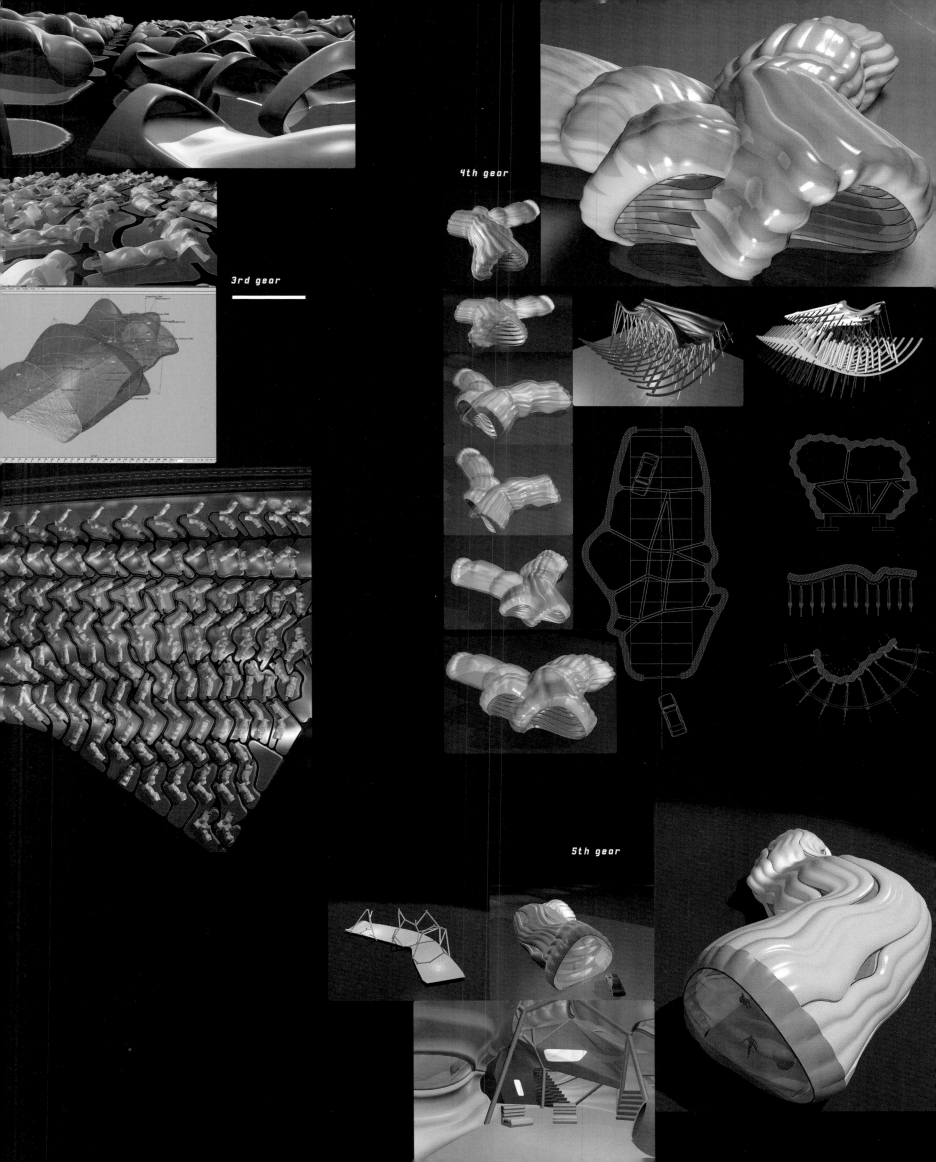

3rd gear

4th gear

5th gear

la Forge

Quatre maisons dans la forge (NIVEAU R+1)

Quatre maisons dans la forge (NIVEAU RDC)

Quatre maisons dans la forge (NIVEAU R-1)

| France |

Odile Decq Benoît Cornette

Odile Decq (1955), Benoît Cornette (1953-1998)

'**A**nswering the question of desire by bringing pleasure' – a programme for present-day architecture that Odile Decq readily refers to by quoting the line from Paul Virilio. Since 1985, Decq & Cornette have been producing an architecture where the incorporation of movement creates tension and complexity in the perception of space, challenging the place of the body in space and architecture. So no project is ever the outcome of a deliberate approach, with the imposition of a form or style. The primary work still involves a re-programming and a redefinition of the programme that tries to get rid of all the conformist features of the commission. The various elements and components that provide the apparent unity of the architecture are analysed one by one, and factored into an order that is no longer defined by spatiality; they are subject to a certain number of operations, which they call inversion, hypertrophy, displacement, shift, deformation, fragmentation . . . Odile Decq also doubles as a teacher, mainly at the Ecole Spéciale d'Architecture in Paris. ◆

Houses for Nomad Living
Brussels, Belgium, project, 2001

These ten or more housing units are part of a project to convert the old veterinary school at Cureghem. Built at the end of the 19th century, this consists of some 15 buildings whose architecture, although highly ordered in appearance, affords considerable scope for interior development. Conceived as an urban project, this operation gave Odile Decq an opportunity to experiment with a truly mixed programme, flexibly combining living space, work and leisure. A series of secondary buildings on the edge of the site (stable, boiler room, forge, etc.) have been converted into living spaces. These houses, which are all different and make use of the existing conditions, are organized in keeping with original scenarios of flexibility based not on movable partitions but on a spatial 'plasticity' and the experimental use of fittings and furniture.

The Stable
The old stable building contains four duplex or triplex 'houses'. The houses are fitted out with programmed 'boxes' that repeat an identical module (about 3.7 by 1.1 metres) and contain kitchen or bathroom elements or perhaps storage units. When the boxes are closed, the spaces are 'deprogrammed' and ready to be appropriated. When they are open, the whole space becomes a generously proportioned kitchen or big bathroom. The boxes vary between each house, each one offering a different implantation and appearance.

The Boiler Room
The old boiler room with its coal cellar has four houses and a cafe that takes advantage of the monumental presence of the boiler and its chimney. Two of the houses are duplexes, with 'night' spaces located up at the top, under the roof. The ancillary rooms are grouped together in a box that also serves as a bedroom/mezzanine. A third house occupies the ground floor and is extended towards the garden. It is divided (day/night) by a fitted-out 'wall'. The 'night' part is itself divided by a 'bath/box', close to the garden. The fourth house is in the basement and is lit from two courtyards and a garden. The boxes here take the form of two longitudinal strips crossing the space all the way to the garden.

The Forge
In the old forge, where four other houses are located, Odile Decq has kept the old hearths along the middle wall. Organized as triplexes, they spread out over two floors, making use of the place's verticality. The basement is lit from above through skylights. Here too it is the singular features of the setting that have determined the architectural individuation of each housing unit and its particular scenario of domestic flexibility. ◆

Pierre Chabard

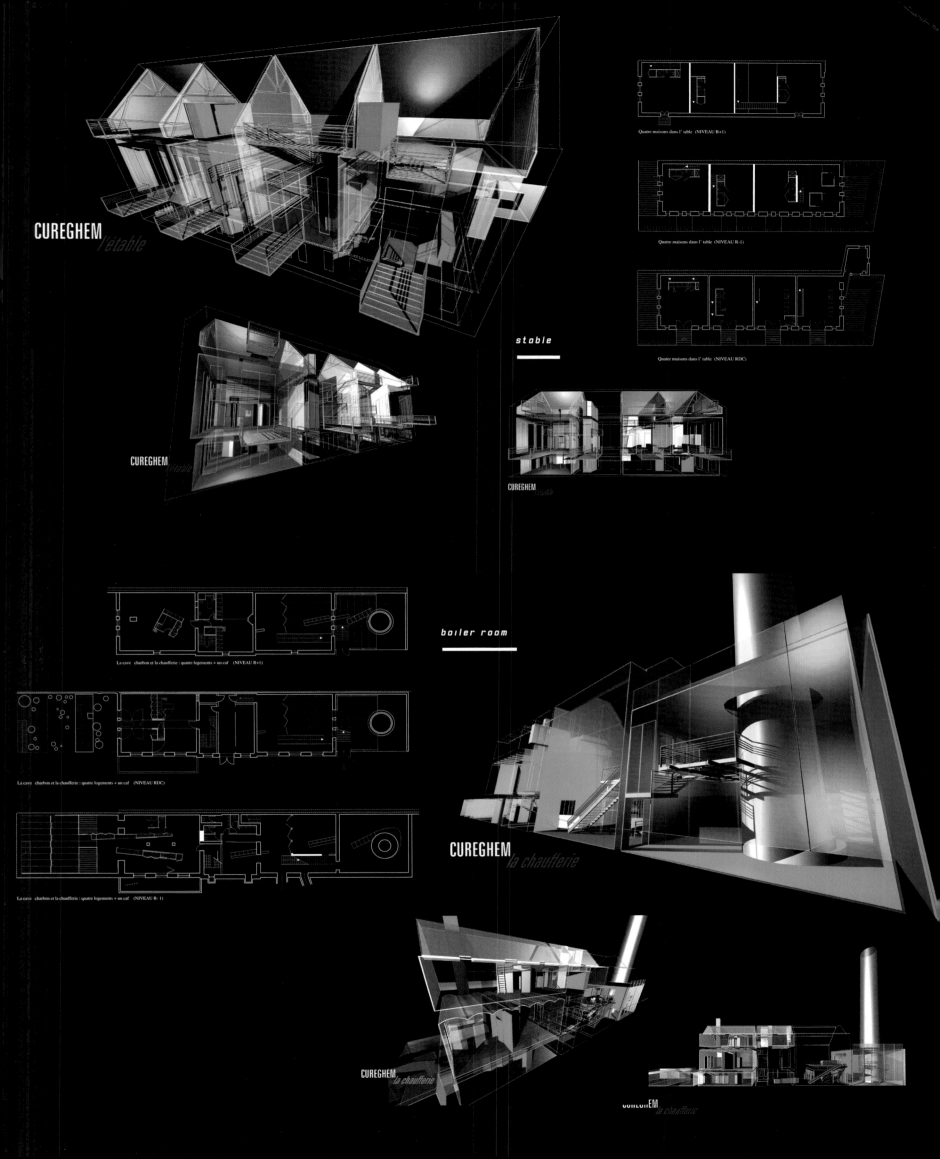

CUREGHEM *l'étable*

CUREGHEM *l'étable*

Quatre maisons dans l' table (NIVEAU R+1)

Quatre maisons dans l' table (NIVEAU R-1)

stable

Quatre maisons dans l' table (NIVEAU RDC)

CUREGHEM *l'étable*

boiler room

La cave charbon et la chaufferie : quatre logements + un caf   (NIVEAU R+1)

La cave charbon et la chaufferie : quatre logements + un caf   (NIVEAU RDC)

CUREGHEM *la chaufferie*

La cave charbon et la chaufferie : quatre logements + un caf   (NIVEAU R- 1)

CUREGHEM *la chaufferie*

CUREGHEM *la chaufferie*

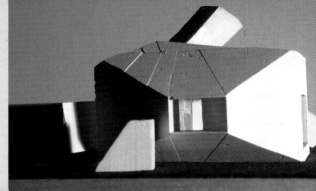

| Netherlands |

OMA (Office for Metropolitan Architecture)

Rem Koolhaas (1944)

The OMA enjoys an outstanding position in the Dutch and international architectural landscape. Most of the works produced by the agency can be regarded as research projects. Over and above its actual works, the agency is primarily a laboratory continuously concerned with finding new solutions to the problems of a society typified by overpopulation and instability. The OMA was founded in 1975, in London, by Rem Koolhaas, in collaboration with Elia and Zoe Zenghelis and Madelon Vriesendorp. In 1978, the Rotterdam agency opened, and duly became the principal agency. As a journalist, writer and scriptwriter before becoming an architect, Rem Koolhaas, who in his youthful years was close to the Situationist movements, has taken up a position as an observer of present-day reality. For him, architecture and city planning are more an extrapolation of what we perceive to be reality than the projection of an ideal order or good intentions; there is no point in wanting to control the future, even though this is, paradoxically, what the architect does. ◆

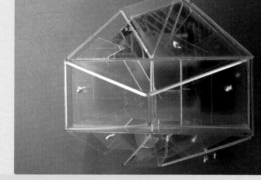

Y2K
Rotterdam, Netherlands, project, 1998
[Rem Koolhaas, Fernando Romero, Erik Schotte, Uwe Herlyn]

Just after completing the Bordeaux house, Koolhaas came up with this project in response to a commission from a client as rich as he is unusual. The man's love of a bit of countryside near Rotterdam prompted him to buy a plot of land and then the fields around it in order to ensure the longevity of his view of this chosen scene so that he could build his house there without worry. The programme he entrusted to Koolhaas is determined by three interconnecting components of his psychology: his hatred of disorder, his millenarianism (which inspired the name of the project) and his ambivalent relationship with his family, as manifested in his desire to differentiate communal spaces from his private environment. But the key element of the programme, the 'simple and stupid' restriction that Koolhaas had to take on board, concerned the integration of the landscape view, the construction of the house 'around' that view. The day rooms are thus organized like a great 'tunnel' that crosses the house from one side to the other, as if the retinal cone had been petrified and become architecture. This tunnel was the first step in the project, the one that dictates the organization of the other interior spaces. These are then built on to the four sides of the tunnel, this process of agglomeration being what produces the external volume of the house. This basic dialectical opposition between the main space, the tunnel, treated as a great empty space, and the rest of the house, treated as a full one, recurs identically at every level, and

particularly in the organization of the secondary spaces. The space is 'sculpted', carved out of the 'mass' of the house. But, as in certain buildings by Borromini, this full form is merely an 'open pouch' that itself contains spaces, empty areas that repeat this same hierarchic principle ad infinitum. In Y2K, the pouch is used particularly as storage space: 'Thus the house would be completely empty, made up of abstract or bluntly concrete spaces, mysterious spaces containing mess, services and other necessary installations'. But the history of this house does not end there. The client's tenseness and doubts about the project, the continual evolution of his desires — making the house turn about its axis, building the pouch in translucent materials, etc. — finally led OMA to withdraw from the project. As an epilogue, Koolhaas, who at the same time had been invited to take part in the international competition for the Casa de Musica in Porto, explains that this abortive Y2K project adapted superbly well to this new concert hall programme. And it was indeed after this strange detour that Koolhaas won the Porto contract in June 1999 and thus prolonged the conceptual history of Y2K. ◆

Pierre Chabard

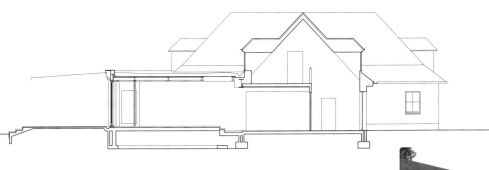

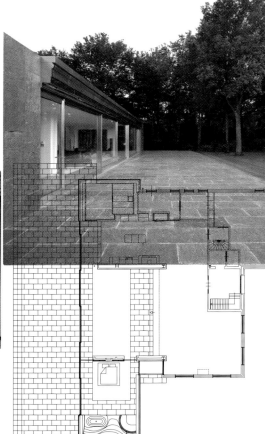

One Architecture

MATTHIJS BOUW (1967), JOOST MEUWISSEN (1950), DONALD VAN DANSIK (1951)

One Architecture was founded in 1994 in Amsterdam, with two members: Joost Meuwissen and Matthijs Bouw. Joost Meuwissen is a critic and theoretician, who also teaches in the city planning faculty at the University of Technology in Graz, Austria. In the 1970s, he played a very important part in introducing the Netherlands on to the international stage. Together with Matthijs Bouw, who is of a younger generation, they form one of the currently most unpredictable and eccentric teams in the Netherlands. Their extension project for the house in Eindhoven illustrates this desire for subversion, which was already present in the early and provocative conceptual works produced by Matthijs Bouw. By respecting the wishes of the clients and introducing references verging on mockery, their approach is akin to that of many contemporary artists, such as Jeff Koons, to whom they readily admit their debt, and Berend Strik, with whom they work on a regular basis. ◆

Extension to a villa near Eindhoven
Netherlands, 1998–99

'Fifteen years ago the client, who loves France, built a house for his family in the style of a French villa. Over the years, he has acquired most of the land around the house in order to keep the view towards the surrounding nature reserve open. Last year he discovered that the relationship between the now immense garden and the small villa needed redefinition. The rather closed villa was not in tune with the family's lifestyle, which centred on the garden.

In a brochure of villa examples we put together for our client, ranging from Palladio to Ben van Berkel and OMA, only Mies's Farnsworth House met with his approval. In the subsequent design, we interpreted Mies in the manner of Schinkel in order to achieve a simple increase in size. Loosely using classical design techniques, we made a splendid extension of the house towards the garden. The anachronistic Mies is loaded with contemporary technical features. The classical stainless-steel cornice, for instance, contains a 5-metre movable awning, a heating and anti-bug system for the terrace, and lighting fixtures reminiscent of those on the front of a car.'

One Architecture got straight to the facts, pragmatically adopting the approach taken by their clients, who had spent 15 years extending their garden. The agency put forward a catalogue of 'dream villas' aping all those glossy magazines full of ideal-home 'cocoons'. Without hesitation, they fitted the desired model. This project integrates the suburban landscape and its discontinuous individual plots, making it the point of departure instead of a stumbling block.

Still, an element of irony is apparent. In passing, the 'great masters' are subjected to the judgement of all and sundry. Conversely, suburbanism is treated as 'pornography', a place authorizing individualized lifestyles 'outside formal rules, propriety and discipline'. If the fluid relationship to the garden, the continuous glazed façade and the free, open plan all come from Mies, the stone base, the classicizing cut of the steel cornice on the façade and the continuity of materials from the base to the walls all take their inspiration from Schinkel. Other quotations are even more explicit. The sliding walls between the living room and the bedrooms are those of OMA's Linthorst house and the floor of the bathroom refers to the architecture of Lars Spuybroek. And yet all this is a long way from postmodernism. The collage is not an attempt to give the building meaning. Rather, it stems from the pragmatic use of tried and trusted solutions. The result is a meticulous, detailed and subtly provocative architectural space. ◆

DESIGN TEAM: Matthijs Bouw, Joost Meuwissen, Frank Toese
Alex de Jong, Stefan Bendiks
CURTAIN: Berend Strik
CONSTRUCTION CONSULTANT: constructiebureau Potter, Amsterdam
INSTALLATION CONSULTANT: HAI Installatietechniek, Amsterdam
CONTRACTOR: Van der Pas, Oss

Model 1
Romeo
and
Julia

Model 2
Farnsworth
House
penetrates
French
villa

Model 3
Penetration
Half way

Model 3
Penetration
Completed

Model 4
Carefully
Withdrawing

> NEWS FLASH
shape your own house !

> SUBSCRIBE TO OUR
  NEWSLETTER

> NEW USER?
create a new account

>USER LOGIN
username:

password:

oosterhuis.nl

Kas Oosterhuis (1951) Ilona Lénard (1948)

Kas Oosterhuis teaches at Delft University of Technology, from which he graduated, and at the the Architectural Association (London). He set up Kas Oosterhuis Architekten in Rotterdam with Ilona Lénard in 1988. For Oosterhuis, complexity of form, of volume, is linked to the complexity of the information being processed and the meanings that are developed. In this regard the practice has always considered computers as a basic tool, one that they were among the first to use. This approach ended up producing forms that are endowed with relatively simple sculptural forms on the outside in contrast to the movement and complexity within. The practice subsequently led them to set up Internet 'workshops' enabling web users to work together on the construction of a given form. Oosterhuis's radical view sees the 'artificial mass' created by humanity as an 'extension of ecological nature', overcoming any possible break between the natural and artificial within one global system. ◆

VariomaticSM
Zoetermeer, Netherlands, 2000

Interactive aspects of parametric designSM: This new concept for a catalogue house is elastic in all directions. In height, depth and width. The clients define the overall dimensions of the house, the place where the kitchen should be or a solar water-heater. They can moreover choose among many materials and colours to finish the volumes: reed, wood, metal, tiles, PVC. The buyers being co-designers, it is virtually impossible to have two identical houses. Variomatic offers actual styling instead of selling architectural 'clichés'.

Relaxed living: This project was originally developed for a Dutch study, of which the basic idea was to show that landscape development, architecture and consumer-friendly building can actually go together. The research results are a response to mass-production housing and ready-made houses of master builders' catalogues.

The Variomatic familySM: The object type of the Variomatic family, the Variomatic S(culpture), is placed on top of the landscape. The landscape type, the Variomatic L(andscape), is literally embedded in the landscape. Moreover, there is a Variomatic Classic S (two floors with roof) and a Variomatic Cabrio L (ground floor with convertible rooftop).

Building up the VariomaticSM: The curved forms of the house offer the biggest possible interior room with regard to the enveloping surface and provide its inhabitants with an enhanced spatial experience. The ground-floor interior is made of stone materials. Around it, a primary steel construction

with secondary wood construction is finished with multiplex on the outside and plasterboard on the inside. The roof is clad with an ultra-light yet very strong and durable sprayed skin (all RAL-colours are available).

DurabilitySM: Thanks to the heat buffers on each wing of the ground-floor living area, the house has less energy loss during the winter and does not get overheated in the summer. Durable building also means compact building. Because of its rounded shape (in plan as well as in section), the house can retain its own energy as long as possible. Durability also means flexibility of usage in the long run. In principle, the warm middle house can be subdivided; only the position of the staircase, the toilet and the technical room is fixed.

Interactive websiteSM: Variomatic offers a new interactive approach to catalogue housing. The client chooses his preferred shape using the images on the website. The elastic geometry of Variomatic is linked to the database where the surfaces, volumes and the expected costs are calculated. After having shaped his/her own Variomatic house, the client can order a scale model or a set of drawings or can directly apply for building permission if (s)he already owns a plot. ◆

oosterhuis.nl

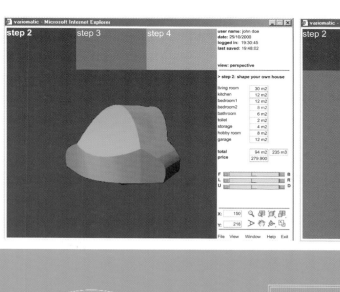
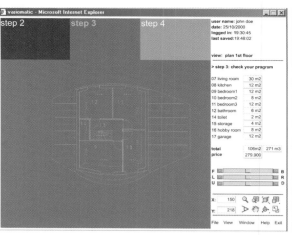
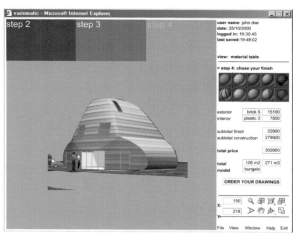
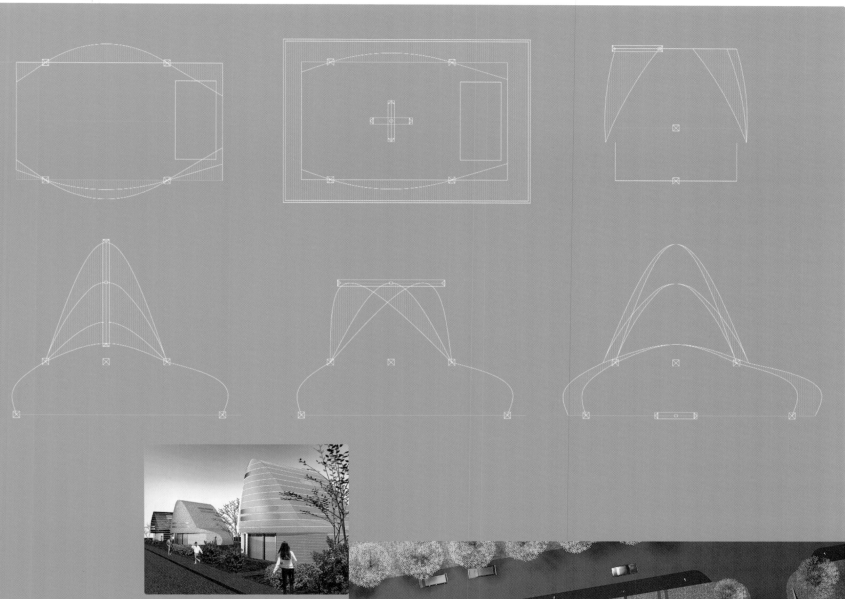

24620 West McNichols

from Detroit

| USA |

Kyong Park DCDC/UDMA |

KYONG PARK

After leaving Storefront for Art and Architecture as its founder (New York, 1982–98), Kyong Park founded the 'International Center for Urban Ecology' in Detroit, a city at the terminal stages of 20th-century urbanism and, therefore, an ideal place to imagine the next state of the city. Within the ICUE project, he invited international artists, architects and others to collaborate with political activists and urban pioneers of Detroit, generating experimental urban fora, such as 'Architecture of Resistance' (1999). As the visiting scholar of urbanism at the University of Detroit Mercy, School of Architecture, he began 'Adamah: A New Equity for Detroit', a fictional utopia about the eastern suburbs of Detroit in the year 2010 and 2075 (with Stephen P. Vogel and students), in addition to producing and directing 'Detroit: Making it Better for You', a 2-channel video project on the construction of Detroit. In '24620', a multimedia travelling house project, Park is working with Detroit Collaborative Design Center (DCDC) and its director, Daniel Pitera. ◆

24620
Orléans, France, installation, 2001 |

'24620' is a multi-media architectural installation, where a simple empty house from Detroit is taken down, cut up and transported across the Atlantic so it can be reassembled in Orléans. Clumsily put back together, the house is a 3-dimensional billboard that expresses and promotes the dysfunctional city as a new tourist destination, where seasoned tourists can experience the phenomena of dismemberment, space, economy and race in a highly realistic environment. As the city from which it originates struggles to cope with the relentless abandonment of spaces, the product of 50 years of depopulation – characterized by scores of empty or burnt houses – this transport is simply a new way of helping Detroit to look better by getting rid of its eyesores. If successful, we expect that more nations and cities would want houses like this, making Detroit the leading exporter of empty houses worldwide. As a proof that there are plenty of them to go around, pieces from hundreds of empty and burnt houses will be stuffed under this one, and pictures of these houses will be displayed inside so that future house adoptions can be more personal.

To further emphasize our humanitarian goal, the house comes equipped with a very special 2-channel video projection called 'Detroit: Making it Better for You', which will present a mosaic of images on the destruction of Detroit, along with visions of its possible future. Its 'drive-by-shooting' video technique is emblematic of the mythology of Detroit as the 'Motor City', offering street-level views of the urban clashes between inner-city emptiness and suburban bliss. Within the contradiction between generations of neglect and current redevelopments of the city cen-

tre, this video paints the conflict between the sustainability of the local community against the greed of the global economy, the struggles of grass-roots community activism against the collusion of political power and industry.

Inspired by the success of reality-based adventure television programmes, 'Detroit: Making it Better for You' aims to combat the three forms of lethargy that weigh on urban thought and actions: the Koyaanisqatsi syndrome that gnaws at academics and professionals; antiquated intellectual monologues, spread by trained eco-terrorists from the Sierra Club or associations like the Gore Institute; the almost religious concept of suburban zones known as the New Urbanism. Conceived as a means of defence against the invasion of generic and franchised cultures from the genome of spaces – a Koolhaasian update on Ayn Rand's 'Atlas Shrugged', now read from Lagos to Pearl River Delta – this video is a premature tribute to Detroit, the last real city to die in this world, at least in its developed sectors. ◆

Kyong Park

Architect: Dan Pitera
Coordinator: Andrew Sturm
Video documentation: Allegra Pitera, Kyong Park
Photo documentation: G. Todd Roberts
Project crew: Saad al-Ajemi, Graig Donnelly, Jason Fowler, Manny Garza,
                           Matt Gerard, Andrew Lehman, Jessica Schulte, Mike Spencer

Technical advisers: Matt Tatarian, Chris Turner, Sean Cruger, Greg Jackunis

ArchiLab 2001

to Orléans

before · · · · · · · · · · · · after

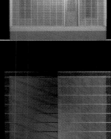

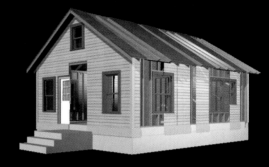

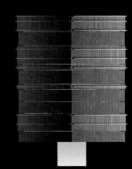

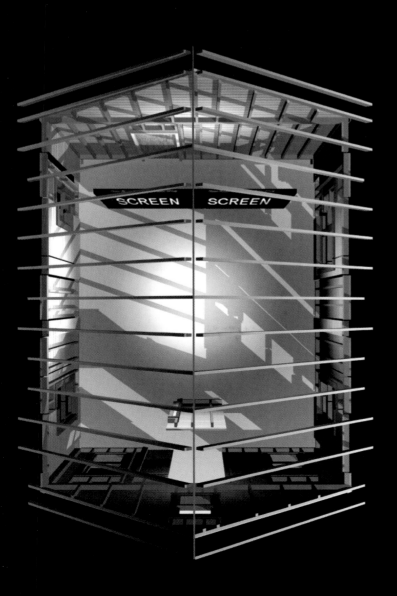

SCREEN SCREEN

| France |

P+L A. with AIR

Laetitia Perrin (1973), Mathieu Lesavre (1972) with Cyrille Hanappe (1969)

Laetitia Perrin and Mathieu Lesavre are graduates of the Ecole d'Architecture de Paris-Villemin. They founded their agency in 1998 after working for Jean Nouvel. They developed their practice though competition designs and by recasting interior spaces, working on all scales. They also got involved with graphic design: for example, they made the promotional stands for the 'Jet' pen and the Christmas visuals for Louis Vuitton. After several years working with an agency in Hong Kong, Cyrille Hanappe, a finalist of the annual French national competition for the best architecture degree in 1998, made a name for himself with his design for 40 housing units in Calais, which came second in the competition and was widely reproduced (*Architecture d'Aujourd'hui, Techniques et Architecture*). The three architects decided to work as a team on the competition for the 'Familistère de Guise' (Guise Phalanstery), organized by the Fondation J.-B. Godin. Their project offers a critical reading of its founding ideas. ◆

Citadium
Guise Phalanstery competition, 2000

'**A** map of the world without utopia on it is not worth looking at, because it excludes the only country where mankind is constantly landing' (Oscar Wilde).

The only aspect of the generous ideas present at its inception that the Godin phalanstery seems to have kept is its architecture. And yet the idea of a safe community, the comfort of a place where everything is designed to promote the quality of life for its residents, is undeniably attractive, even if the accompanying ideas of social control will now seem obsolete.

Community values seem to have been supplanted by those of sharing and exchange, of encounter and openness to others. The notion of collectivity has replaced that of community.

For this contemporary take on Godin's project, we are proposing a place that constitutes a centre for living and collective activities, a place that is open to the outside world and at the same time attentive to solving the problems of proximity that condition everyday life.

The Citadium is located on sloping terrain, with, in the background, a clear view of the town of Guise and the phalanstery. The territory is organized around a programmatic LOOP, made up of a multiplicity of sequences.

At the centre, adjacent to a stone square, a district library and an auditorium bring up to date the programmes proposed by Godin. The general form of the central building is designed as a direct homage to the island of Utopia, which 'forms a semicircle 500 leagues around, and has the form of a crescent'.

The large garden becomes gradually more private as one approaches the buildings. The plants standing at right angles to the façades define virtual limits without uselessly partitioning off the space. The space of the garden is prolonged in the space that continues towards the interiors of the housing. The idea of progression is also illustrated outside the LOOP. A series of 'active limits' such as the workshops or small shops/the pedestrian path/the private allotments/the car parks/the vehicular thoroughfares soften the distinction between inhabitants and visitors.

The housing is based on the principle of an 'interactive strip': a passageway (135 centimetre) along the front serves the whole housing unit. The partitions open on to this corridor, which allows all the rooms to enjoy light from two directions and to be extendable. Also, it would be possible for two apartments with separate entrances to share a bedroom. This system makes it possible to experiment with innovative modes of collective life involving autonomous groups. ◆

P+L A with AIR

TYPOLOGIE DE LOGEMENT T3 1/50°

SURFACE TOTALE
70 m²

TYPOLOGIE DE LOGEMENTS 1/100°

T5 DUPLEX
niveau haut

T5 SIMPLEX
Logement pour deux
familles monoparentales
101 m²

T5 DUPLEX
niveau bas
102 m²

T4 SIMPLEX
85 m²

T2 SIMPLEX
54 m²

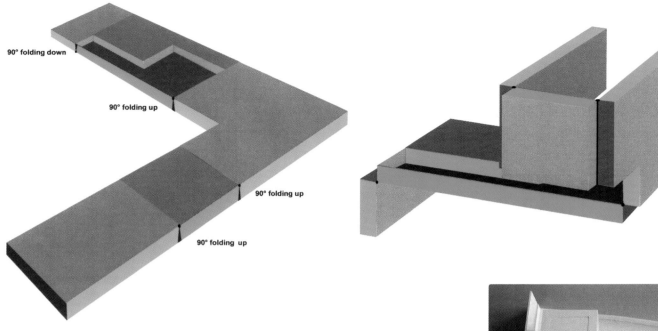

90° folding down

90° folding up

90° folding up

90° folding up

| Austria |

Pauhof

Michael Hofstätter (1953), Wolfang Pauzenberg (1955)

Michael Hofstätter and Wolfgang Pauzenberg, who both teach architecture at the Vienna Technical University, set up the Pauhof agency in 1986. The work of these two Viennese architects includes many different projects (submitted in particular to international competitions), exhibition design, installations and one or two rare and masterful constructed works. The rigorous and radical architecture of Pauhof explores the paths of a critical minimalism and a basic abstraction, which are both quite close to conceptual art. With an approach that both strips down and intensifies the modernist vocabulary, Pauhof is in fact seeking a real formal independence of the architectural object. This object is freed from all stylistic, historical and contextual reference, and stripped of all heteronomous determination, and as such is worked in a specific way and becomes just architecture. As a negative response to the excesses of Viennese postmodernism, this architectural self-reference is the very condition, for Pauhof, of a possible connection with the context, the city, and, above all, the subject summoned in its full power of perception. ◆

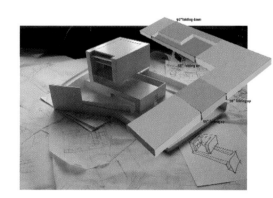

ST House
Linz, Austria, 2000–present

Particularly when we design a housing project, the idea of the urban whole is always a crucial part of the basic concept. It isn't, however, the formal adaptation that we seek, but the gulf between chaos and order, without which urban freedom, vitality, would not be possible in the first place. In this way possibilities for interpretation arise in a specific situation, beyond ostensible images of harmony, which hardly ever correspond to social reality anyway. But what is social reality today? The threat to the individual posed by overcommunication, which generally remains shallow, or the fragmentation of society through indiscriminate consumer behaviour or, on the other hand, perhaps the chance for individual originality through precisely this unprecedented spectrum of choice. If we transform this into the urban structure, we come up with either complete arbitrariness or differing wealth, or both at once. That would mean indifference. And it is precisely for these zones of urban indifference that we developed the ST house as a city dwelling whose precision of contextual integration allows infiltrations but whose form claims architectonic autonomy – a tensely fascinating contradiction that we value highly. The formations must be complex and open, must have dynamic sequences and calculated interstices, but all under the premise of a strong, orthogonal tectonics.

In the ST house – situated on a south-facing slope, planned for two clients from different generations and with varying demands – it is not the usual exterior walls that mark off the surrounding area. Here, it is a flat structure with several bends – 1.5 metres thick and 6.3 metres/10.4 metres wide – that protrudes on one of its narrow sides from the natural ground surface, folding out from there into a framework that first rests on a one-storey service tract before rising up, self-supporting, to embrace both upper floors. The usual separation of a house into façades, roofs, exterior and interior spaces has been done away with here. One ought perhaps to speak of a spatial continuum in which flat secondary rooms enclose the large main rooms so that these are given a specific orientation and make reference to the exterior. Interstices are created, whose glazed surfaces define climatic rather than optical borders. ◆

Pauhof

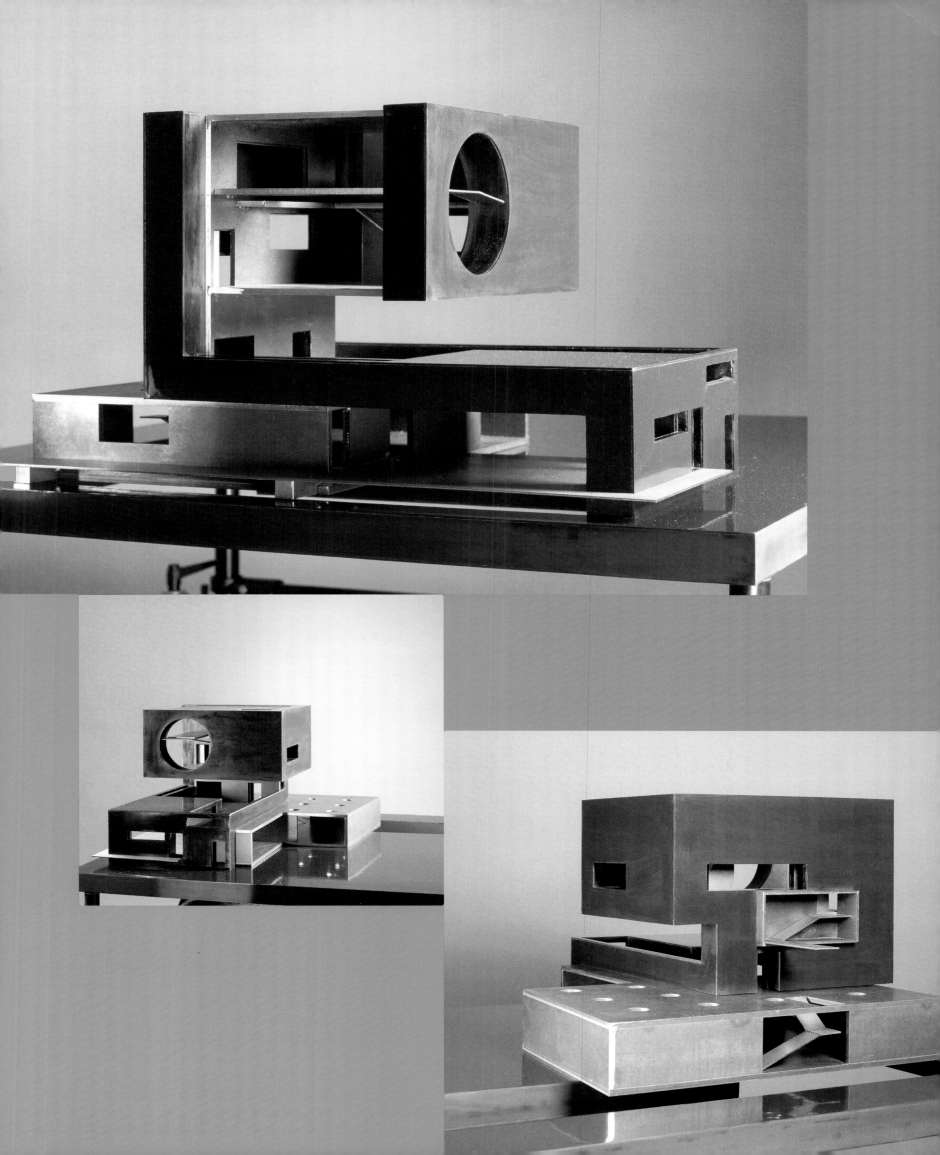

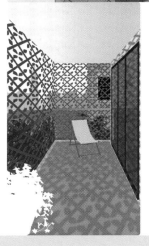

| FRANCE |

Périphériques

LOUIS PAILLARD (1960), ANNE FRANÇOISE JUMEAU (1962), EMANUELLE MARIN-TROTTIN (1967), DAVID TROTTIN (1965)

WHY PÉRIPHÉRIQUES?

BECAUSE! Périphériques Architects consists of two architects' agencies, Marin-Trottin and Paillard-Jumeau, plus all our 'super-collaborators'. This duality allows us to multiply the possibilities of contemporary architecture. The positions we take are radical ones. We believe that architectural activity must boldly 'play' according to its own self-imposed rules. And, as we all know, to start a game, to play, there have to be at least two of you. In our projects, therefore, we are going to try to apply an attitude that turns aside the demand (programme, site, budget, techniques, restrictions) expressed, often blandly, by the client and thus invent our own 'rules', a bit like those Danish filmmakers who upset the world of cinema with their Dogme concept. Laying false trails and being where we are not expected are thus part of our 'game'. Which is why we are publishers (IN-EX projects publisher), writers and reporters for an architecture journal (IN-EX project 01-02), organizers of and partners in events and exhibitions ('36 Models for a House', 'My Home Is Yours/Your Home Is Mine', etc.) both in France and abroad, and 'producers' (again, as in the movies) of town-planning projects where we invited colleagues to come and build (Urban Planning at Rezé in Brittany). But of course, we are also architects and we want to build big and often (see our monograph *Beaucoup-Minnesota*)! Generationally and historically, it's our turn: we are the post-*ACTUEL** baby-boomers! That is why we believe in a certain professional ethics: this means SHARING (doing projects as a group, inviting other architects: MVRDV and J. Moussafir for the Musée du Quai Branly; ACTAR, STALKER and T. Lacoste for Urban Planning at Rezé and Jakob + MacFarlane for the Café-Musiques at Savigny-le-Temple) and NEGOTIATION, which is the direct consequence of SHARING! This 'anti-ego' attitude comes naturally to us. We think that an ego multiplied by 2, 4 or 8 individuals is bound to be a more powerful tool for developing ideas. Because of course it is ideas – good ones, new ones, unexpected, odd, poetical or even bizarre ones – that motivate us to transform the 'hyper-reality' around us. ◆

* A French magazine synonymous with the '68 'me generation'

36 dwelling units for 5 houses
Paris, France, competition, 2000

Taking advantage of the land's closeness to the future 'green corridor' running between Boulevard Richard-Lenoir and the Saint-Ambroise church, Périphériques sites the housing units on the edge of the road, basing them on the dimensions of the urban house, while clearing courtyard areas at the back so as to be open to the future garden. The housing was divided into several units in order to afford vistas between the walls, views towards the park that lighten the presence of the opposite buildings. These passages, called 'viales', together with work on fragmented volumes, the lower slopes of the roofs and the use of 'more intimate' materials, all help to recreate an interior perception characteristic of the urban island, one that can be visually appropriated and is open to a diversity of uses. Two types of facing were chosen for the façades: a plastic climbing plants pattern on the façades overlooking the 'viales', designed to support real plants, and zinc 'scales', whose flexibility can be adapted to fit precisely over broken volumes. These form a continuous cladding over the main façades and the 'sitting dog' roofs. This work on the subtle integration of volumes and the reinterpretation of references goes hand in hand with work on openings. The windows constitute a whole project in themselves, protruding slightly from the façades. They are technically sophisticated: they have integrated blinds; they promote comfort, with reflective glass to protect privacy; and they are of multiple uses, the angles chosen to vary orientations and views, giving on to the garden or the sky. ◆

Bénédicte Grosjean

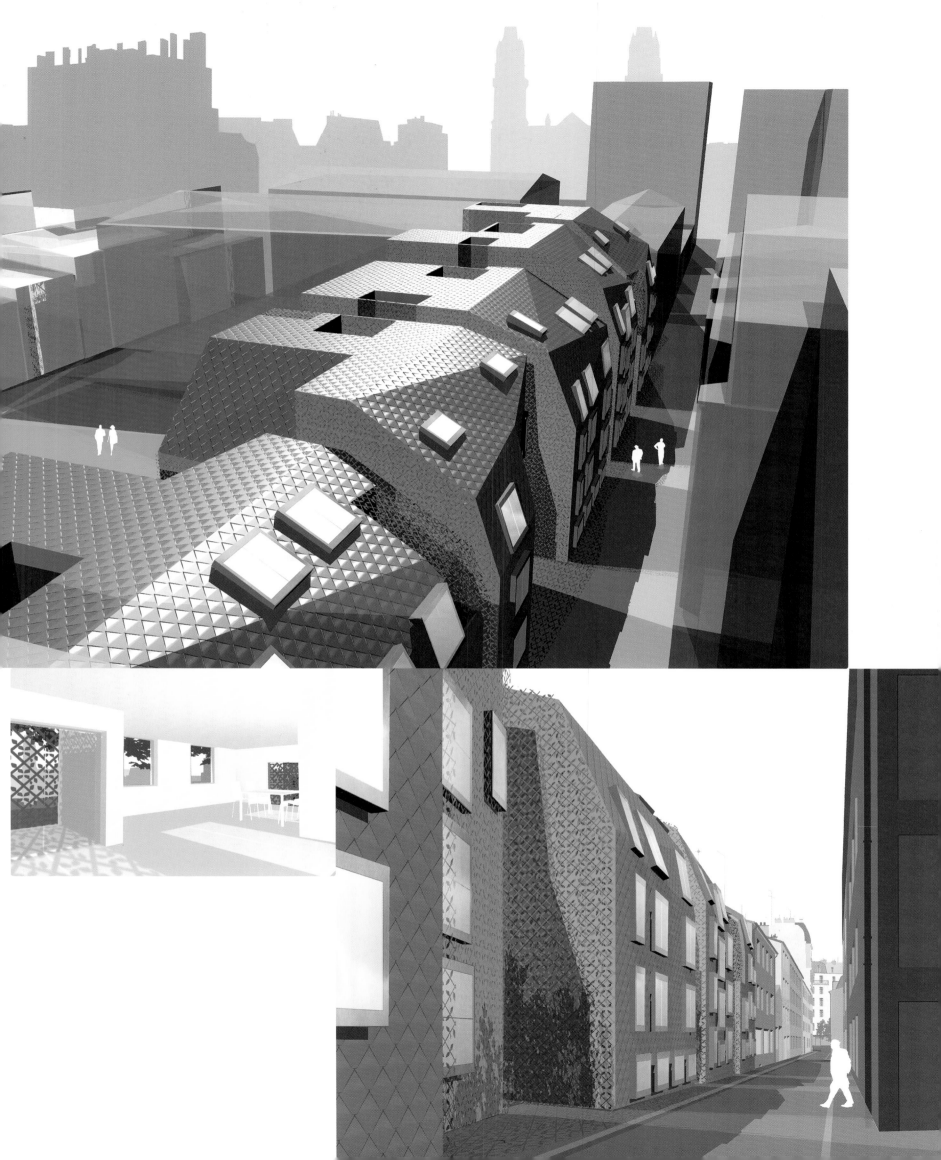

Dominique Perrault |

DOMINIQUE PERRAULT (1953)

As creator of the IESEE, an engineering school at Marne-la-Vallée (1984–87), and the Berlier Industrial Building in Paris (1986–90), Dominique Perrault won the international competition for the François-Mitterrand Bibliothèque de France in 1989, as well as the international competition for the Olympic Swimming Pool and Vélodrome in Berlin in 1992, the year in which he opened an agency in Berlin, 11 years after opening his Paris agency. Dominique Perrault also created the Usinor-Sacilor Conference Centre at Saint-Germain en Laye, the Mayenne Departmental Archives at Laval and the Meuse Departmental Administrative Centre at Bar-le-Duc, as well as various urban studies (the Island of Nantes, the Garonne embankments in Bordeaux, etc.). In 1993, he was awarded the Grand Prix National d'Architecture. Drawing his inspiration from Land Art, contemporary literature and music, Dominique Perrault is exploring all the connections between art, nature and architecture. He pursues his quest, project after project, for a 'zero degree' in architecture, a state of abstraction, of silence, where architecture could dissolve, disappear, becoming a pure and transparent spatiality. ◆

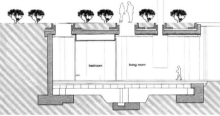

Villa One
Saint Cast, France, 1992–95

Is this house a house? That is the question, or the puzzle, that we set out to build. The presence or absence of architecture, a permanent theme in my work, which is more interested in landscape as the element that brings together architecture and nature. Is it possible to live underground? Can we go back to the cave living of the dawn of humanity, recapturing the original feeling of man's presence on earth? This architecture is an experiment that is constantly being renewed, an attempt to understand, to feel, an attempt to live better with and in our environment. This search for sensuous emotions that can be understood only by experiencing them physically brings to mind Francis Bacon's ideas about emotion in painting, which should make itself felt in the brain without transiting through the intellect. Genius loci, the joy of existing – these are some of the good reasons we architects have for building, thus showing that commonplaces and conventional assumptions do not constitute the rules of art, to which the conformism of our contemporary society refer much too often. ◆

Dominique Perrault

There are houses without ideas: rooms are put together at random and life goes on amidst the jumble of walls. There are also ideas without houses where we shiver, lost in the winter and the cold of impersonal concepts. Even when it's sweltering.

Dominique Perrault has managed to combine ideas with warmth – and more: the most lofty radicalism with freedom for all. Impishly overriding contradictions. As secretive and invisible as can be, not the slightest bit ostentatious, his house is also the most open building I know of. Dug into the hillside with which it merges. One could also say that the lawn that extends it enters it like a gentle green tide.

Likewise with the length of the huge 'living room': one could feel lost there, except that, for every moment of life, the play of mobile partitions allows you to create the space you need.

As a voyeur fascinated by everyday life, looking in from the outside, I imagine the scenes that are played out here, undisturbed; a lady does the ironing, children play, animals dream, a fire crackles in front of a woman reading, a man at the back is drawing. Like the compartments of a train, constantly modifiable, a train moving silently on, like life itself. Every house, whether lazy or wilful, is a moral, that is to say, a design. And every half measure is already a betrayal, that is to say, a wrench. This comfort born of boldness in nothern Brittany is deserving of praise. ◆

Erik Orsenna

Platane Architecte |

PLATANE BÉRÈS (1964)

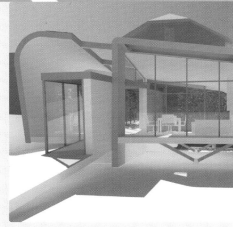

Platane Bérès graduated in 1990 from the Paris-Belleville School of Architecture, where he studied under Henri Ciriani, and has been working in Paris since then. With an attentive eye on the roles delegated to imagery and on what he calls 'sign-objects', which appeared with the digital technologies, he is exploring the influence of animated images on the design and reception of projects. To borrow his own words: 'Inhabiting is no longer being in a relationship, be it head on, static or relational, between an absolute exterior and an interior. These days, inhabiting means being in transit in a continuous space between a more exterior previous event and the more interior next event itself.'

A conspicuous presence in many competitions, Platane Bérès is best known for his two apartment blocks in Paris, one of which, for the Paris water board (SAGEP), succeeds in combining the residential function with industrial water-treatment facilities. He also works as a teacher in the computer laboratory at the Ecole Spéciale d'Architecture in Paris. ◆

Descamps House
50-square-metre extension, Paris (concept)

When a family begins to feel cramped, hemmed in by the walls of its house close to Paris, it is first of all the idea of reinterpreting everyday use and the existing spaces that speaks to architect Platane Bérès. The garden area is by no means small, but is little used because it falls away too steeply from the living spaces. All the necessary functions are there, but their layout needs changing. Beginning with the given and condensing the 'necessary' into a fresh vision of the volume opens the way to the pleasure of the 'little something extra' that is the extension – domain of the non-given – and so to ultimate 'sufficiency'.

How is the level of the living room to be linked to that of the garden? The architect suggests the simple means of appropriating the space: a sloping ramp, a roofed and glassed-in passageway. And where is this 'little extra', this breathing space for the house, to be put? It is to be a kind of wayside stop during the descent into the garden. As Platane Bérès has written, 'Space as such does not exist. The feeling of space arises, physically or mentally, as we move about; space exists in duration. All effects of tension, distortion, depth and transparency have to do with movement through space. In a photograph they are invisible. So this is what creates the spatial emotion contained in the experience of spatial movement'.

And as the journey unreels in time and space, a curved covering is grafted on to it, an outline that interrupts it just long enough to generate a pause, a widening, an opening out. Almost hovering above the garden, a space takes shape within a shell of laminated wood, an open ring floating between interior and exterior, between garden and terrace.

The project is also the illustration and development of a finely honed assessment of the influence of computer design on architectural process. 'By infinitely multiplying points of view, the computer wipes them all out. When you create your project inside the machine, you're enveloped – you could almost say imprisoned – in the projection. With the machine all the hidden parts of the project become visible, everything can become the subject of a drawing, of an act of will. From beginning to end of the project and at every level, your intentions hook into objects and turn them into signs.' And so, in apparent contradiction with its openness, it is from the inside outwards that this place was imagined and its contours laid down, in eye-height perspectives caught in movement as nearly as possible to its moments of use. ◆

Bénédicte Grosjean

| GERMANY |

Popp. Planungen Berlin |

WOLFRAM POPP (1957)

Having obtained his architecture degree after attending courses for only three semesters (he found them too rigid), Wolfram Popp presents himself as self-taught, rather autonomous and joyously stubborn. Refusing to think in terms of categories such as knowledge or experimentation, concept or detail, he is also equally dubious about the German tendency to separate theory from practice. This was the message of the 'power and impotence of ideas' seminars that he organized at the Technische Schule in Berlin. Thus 'mediummulti', his 1995 loft renovation on behalf of the Berlin multimedia firm Pixel Park, grew out of a constant movement back and forth between ideas and production, personal and collective work, experiment and rationalization. This flexibility is clearly expressed in the mobility of the architecture he proposes, with its boomerangs, spirals, 'surf' and 'swing'. His most recent substantial piece, the Platform House, is inventive too, by virtue of its original technical details but also because of its bold financial plan: the 'firm' supposed to buy the building and inspire confidence in investors was founded by the architect himself. ◆

Platform House
Choriner Straße, Berlin, 1998

Wolfram Popp built the 7-storey Platform House on Choriner Straße in Berlin-Prenzlauer Berg (ten apartments, two offices, one shop) with his own development company, at the same time refuting the well-established view that nothing new could be developed in residential architecture. Since Wolfram Popp professedly designs from the inside out, the concept of dwelling was central to the project.

Each of the two apartments per floor, measuring 108 and 79 square metres respectively, consists of a main area and a service zone that runs the full depth of the unit. The two are so sensitively correlated, both with one another and with the exterior, that the whole is a successful combination of spaciousness, comfort and privacy. Wolfram Popp doesn´t build closed rooms, but rather areas whose borders remain open and alterable, thereby offering a variety of options for use.

Two elements determine these relations. First, there are the platforms – hence the name – which are elevated platforms, each 40 centimetres high and 1.8 metres deep, running along the entire width of the apartment, at front and rear. These special spatial zones can be used as intimate and mediating areas between interior and exterior, especially when the ceiling-high French doors, which can be rotated 180 degrees, are opened, so that platform and balcony combine to form a generous loggia.

The second essential space-articulating element is what he calls the 'wall gills', reaching though the entire depth of the unit, and separating the main room from the service area. It consist of 12 wooden ceiling-high panels that run on 2 tracks above and 1 below, and can thus be slid as well as rotated. Through these gills, the space can be orchestrated according to need. Kitchen and bath can be either open or closed zones, and the entryway can either be a small hallway or disappear entirely. It goes without saying that these gill walls, along with most of the other built-in features and construction details, were discoveries of Wolfram Popp. With the exceptions of the reinforced-concrete structure and the prefabricated floors of exposed concrete, there are only specially developed prototypes. These include the sanitary facilities and even the large entry doors, which slide rather than open in the usual fashion. From overall conception to the tiniest detail, everything is placed for the sake of functionality and comfort. ◆

Angelika Schnell

popp planungen berlin Choriner Str.56 D-10435 Berlin
tel +49(0)30.440 516-74 fax -77 email popp@popp-planungen.de
wolfram popp

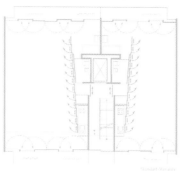

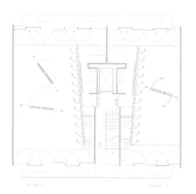

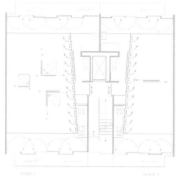

Estradenhaus

7 geschossiges Wohn- und Geschäftshaus in Berlin-Prenzlauer Berg

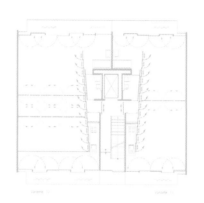

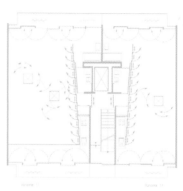

| NETHERLANDS |

Bas Princen

Bas Princen (1975)

Bas Princen graduated from the Eindhoven Academy of Design in 1998, attended the Berlage Institute and founded tjJlp designers in Rotterdam in 2000. He has never really designed housing. He cannot be considered an architect in this field if one considers housing as an object, something that one may buy. His work can nevertheless be regarded as having to do with the subject, if we regard ways of living in inhabited places and the spontaneous appropriation of abandoned spaces and plots of land without a specific function as both architecture and urban development. Bas Princen's photos show us bits of landscape not as an illustration of reality but as images of a potential reality to do with this landscape. They are often places that are first overlooked and start to trouble us only later; they are too abandoned for us to consider them as part of nature, whose initial function we forgot a long time ago, even when they have retained traces of it. What interests Bas Princen and what he photographs is when spontaneous appropriation of these places and of the signs of activities that have fashioned them reveals them in their real nature and restores a new reality to them; it is the changes in the landscape, which, through new uses, acquire a different meaning. ◆

Mutating Landscape
(Pure Pleasure Seekers), photos, 1999–2000

It is Sunday morning, 25th March 2001, 11:20 am. A group of 25 people from all over the Netherlands are gathering in the harbour of Rotterdam. Each of them is carrying: a tripod, a professional telelens camera, a mobile phone and a pair of binoculars. Yesterday they received a message from the Dutch birding association to say that the Provençal 'grasmus' (sylvia undata) was spotted sitting on a fence post in the harbour. Very common to the south of Europe, this bird can even be found in Brittany, but in the Netherlands it has been seen only once: in April of 1959! The group starts searching for the bird; at 12:50 am, they find it, gather around it in a small circle and shoot close-ups. At 1:05 pm, they return to their cars, where they exchange photos of their previous spotting.

I pack my camera too, another slow hunt is finished. Swimming in a marble quarry, climbing over a mound of rubbish and tracking birds in the harbour, with the right piece of equipment and information; anything is a potential field of play. The amateur will spend all his time and money to live his desire; to conquer the landscape by means of a product, a plaything. Every individual or group is a sample of a network, comprising specific technological innovations and communication codes, through which the use of landscape becomes lighter and increasingly temporal. Whether the landscape can be described conventionally, through designed surfaces, is therefore questionable. Rather, it is described through quickly evaporating forms of urbanism, pure pleasure colonization.

In this regard I am looking at the way people spend their spare time, mostly their leisure activities. The lifestyle nowadays seems to be more influenced by the equipment surrounding the individual rather than the place: places are not fixed. The same equipment in another landscape makes a new adventurous experience. So, the house is not the most interesting place to let the lifestyle define the programme, but rather the place where the individual is using his equipment, the periphery of the city, or the abandoned cultivated landscape, the spot where people are able to 'live their Identity'. What interests me most is the effect these groups have on the landscape, how they find and inhabit a space and how they seem to know how to make the most of leftovers.

The photographs of these temporary territories show just a few out of thousands of possible combinations of habitation. The project in this sense is not a material or an object, but an Arcadian perspective for the artificial/cultivated landscape. ◆

Bas Princen

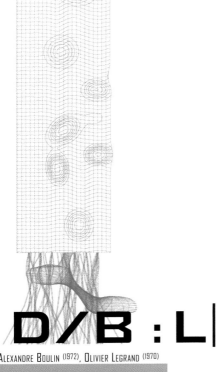

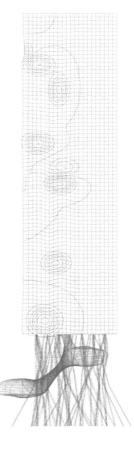

| France |

|R & Sie. D/B:L|

François Roche (1961), Stéphanie Lavaux (1966), Gilles Désévedavy (1963), Alexandre Boulin (1972), Olivier Legrand (1970)

At R & Sie. D/B:L 'making do to make less' signals a determination to develop within architecture a critical experience that will effect a mutation of its contextual parameters. Scenarios involving hybridization, grafting, cloning and morphing give rise to endless transformations of architecture in which the standard object/subject, object/territory polarities are abolished. Experimental and inventive, R & Sie. D/B:L architecture sets out to be deeply critical and 'deceptive', an architecture that 'often throws up a non-form seemingly made of low-grade materials', 'an architecture gone adrift', as Frédéric Migayrou puts it. Closely associated with the art world, the agency is active in many different fields: exhibitions at 'La Beauté' in Avignon in 2000, French and international pavilions at the Venice Biennale, event organization and publishing, coupled with François Roche's original approach to teaching at the ENSBA Paris and the Bartlett School in London. ◆

[Un]Plug Building & Friday Wear
Building of 'domestic offices' at La Défense, Paris, France, project, 2000

[Un]Plug Building was a commission from the R&D division of French national electricity supplier EDF, at the suggestion of Ante Prima, for a block of 352 offices and 22 conference rooms, with 16 offices per floor and 23 floors totalling 9,839 square metres.

Concept: The project proposes a 'concept building' along the lines of what the automobile industry is doing with its 'concept cars' that 'react' on contact with renewable energies. Hairy with solar sensors and swollen with photovoltaic cells, its curtain-façades are all energy-producing membranes. Thus the architecture simultaneously consumes and generates energy for injection into the network. Moreover, the building sets out to introduce work-related domestic-style practices. In the world of delocalized work spawned by the new technologies, two systems have intersected: one involves working at home, the other is the start-up 'live and sleep at the office' approach. This practice, among others, got the seal of approval a few years back with Friday Wear (wear what you like on Friday), which has now become Monday-to-Friday Wear. Are we looking at the latest metamorphosis of all-conquering capitalism here, or a whole new way of life? The project presents the tertiary sector not as an extension of the home but as a new social and tribal dimension in which architecture has to cope with sleeping, working, eating, screwing and all the rest. The organic aspect – the hairiness and the piercing – is the fortuitous expression of this approach.

The Renewable Energy Principle: The project is based on the transformation – the mutation – of a standard type of tall office building via contact with renewable energy, using vacuum-tube solar sensors and single-crystal photovoltaic panels. Thus the façade becomes 'reactive' to the new energy input. Several processes are involved:

Incorporation of excrescences of the 'ox-tongue fungus' type, with resultant swelling of the building's skin, or façade. These contain the conference rooms and include 400 square metres of photovoltaic panels for electricity supply.

Creation of a 'hairy' wall allowing for implantation of 4,500 linear metres of tubular solar sensors, for heating.

Integration into the structure of this curtain-façade of all systems – plumbing, electricity, etc. – allowing for exchanges within the building.

Disconnection of the building from the earth of the city, so as to utilize the plug or unplug mode in relation to the urban electrical network. ◆

François Roche

| GERMANY/USA |

Dagmar Richter Studio |

DAGMAR RICHTER (1955)

A graduate of the Royal Art Academy of Copenhagen and the Frankfurt Städelschule, where she studied under Peter Cook, Dagmar Richter divides her practice between Europe and the United States. After working in Copenhagen from 1982 to 1986, she spent 1986 to 1989 in Cambridge, Massachusetts, and in 1987 founded the Dagmar Richter Studio in both Berlin and Los Angeles. She has been teaching since 1991 in the United States – University of Illinois, SCI-Arc, Columbia, UCLA – and since 1999 at the Berlin Kunsthochschule. Her work, which has attracted considerable attention in many international competitions – notably West Coast Gateway (1988), Shinkenshiku-cha Membrane (1994), Time Capsule (1999), etc. – adopts a radically critical, analytical stance. Taking reality as an indecipherable text of which any human construction can provide only a skewed reading, she sees architecture as above all 'an art of copying, appropriation and recombination'. No longer inscription but description, it is a purely provisional means of understanding and representing the complexity of the world. ◆

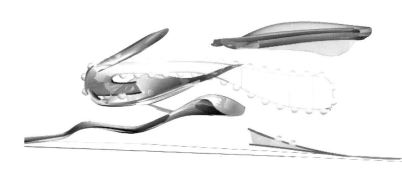

domestiCITY
project, 2000
(Dagmar Richter with Markus Sohst, Anthony Guida, Nina Yoon and Andrew Obermeyer)

This project offers a radical approach to the contemporary circumstances of domesticity. In the course of the 20th century the idea of the house as private interior space and the absolute antithesis of the external public domain underwent gradual breakdown. The ongoing development of the televisual and electronic media rendered the house permeable to the outside world, both as spectacle and point of view. Endlessly put on show and laid bare, the house has become 'un-private'. Yet, says Richter, this is only a partial view of the situation. The trend towards media exposure of the house went inextricably hand in hand with a move towards privatization of the public domain, itself transformed into 'an open urban field of privacy intimately meshed with domestic experiences networked by the car, the plane, the telephone and the Internet'. Examples are the massive expansion of home delivery and mail order selling of all kinds of consumer goods, which has extended the domestic space well beyond the strict limits of the house itself and projected even its most ontological functions towards the outside. For Richter, 'The whole world has become our home'. In this context each household becomes the local node – defined by its pure, unique location – of a general domesticity. Each of these nodes becomes the centre of an individual construction that reformulates, out of this unique situation, the totality of the city and the world, of the overlapping spheres of the real and the virtual.

Dagmar Richter uses the project to suggest the architecture of a house – or an anti-house – that fits with this new definition of domesticity: uniqueness of location, privatization of the world. Freed of all the functions it can delegate to the outside – eating in restaurants, sleeping in hotels, etc. – the house is now no more than the unique, subjective venue for construction of an individual identity and a private version of reality. What, then, remains of the 'house'? The owner's collection of objects, punctuating his biography, filling out his memory; his pet, that absolute symbol of the household; the 'front' of the house as a provisional stage for self-representation – putting the car on show, etc.; and the 'back' for a series of typically private rituals – gardening, barbecues, parties, etc. The actual architecture of the house lies in the intimately harmonious interlacing of the once-rival strips that are front yard and back yard. Rid of all functional demands, the house space fulfils the modernist 'open plan' dream in a shift to pure flexibility. ◆

Pierre Chabard

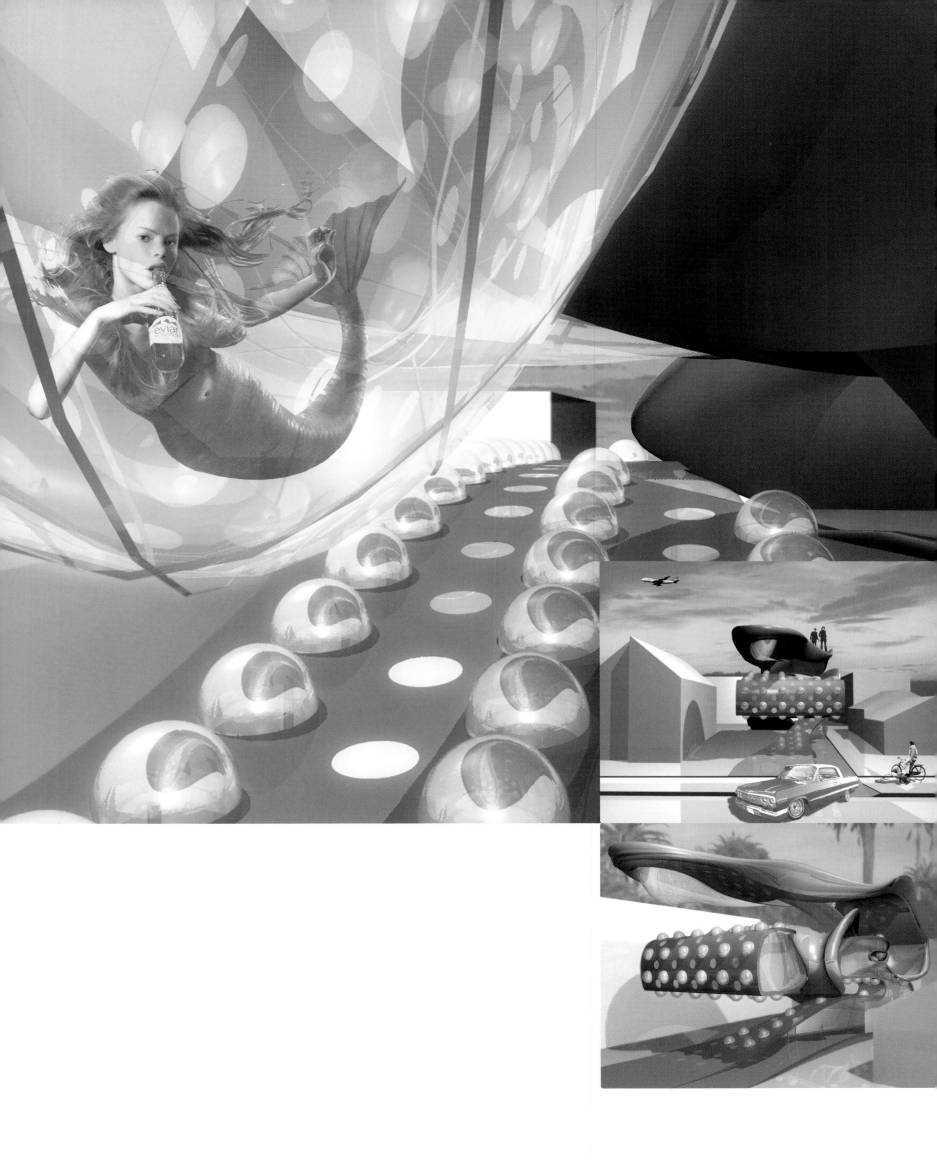

Housing, Strassgang, Graz, 1994

| Austria |

Riegler Riewe |

FLORIAN RIEGLER (1954), ROGER RIEWE (1959)

Based in Graz since 1987, Riegler and Riewe have designed several housing projects, as well as Graz Airport, while at the same time pursuing international teaching careers. For Riegler and Riewe, the architect's task consists in 'developing precise but open structures, which function as a frame for the complex flow of images of their use'. Thus they declare that their work has less to do with architecture itself than with its use and evolution in time. Riegler and Riewe raise questions about the reach of the abstract in the development of the real. Their housing units often deal with an in-between space that can be attached at random to the living room or the kitchen, giving free rein to appropriation. Drawing on structuralist language but avoiding the pitfall of the monumental, the architecture of Riegler Riewe develops stripped-down geometries, a painstaking attention to detail and sophisticated materials, even in very cheap housing units, like the Strassgang homes in Graz, where the sliding shutters, made of nylon fabric, subtly modulate the repetitive and static structure of the façade. ◆

The Abstract and the Real
In collaboration with Bas Princen, photographer

'**O**ur architecture is not one of built images. Creating open and yet precise structures, it provides the framework for the complex flux of images of use', say Riegler and Riewe. Indeed, there seems to be coincidence with structuralism, but only to a certain extent, because Riegler Riewe seem to have a healthy mistrust of the idea that life can really be captured in regular structures; nor are they interested in structuralism as a type of mimicry where the building becomes one with the town on an abstract level. By contrast, their designs appear almost like unavoidable bodies in their context. In this sense, they seem to be more influenced by the typological and monumental approach of the Tendenza. But their buildings are too modest to be monumental and they seem to consider typologies as a tricky business as well, because the idea behind them is that life will always unfold in more or less the same way.

Riegler Riewe's ground plans can be inhabited in many different ways and do not even show any real preference of the architect for a particular type of organization. If there are nevertheless certain parallels with structuralism, then it is the value Riegler and Riewe attribute to the 'in-between', reminiscent of the early Aldo van Eyck and even more of Herman Hertzberger. This is where the tenants' creativity is tested: whether they annex this room to the living room or the kitchen, whether it becomes a playground for the children, an interior terrace or an extension of the living room. In the residential complex in Mautern, however, the tension inherent in this in-between space is further heightened by maximizing the distance between the kitchen and living room and locating the other rooms between them. Like the open middle floor in Koolhaas's villas, the corridors in Riegler Riewe's apartments act like minute social condensers. But how this works is not easily illustrated in the design phase. Bas Princen's photographs of three Riegler Riewe residential projects show what happens if life takes over architecture. Although the photographs are beautiful, they are not flattering. Quite the contrary: they show architecture overgrown and worn, uncomfortable and often almost totally hidden under furniture, decoration, toys, plants, trees and improvised additions. But everybody is alive. Almost nothing is in keeping with the expected logic: the inhabitants have their own logic. ◆

Bart Lootsma

Housing, Casa Nostra, Graz, 1992

Housing, Mautern, 1992

| Spain |

S'A Arquitectos |

Carlos Sant'Ana (1973)

A graduate of the architecture faculty of Lisbon Technical University (1996) and the Polytechnic University of Barcelona (1999), Carlos Sant'Ana now divides his activity between these two cities, where he has become expert in questions of large-scale work, environmental issues and the new tools of architectural design while studying for several masters and postgraduate degrees. In Barcelona Sant'Ana has also had the opportunity to work with the team of Actar Arquitectura. Like them he thinks of himself as an 'actor of architecture', a producer of projects and books as well as exhibitions. The creation of a website in collaboration with Eva Disseny is just one of his related activities. Concerned to 're-democratize' architecture by linking it with and making it responsive to the local-global data flow, he eagerly explores the themes of flexibility and mobility. Thus, in his EuroPAN-DOM project he has developed a design that can take on board urban growth and spontaneous architectural development.

◆

NUC – Nomad Use Camaleonics |
Project, 2000

'NUC - Nomad Use Camaleonics' is a house designed for 'nomads', for those who want to have a house without owning land; to have a home but not a fixed place; to choose and then change; to belong to no background but to draw on all roots: a room with a view, in nature, isolated but connected. Also essential is the desire to adapt one's own way of life: there are no stereotyped ways of life – not any longer. Everything can be adapted and personalized: clothes and hair, food and beliefs, tattoos and screen savers. Self-transformation, flexibility – it's all possible. So why not with houses?

Sant'Ana seeks to follow his desires as closely as possible by generating a system that allows him to integrate a growing number of formal and programmatic variables, independently of any set physical context.

He has designed a single, prefabricated module, which repeats itself by turning around an axis. One flat side, one round side, one glassed-in, the other opening out: each desired function fits in and finds its place. The LIVING section opens up on the left and the kitchen faces right. The space breathes, widening towards the top. In contrast, the bedroom and the dining room widen downwards, towards the living area. The bathroom is toplit, and offers itself up to the sun like a swimming pool. The garage is anchored to the ground and the garden opens to the sky, the bottom being filled with earth.

The principle thus developed is exploited in every detail: by joining up, end to end, the modules produce extra spaces between them at every quarter-turn. These offer new sideways views and allow rays of light to play over the surfaces.

The desire for original personal appropriation and adaptation really comes into play in relation to the quality of the materials and the diversity of textures. Here it can adopt a playful, natural or 'hip' character. It would be possible to download the extremely rich cladding for the surfaces of the building from the web. At the same time, this 'digital skin', which simulates the scales of a chameleon, is above all a reference to and reminder of nature. It is a means of integration into the environment, whatever this may be.

◆

Bénédicte Grosjean

S2   S5   S6   S7   S8

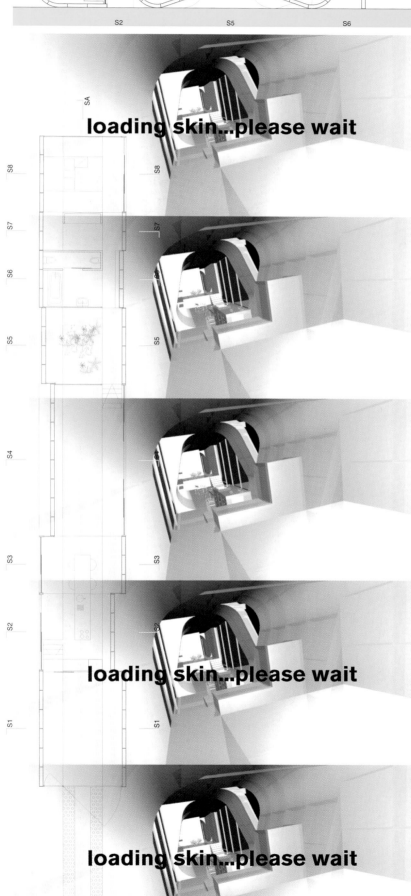

loading skin...please wait

loading skin...please wait

loading skin...please wait

loading skin...please wait

loading skin...please wai

loading skin...please

T2 Tipo A
C 8 m2
S+C+D 42 m2
D1 11 m2
D2 9 m2
D3 9 m2
B 3.5 m2
B 3.5 m2

T2 Tipo B
C 8 m2
S+C+D 30 m2
D1 10 m2
D2 8 m2
D3 8.5 m2
B 3.5 m2
B 3.5 m2

T2 Tipo C
C 8 m2
S+C+D 37.2 m2
D1 11m2
D2 8.5 m2
D3 8.5 m2
B 3.5 m2
B 3.5 m2

T2 Tipo D
C 8 m2
S+C+D 43 m2
D1 11 m2
D2 8.5 m2
D3 8.5 m2
B 3.5 m2
B 3.5 m2

T2 Tipo E
C 8 m2
S+C+D 41 m2
D1 10 m2
D2 8.5 m2
D3 8.5 m2
B 3.5 m2
B 2.5 m2

T2 Tipo F
C 8 m2
S+C+D 26 m2
D1 11m2
D2 10 m2
B 3.5 m2

| Spain |

S & A a

Federico Soriano (1961), Dolores Palacios (1960)

For Federico Soriano, architecture is a matter, first and foremost, of a careful working-out of semantics. This observation refers not only to his strictly literary and discursive activities: he was editor of *Arquitectura* from 1991 to 1994 and then founded the review *Fisuras de la cultura contemporanea* (1994). Since 1991, he has also been teaching at the Escuela Técnica Superior de Arquitectura in Madrid. His actual architectural praxis, which is nearer to the art of poetry than to architectonics, can be understood only in this ongoing quest for meaning, in this exploration of the evocative power of architecture. The Museo de los Niños (Valencia, 1999) refers to the theme of the primitive cave in fairy tales; the Euskalduna building (Bilbao, 1998), with its rusty steel shell, calls to mind cargo run aground in old shipyards. Each project is presented like an architectural fiction or phenomenological graph, seeking to weave bonds with a context.

◆

Six Chimneys
Barakaldo, Spain, project, 1999

The Six Chimneys housing project (Bilbao, 1999) is a manifesto of city planning: the issue is not whether to construct in brick or steel, the important thing is not the social housing programme or the price of a housing unit per floor, and there is no crossing of uses and forms. The project must put forward an image, a metaphor rather than a plan, envisaging that the city may take over these banks of the Ria, a zone filled with industrial buildings, warehouses and tall chimneys. The six long and slender housing towers represent an interpretation of the industrial skyline of the Ria. The disposition of the shipyards and steel works influences the way they are grouped together. The way the urban programme is dealt with also contrasts fiercely with any vision of urban composition. The density is too low for traditional urban tools, which divide a territory into a series of blocks, technological estates, sports complexes and green belts. The area has to be approached like a strange and foreign land, a forest caught in the city or a room caught in industry, and it has to be formulated in a continual configuration. Not parcels but buildings which form groups and are either isolated or in contact. No zoning grid but a beech forest, covering and hiding the playing fields.

The noisy and fast-moving traffic is channelled by the peripheral road system, which serves the sites planned for economic and technological activities in the Ria 2000 programme. A penetrating road, for slow-moving

traffic, links the centre of Barakaldo with the new residential towers and the sports facilities, while their accessibility from neighbouring city areas is completed by trams. The break formed by the railway, which used to cut the area in two, is now just a line passing through the forest. The six towers rise above a parking area and their silhouettes, sheathed in a subtle envelope, seem to move slowly, because of the rotation of the plan for the apartments around the vertical distribution core, gradually orienting the bedrooms and terraces towards different views.

The architecture takes the form of an attempt to bring out or to the surface the context and its residual traces in the project. The memory of the skyline of the industrial city is reinterpreted and enhanced in order to create a moving and plant-rich landscape, playing illusorily with self-generation. ◆

Bénédicte Grosjean

BARAKALDO. LAS TORRES.

CLIMATICSTRIPE   CLIMATICSTRIPE+THICKWALL   CLIMATICSTRIPE+THICKWALL+VARIABLESTRIPE   CLIMATICSTRIPE+THICKWALL+VARIABLESTRIPE+ROOF

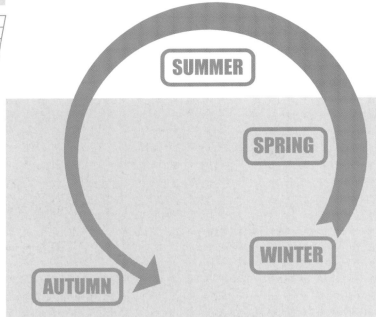

SUMMER

SPRING

WINTER

AUTUMN

| Slovenia |

Sadar Vuga Arhitekti |

Jurij Sadar (1963), Bostjan Vuga (1966)

The Slovenian architects and engineers Jurij Sadar and Bostjan Vuga are graduates of the University of Ljubljana and have been working together since 1992. Vuga studied at the Architectural Association for a year before they founded their agency in 1996. The chief concern of their architecture is to be open to all the different disciplines and activities that have a bearing on construction (engineering, economics, landscape, media, etc.) as well as to all kinds of outside influences (art, fashion, new media, etc.), not to mention the general European architectural context (the OCEAN Net network). Noted presences in a number of international competitions, their pragmatic yet experimental projects are striking in their formal radicality. In Ljubljana, Sadar and Vuga designed the chamber of commerce building (completed in 1999), an extension for the National Gallery (under construction) and the DOM Mueller department stores (completed in 2000). ◆

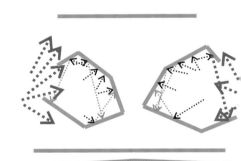

Nomad House
Ljubljana, Slovenia, project, 2000
(Jurij Sadar, Bostjan Vuga, Tatjana Kercmar and Miha Praznik)

The nomadism of this house is not manifested by any kind of physical movement: the Nomad House does not 'drift' but, on the contrary, is immobile, anchored to its local site and almost dependent on this geographical location. It will never leave the residential suburb of Ljubljana for which Sadar and Vuga designed it. Rather, it is the occupier himself who will experience the house as a constantly metamorphosing environment, a terrain of endlessly renewed migrations. Permeable to climatic variations and to the changing seasons, the Nomad House responds to the cyclical transformations of lifestyles and the uses that these imply, making it possible to construct the conditions of a domestic nomadism. Sadar and Vuga's first gesture was to design two protective walls as a means of dealing with climatic flux. These are folded inwards, like two parentheses, on to an 'inner space', which they insulate from the variations outside. Carefully positioned in relation to the many different seasonal movements of the sun, they are slightly staggered, thus making it possible to fit in, to the south, an entranceway/sliding door and, to the north, a large picture window opening up the north/west corner of the living room. The second gesture in this project was to include twin patios, each abutting one of these two walls. These two pockets of outside space, which are open to all the variations of weather and time, enrich the house with a multiplicity of possibilities: eating outside or inside, being in the shade or in the sun, being sheltered or looking out on the scenery, etc. Their positions encourage displacements, movements and uses that vary in accordance with the seasons and times of day. In the winter, for example, life centres on the light of the east side patio (kitchen, 'between-patios', living room), whereas in the summer the daily movements will form a broader arc, going from one patio to the other via the north-facing terrace. The third gesture in the Nomad House project concerns its roof. Made from prefabricated metal panels, it spreads out like a domestic landscape, like an artificial topography hanging above the house. Like a thick, snowy coat, its eaves envelop and cover the transitional spaces outside. ◆

Pierre Chabard

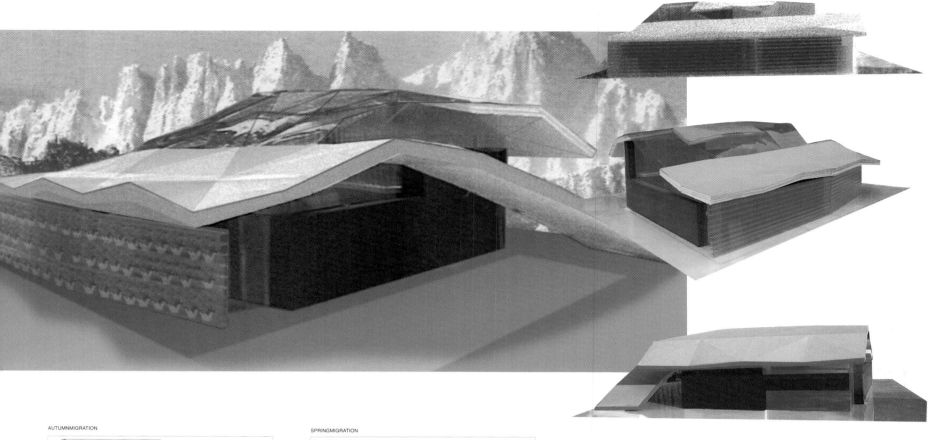

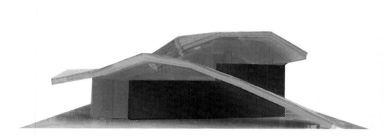

AUTUMNMIGRATION

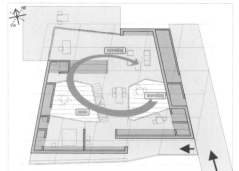

SPRINGMIGRATION

WINTERMIGRATION

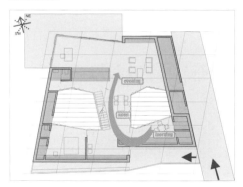

SUMMERMIGRATION

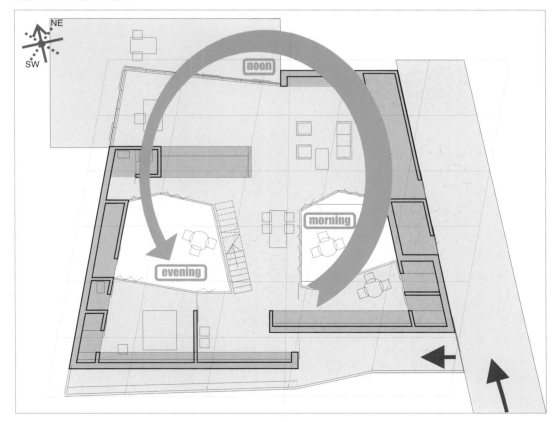

| USA |

Michele Saee |

MICHELE SAEE (1956)

Michele Saee is an experienced builder who trained with Morphosis before setting up his own agency in Los Angeles, in 1985. His architecture, which is invariably unstable and almost in an unfinished state, looks like a collection of floating, sculptural forms and materials interacting with light, always connected with the outside world. It is divided up into successive envelopes, which stand out on undulating surfaces like the different parts of an item of clothing covering a composite and moving body. All Michele Saee's architecture brings on a crisis of established identities, be it the identity of the notion of form, the notion of plane and surface, the notion of inhabiting or the closed identity of project, construction methods and engineering. This architecture replaces these issues of identity with a temporal dimension which sets it up as an 'authority' striving to define an architecture that refuses to be the application of an order or model. ◆

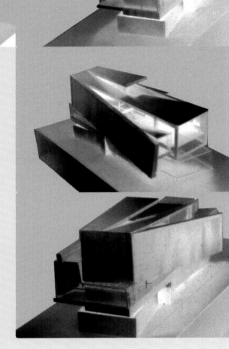

Linnie Residence
Los Angeles, USA, project, 2001

Michele Saee has designed numerous house projects in California (Sprecher House, 1985; Jones-Chapman Residence, 1988; Meivshana House and Sun House, 1990; Acks House, 1994; Golzari Guest House and IS House, 1996, etc.). In his work, these projects together function as an area of formal experimentation and conceptual exploration, as the laboratory for a complex and demanding architectural practice that is constantly questioning its own assumptions and foundations. But, above all, through these houses Saee is articulating a critical analysis of the urban context in which they are all located: the tentacular metropolitan area of Los Angeles and southern California, structured in a horizontal succession of residential districts full of detached houses. As the shifting and negative origin of the spatiality that he explores in his architecture, Saee conceives of this territory as a space of dislocation and disorientation, an anti-Euclidean space that throws the geometrical organization of the traditional nuclear town into crisis; a 'non-town' that is defined by its physical and built structures but equally by the emptiness between them, the 'in-between'. This intermediary condition of space also reflects the organization of society itself as an archipelago of communities, peoples, cultures and traditions, manifesting a heterogeneous social and spatial order that backs up the inherited hierarchies. Attentive to the aleatory development

of this space that he himself inhabits, Saee wishes to integrate into his architecture, and into the very process of its conception, the state of indistinctness and incertitude that it manifests and by which it is conditioned. The Linnie Residence reflects this search for an indeterminate architecture whose form is produced by a free and open genetic process. The living spaces open into the in-between, into the interstices created by the forms of the house. Lacking any programmatic determinants or any typological legitimization, these forms spread out almost randomly, converging and diverting and answering one another in a theory of folds and enfoldments. The house gives the impression of a complex, potential landscape, an immanent landscape that will be realized only in the future of a 'dwelling' that the architect cannot foresee but that he can almost blindly endow with a multitude of possibilities for effectiveness. ◆

Pierre Chabard

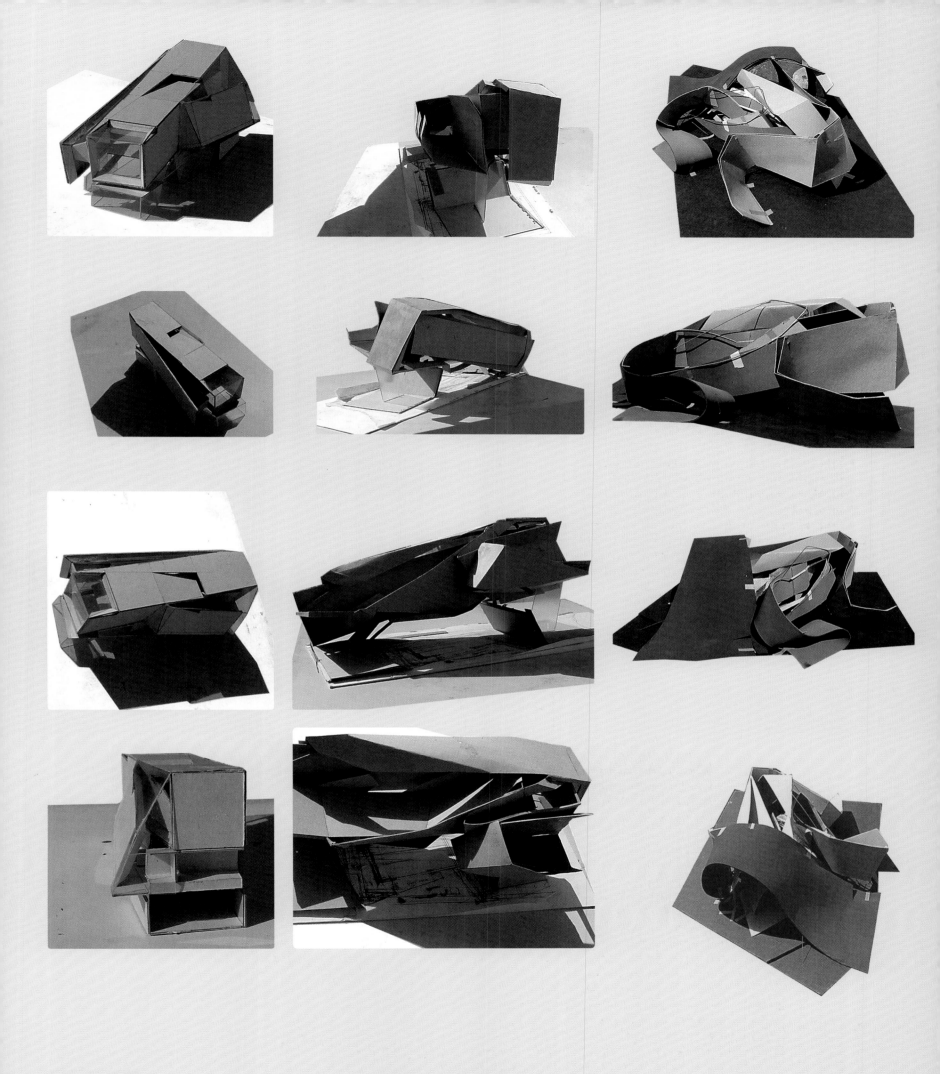

| France |

Scape

Duncan Owen Lewis (1959), Hervé Potin (1972), Pascal Riffaud (1969), Benoit Fillon (1970), Denis Brillet (1971), Stéphane Lagré (1969)

Scape is a laboratory of 6 architects. A merger of their 3 agencies (Lewis, Potin & Lewis, Block and Data 0.10), Scape sees itself as a true experimental platform for architectural research and production. Applying a rigorously transversal approach, its members are active at all levels from the urban scene to natural spaces. The overall dynamic of the group's projects has its conceptual origins in the term 'scape', whose lexical implications have to do with the transformation of the environment into landscape and of space into territory. Within the flux of project situations, Scape uses a series of controlled conceptual shifts to bring to light avenues not yet explored by the group. ◆

Tartan Lands
Glasgow, Scotland, project, 2001

In its combining of plant life and habitat, the project plays on the fluctuation between vegetable matter and textile, 'constructed' and 'modelled' landscape, via a ceaseless interplay of matter and form in which neither ever gains the upper hand. No question here of architecture camouflaged by nature or of nature instrumentalized by architecture; the essence is the give and take between true and false, legible and opaque, hidden and manifest. In this spirit the project encourages a playful relationship with textile pattern, shifting clothing concepts towards building. Here the kilt plays the role of a profound clothing icon, the geometrical matrix of the tartan providing infinite variations according to clan territory and identity. The tartan, be it the Macleod, MacBeth, Mackenzie, Stewart or whatever, is partly a territorial tool: more than a mere pattern, it uses the individual's territory to situate him in the landscape. It is this dual structure – pattern/identity, person/landscape – that gives the project its direction. In its very make-up the tartan is a representation of depth, a spatial depiction produced by the intermingling of warp and weft. The warp marks out the extent of the territory, the weft defines its boundaries and the whole describes the individual's loyalties. The kilt weaves a relationship – between local and global, body and envelope, environment and territories – in an inversion of the evolutionary order, a phylum that brings clothing into architecture. Drawn-out and double-woven, the façade creates depth, an extension into a living space made adaptably receptive to use and to the plant kingdom. This intervening space is colonized by vegetable matter, which develops or regresses like a more or less dense filling that the user arranges and domesticates in the interests of livability. The façade gives concrete expression to 'fluctuating' territories that vitalize or abort emerging interstitial areas: here proliferation makes space dilate, there life is extinguished and space shrinks, letting light filter through. Time permeates the project, generating outgrowths due to heat as the damp zones to the north are colonized. Structured like a tartan, this 'filled' space extends the scope of the building, evokes something more than a dramatic separation between the urban and the domestic: for it induces over time real processes of appropriation, nomadic and endlessly mutating. The garment is shaped by use and energy flow; time folds and unfolds the depth, breathing life into bodies. The internal space shapes and models itself according to the movements of weaving, and vice versa. The project is reminiscent of a habitable topiary dynamically sculpted by the scattering of relief-moulded sheets of vegetable matter bearing a tartan pattern. The sheets suggest a lacy skin, reminding us of the tracery of French formal gardens as they let light filter through a second, more fragile skin on which, this time, the tartan pattern is directly imprinted. ◆

Scape

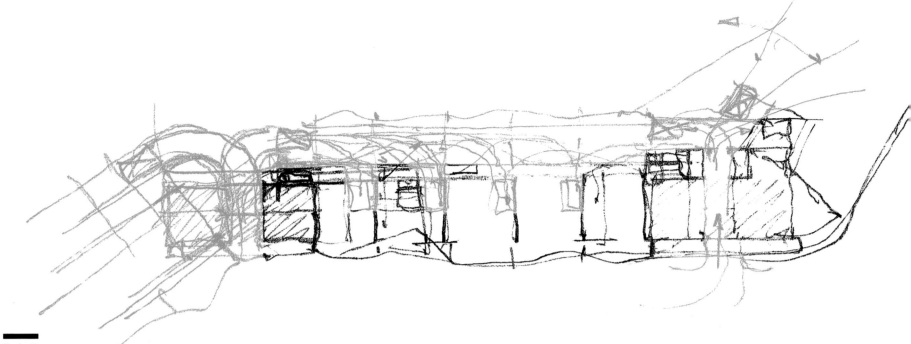

| France |

Agence François Seigneur |

François Seigneur (1942)

Unconventional, intellectually fertile and surprising, François Seigneur has spent more than 30 years exploring the field of architecture, revisiting its problems, doing away with recognized frontiers and testing the limits of fixed assignments. An alumnus of the Boulle and Arts Déco (ENSAD) applied arts schools, he began moving in this direction in the footsteps of Claude Parent, with whom he worked in the days of Architecture Principe and 'Fonction Oblique'. Between 1970 and 1974 he worked in partnership with Jean Nouvel and then Gilbert Lézénès. During the 1980s, after a number of years spent outside the circuit in the Cévennes mountains, he worked periodically with various architects (Nouvel, Hauvette, Viguier & Jodry, etc.) and his name was linked with a number of major projects (Institut du Monde Arabe, Némausus, the French Pavilion at Seville). In 1992, he received a degree in architecture and founded his own agency in Paris, moving to Arles in 1999 to work with Sylvie de la Dure. Combining architecture, painting, installation, graphic art and scenography, his practice is driven by experiment and critique, and resolutely oriented towards social issues. ◆

Car-house
Project, 2000

This experimental project sets out to re-examine the position of the motor car in relation to the city and housing. An attentive observer of the age, Seigneur has noted all the different kinds of appropriation, projection, subversion and instrumentalization to which the car has been subjected in the contemporary world. Looking beyond its function as an A-to-B device, it has become a place in its own right with numerous uses and meanings — somewhere to work, eat, sleep, listen to music, make phone calls, protect oneself, express one's personality, etc. A technological prosthesis, cabin dwelling and mobile outdoor extension of the home. The domestic character of the car is obvious and leads dialectically to the question underpinning this project: how should domestic architecture treat the relationship between car and house? As Seigneur sees it, this question brings to light a major social, architectural and urban rift: for while suburban housing has totally absorbed and integrated the car — which, indeed, is one of its technological conditions of possibility and major attributes — collective housing denies its existence, at the very least burying it in its underground parking areas. These very costly infrastructures and non-places are a burden on budgets and cause an economic imbalance in the construction of collective housing that favours the car without taking advantage of its domestic potential when not out on the road (in other words, 95 % of the time). In this project Seigneur proposes to create an extra room in each flat so that the car can be parked 'at home'. A transitional space between interior and exterior, it is part of each entranceway. Naturally or mechanically ventilated, phonically insulated from the other rooms, it does not disturb the other areas of the housing. On the contrary, when 'equipped' with its car, it enriches the domestic space with new possibilities: spare bedroom, (insulated) music room, place for teleworking, place for loading and unloading (shopping, moving, going on holiday, etc.). Bringing the car into the home also means that you can show it off, exhibit it like a designer object, a precious possession. The huge lift required to raise the cars is at the centre of the plan, thus liberating the façades. It can also be used to carry other loads, to service the building's terrace roof, which is made into allotments. Reconciling home and automobile, this project also initiates a reconquest of the public space of the street, which is currently 'privatized' by parking. ◆

Pierre Chabard

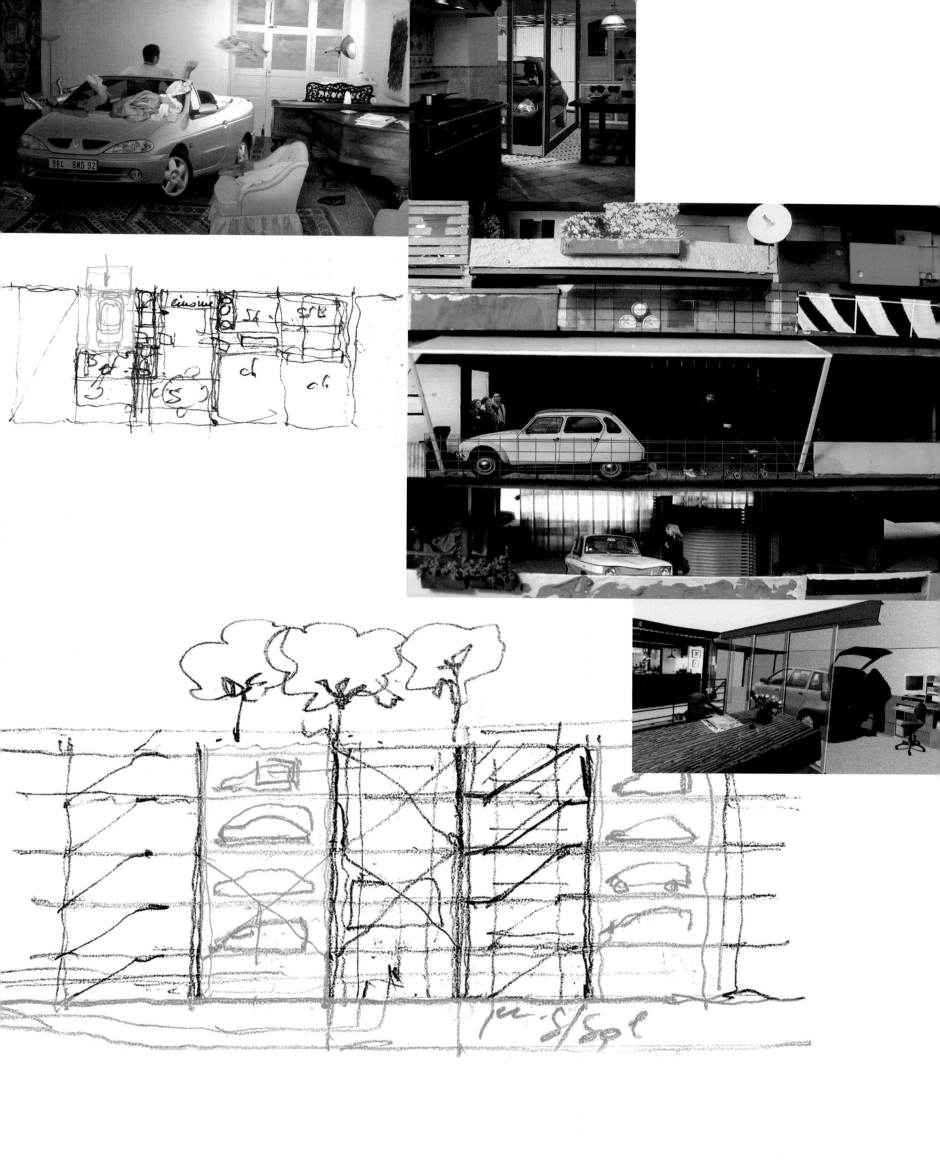

Smith-Miller + Hawkinson |

HENRY SMITH-MILLER (1942), LAURIE HAWKINSON (1952)

New York architect Henry Smith-Miller, a former associate of Michael Graves and Richard Meier, and Californian artist Laurie Hawkinson, who studied at Berkeley and then Cooper Union, where she trained in architecture, joined forces in 1983. They are deeply involved in contemporary architectural issues and strive to weave together theory and action, design and execution, praxis and instruction. The architecture of Smith-Miller & Hawkinson draws both from a sophisticated and proven art of construction (at work, in particular, in the Glass Museum, Corning, NY, 1994), and from an openness and availability to contemporary culture in all its forms. The decidedly cross-disciplinary praxis of Smith-Miller & Hawkinson also often looks for fertile associations in other areas of thought and other disciplines: with the artist Barbara Kruger and the landscape artist Nicholas Quennell (Imperfect Utopia: a Park for the New World, 1987–96, Elliot Bay Waterfront, Seattle, 1989), with the artist and writer Silvia Kolbowski, and with the architect and historian Kenneth Frampton (MAXmin House, 1993). ◆

Broken Bar Ranch
Colorado, USA, 2001–present

The 'broken-bar' organization of the house on a remote mesa in the Colorado (USA) Rocky Mountain wilderness reinterprets and re-presents the American dream. Located on the wooded edge of a vast alluvial meadow, the site (and house) enjoys a nearly 270-degree view of its surroundings, several million acres of forest and mountainscape.

The project's formal origins lie in the 'long house', a native American communal dwelling – a single large room dedicated to social gatherings and usually sited by local topography and ritual. The 'broken bar' runs from east to west, linking mountain to valley, is closed to the north like the edge of a forest, and open to the south, the prairie. The serpentine approach road refers first to local topographies, a grove of ancient ponderosas (trees), then remote topographies, the mountain ranges, before leading the visitor to the building's opaque north wall. The entrance to the building recalls the approach sequence; first oblique, then frontal and finally oblique. Passing through the north wall at the building's 'broken' section, one remains 'exterior', only to discover the 'hidden' domestic wing of the building.

The building's skin wraps and folds over its interior. A large 'flap' or visor shades the south-facing spaces, qualifying the view while offering protection from the environment. Windows and doors are set in the extrusion's fissures and folded surfaces. The building's simple extrusion (section) is broken at the confluence of diverse typologies and conflicting programmatic needs. These breaks afford visual access to and through the interior of the building, counteracting the implications of chosen typologies and producing a 'third typology' – a negotiated stasis. Interior materials, plywood panelling, and exterior materials, plank siding, slip past glazed and unglazed openings to re-qualify exterior and interior and to reinforce the presence of the site in the building. The project weaves the historical and contemporary, the indigenous and foreign, into a fabric unique to its site. ◆

Henry Smith-Miller

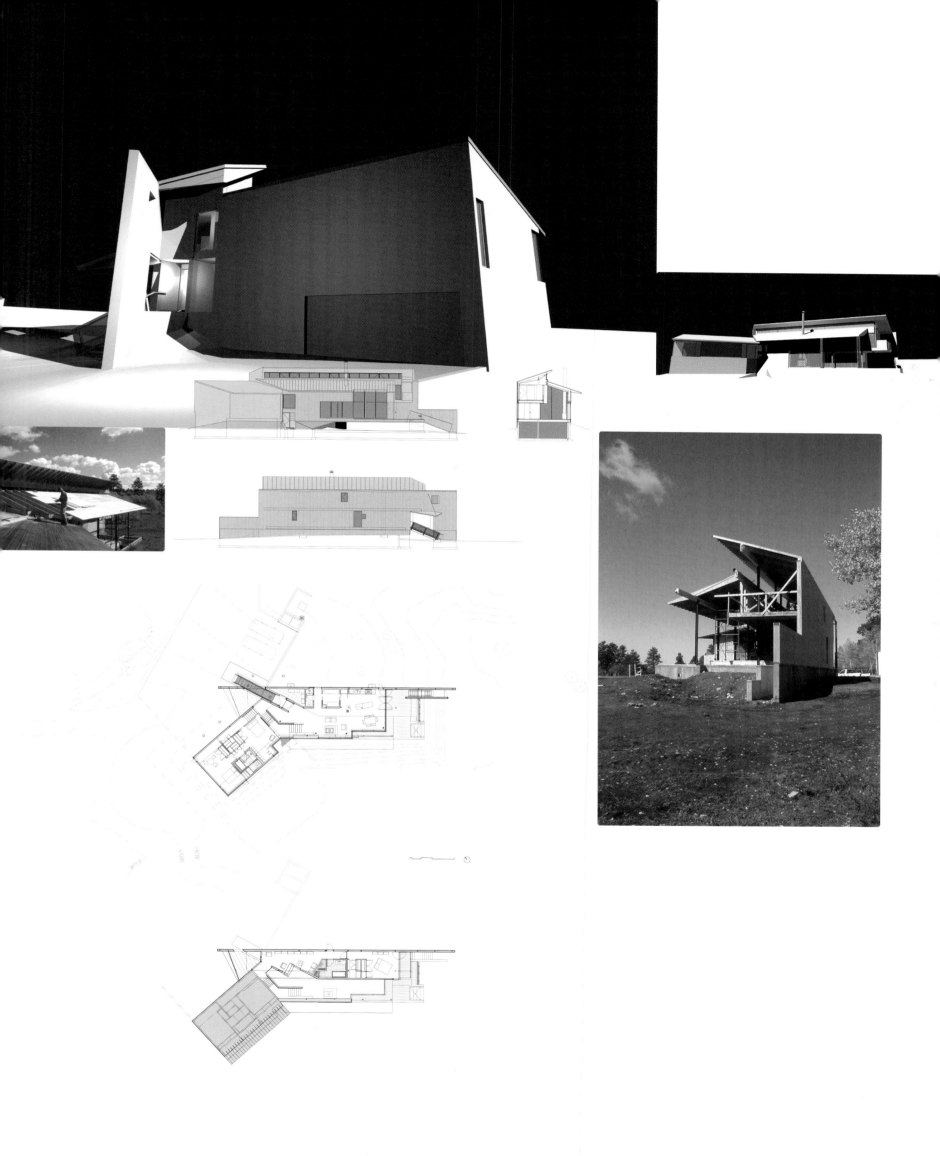

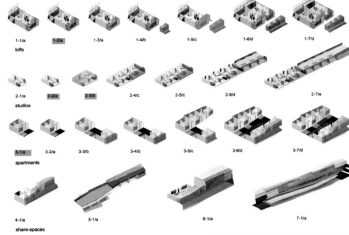

1-1/a | 1-2/a | 1-3/a | 1-4/b | 1-5/c | 1-6/d | 1-7/d
lofts

2-1/a | 2-2/a | 2-3/b | 2-4/c | 2-5/c | 2-6/d | 2-7/e
studios

3-1/a | 3-2/a | 3-3/b | 3-4/b | 3-5/c | 3-6/d | 3-7/d
apartments

4-1/a | 5-1/a | 6-1/a | 7-1/a
share-spaces

alternative living/work/leisure configurations determined
by users daily routine (see diagram)

Gradate Housing, project 1998–2000

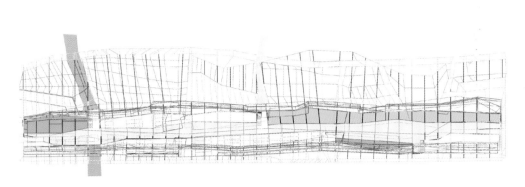

| USA |

su11 Architecture & Design

Ferda Kolatan (1966), Erich Schoenenberger (1966)

New York-based su11 is a platform devoted to conceptualizing and practising experimental architecture and design. Headed by Ferda Kolatan and Erich Schoenenberger, su11 seeks to combine various different fields and aspects of design in order to achieve more adaptive and integrated solutions. They are interested in rethinking and conceptualizing architectural space in relation to the increasingly changing lifestyle of our digital age and its complex programmatic configurations in urban culture. Design is defined as an opportunity to create an environment that participates in a daily exchange with its users and has the ability to transform in order to meet programmatic changes over time. su11's work includes architectural projects, both residential and commercial, furniture design and urban planning. ◆

Composite Housing

'Composite Housing' is a twofold approach to developing a new way of thinking about prefabrication and mass customization by means of new design concepts, material technologies and a contemporary marketing strategy. The skeleton of this single-family, free-standing house is a wood or steel frame, erected in accordance with traditional regional practice. This first phase of construction is entrusted to local contractors chosen for their competence. This solution is quick and easy and also allows the use of local labour.

The second phase of this project deals with prefabricated 'Add-On' units, which complement the on-site structure to create fully functional buildings. Add-On units are conceptualized as a sort of appliance–extension. They blur the boundaries between appliance, furniture and space, creating an architectural element that defies easy categorization. Appliances are frequently updated within a household following the latest innovations. The flexibility of the owner to exchange these products as he wishes is extended to the Add-On units and therefore impacts the programmatic and spatial configuration of his home. These units come in different variations and would be produced by third parties to ensure a competitive market and ongoing progressive innovation. The owner can configure his house by his personal choice of Add-On units, order them via the Web and have them delivered and installed on-site. Over the years he may update some of them to satisfy his change in taste or to accommodate a different programmatic concept.

Gradate Housing

This project seeks to provide an adaptive housing concept, which maintains a high level of programmatic flexibility over time by temporarily extending typically private and enclosed spaces into a more public and accessible realm. Different housing types, such as studios, lofts and apartments, are configured by the user's schedule and combined in a way that allows maximum transformation. But not only the insides of the units are flexible: the corridors of the buildings become vacant, in-between spaces ready to be utilized by the most dominant programmes. The growth and shape of the whole building are also determined by the most progressive, programmatic applications. The term 'Gradate Housing' describes how the 'intermediate' becomes the key infrastructure for this project. The spaces shift through different grades of programme, over time, without freezing at a certain condition. Pocket spaces and corridors function as filters between grades of private and public life. The residents' activities define the building shape. Conversely, the building layout enables the residents to combine and coordinate their activities. ◆

su11

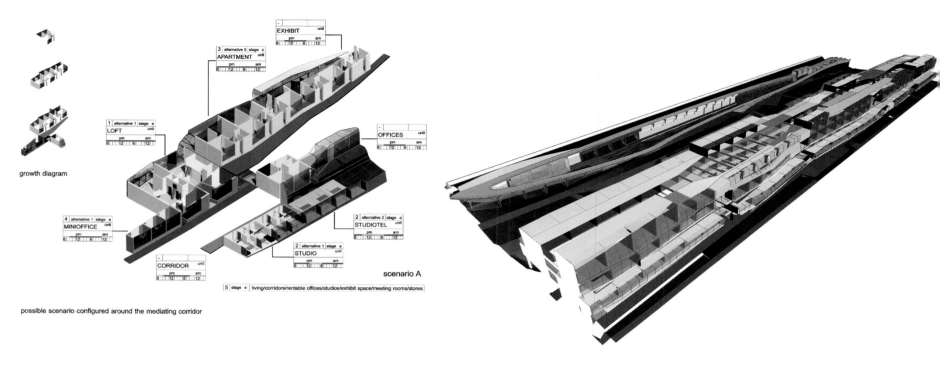

growth diagram

EXHIBIT

APARTMENT

LOFT

OFFICES

MINIOFFICE

STUDIOTEL

STUDIO

CORRIDOR

scenario A

possible scenario configured around the mediating corridor

5 stage e living/corridors/rentable offices/studios/exhibit space/meeting rooms/stores

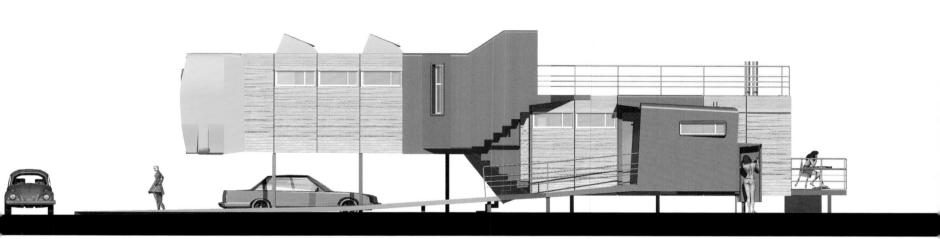

Composite Housing, project 1998-2000

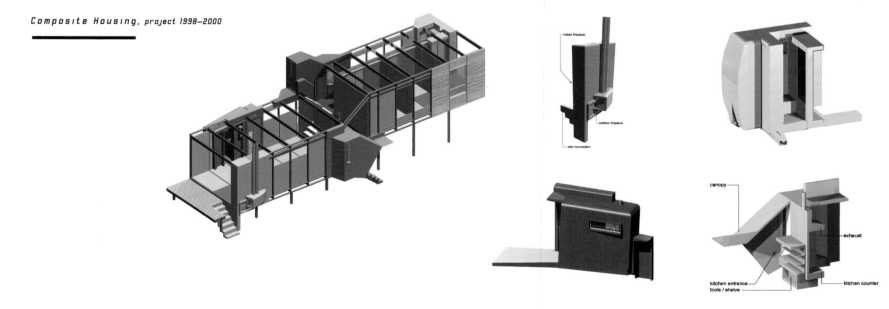

indoor fireplace

outdoor fireplace

stair connection

canopy

exhaust

kitchen entrance
tools / shelve

kitchen counter

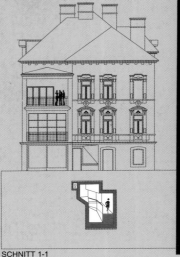

SCHNITT 1-1

| AUSTRIA |

the nextENTERprise Architekten

ERNST J. FUCHS (1963), MARIE THÉRÈSE HARNONCOURT (1967)

Ernst J. Fuchs and Marie Thérèse Harnoncourt are graduates of the University of Applied Arts in Vienna, where they were, in particular, students of Wolf D. Prix, and have been working together since the early 1990s. In 1994, in Vienna, they founded the Poor Boy's Enterprise with Florian Haydn, which became the nextENTERprise, after the latter's departure in 2000. As authors of artistic and experimental installations (Zustands Design, 1991–2000) and rare but demanding architectural works (Zirl House, 1997; Message in the Bottle, 2000), these two Viennese architects single out the importance of form (for which they eschew any kind of preconception) solely by validating the complex processes of which it is the product. The 'off-space' is one of these processes: a spatial tool that reacts to the social fabric, which belongs to whoever takes it and whose structure can be used by each person as a mental space. The project of an indoor swimming pool as an annex to an existing house that cannot be extended with a garden is an application of the 'off-space' idea to living. Here it generates a floating underground cavity, linked to the house by an elongated ramp. ◆

Off-Space/Spaced Out
Private underground swimming pool, Vienna, 1998–2001

New ways of living in the networked information society have broken down the boundaries between role-specific work and leisure (the idol of regeneration), between self-presentation to the world around and the stylization of privacy, between the clichéd usage of architecture and variable interpretations of spatial agendas. Just as the home used to be a domain for retreat inter alia, to prepare a new personality, and also a tabernacle to intimate self-reference, so the contemporary urban lifestyle/home is tending to become a conglomeration of complex situations for meeting requirements and of strategies for satisfying these. Accordingly, the bedroom houses the electronic bank teller, business partners are simultaneously utilized as friends, supper unexpectedly turns into the project 'dinner', etc.

Nevertheless, this new way of living clings to the original forms of the middle-class private sphere – the coffee shop, bar, church, hotel or shopping mall remain highly attractive. Even if physically defined distance is rendered relative by virtual media spaces, the fascination held by conventional far-off places remains intact – a spectrum of strategies for individual and collective distancing that opens up between imagined space, experiential worlds and forms of the beyond. In the face of the omnipresence of the media, however, the so-called 'network' no longer accords to any spatial-temporal distance. The server is ubiquitous; the paradigm of transferability has become obsolete. And yet this situation does not affect 'distant spaces', whether mental, emotional and spiritual, those machines for dreams and desires to which people have recourse with imagination and vision. The fantastic imaginings of the Orientalists in the 19th century, for instance, created 'spaces' with foreign, 'distant' contents.

The generation of distance is achieved not only by distancing oneself spatially; changing oneself is at the centre of what is going on, the way we reflect and experience ourselves in our own transformation – the threshold is a temporal one. It is not an imagined place that is distant but the obsession of the self-relation in the transition. Nowadays visions do not produce any futures, they are incorporated as a utopian impetus of the present.

Spaces are not random bearers of functions, significance and symbolism per se – we take the content with us, updating it elsewhere. A conceptual architecture that is aware of these flexible – and conditioned as empty contents – forms of treatment by their users, with functional or symbolic requirements for architectural settings, cannot remain satisfied with the limitation of a monologue in terms of the spatial structure. Complex spatial successions 'live' from phantasms of construed distant spaces – vanishing points, 'escape boxes', dream spaces, the alter locus or anti-space, etc. The instrument of distant space is what initially puts the architectural factor space at someone's disposal: 'real' virtuality versus virtual reality. ◆

Herbert Lachmayer,
Jeanette Pache

SCHNITT 4-4

| MALAYSIA |

T. R. Hamzah & Yeang Sdn. Bhd. |

KEN YEANG (1948), TENGKU ROBERT HAMZAH

Trained at the Architectural Association (1966–71) and at Cambridge University (1971–75), where he obtained his PhD ('A Theoretical Framework for the Incorporation of Ecological Considerations in the Design Environment', 1981), Ken Yeang, who is of Malaysian origin, is one of the pioneers of bioclimatic architecture. For the past 25 years, from both a theoretical and a practical angle, he has been developing a true ecological expertise in the architecture of very large buildings (which are nevertheless regarded as the most harmful to the environment). As a partner in T. R. Hamzah & Yeang, which was founded in Kuala Lumpur in 1976, he has designed and built, together with his colleague Hamzah, of the AA School, a very large number of colossal edifices, including his famous 'green skyscrapers'. Integrated in the dynamics of nature (sun, wind, climate, etc.), and economical in terms of matter and energy, these giants have proven their viability in both ecological and economic terms and are winning over numerous developers: Yeang is currently building the National Library in Singapore, a shopping mall in Stuttgart and 3 apartment towers in London. ◆

City in the Sky
Elephant & Castle Eco-Towers
London, project, 2000
(Ken Yeang with Chong Woon Wee, Ridzwa Fathan, Portia Reynolds, Ooi Tee Lee, Loh Hock Jin, Ong Eng Huat)

These three 'Eco-Towers' by Hamzah and Yeang are part of an ambitious project to regenerate the Elephant & Castle district, a vast expanse of 730 hectares in south central London. The general programme includes 100,000 square metres of shops, 3,500 housing units and 1,100 public housing units as well as 50,000 square metres of office space, a hotel, facilities and services, a new public transport network and three new parks, the largest covering 60 hectares. The new station divides the site in two: the 'left bank' is entrusted to Foster & Partners, while the 'right bank' is shared between Benoy Limited, H.T.A. Architects and T. R. Hamzah & Yeang.

In keeping with their idea of the Eco-Tower, or 'green skyscraper', Hamzah and Yeang have conceived their project as if it were a genuine 'ecosystem', an organized urban and geographical fragment, a 'microcosm' comprising all the different elements that constitute a complete community (housing, amenities, parks and gardens, shops, leisure centres, etc.), only turned upright in towers, like a kind of 'city in the sky'. Their Eco-Towers ultimately offer a real habitat in the naturalist sense of the term, one whose every aspect has been conceived as part of an integrated whole. The ecological character of this city in the sky has both a social and an environmental dimension.

Socially, Hamzah and Yeang have favoured a resolutely mixed programme (vertical zoning leading to a harmonious distribution of infrastructure and services, and the possibility of nearby work for residents) as well as social mixing (residents are grouped together by category of housing: studio flats, family flats, prestige flats, all contained in the same building). From an architectural point of view, Hamzah and Yeang have sought to generate a multiplicity of sophisticated transitions between open spaces ('parks in the sky'), semi-private spaces (inner courtyards, light shafts) and open private spaces (balconies, etc.).

In terms of environmental ecology, Hamzah and Yeang take a global and systemic, or holistic, approach. In other words, they seek to balance the different logics, parameters and functions at work in a given situation, as well as the many different kinds of interplay between them. Because they are part of a specific urban and geographic environment, the Eco-Towers are expected to contribute towards its general equilibrium by generating biodiversity, by increasing the 'organic mass' of plant life and by controlling exchanges of matter and light with their environment. On the inside, every aspect of the building's configuration, orientation and structure is designed to minimize the use of heavy energy (electro-mechanical systems) and make rational use of the site's potential and its natural energy sources. ◆

Pierre Chabard

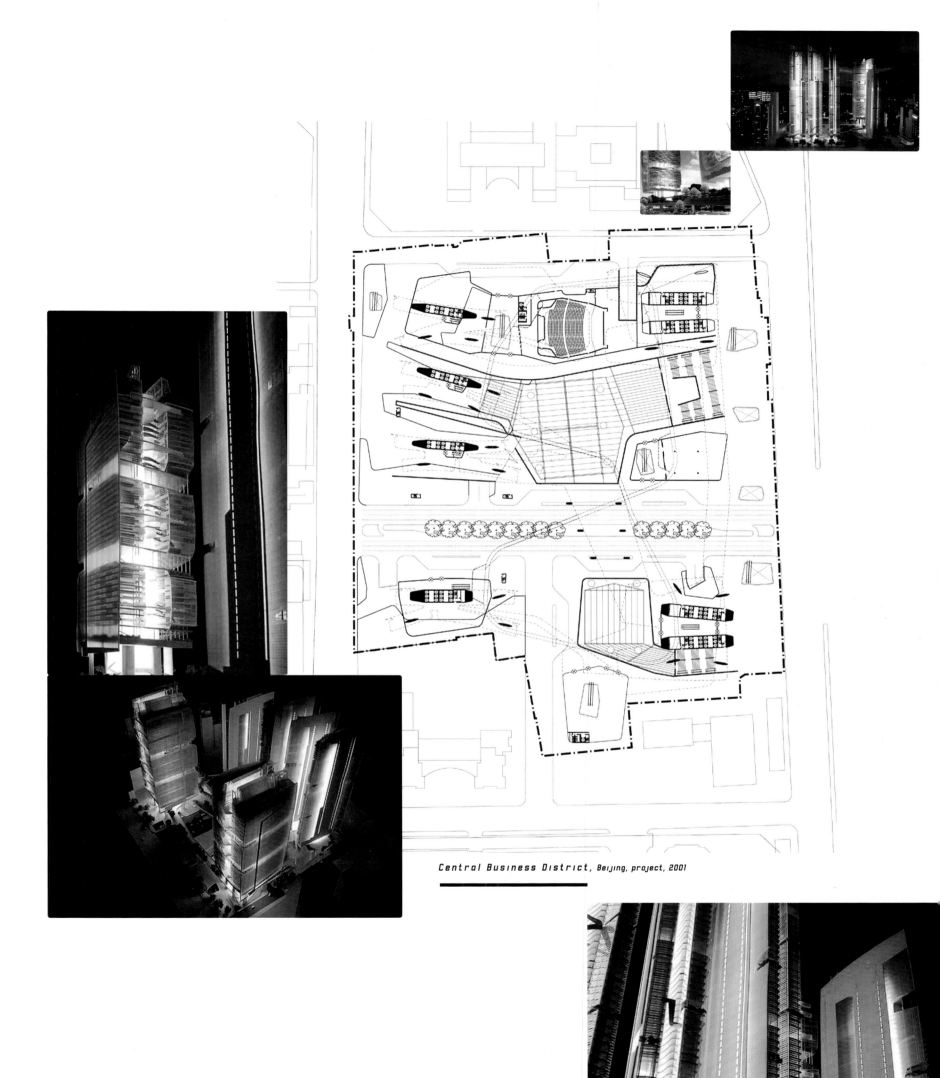

Central Business District, Beijing, project, 2001

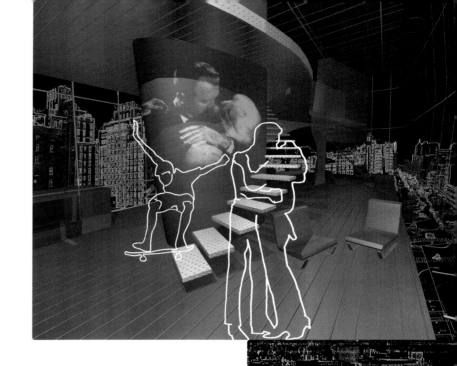

| France/USA |

Bernard Tschumi Architects |

BERNARD TSCHUMI (1944)

Author of several emblematic projects (The Manhattan Transcript, 1976–81; the Parc de la Villette, 1983–95) and of several major books (*Architecture and Disjunction*, 1994; *Event Cities* [Praxis], 1994), Bernard Tschumi has left his mark on and informed the architectural debate over the past 15 years. He was associated in 1988 with 'Deconstructivist Architecture', presented by Mark Wigley at the MoMA, and he focuses, above all, on a fruitful combination between architecture and contemporary philosophy (Jacques Derrida, Gilles Deleuze). Where the latter is concerned, he has notably extended thinking about space and cinematographic time, by applying it to architecture. Like that moving form represented by the cinema, Tschumi's architecture basically resists inscription; it comes into being only in the ephemeral, unstable and evolving moment of its encounter with the subject and with the body or bodies in motion. In search of an architectural generation (and therefore expression) of 'the event', Bernard Tschumi conceives of architecture merely as an extension of social space in its continual changes. ◆

Glass House in the Sky |
New York, USA, project 2000 |

The House responds to a contemporary desire for infinite space in the dense metropolis. It is a reaction against the recurring dream of suburbia; rather than abandoning the city and recreating an artificial urban experience outside it, the House addresses the city by existing both within and above it.

The architecture of this 'Glass House in the Sky' plays on an opposition between its industrial-looking rectangular envelope and the lush curvature of its inner volumes. The strict glass-and-steel detailing of its exterior contrasts with the soft velvet or silk curtains, rounded and polished marble, curved translucent glass and exotic wood veneers of the interiors. The services and circulation are contained in an undulating 'sandwich' wall that also helps define the living spaces. The wall expands and folds back on itself, enclosing spaces for privacy, and opening to allow rooms and corridors to flow continuously into one another. It provides the 'subconscious' of the House, adjusting to the specific desires of the user. Separations can be made by sliding partitions and curtains out of the services wall, thus allowing for more privacy. Bathrooms are contained in a large 'liquid', or 'wet', wall that extends through the house. This wet wall surface, made of a composite of glass and boat-like resin, changes between transparency/translucency and opacity. Its other side is a 'digital' wall. If making one's lifestyle public suits the occupants, this curved digital wall, which acts as a projection screen, could exhibit enlarged images of the most intimate moments of its occupants' everyday life. Should they prefer more restrained anonymity, other messages can be projected, from advertising slogans to exhibitions of their video art collection. The digital wall appears as a media installation of soft, pliable electronic images. The technical constraints of the House are small. In the unlikely event that the roof could not support the additional load, structural support would reach to the load-bearing walls or columns of the existing building. The intermediate floor of the House is cantilevered from within the undulating double wall. Services (water, electricity, etc.) simply 'plug into' the existing facilities. Elevator access is generally available to the top floors and, occasionally, to the roofs of the urban buildings. Various permits would have to be obtained, especially since the Landmarks Preservation Commission has generally been conservative about roof additions in historic neighbourhoods. ◆

Bernard Tschumi

| NETHERLANDS |

West 8 Landscape Architects & Urban Planners |

ADRIAAN GEUZE (1960)

Upon completing a degree in landscape architecture at the University of Wageningen in 1987, Adriaan Geuze founded West 8 Landscape Architects in Rotterdam and is active in all aspects of landscape design. Through such large-scale projects as the zoning and organization of Schiphol airport (1991), the design of city squares like the Schouwburgplein in Rotterdam, or the design of gardens such as the one around the art centre in Dordrecht, the ideas of Adriaan Geuze have had a powerful influence on the urban landscape of the Netherlands.

West 8 challenges the boundaries between architecture, design and city planning, situating their intervention where all these disciplines meet, on extreme scales, from the object to urban development. Their philosophy is rooted in an optimistic attitude towards the contemporary landscape, which, for them, expresses both the vulnerability and the euphoria of mass culture.

They are interested in the urban landscape both in its complexity and in its ordinariness, coming up with often unexpected solutions where there is a mixture of the natural and the artificial. ◆

Borneo Sporenburg Master Plan |
Amsterdam, Netherlands, 1993–97

Whereas the urban development plan for the third extension of the Amsterdam docklands stipulated a density of 100 housing units per hectare, developers pointed to a clear market preference for single-family, suburban-style dwellings with direct access to the street. In view of this paradox in which the wish for density clashes with the movement towards individualization of housing, which has been increasingly prominent in the Netherlands since the first criticisms of the Vinex Plan, a competition was organized in order to define this new typology.

West 8's winning entry is inspired by the villages on the edge of the old Zuiderzee. It reinterprets the typology of Amsterdam's canal houses by using thin and tightly packed strips of land. The density is further increased by removing the traditional opposition between frontage and back garden: placed back to back, the constructions present only a main façade, but they do gain an internal patio. This 'gruyère solution', which imposes 30 to 50 % of empty land per plot, chooses to attribute all the open space to individual plots rather than creating external public spaces. Because the sea is omnipresent here, it is possible to offer a 'blue landscape' by way of 'parks and gardens'.

Some 60 architects contributed to the plan, proposing prototype houses meeting the requirement that they be designed around a natural light shaft, offering a hidden, familial and introverted space that comes as a surprise after the rough, open landscape of the harbour. Another important rule in the guidelines of West 8 stipulates a minimum ceiling height of 3.5 metres for the first floor of the houses (the Dutch standard is 2.4 metres), which improves the luminosity of the house and, in the long term, ensures the versatility of the ground-floor level, where roads and shops, cafes and offices can create a mixed urban texture. The key problem of parking was resolved by combining different solutions: individual garages, parallel car parks alongside the blocks and a half-buried collective lot. A number of fine plots along the canals were also sold to private owners who formed a group and decided to adopt a joint plan for a living room two floors high overlooking the water. This principle of integrating individual projects has spread and many town planning projects in the Netherlands now assign a certain number of plots to private use.

In the general plan, this 'sea of houses' is broken up by three public housing blocks, the 'meteorites'. Designed by prestigious agencies, they serve as landmarks structuring the harbour area. West 8 also designed the public spaces, employing a restraint that would set off the architectural diversity of the different buildings.

◆

Client: New Deal
Credits: Adriaan Geuze, Wim Kloosterboer, Yushi Uehara, Sebastiaan Riquois

Bénédicte Grosjean

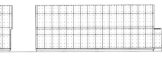

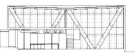

| JAPAN |

Hideyuki Yamashita |

HIDEYUKI YAMASHITA (1961)

A graduate of the Tokyo Institute of Technology (1984, atelier headed by Kazuo Shinohara), Hideyuki Yamashita was taught by Peter Cook at the Frankfurt Städelschule in 1986. He has lived in Tokyo since 1991. He founded Infagenda, Inc. in 1999 and has taught as an associate professor at the Institute of Design in Nagaoka since 2000. In 1993, he developed the concept of the 'Nested Cube in Process', a structure within a structure in which form is the result of the interlocking of different systems of construction that mirror one another, elaborating a 'recursive space and the kernel of a structural system supporting a combination of associated spaces' (Yamashita). This theoretical and conceptual research takes a number of complex forms and constitutes the generative matrix of his architecture. It articulates a number of notions that are transferred more or less directly to his architecture: recursion, the continuous interlocking of scales, the interrelation of spaces, auto-normative architecture, etc. ◆

TM-House
Tokyo, Japan, 2000–present
(Hideyuki Yamashita/architect, Alan Burden/engineer, Shigeo Ogawa/photographer)

TM-House, like 'House in Tokyo' (completed in 1999), is one of a series of buildings based on the 'Nested Cube' concept. In TM-House, full-width sliding doors are installed in the south elevation of a two-storey reinforced structure. The 'W' structure connecting the floor and the roof plates acts as a truss, allowing both sides to be opened freely. TM-House stands on four ground-bearing points. In contrast to its static exterior shape, the interior expresses dynamism. The W structure leads the other structural members. All the pieces except for the long wall of the north function as structural members. The W structure supports the most of the weight of the building. Two bearing walls resisting seismic movement are also suspended from the top of the W structure. Consequently, most of the total weight disperses and concentrates on the feet of the W structure to be supported by the four strip foundations. The whole south side is open. Sunlight enters the void space through the stepped building elevation. The glass screens are all movable and may slide the full width. Each sliding unit is a normal ready-made aluminium extrusion. The opening reminds us of the *engawa* system (terrace equipped with sliding screens in traditional Japanese architecture). The whole north side is closed so that the building becomes an enclosure with one side fully opened. The whole north wall will carry shelving for books and records. The two W structures will permit the whole north side to be fully opened in future. At present it is a fair-faced concrete wall that gives a sharp contrast of light and shadow between the south and the north sides. The dining and cooking space, sanitary facilities and bathroom, air-conditioning units and electrical terminal are packed together. The other spaces are semi-exterior and therefore not regulated according to ordinary house function. ◆

Hideyuki Yamashita

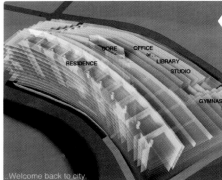

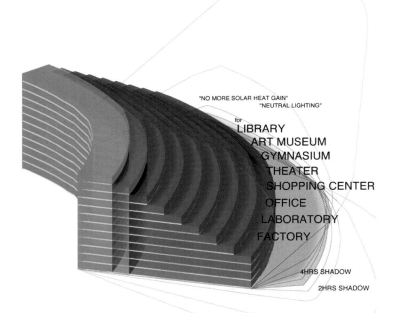

"NO MORE SOLAR HEAT GAIN"
"NEUTRAL LIGHTING"

for
LIBRARY
ART MUSEUM
GYMNASIUM
THEATER
SHOPPING CENTER
OFFICE
LABORATORY
FACTORY

4HRS SHADOW
2HRS SHADOW

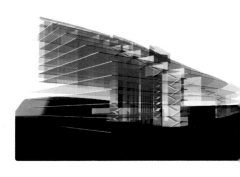

| JAPAN |

Shoei Yoh & Architects

SHOEI YOH HAMURA (1940)

Shoei Yoh has shunned the Tokyo megalopolis, to live, work and teach in Fukuoka, where he set up his agency in 1970. An economist by training, in the early 1960s he studied at the School of Fine and Applied Arts at the University of Springfield, Ohio, and set his sights on architecture. His many and varied works are the culmination of much rigorous experimental labour, which can be seen in the architecture of several of his houses: Stainless House with Light Lattice, 1981; Glass House with Breathing Grating, 1983; Glass House between Sea and Sky, 1991; Six Cubes in Light, 1994; Sundial House, 1996, etc. For Yoh, these houses all represent 'prototypes', and opportunities to experiment with materials and with arrangements of space and light, within a minimalist quest for formal simplicity as well as an ever greater economy of technical means. Shoei Yoh's work stands at the cross-roads of Western modernist thinking and Japanese culture, and explores a sensitive path combining minimalism and complexity, ecology and technology, nature and architecture. ◆

Solar-Oriented City 2001

Warm housing to the south; temperate spaces to the north (in the northern hemisphere), project, 1994–2001

Shoei Yoh has been working on this concept–project since 1994, and is now trying to produce a prototype with the collaboration of the Japan Urban Development Center. A combination of engineering, architecture and town planning, Solar-Oriented City 2001 is a contemporary take on what is a recurrent issue in 20th-century urbanism: that of access to sunlight in megacities. After countless architects, town planners, doctors and hygiene experts, it is now Shoei Yoh's turn to grapple with what may seem an impossible paradox: providing equitable access to sunlight in a densely populated and built-up environment; allowing the possibility of enjoying a personal relationship to this collective 'benefit' in the middle of the city. Shoei Yoh's project fundamentally reaffirms the beneficial character of the sun, which is discussed in terms of several different themes or values (light, warmth, energy curative properties, etc.). According to him, offering equitable access to the sun, far from being a simple 'bonus', is the necessary compensation for living in a big city and putting up with its daily drawbacks and even absurdities. Observing city folks' Sunday migrations towards parks and gardens and away from their dark and cramped homes, observing the financial cost of the air-conditioning systems used by public spaces in their struggle against temperature variations and the assaults of the sun, Shoei Yoh plans to offer a global response, one that is synthetic and integrated into the numerous problems deriving

from the initial paradox. The answer is formulated through architecture, in the concept of the Solar-Oriented City. This project consists of a vertical and horizontal redistribution of functions: the southern façade is dedicated to habitation, the northern façade to amenities (libraries, museums, factories, laboratories, etc.). The building is thus stratified into three vertical layers. The southern layer is designed to offer maximum sunlight in the living units; the northern layer, using thicker walls, seeks protection from the sun and fits into the shadow of the southern part. Between the two layers there is a service and circulation interface. The general form of the building is the result of the optimization of the sum of restrictions, undertaken according to a genuine scientific procedure, which involves making diagrams of shadows, calculations of thermal performance, economic parameters, optimization of movement, etc. A hi-tech take on Le Corbusier's 'Ville Radieuse', Solar-Oriented City aims to reconcile citizens with their megacity. ◆

Pierre Chabard

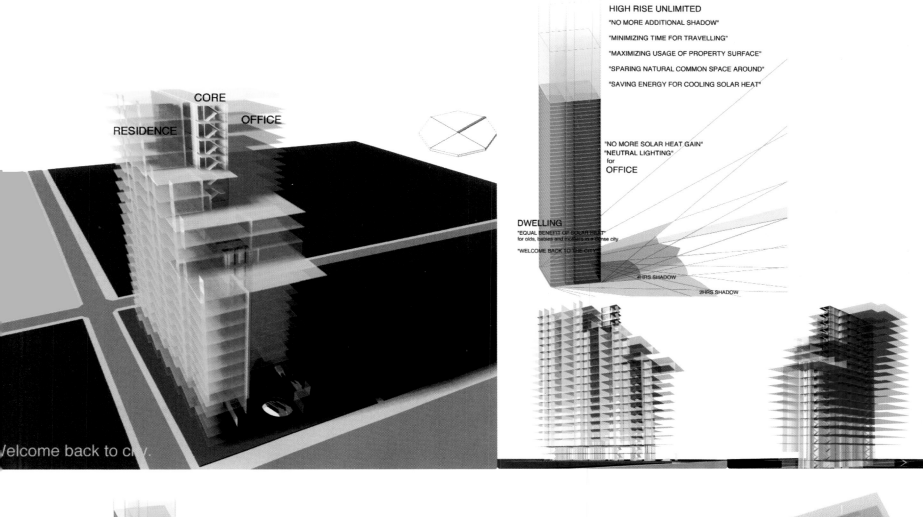

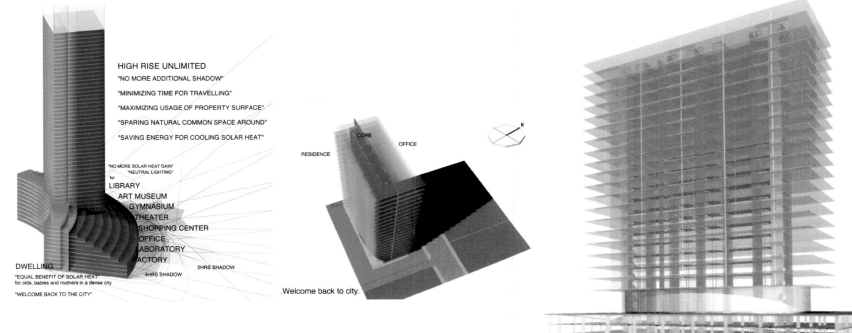

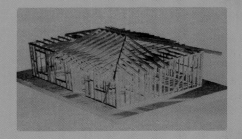

| USA |

Z+ (Zellner+Associates: Architecture & Research)

PETER ANTHONY ZELLNER (1969)

Peter Anthony Zellner is a young American architect with a degree from the Royal Melbourne Institute of Technology in Victoria, and more recently a graduate of Harvard University, in Cambridge, MA ('Harvard Project on the City' under the direction of Rem Koolhaas). Today, he runs Z+ in Santa Monica, California. He is the author of two books: *Pacific Edge: Contemporary Architecture on the Pacific Rim* (1998) and *Hybrid Space: New Forms in Digital Architecture* (1999). Living and working in the United States, he has nevertheless imported from his native Australia unusual knowledge about transitional suburban zones. In the area created by this confrontation, and with a curiosity about apparent juxtapositions of urban development and the natural environment, Peter Zellner designs an architecture that embraces both an urban setting with often intense development and a natural environment that is sometimes intact. He juggles with assemblages and interstices, folds and shifts, showing a preference for what Klaus-Klaas Lœhnert calls 'dissolution, adventure and uncertainty'. ◆

The Future is Domestic
New dwelling prototype, California, USA, project, 2001

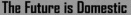

Redundancy: between 1990 and 2000, over 15 million private homes were built in the United States.* Using 'off-the-shelf' plans, the majority of these dwellings were constructed by monolithic commercial home-building companies like Centex, Kaufman and Broad, Pulte, Champion and the Lennar Corporation. Less than 5 % of these homes were designed by registered architects.

The almost total elimination of the architect from the commercial home-production process suggests that – at least in the United States – architects are increasingly incapable of influencing the housing market, let alone subverting its forms of production.

Fiction: 87 years after Le Corbusier and Pierre Jeanneret developed the Maison 'Domino' as a means of aligning the production of the single family dwelling with industrial construction processes, the architectural avant-garde habitually returns to the investigation of various systems for the mass-production (or more lately the mass-customization) of the housing unit. The irony that is lost on this generation of architects is that the production homebuilding industry has inherited the legacy of Le Corbusier's vision by other means. By focusing directly on systems of manufacturing, distribution and delivery, commercial homebuilders have broadly realized the technological and typological promise of the 'Domino' programme without resorting to the fiction of contemporary formal invention.

The future is domestic: operating like car manufacturers, American commercial homebuilders now market entire communities like sequential yet flexible product lines. Buyers then customize their basic production home purchases by ordering options from catalogues of thousands of 'extras' on view over the Internet or in company design centres. Finally teams of contractors serially assemble housing units derived from variations made to generic framing and cladding routines. On average the commercial home production and delivery process takes 4 to 6 months.

To a certain degree, the apparent success of this seamless, speculative coordination of materials, concepts and labour defines the inevitable context with which American architects will have to engage if they are to undertake what Manuel Gausa has anticipated – nothing less than a 'reversible colonization of the territory'.

Coda: the texts, model and drawings presented here are a direct response to the call made by ArchiLab's organizers for research-oriented architecture. More specifically, these articles are focused on examining the state of standardized housing today. By definition they are appropriations. They are explicitly not intended to be understood as the work of the architect. Instead they should be seen as reflections on domestic field and the phenomenon of standardization.

* Source: US Census 2000

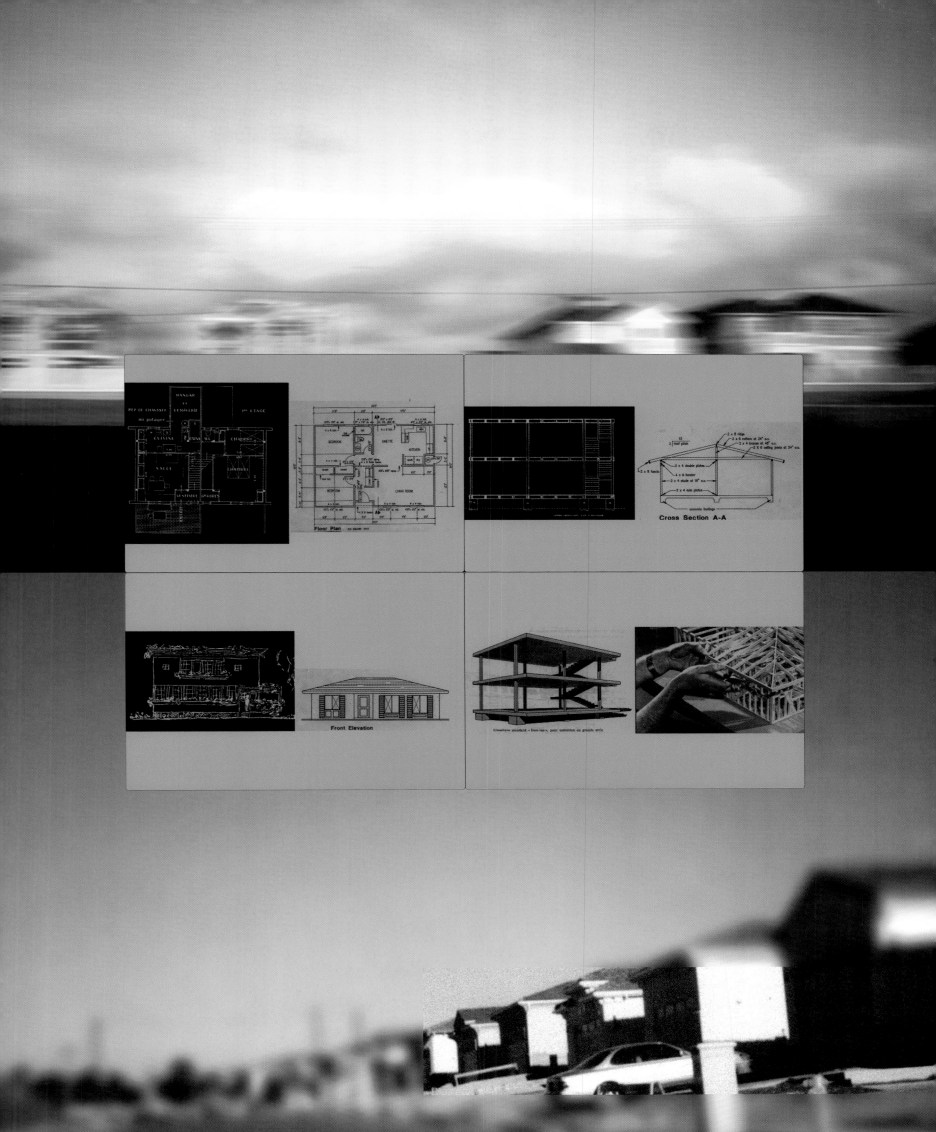

    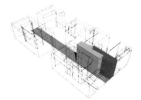

GERMANY

Zanderroth Architekten

SASCHA ZANDER (1968), CHRISTIAN ROTH (1970)

Zanderroth is a new Berlin-based agency founded in 1999 by two architects with a notable European pedigree. Sascha Zander studied architecture at the Barlett School in London, where he was taught by Peter Cook. Christian Roth began his career in Spain, at the ETSA in Madrid. The two architects met in 1995–96 at the Düsseldorf Kunstakademie, where they were students of Carme Piños and Elia Zenghelis, and then completed their studies together at the RWTH in Aachen. Their projects include architecture and town planning (Europan 4 and 5) and public and residential projects. Their work indicates a strong interest in and preference for metropolitan issues and the question of the urban habitat. ly 43, their first realization, manifests considerable mastery of the most restrictive urban situations and a pragmatic sense of 'opportunity': it was they who gave the commissioning body the idea for this operation. ◆

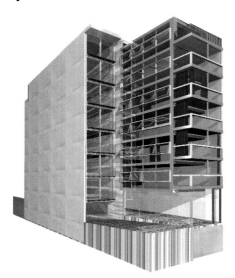

ly 43 Housing
Berlin, Germany, 2001

It is situated in Prenzlauer Berg, a district with a late 18th-century urban structure, dominated by the typical Berlin 'block' typology, which the Berliners adore. Owing to an anomaly in the apportionment of the land, the site does not conform to the usual plan: 10 metres wide, it is bounded by the blank walls of neighbouring buildings, 35 and 45 metres long.

The solution is a scheme adapted to the parameters of the site. We started with a volume 10 metres wide, 26 metres long and 22 metres high, which was cut by a Z-shaped line. The resulting two volumes were moved in such a way as to create three voids: 2 for light, the one in the middle for access. One of the volumes was lifted a half-storey-height to permit access to the central void. This strategy weakens the contradiction between street and garden of the 'block' typology. All the dwellings are oriented to both sides, enjoying a view 100 metres long over a city square to one side, and over the garden, to the other; the edge of the block becomes permeable: a passage for pedestrians and access to the building.

The apartments, whose surface area is about 110 square metres, measure 26 metres in depth and vary in width from 3.3 to 5.7 metres. There are two specific plans. The large living room (kitchen/living) consists of two parts: one, quite intimate, is oriented to the blank wall of the neighbouring building and one called 'mirame' ('look at me' in Spanish), gives on to the outside. The latter is lifted about 40 centimetres to give the other more intimacy (the façade is fully glazed!). Anyone who crosses the step chooses to become exposed. The private areas of the dwelling consist of a room equipped for bathing and storing.

The difference of level in the living area is not an arbitrary decorative element but the result of structural engineering. The urbanistic intention to make the edge of the block permeable required suspending the building. Apart from the access void in the middle, the building does not touch the ground. To achieve such huge unsupported areas, the structural engineer designed a Vierendeel beam, which rises vertically through 6 floors that support the ceiling, and these at the same time prevent it from collapsing (Baron Münchhausen). The thickness of this beam is used for the differentiation of rooms (the above-mentioned step). This structure requires a symmetrical plan for the forces to meet in the mirror point of the building, where they neutralize. ◆

Zanderroth

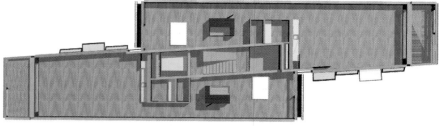

A BOX MADE OF WOOD BUILT
UPON THE ASHES OF A
BOX MADE OF WOOD

A BOX MADE OF WOOD BUILT
UPON THE ASHES OF A
BOX MADE OF WOOD

UNE BOÎTE F

A BOX MADE OF WOOD BUILT
UPON THE ASHES OF A
BOX MADE OF WOOD

BÂTIE SUR

A BOX MADE OF WOOD BUILT
UPON THE ASHES OF A
BOX MADE OF WOOD

D'UNE BOÎTE

A BOX MADE OF WOOD BUILT
UPON THE ASHES OF A
BOX MADE OF WOOD

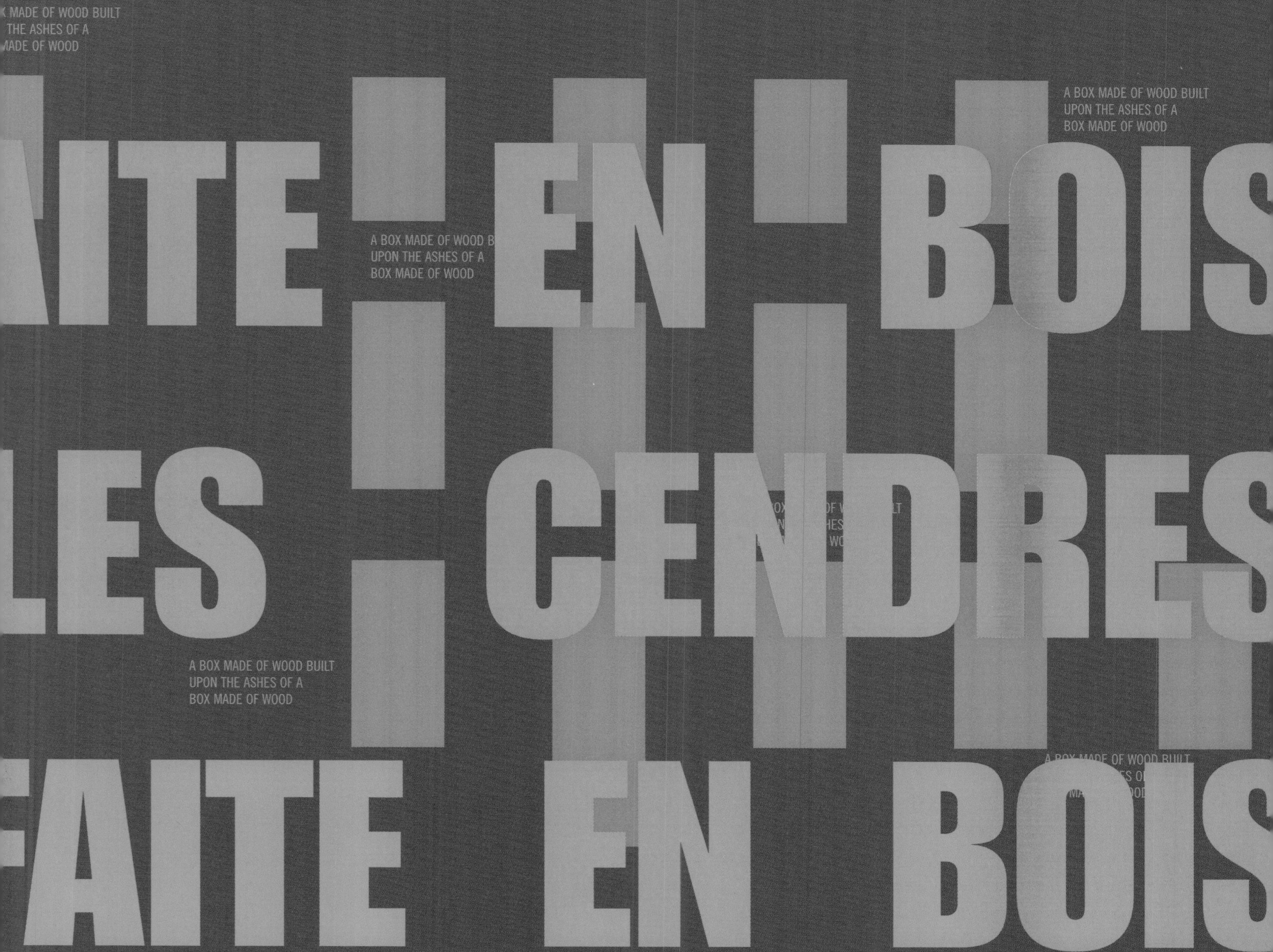

AITE EN BOIS

K MADE OF WOOD BUILT
THE ASHES OF A
MADE OF WOOD

A BOX MADE OF WOOD BUILT
UPON THE ASHES OF A
BOX MADE OF WOOD

A BOX MADE OF WOOD B
UPON THE ASHES OF A
BOX MADE OF WOOD

LES CENDRES

A BOX MADE OF WOOD BUILT
UPON THE ASHES OF A
BOX MADE OF WOOD

A BOX MADE OF WOOD BUILT
UPON THE ASHES OF
MADE OF WOOD

FAITE EN BOIS

Lawrence Weiner, 1974
courtesy FRAC Rhône-Alpes

architect
biograpies

Marie-Ange Brayer
Director of the FRAC Centre, Orléans
Art and architecture critic, France

Manuel Gausa
Architect and critic, Spain

Christian Girard
Architect and teacher, France

Bart Lootsma
Critic, Netherlands

Frédéric Migayrou
Chief curator, architecture department,
Centre Pompidou, Paris

Andreas Ruby
Architectural critic, Germany

Béatrice Simonot
Sociologist and teacher, France

Ábalos & Herreros (Spain)

Founded in Madrid in 1984.

Iñaki Ábalos (1956), Juan Herreros (1958)

1984-88	Professors of construction, Escuela Técnica Superior de Arquitectura, Madrid.
1988	Prize, Community of Madrid, Le Corbusier exhibition : 'The Skyscraper'.
1988 ›	Professors of planning, ETSA Madrid.
1991	Prize, Community of Madrid, RENFE project.
1992 ›	Directors and coordinators, Liga Multimedia International.
1997	COAM architecture prize / Prize of the Community of Madrid (Gaudillo House project).
1996-97	Buell Book Fellows and visiting professors, Columbia University, New York.
1997-99	Diploma Unit Masters, Architectural Association, London.
1998-99	Visiting professors, Ecole Polytechnique Fédérale de Lausanne.
1997	Authors, *Áreas de impunidad*, Monograph.
1997 ›	Editors of *ExitLMI, Documentos de arquitectura*.
1999	Prize, Municipality of Barcelona, Fabrications.

Angel Jaramillo (1968)

1997	Associate architect.

www.abalos-herreros.com

Actar Arquitectura (Spain)

Founded in Barcelona in 1994.

Manuel Gausa Navarro (1959)

1986	Higher architectural diploma, Escuela Técnica Superior de Arquitectura, Barcelona.
1991-00	Director of the review *Quaderns d'arquitectura i urbanisme*.
1994	Member, International team of expert critics from Europan.
1995-99	Professor of planning, Escuela Técnica Superior de Arquitectura, Barcelona.
1998	Co-founder and co-director, Metapolis, with Vicente Guallart and Willy Müller. Organization 1st and 2nd Metapolis Architecture Festival, Barcelona. Publisher, *Met 0.1*, Actar, Barcelona / *Met 0.2*, Actar, Barcelona.
2000	Director, postgraduate programme on advanced architecture and digital cities.

Aureli Santos Ruiz (1960)

1986	Higher architectural diploma, Escuela Técnica Superior de Arquitectura, Barcelona.
1987-88	Associate judge, 'Diseño en España' exhibition, Europalia, Brussels.
1988-00	Architect in chief for public buildings and housing, Historic Centre of Barcelona.
1993	Associate judge, 'Dura Realidad' exhibition, Barcelona.
1996	Judge, 'Cine y Arquitectura' seminar, XIX Congress UIA, Barcelona.

Ignasi Pérez Arnal (1965)

1992	Higher architectural diploma, Escuela Técnica Superior de Arquitectura, Barcelona.
1993	Master of Construction and Technology, Polytechnic University of Catalonia.
1995	Grand Master, Escuela Técnica Superior de Arquitectura, Barcelona.
1997	Director of the international studio Inovar la vivienda en la Barceloneta, PU, Catalonia.

Oleguer Gelpi (1964)

1986-87	Student, Escuela Técnica Superior de Arquitectura, Barcelona.
1993	Judge, international consultation 'After expo', Seville.
1992-97	Member of the editorial team, review *Quaderns d'arquitectura i urbanisme*.
1992-99	Head, Internet Department of the Order of Architects of Catalonia.

Florence Raveau (1965)

1991	Diploma, École d'Architecture de Paris-la-Défense.
1992	Master of design, Espacios urbanos, Barcelona.
1997 ›	Member of the editorial team, review *Quaderns d'arquitectura i urbanisme*.
1998-99	Coordination of the Forum, Escuela Superior de Arquitectura, International University of Catalonia.

www.actar.es

Alejandro Aravena (Chile/USA)

Santiago.

Alejandro Aravena (1967)

1991	Jury Special Mention, 5th Venice Biennale.
1992	Diploma of Architecture, Catholic University of Santiago.
	Specialization in Theory and History, University Architecture Institute of Venice.
	Studies in engraving, Academy of Fine Arts, Venice.
1992 ›	Professor of history and planning, Catholic University of Santiago.
1998 ›	Director of the Department of History and Planning, Catholic University of Santiago.
1997 ›	Collaborator, review Casabella.
1999	Visiting professor, Architectural Association, London.
2000-03	Visiting professor, Harvard GSD.
2000	1st prize, 12th Santiago Biennale.
	Prize for best architect under 40 from the Chilean Architectural Association.
	Co-author, Los hechos de la arquitectura ('The architectural facts').

archi media (France)

Founded in Paris in 1992.

Fiona Meadows (1967)

	Scholarship laureate Monbusho (Japan), Lavoisier (France), Communauté Française de Belgique, Envers des Villes (France).
1991	Architecture degree DPLG.
1995	Diploma, DEA architecture and urban planning.
1995 ›	Teacher, 3rd cycle, École d'Architecture Paris-la-Villette.
1997 ›	Working towards a doctorate, Université de Paris 8.

Frédéric Nantois (1965)

	Scholarship laureate Lavoisier (France), Villa Médicis hors les murs, Communauté Française de Belgique, Envers des Villes (France).
1990	Architecture degree DPLG.
1995	Diploma, DEA communications and multimedia.
1996 ›	Working towards a doctorate, Université de Paris 8.
2000 ›	Research associate at GRAI.

Archi-Tectonics (USA)

Founded in New York in 1994.

Winka Dubbeldam (1960)

1983	Diploma, Academy of Art, Rotterdam.
1988	Travelling scholarship in five Brazilian cities.
1984-90	Collaboration, BOA Architects, Rotterdam.
1990	Diploma, Academy of Architecture, Rotterdam.
	Collaboration, Steven Holl Architects, New York.
1991	Collaboration, Bernard Tschumi Architects, New York.
1992-94	Collaboration, Eisenman Architects, New York.
1992	Master, architecture, Columbia University, New York.
1993	Scholarship, National Foundation for Arts, Design and Architecture.
1995	Scholarship from the Dutch Art & Architecture Foundation for the monograph Winka Dubbeldam Architect, 010 Publishers, Rotterdam.
1995›	Teaching, University of Pennsylvania, Philadelphia, PA.
1997	Scholarship to study in the metropolitan areas of South-east Asia.
1997›	Teaching, Columbia University, New York.

Architekturbüro Bolles + Wilson (Germany)

Founded in London in 1980, in Münster in 1989.

Peter Wilson (1950)

1969-71	Architecture course, Melbourne.
1972-74	Architecture course, Architectural Association, London.
1976-88	Teaching, Unit Master, Architectural Association, London.
1978	Teaching, Summer Academy, Berlin.
1987-89	Workshop for A+U, Tokyo.
1994-96	Visiting professor, Kunsthochschule Weißensee, Berlin.
1994-95-97	Teaching, Berlage Academy, Amsterdam.
1997-98	Teaching, IAAS, Venice.
1998	Teaching, NAI Summer Academy, Rotterdam.
1998 ›	Degree panel, Architectural Association, London / University of Cambridge.

Julia Bolles Wilson (1948)

1968-76	Architecture course, University of Karlsruhe.
1978-79	Architecture course, Architectural Association, London.
1981-86	Teaching, Chelsea School of Art, London.
1996 ›	Professor, Architectural Design, University of Applied Sciences, Münster.
1994	Judge, international competition, Alster, Hamburg.
1998	Judge, competition, German Federal Office for Environmental Design, Dessau.
1998	Prize (nominated), Carlsberg, Denmark.
2000	Judge, competition, Urban Design of the ICE-Railway Station, Cologne.
2000	Mies van der Rohe Prize (nominated).

Asymptote (USA)

Founded in New York in 1988.

Lise-Anne Couture (1959)

1986	Master of Architecture, Yale University.
	Muschenheim Scholarship, University of Michigan, Ann Arbor.
1999 ›	Teaching, Parson School of Design / Columbia University, New York / University of Michigan, Ann Arbor / Städelschule, Frankfurt / Harvard University / University of Montreal.
1990 ›	Professor, Parson School of Design, New York.

Hani Rashid (1958)

1985	Master of architecture, Cranbrook Academy of Art, Michigan (USA).
1994	Author, LAX : the LAL experiment AGIT(N)ATION Pseudo architecture, SITES, Lumen Books.
1989 ›	Professor, Columbia University Graduate School of Architecture.
1999 ›	Teaching, Graduate School of Architecture and Urban Planning, Columbia University / Harvard University / Städelschule, Frankfurt / Royal Danish Academy, Copenhagen / Berlage Institute, Amsterdam / Technical University, Vienna / Lund University, Sweden.

www.asymptote.net

Atelier Hitoshi Abe (Japan)

Founded in Sendai in 1992.

Hitoshi Abe (1962)

1989	Master of Architecture, Southern California Institute of Architecture.
1988-92	Collaboration, Coop Himmelb(l)au agency, Los Angeles.
1992	PhD in architecture, Tohoku University.
1994 ›	Director of Hitoshi Abe, Architectural Design Laboratory, Tohoku Institute of Technology. Teaching, Tohoku University / Miyagi National College of Technology.
1995	Tohoku Steel Architecture Award '94.
1997	Prize (4th), Twenty Young Architects, 8th World Triennale of Architecture, INTERARCH.
1998	Prize, 14th Yoshioka Architectural Award.
1999	Prize (citation), Tohoku Architectural Award '98.

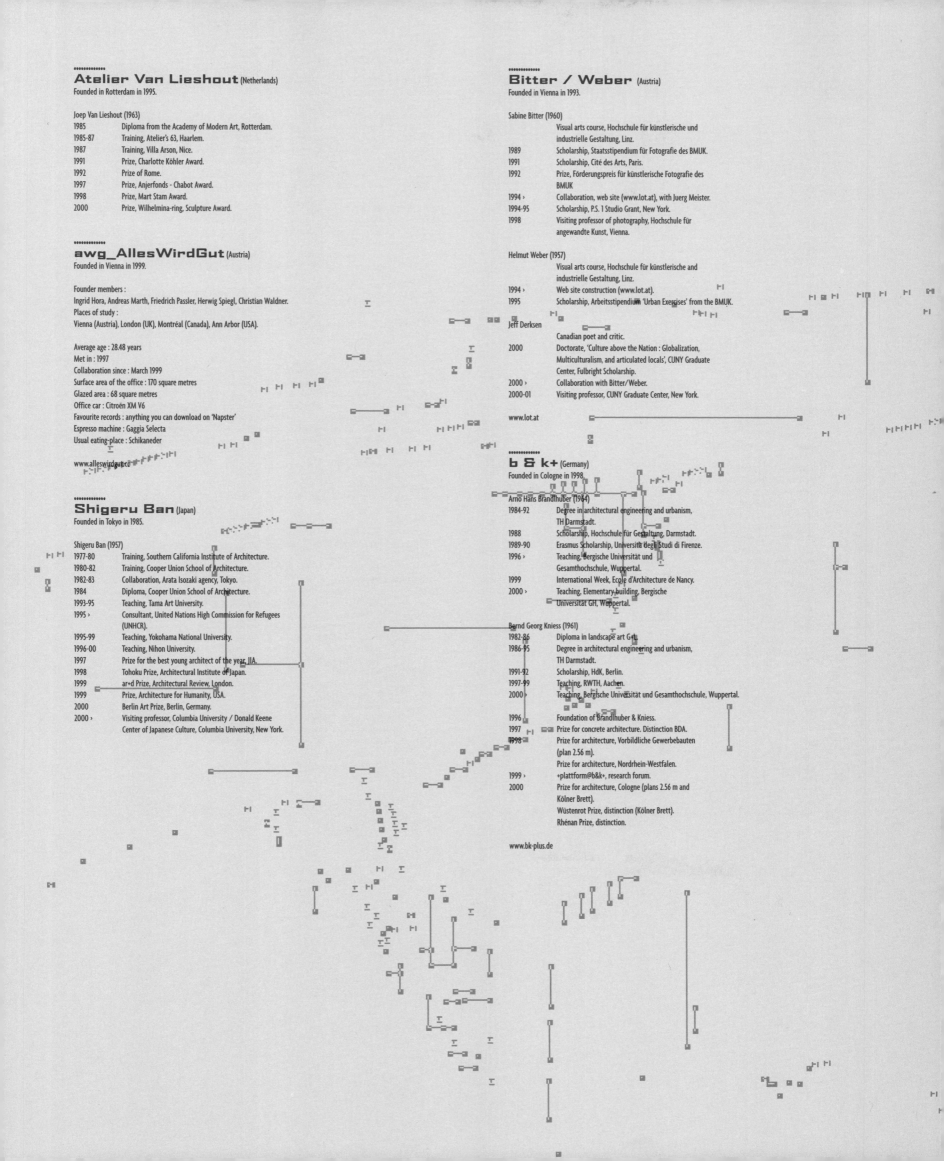

Atelier Van Lieshout (Netherlands)
Founded in Rotterdam in 1995.

Joep Van Lieshout (1963)
1985	Diploma from the Academy of Modern Art, Rotterdam.
1985-87	Training, Atelier's 63, Haarlem.
1987	Training, Villa Arson, Nice.
1991	Prize, Charlotte Köhler Award.
1992	Prize of Rome.
1997	Prize, Anjerfonds - Chabot Award.
1998	Prize, Mart Stam Award.
2000	Prize, Wilhelmina-ring, Sculpture Award.

awg_AllesWirdGut (Austria)
Founded in Vienna in 1999.

Founder members :
Ingrid Hora, Andreas Marth, Friedrich Passler, Herwig Spiegl, Christian Waldner.
Places of study :
Vienna (Austria), London (UK), Montréal (Canada), Ann Arbor (USA).

Average age : 28.48 years
Met in : 1997
Collaboration since : March 1999
Surface area of the office : 170 square metres
Glazed area : 68 square metres
Office car : Citroën XM V6
Favourite records : anything you can download on 'Napster'
Espresso machine : Gaggia Selecta
Usual eating-place : Schikaneder

www.alleswirdgut.cc

Shigeru Ban (Japan)
Founded in Tokyo in 1985.

Shigeru Ban (1957)
1977-80	Training, Southern California Institute of Architecture.
1980-82	Training, Cooper Union School of Architecture.
1982-83	Collaboration, Arata Isozaki agency, Tokyo.
1984	Diploma, Cooper Union School of Architecture.
1993-95	Teaching, Tama Art University.
1995 ›	Consultant, United Nations High Commission for Refugees (UNHCR).
1995-99	Teaching, Yokohama National University.
1996-00	Teaching, Nihon University.
1997	Prize for the best young architect of the year, JIA.
1998	Tohoku Prize, Architectural Institute of Japan.
1999	ar+d Prize, Architectural Review, London.
1999	Prize, Architecture for Humanity, USA.
2000	Berlin Art Prize, Berlin, Germany.
2000 ›	Visiting professor, Columbia University / Donald Keene Center of Japanese Culture, Columbia University, New York.

Bitter / Weber (Austria)
Founded in Vienna in 1993.

Sabine Bitter (1960)
	Visual arts course, Hochschule für künstlerische und industrielle Gestaltung, Linz.
1989	Scholarship, Staatsstipendium für Fotografie des BMUK.
1991	Scholarship, Cité des Arts, Paris.
1992	Prize, Förderungspreis für künstlerische Fotografie des BMUK
1994 ›	Collaboration, web site (www.lot.at), with Juerg Meister.
1994-95	Scholarship, P.S. 1 Studio Grant, New York.
1998	Visiting professor of photography, Hochschule für angewandte Kunst, Vienna.

Helmut Weber (1957)
	Visual arts course, Hochschule für künstlerische and industrielle Gestaltung, Linz.
1994 ›	Web site construction (www.lot.at).
1995	Scholarship, Arbeitsstipendium 'Urban Exercises' from the BMUK.

Jeff Derksen
	Canadian poet and critic.
2000	Doctorate, 'Culture above the Nation : Globalization, Multiculturalism, and articulated locals', CUNY Graduate Center, Fulbright Scholarship.
2000 ›	Collaboration with Bitter/Weber.
2000-01	Visiting professor, CUNY Graduate Center, New York.

www.lot.at

b & k+ (Germany)
Founded in Cologne in 1998.

Arno Hans Brandlhuber (1964)
1984-92	Degree in architectural engineering and urbanism, TH Darmstadt.
1988	Scholarship, Hochschule für Gestaltung, Darmstadt.
1989-90	Erasmus Scholarship, Università degli Studi di Firenze.
1996 ›	Teaching, Bergische Universität und Gesamthochschule, Wuppertal.
1999	International Week, Ecole d'Architecture de Nancy.
2000 ›	Teaching, Elementary building, Bergische Universität GH, Wuppertal.

Bernd Georg Kniess (1961)
1982-86	Diploma in landscape art GH.
1986-95	Degree in architectural engineering and urbanism, TH Darmstadt.
1991-92	Scholarship, HdK, Berlin.
1997-99	Teaching, RWTH, Aachen.
2000 ›	Teaching, Bergische Universität und Gesamthochschule, Wuppertal.
1996	Foundation of Brandlhuber & Kniess.
1997	Prize for concrete architecture. Distinction BDA.
1998	Prize for architecture, Vorbildliche Gewerbebauten (plan 2.56 m). Prize for architecture, Nordrhein-Westfalen.
1999 ›	+plattform@b&k+, research forum.
2000	Prize for architecture, Cologne (plans 2.56 m and Kölner Brett). Wüstenrot Prize, distinction (Kölner Brett). Rhénan Prize, distinction.

www.bk-plus.de

BKK3 ZT (Austria)
Founded in Vienna in 1999.

Johann Winter (1949)
	Degree from the Technical University of Vienna.
1985-93	Foundation, BauKünstlerKollektiv, with Peter Raab and Josef Zapletal
1993-99	Foundation, Agence BKK-2.

Franz Sumnitsch (1961)
	Training, Technical University of Graz.
	Collaboration, Gunther Domenig.
1993-99	Foundation, Agence BKK-2.
1995	Prize, Upper Austrian Culture Award (Gänserndorf library project).
1996	Adolf Loos Prize for architecture (Wohnheim Sargfabrik project).
1996	ZVA Prize (Wohnheim Sargfabrik project).

Regina Gschwendtner (1971)
Christoph Mörkl (1970)
Verena Kukla (1974)
	Studies, Technical University of Vienna.
1999	Collaboration, Agence BKK3.

2 4 4

Andrea Branzi (Italy)
Milan.

Andrea Branzi (1938)
	Architecture and design studies, Florence.
› 1971	Co-founder of Archizoom.
1972	Italy exhibition : 'The New Domestic Landscape', MoMA, with Archizoom.
1972-75	Collaboration, review *Casabella*.
1970s	Member of CDM (Consulenti Design Milano), of Alchimia, of Memphis.
1977	Coordination, 'Il design italiano degli anni '50' exhibition, Milan.
1978	Compas d'Or, with Consulenti Design Milano.
1983	Co-founder of Domus Academy, Milan.
1983	International prize, Buenos Aires Biennale, with Domus Academy.
1983-84	Teaching, Faculty of architecture, Palermo.
1983-87	Editor of *Modo*, magazine of architecture and design.
1986-90	European Community, development of design in Europe.
1987	Compas d'Or, Special Award.
1989	Robert Maxwell Prize, Royal College of Art, London (seven theses on design).
1990	Judge, 'Il Dolce Stil Novo (della Casa)' exhibition, Florence.
1990	Coordination, 'Les Capitales européennes du nouveau design', Centre Pompidou, Paris.
1991	Consultant, Biennial Interiors Exhibition, Courtrai, Belgium.
1991	Baden Württemberg Prize, with Up&Up (table Quadrio).
1991 ›	Director, Domus Design Agency, Tokyo.
2000	'Fondation pour l'Architecture' exhibition, Brussels

Bureau Venhuizen (Netherlands)
Founded in Rotterdam in 1998.

Hans Venhuizen (1961)
1982-84	Town planning course, University of Nijmegen.
1986-92	Architectural design/ monumental art course, art school, Arnhem.
1996-97	Master, urban design, art school, Berlin-Weißensee.
1995-01	Visiting professor, schools of arts and architecture in Arnhem, Rotterdam, Tilburg (Netherlands), Bergen, Trondheim (Norway).
1992-98	Scholarships from the National Foundation of Design, Arts and Architecture, Amsterdam.

Cero 9 (Spain)
Founded in Madrid in 1997.

Cristina Díaz Moreno (1971)
1998	Diploma from the Escuela Técnica Superior de Arquitectura de Madrid.
1995-96	Bartlett School of Architecture.
	Visiting professor, ESARQ of the International University of Catalonia / EPSA of the Polytechnic University of Alicante.
	Associate professor, UEM.
	Assistant professor at the ETSA, Madrid.
2000 ›	Committee member, 'Arquitecturas Silenciosas', Ministry for Innovation, Spain.

Efrén Garcia Grinda (1966)
1992	Diploma from the Escuela Técnica Superior de Arquitectura de Madrid.
	Visiting professor, ESARQ of the International University of Catalonia / EPSA of the Polytechnic University of Alicante.
	Associate professor, UEM.
	Associate professor at the ETSA, Madrid.
2000 ›	Committee member, 'Arquitecturas Silenciosas', Ministry for Innovation, Spain.

Santiago Cirugeda Parejo (Spain)
Founded in Seville in 1994.

Santiago Cirugeda Parejo (1971)
	Training, Escuela Tecnica Superior de Arquitectura, Seville, Spain.
1997	Teaching, 'Urban planning', public art, School of Scenography, Seville.
1998	Teaching, 'Dripping shit', public art, School of Scenography, Seville.
1999	Teaching, 'Intervenciones urbanas, un lugar desde la institución', FIDAS, School of Scenography, Seville.
	Teaching, 'Danza vertical-Danza arquitectura', ENDANZA, Seville.
	Seminars, Academy of Performing Arts, Perth, Australia / Theatre Institute, Seville / ETSAV, Barcelona / ESARQ, Barcelona / Technical University of Lisbon, Portugal / Centre of Contemporary Culture, Barcelona / ETSA, Granada.

Herman Tschernko, architect, 2000.
Santiago Balbotín, architect, 1998.
Ignacio Pretel, lawyer, 1998.
Beatriz Acedo, lawyer, 1997.

Preston Scott Cohen (USA)
New York.

Preston Scott Cohen (1961)
1983	Diploma in architecture, Rhode Island School of Design.
1985	Master of architecture, Graduate School of Design, Harvard University.
	Associate professor, Graduate School of Design, Harvard University.
	Teaching, Princeton University / Ohio State University / RISD, Rome.
1992	Winner, Young Architects Competition, Architectural League, New York.
1995	Co-author, *Eric Owen Moss : The Box*, Princeton Architectural Press.
1996	Selected among 'Emerging Voices', Venice Architecture Biennale.
1998	Winner, Progressive Architectural Award.
2000	Winner, Progressive Architectural Award.
	Author, *Contested Symmetries and Other Predicaments in Architecture*, Princeton Architectural Press.
	Author, *Permutations of Descriptive Geometry*.
	Author, *On the Terminal Line*, Architectural Association, London.

www.gsd.harvard.edu/faculty/cohen/profile.html

Peter Cook (UK)

Cook and Hawley Architects
Founded in London in 1978.

Peter Cook (1936)

	President, Bartlett School of Architecture, University College, London.
	Member, Royal Institute of British Architects / Bund Deutscher Architekten / Architektenkammer Hessen / Royal Society of Arts / Académie Européenne des Sciences et des Arts.
1953-58	Training, Bournemouth College of Art.
1958-60	Training, Architectural Association, London.
1961-76	Founder member, Archigram group, London.
1964-89	Teaching, Architectural Association, London.
1970-72	Director, Institute of Contemporary Art, London.
1972-78	Director, Art Newt, London.
1984›	Professor, Hochschule für Bildende Künste, Frankfurt am Main.
1990	Los Angeles Prize, American Institute of Architects.
1990›	Professor, Bartlett School of Architecture, London.
1997	Jean Tschumi Prize, Union Internationale des Architectes.
1998-99	Teaching, Rice University, Houston.

Coop Himmelb(l)au (Austria)

Founded in Vienna in 1968.

Wolf D. Prix (1942)

	Training, Technische Universität, Vienna / Architectural Association, London / Southern California Institute of Architecture, Los Angeles.
	Professor, University of Applied Arts, Vienna / Southern California Institute of Architecture, Los Angeles.
1984	Teaching, Architectural Association, London.
1990	Teaching, Harvard University, Cambridge, MA.
1995-97	Member, Architectural Counsellor, Federal Ministry of Science, Research and Arts, Austria.
1998›	Teaching, Columbia University, New York.
	Member, Association of Austrian Architects and Association of Architects, Santa Clara, Cuba.

Helmut Swiczinsky (1942)

	Training, Technische Universität, Vienna / Architectural Association, London.
1999	Honourable mention, German Architecture Award / Architecture Award for Cement Structure / Erich Schelling Architecture Prize / Großer Österreichischer Staatspreis.
	Member, Académie Européenne des Sciences et des Arts.
2000	Musée des Confluences competition prize, Lyon.

www.coop.himmelblau.at

dECOi (France)

Founded in Paris in 1991.

Mark Goulthorpe (1963)

1984-85	Collaboration, Building Design Partnership, London.
1988	Degree, B. Arch., University of Liverpool.
1988-92	Collaboration, Richard Meier, New York.
1990	Prize from the Royal Academy, Centre for the Performing Arts, Glasgow.
1993	Prize (2nd place), La casa piu bella del mondo, Milan.
1993	Prize, Les Albums de la jeune architecture, Ministère de l'Équipement, France.
	Prize, Young Architects Forum, Architectural League of New York.
1996	Selected, Venice Architecture Biennale.
1999	Prix, Young Architect of the Year, BD Journal.
1999	Prix, Birmingham Hippodrome Interactive Art Competition.
2000	Selected, Venice Architecture Biennale.
	Teaching, Architectural Association, London / University of Kassel, Germany.
	Visiting professor, École Spéciale de Paris / University of Llubljana, Slovenia.

Diller + Scofidio (USA)

Founded in New York in 1979.

Elisabeth Diller (1954)

	Professor, Princeton University, Princeton, NJ.
1979	Degree, Cooper Union School of Architecture, New York.
1981-90	Teaching, Cooper Union School of Architecture, New York.

Ricardo Scofidio (1935)

	Professor, Cooper Union School of Architecture, New York.
1952-55	Training, Cooper Union School of Architecture, New York.
1960	Degree, architecture, Columbia University, New York.
1987	Prize, Bessie Schoenberg Dance and Performance.
	Authors, *Bodybuildings : architectural facts and fictions*, New York : Storefront for Art + Architecture.
1990	Prize, Tiffany Foundation for Emerging Artists.
1991	Prize, Progressive Architecture for the Slow House /
	Authors, *Flesh*, New York : Rizzoli.
2000	Selected, Venice Architecture Biennale.
	Prizes : MacArthur Foundation Award, Obie for Creative Achievement (for 'Jet Lag') / James Beard Foundation Award (for 'Brasserie') / Progressive Architecture Design Award (for the 'Blur Building') / MacDermott Award.
	Scholarships : Graham Foundation / Chicago Institute for Architecture and Urbanism / New York Foundation for the Arts.

Pierre du Besset & Dominique Lyon (France)

Founded in Paris in 1986.

Pierre du Besset (1949)
Dominique Lyon (1954)

1994	Author, *Point de vue, usage du monde*, Carte Segrete.
1995	Teaching, School of Fine Arts, Vienna.
1997	Author, *Les Avatars de l'architecture ordinaire*, Paris : Sens & Tonka.
1998	Teaching, École Spéciale d'Architecture, Paris.
1999	Teaching, Columbia University, New York.
	Author, *Le Corbusier vivant*, Paris : Telleri.

EDGE (HK) (China)

Founded in Hong Kong in 1998.

Gary Chang (1962)

1987	Degree in architecture, University of Hong Kong.
1987	Scholarship, Hong Kong Land Travel Grant.
1987	Collaboration, P&T Architects and Engineers, Hong Kong.
1990	Prize, 25th Central Glass International Design Competition.
1994	Foundation of EDGE, with Michael Chan.
1997	Prize, Young Architect, Foundation Hsin Chong K. N. Godfrey Yeh.
1998	Jury, Hong Kong Institute of Architects Annual Awards.
1998	Prize, Chartered Society of Designers, Hong Kong Design.
1999	Prize, Asia Pacific Interior Awards.
2000	Prize, Asia Pacific Interior Awards.

www.edge.hk.com

EMERGENT Design (USA)

Founded in Los Angeles in 1999.

Tom Wiscombe (1970)

1990-92	Collaboration, Timberline Geodesics, Berkeley.
1992	Degree in architecture, University of California, Berkeley.
1992-99	Collaboration, Coop Himmelb(l)au, Vienna/Los Angeles.
1995-96	Teaching, University of Applied Arts, Vienna.
1999	Master of architecture, University of California, Berkeley.
1999	Teaching, Woodbury University, Burbank.
1999 ›	Teaching, SCI-Arc, Los Angeles.

www.emergentdesigninc.com

Shuhei Endo Architect Institute (Japan)
Founded in Osaka in 1988.

Shuhei Endo (1960)

1986	Master, Kyoto University of Art.
1986-88	Collaboration, Osamu Ishii & Biken Associates, Osaka.
1998	Prize, Japanese Federation of Architects, Association of Engineer-Builders.
1998›	Teaching, Kinki University, Kobe / Design School / Fukui Institute of Technology.
	East Asia Prize, Italy.
	Prize, Marble Architectural Award.

Didier Fiuza Faustino (France/Portugal)
Architect in Paris and Lisbon since 1996.

Didier Fiuza Faustino (1968)

1995	Diploma, École d'Architecture de Paris-Villemin.
1996	Co-founder, Laboratoire d'Architectures Performances et Sons (LAPS), Paris.
1997	Co-founder, Atelier Pluridisciplinaire 'le Fauteuil vert', Paris.
1998	Co-founder, co-director and artistic director of the review Numeromagazine, Lisbon.

Field Operations (USA)
Founded in New York / Philadelphia in 1999.

Stan Allen (1956)

	Associate professor, Columbia University, New York.
1981	Degree in architecture, The Cooper Union, New York.
1981-83	Collaboration, Richard Meier & Partners, New York.
1983-85	Collaboration, Rafael Moneo, Spain.
1987	Master of architecture, Princeton University.
1986	Architecture scholarship, New York Foundation for the Arts.
1988	Winner, Young Architects Competition, Architectural League of New York.
1990	Architecture scholarship, New York Foundation for the Arts.
1990s	Editor in chief of the review Assemblage.
1991	Prize, National Endowment of Arts.
1992	Prize, New York State Council on the Arts.
1993	Prize, Graham Foundation.
1995	Editor, Lusitania, special edition on 'Architecture and Urbanism'.
1999	Author, theoretical essay Practice : architecture, technique and representation, Princeton.
1999	Association with James Corner (1961), urban planner and landscape artist.

Manuelle Gautrand Architectes (France)
Founded in Lyon in 1991 / in Paris in 1993.

Manuelle Gautrand (1961)

1985	Diploma in architecture.
1986-90	Collaboration, various agencies in Paris.
1992	Prize, Les Albums de la jeune architecture, Ministère de l'Équipement.
1992›	Architectural adviser, Rectorship of Isère.
1994	Prize (nomination) for a first work, le Moniteur (for the cinema at Villefontaine).
1999›	Teaching, École d'Architecture, Paris-Val-de-Seine.
	Architectural consultant, Mission Interministérielle pour la Qualité des Constructions Publiques (MIQCP).
2000	French AMO Prize 'Architecture et lieux de travail', Association AMO, Ministère de la Culture.
2000-01	Teaching, École Spéciale d'Architecture, Paris.

www.manuelle-gautrand.com

Vicente Guallart (Spain)
Founded in Barcelona in 1993.

Vicente Guallart (1963)

	Director, postgraduate programme, Arquitectura Avanzada y Ciudades Digitales, Polytechnic Foundation of Catalonia.
	Director, Metapolis.
	Co-director, Project Media House I+3D, Media Lab.
	Author, Media, Mountain and Architecture, Actar / Single Housing, Actar / Metapolis Barcelona, Actar.
1989	Diploma in architecture, Escuela Técnica Superior de Arquitectura, Valencia.
1992	Doctorate in architecture, Escuela Técnica Superior de Arquitectura, Barcelona.
1989-93	Foundation, Map Architects, with José Luis Mateo.
1992	FAD Prize.
1995	Moebius Prize, production 'CD-ROM Architecture'
1996	Milia d'or, Cannes, France.
1997	Prize (finalist), 4th Spanish Architecture Biennale.
1998	Co-founder of Metapolis, with Manuel Gausa and Willy Müller.
	Organisation 1st and 2nd Metapolis Festival of Architecture, Barcelona. Publisher, Met 0.1, Actar, Barcelona / Met 0.2, Actar, Barcelona.

IaN+ (Italy)
Founded in Rome in 1997.

Carmelo Baglivo (1964)

1993	Diploma in architecture, La Sapienza University, Rome.
1994	6th international seminar 'Naples, Architecture and City', by Domus / the Frankfurt Museum / University of Naples.
	Collaborations, Max Dudler, Berlin / Paris / Rome.

Luca Galofaro (1965)

1990	Diploma in architecture, La Sapienza University, Rome.
1993	Master of spatial science, International Space University, Alabama, USA.
	Collaboration, Peter Eisenman Architects, New York.
1997	Author, 'Eero Saarinen', in Testo & Immagine, ed. Bruno Zevi.
2000	Author, 'Chicago Tribune Competition', in Testo & Immagine, ed. Bruno Zevi.

Stefania Manna (1969)

1996	Diploma in civil engineering, La Sapienza University, Rome.
1993 ›	Working towards a doctorate, La Sapienza University, Rome.
	Research in cooperation with the universities of Helsinki and Oulu, Finland.
1998	Organization, 'American Architecture @ the Edge of Millennium' exhibition, Rome / UCLA, Los Angeles / Parson School of Design, New York.

Osamu Ishiyama Lab. (Japan)
Founded in Tokyo in 1968.

Osamu Ishiyama (1944)

1966	Degree, B. Arch, Waseda University, Tokyo.
1968	Master of engineering, Waseda University, Tokyo.
	Foundation, Dam-Dan Space Workshop, Tokyo.
1968›	Professor, Waseda University, Tokyo.
1972	Foundation, Dam-Dan Corporation, Tokyo.
1984	Author, Akihabara-kankakude jutakuwo kangaeru ['Building a house in the sense of Akihabara'], Tokyo : Shobunsha.
1985	Isoya Yoshida Prize (for the Izu Choliachi Sakan art museum).
1986	Author, Warau jucatu ['The house that makes you laugh'], Tokyo : Chikuma-Shobo.
1991	Author, Gendaino shokunin ['Artisans of today'], Tokyo : Shobunsha.
1993	Author, Jutakubyo wa naoranai ['The sickness of the house'], Tokyo : Shobunsha.
1994	Author, Sekai-ichino machitsukurida ['We have built the most beautiful town in the world'], Tokyo : Shobunsha.
1995	Prize, Japanese Architectural Institute (for the Rias-Ark art museum).

Jakob + MacFarlane (France)
Founded in Paris in 1992.

Dominique Jakob (1966)
1991	Diploma, École d'Architecture de Paris-Villemin.
1994›	Teaching, École d'Architecture de Paris-Villemin.
1999	Teaching, École Spéciale d'Architecture, Paris.

Brendan MacFarlane (1961)
1984	Degree, B. Arch., Southern California Institute of Architecture, Los Angeles.
1988	Teaching, Graduate School of Design, Harvard University, Cambridge, MA / Southern California Institute of Architecture, Los Angeles.
1990	Degree, M. Arch., Graduate School of Design, Harvard University, Cambridge, MA.
1995›	Teaching, École d'Architecture de Paris-la-Villette, Paris.
1998-99	Teaching, Bartlett School, London.
1999	Teaching, École Spéciale d'Architecture, Paris.
1995	Co-founders, Association Périphériques, with E. Marin-Trottin and D. Trottin.

Jones, Partners: Architecture (USA)
Founded in San Francisco in 1993 / Los Angeles.

Wes Jones (1958)
1978	Graduate, United States Military Academy, West Point.
1980	Degree, University of California, Berkeley.
	Foundation, ELS Design Group, Berkeley.
1983	Master, Graduate School of Design, Harvard University, Cambridge, MA.
	Collaboration, Eisenman / Robertson, New York.
	Teaching, Graduate School of Design, Harvard University, Cambridge, MA.
1984	Teaching, Columbia University, New York.
1985	Prize, American Academy of Rome.
1987	Foundation, Holt Hinshaw Pfau Jones, San Francisco.
	Scholarship, New York Foundation for the Arts.
	Prize, Progressive Architecture (for 'Right Away Ready Mix').
1988	Teaching, College of Environmental Design, University of California, Berkeley.
	Teaching, Graduate School of Architecture and Urban Planning, University of California, Los Angeles.
1989	Prize, Progressive Architecture (for 'Astronauts Memorial').
	Teaching, Graduate School of Architecture and Urban Planning, Rice University.
1990	Professor, Graduate School of Design, Harvard University, Cambridge, MA.
1991	Foundation, Holt Hinshaw Jones, San Francisco.
1997	Author, Instrumental Form, Princeton : Princeton Architectural Press.

www.jonespartners.com

Kalhöfer-Korschildgen (Germany)
Founded in Aachen in 1995 / in Cologne in 2000.

Gerhard Kalhöfer (1962)
1984	History of art course, University of Marburg.
1984-92	Diploma in architecture, RWTH, Aix-la-Chapelle.
1990-92	Scholarship, Düsseldorf Academy of Arts.
	Collaboration, Eisele+Fritz, Darmstadt / Jean Nouvel, Paris / Architecture Studio, Paris.
1997 ›	Teaching, Academy of Architecture, Maastricht / Netherlands / FH Cologne.
1998 ›	Professor, theory and architecture, FH Mainz.

Stefan Korschildgen
1982-84	Training as a ship's carpenter.
1984-92	Diploma in architecture, RWTH, Aix-la-Chapelle.
1990-92	Scholarship, Düsseldorf Academy of Arts.
	Collaboration, Szyszkowitz + Kowalski, Graz / Overdiek + Petzinka, Düsseldorf / Olson + Sundberg, Seattle.
1997 ›	Teaching, RWTH, Aix-la-Chapelle.
2001 ›	Professor, interior architecture, FH Düsseldorf.

Mathias Klotz (Chile)
Founded in Santiago in 1991.

Mathias Klotz (1965)
1991	Diploma, Catholic University of Chile.
1994	Prize, 2nd Biennale at Concepción, Chile.
1995	Prize, Promotion of Young Architects, College of Architects of Chile.
	Prize, 10th Chile Architecture Biennale.
1996-98	Teaching, Central University of Santiago.
1996-00	Teaching, Federico Santa María de Valparaíso University.

KOL/MAC (USA)
Founded in New York in 1988.

Ayse Sulan Kolatan (1958)
1983	Engineering diploma, RWTH Aachen, Aix-la-Chapelle, Germany.
1984	Master, Architecture and Urban Design, Columbia University, New York.
1989	Teaching, Barnard College, Columbia University, New York.
1990›	Teaching, Columbia University, New York.
1993	Teaching, Ohio State University, Columbus, OH.
1994	Teaching, University of Pennsylvania, Philadelphia, PA.

William J. MacDonald (1956)
1977-78	Training, Architectural Association, London.
1979	Degree in architecture, Syracuse University, Syracuse, NY.
1981	Master, Architecture and Urban Design, Columbia University, New York.
1982-85	Teaching, University of Virginia, Charlottesville, VA.
1985›	Teaching, Columbia University, New York.
1993	Teaching, Ohio State University, Columbus, OH.
1994	Teaching, University of Pennsylvania, Philadelphia, PA.

www.kolatanmacdonaldstudio.com

Tom Kovac (Australia)
Founded in Melbourne in 1990.

Tom Kovac (1958)
1970	Settled in Australia.
1986	Architecture diploma, Royal Melbourne Institute of Technology, Melbourne.
1991	Prize, RAIA.
1994	Foundation of Galerie Curve Architecture, Melbourne.
1996-97	Teaching, Royal Melbourne Institute of Technology, Melbourne.
1997	Master of architecture, Royal Melbourne Institute of Technology, Melbourne.
2000	Selected for the Venice Architecture Biennale.
	Exhibition, NAI, Rotterdam /Aedes Gallery, Berlin.
2001	Teaching, University of Ljubljana, Slovenia.

Kengo Kuma & Associates (Japan)
Founded in Tokyo in 1990.

Kengo Kuma (1954)
1979	Master of architecture, Engineering faculty, University of Tokyo.
1985-86	Scholarship from the Asian Cultural Council.
	Visiting professor, Columbia University, New York.
1987	Foundation of Spatial Design Studio.
1994	Author, An Introduction to Architectural History and Ideology, Chikuma Publishing, Japan.
	Author, The Catastrophe of Architectural Desire, Shinyosha, Japan.
	Jury, Columbia University, New York.
1995	Author, Beyond the Architectural Crisis, TOTO Publishing, Japan.
	JCD Design Award, Cultural/Public Institutions.
1997	Prize, Architectural Institute of Japan.
	AIA DuPont Benedictus Award.
1998-99	Professor, Faculty of Environmental Science, University of Keio.
2000	Prize, INTER INTRA SPACE, design selection.
	Prize, Architectural Institute of Japan.

Lacaton & Vassal (France)
Founded in Bordeaux in 1987.

Anne Lacaton (1955)
1980	Diploma, École d'Architecture de Bordeaux.
1984	DESS in city planning, Bordeaux.
1994-99	Teaching, École des Beaux-Arts, Bordeaux.

Jean Philippe Vassal (1954)
1980	Diploma, École d'Architecture de Bordeaux.
1980-85	Architect–city planner in Niger.
1992-99	Teaching, École d'Architecture de Bordeaux.
1994-99	Teaching, École des Beaux-Arts, Bordeaux.

1991	Laureates, Albums de la Jeune Architecture.
1996	Prize (nominees), Equerre d'Argent du Moniteur.
1997	Selected for 5th European Architecture Mies van der Rohe Award.
1999	Grand Prix National d'Architecture Jeune Talent, Ministère de la Culture, France.

LCM (Mexico)
Laboratorio de la Ciudad de México
Founded in Mexico in 1999.

Fernando Romero (1971)
1995	Diploma, Universidad Iberoamericana.
	President, Student Society.
	Organizer, First International Architecture Congress, Mexico.
1996	Collaboration, Enric Miralles, Barcelona.
1997	Collaboration, Jean Nouvel, Paris.
1997-00	Collaboration, Rem Koolhaas, OMA.
2000	Selected for the Venice Architecture Biennale.
2000	Co-author, ZMVM, *Analysis of the Transformation of Mexico City*, National Council of Arts, Mexico.

Leeser Architecture (USA)
Founded in New York in 1989.

Thomas Leeser (1952)
	Training, Industrial design, Hanover, Germany.
	Master architect–engineer, Technische Universität Darmstadt, Germany.
1970	Foundation, Art Run, Frankfurt am Main, Germany.
1978-80	Collaboration, Architekturbüro Ludwig E. Leeser, Frankfurt am Main.
1980-89	Collaboration, Peter Eisenman.
1985	Stone Lion Award, 3rd Venice Biennale.
	Teaching, Parsons School of Design /Columbia University, New York /Illinois Institute of Technology, Chicago, Princeton University /The Cooper University, New York /ETH Zurich.
1986	Co-author, *Moving Arrows, Eros and Other Errors: An Architecture of Absence*, A.A. Publications, London.
1989	AIA Honour Award, IBA Museum and Social Housing Project, Berlin.
1996	Scholarship, New York Foundation for the Arts.
1997	Co-author, *Chora L Works : A Collaboration between P. Eisenman & Jacques Derrida*, Monacelli Press, New York/London.
1998	Foundation, Bureau for Major Projects, Melbourne.
2000	3rd prize, virtual environmental design, International Competition ETH, Zurich.

Jörg Leeser (1967)
1986-97	Training, Ecole d'Architecture RWTH de Aix-la-Chapelle /Bartlett School of Architecture, London.
1994-98	Leeser Architecture Agency, New York.
1997-98	Design Director, *Intelligent Agent, Journal for Interactive Media*, New York.
1999-00	Collaboration, b&k+, Cologne.
2000	Agency BeL, with Anne-Juchen Bernardt, Cologne.
1998	Research, Rensselaer Polytechnic Institute, New York.
1999 ›	Teaching, École d'Architecture, RWTH de Aix-la-Chapelle.

www.leeser.com

LOT/EK (USA)
Founded in New York in 1993.

Ada Tolla (1964)
1989	Diploma in architecture, University of Naples.
1991	Diploma, Advanced Architectural Studies, Columbia University, New York.

Giuseppe Lignano (1963)
1989	Diploma in architecture, University of Naples.
1991	Diploma, Advanced Architectural Studies, Columbia University, New York.

2000	Installation, 'Mixer', with Henri Urbach Architecture and Joystick Nation.
	Authors, *Mixer*, with preface by Mark Robbins, Edizioni Press, New York.
2000›	Teaching, Parsons School of Design, New York.
2001	Authors, *Urban Scan*, with preface by Philip Nobel, PAP, New York.
	Installation, 'Inspiro-Trainer', MoMA, New York.
	Collection, San Francisco Museum of Modern Art.

www.lotekarchitecture.com

Mantiastudio (Italy)
Founded in Rome in 1999.

Giuseppe Mantia (1964)
1991	Diploma in architecture, Venice University Institute of Architecture.
	Collaboration, Gregotti Associati International Office, Milan, Venice.
1996	Foundation of No Where Architects, with Karl Amann, Amsterdam.
1998	Master of architecture, Berlage Institute, Amsterdam.
	Collaboration, Gonçalo Souza Byrne & Associates, Lisbon /De Architekten Cie., Amsterdam.
	Exhibitions, 'New Italian Blood', Stockholm /'Unlimited NL-G7', Galerie de Apple, Amsterdam /'The New Architecture', Cini Foundation, Venice /Biennale of Young Mediterranean and European Architects, Rome.
	Publication, *Studi Mantia*, Libreria Dedalo, Rome.

maO/emmeazero studio d'architettura (Italy)
Founded in Rome in 1996.

Tommaso Avellino (1966)
Frederico Cavalli (1966)
Massimo Ciuffini (1966)
Ketty Di Tardo (1968)
Alberto Iacovoni (1966)
Luca La Torre (1964)

1991-92	Collaboration, Ketoff et Petit studio, Paris.
1997-98	Audi Prize, 'Life in Movement'.
1998	Research scholarship in the Netherlands on 'The transformation of urban voids in the post-industrial town', Netherlands intervention policy.
1996	Doctorate, under the direction of Giorgio Muratore, Faculty of Architecture, University La Sapienza, Rome.
1998	Thesis prize, INU /DEI.
1999-00	Selection for Gerico :'0+20+20 giovani architetti Italiani', Rome (1999) /Prague (2000).
2000	Selection for Venice Architecture Biennale (with IaN+).
	Selection for Stanze aperte sulla giovane architettura Italiana, Order of Architects, Milan.
	Installation, 'Tappeto Volante', Orestiadi Foundation, Italian Ministry for Foreign Affairs, Rome (with Stalker).

J. Mayer H. Architekten (Germany)
Founded in Berlin in 1996.

Jürgen Mayer H. (1965)
	Training, University of Stuttgart.
	Training, The Cooper Union School of Architecture, New York.
	Training, Princeton University, Princeton, NJ.
›1996	Collaboration, Büro Prof. J. P. Kleihues, Berlin.
1996›	Teaching, Hochschule der Künste, Berlin.
2000	Teaching, Graduate School of Design, Harvard University, Cambridge, MA.

www.jmayerh.de

Minifie Nixon (Australia)

Founded in Melbourne in 1999.

Fiona Nixon (1968)

1991	Diploma in architecture, Royal Melbourne Institute of Technology.
1996-97	Teaching, La Salle College of the Arts, Singapore.
1999	Teaching, University of Melbourne.
1999 ›	Teaching, Royal Melbourne Institute of Technology.
1999	Master of technology (computing), Royal Melbourne Institute of Technology.

Paul Minifie (1965)

1992	Co-author, *Backlogue, Journal of the Half Time Club*, Volume One.
1993	Diploma in architecture, Royal Melbourne Institute of Technology.
1995 ›	Teaching, Royal Melbourne Institute of Technology.
1996	Master of architecture, Royal Melbourne Institute of Technology.

Pablo Molestina (Ecuador)

MDK Architekten Group (Germany)

Pablo Molestina (1955)

1976	Degree in architecture, Yale University, New Haven, USA.
1976	Training, Architectural Association, London.
1978	Training, Graduate School of Design, Harvard University, Cambridge, MA.
1979	Training, ILAUD, Urbino, Italy.
1980-82	Teaching, Design Program, Massachusetts Institute of Technology (MIT), Cambridge, MA.
1982	Master of architecture, MIT, Cambridge.
	Collaboration, Hassan Fathy, Egypt.
1989	Teaching, Housing Prototypes, MIT, Cambridge.
1991	Agency with Michael Kraus, Germany.
2000-01	Visiting professor, Bauhaus, Dessau, Germany.

Moussafir Architectes Associés (France)

Founded in Paris in 1992.

Jacques Moussafir (1957)

1984	Licentiate in history of art, Université Paris I.
1985-92	Collaboration, Bernard Kohn, Paris (Cité Judiciaire, Clermont-Ferrand) /Christian Hauvette, Henri Gaudin, Paris (Stade Charléty) /Dominique Perrault, Paris (TGB) /Francis Soler (CCIP).
1993	Diploma, École d'Architecture Paris-Tolbiac.
1996	Exhibition, 'Concours Perdus', Galerie Uzzan, Paris.
1997	Exhibition, 'À la recherche de la maison modèle', Association Périphériques, Paris.
2000-03	Member, National commission of the 1% dedicated to ornamental works on public buildings, Ministère de la Culture.

Willy Müller Arquitecto (Spain)

In association with THB Consulting, founded in Barcelona in 1997.

Willy Müller (1961)

1984	Degree in architecture, University of La Plata, Argentina.
1984-85	Teaching, FAU, University of La Plata, Argentina.
1987	Prize, Spanish National Design Competition, Valencia, Spain.
1988	Prize, International Design Competition, Shinkenchiku, Japan.
1993-94	Member of panel, Autografías exhibitions, Barcelona.
1995	Member of panel, Ferros exhibitions, COAC, Barcelona.
	Conceptualization, Antonio Bonnet Castellana exhibitions, COAC, Spanish Ministry of Development.
1996	Prize, 'Young Architects' exhibition, COAC.
	Co-director, Atelier Barcelona Barceloneta, Master La Grande Escala, Escuela Técnica Superior de Arquitectura, Barcelona.
1996	Teaching, Cinema y arquitectura, cycle IUA Conference, Barcelona.
1997-00	Teaching, Higher School of Architecture, International University of Catalonia.
1998	Co-founder of Metapolis, with Manuel Gausa and Vicente Gallart.
	Organization of 1st and 2nd Metapolis Festival of Architecture, Barcelona.
	Publication, *Met 0.1*, Actar, Barcelona /*Met 0.2*, Actar, Barcelona.
1999	Direction, Fingers studio, 'Polders, Islands, Build the Sea'.

www.willy-müller.com

MVRDV (Netherlands)

Founded in Rotterdam in 1991.

Winny Maas (1959)

1978-83	Training, landscaping, RHSTL, Boskoop, Netherlands.
1984-90	Training, Faculty of Architecture and Town Planning, Technical University of Delft.
	Collaboration, OMA /Ben van Berkel.
	Teaching, Architectural Association /Berlage Institute, Amsterdam /Technical Universities, Delft, Eindhoven, Wuppertal, Berlin, Barcelona, Oslo, Stuttgart, Bergen, Vienna, Lausanne, Graz /Architecture Academies, Amsterdam, Rotterdam, Tilburg, Groningen, Arnhem.

Jacob van Rijs (1964)

1984-90	Training, Faculty of Architecture and Town Planning, Technical University of Delft.
1983-84	Mention, Archiprix, The Hague Free Academy.
	Collaboration, OMA, Rotterdam.
	Teaching, Architectural Association /Berlage Institute, Amsterdam /Technical Universities, Delft, Eindhoven, Stuttgart, Karlsruhe /Architecture Academies, Amsterdam, Rotterdam, Tilburg, Arnhem.

Nathalie de Vries (1965)

1984-90	Training, Faculty of Architecture and Town Planning, Technical University of Delft.
	Collaboration, Ben van Berkel.
	Co-author, *Eating Brazil*, 010 Publishers, Rotterdam.
	Teaching, Berlage Institute, Amsterdam /Architecture Academy, Arnhem /Technical University, Delft.
1992	Authors, *Statics*, Office Publication.
1997	Concrete Award, Betonvereniging ('Villa VPRO' project).
	Merkelbach Prize, Amsterdam Fund for the Arts ('WoZoCo' project).
	Dudok Prize, Municipality of Hilversum.
1998	Authors, *FARMAX*, 010 Publishers, Rotterdam.
	National Steel Prize (mention) ('Double House'project).
1999	Authors, *MetaCITY/DATATOWN*, 010 Publishers, Rotterdam.
	Belmont Prize, Forberg Schneider Stiftung (Netherlands Pavilion Expo 2000).
	Finalist, VI Mies van der Rohe Award ('WoZoCo'project).
2000	Authors, *Costa Iberica*, Actar, Barcelona.
	Fritz Schumacher Prize, Hanover, Germany.
	1st Prize, J. A. van Eck, BNA, Amsterdam ('WoZoCo' project).
	Prize, International Media Art ('MetaCITY/DATATOWN' project).

Ibrahima N'Doye (France/Senegal)

Divides his working time between Paris and Dakar.

Ibrahima N'Doye (1973)

1999	Diploma, École d'Architecture Paris-Villemin.
2000	Exhibition, Institut Français d'Architecture, Paris.
	Mention, Europan-DOM competition (in association with the Caméléon agency).
2001	Diploma, CEAA Théories et projets de l'architecture, École d'Architecture Paris-la-Villette.

Naito Architects + Associates (Japan)

Founded in Tokyo in 1981.

Hiroshi Naito (1950)

1974	B. Arch., Waseda University, Tokyo.
	Murano Prize (for his degree project).
1974-76	Master of architecture, under the direction of Prof. Takamasa Yoshizaka, Waseda, Tokyo.
1976-78	Collaboration, Fernand Higueras, architect, Madrid.
1979-81	Collaboration, Kiyonori Kikutake, architect, Tokyo.
1986-88	Teaching, Waseda University, Tokyo.
1990-95	Teaching, Waseda University, Tokyo.
1993	Art Encouragement Prize, Japanese Ministry of Education.
	Prize, Architectural Institute of Japan for Design.
	Isoya Yoshida Memorial Prize.
1998	Kumamoto Landscape Prize.
	Selection for '100 Public Architecture', Japanese Ministry of Construction.
1998›	Teaching, University of Tokyo.

Taeg Nishimoto + Allied Architects (USA)

Founded in New York in 1989.

Taeg Nishimoto (1955)

1978	Degree in architecture, Waseda University, Tokyo.
1981	Master, Waseda University, Tokyo.
1983	Diploma, Graduate School of Design, Cornell University, Ithaca, New York.
1985>	Teaching, Columbia University, New York.
1989>	Teaching, Pratt Institute, New York.
1991	New York Chapter AIA's Design Award (for 'Super Pier - 1 + 2').
1993	Installation, 'Re-f(r)action 1', Galerie Rotunda, New York.
1995	Installation, 'Re-f(r)action 2', Pratt Institute, Brooklyn, New York.

Njiric + Njiric Arhitekti (Croatia)

Founded in Zagreb in 1996.

Helena Njiric (1963)

1987	Rector's Award (Rowing Club).
1989	Diploma in architecture, University of Zagreb.
1990-95	Independent architect, Zagreb.
1997-99	Jury, HAB, Weimar /ETSAB, Barcelona /TU, Vienna /AA, London /ETH, Zurich.
	Teaching, Amsterdam, Zagreb, Merano, Maribor, Gorizia, Brescia, Barcelona.
1998-99	Teaching, Technical University, Graz, Austria /University of Zagreb.

Hrvoje Njiric (1960)

1985	Rector's Award ('Pharmacy Museum' project)
1986	Diploma in architecture, University of Zagreb.
	Forest Edge House, APZ Award, Best Graduate in 1986.
1990-95	Independent architect, Zagreb.
1997-99	Jury, HAB, Weimar /ETSAB, Barcelona, /TU, Vienna, /AA, London /ETH, Zurich.
	Teaching, Amsterdam, Zagreb, Merano, Maribor, Gorizia, Brescia, Barcelona.
1998-99	Teaching, Technical University, Graz, Austria.
1999	Visiting professor, Technical University, Graz.

NL Architects (Netherlands)

Founded in Amsterdam in 1997.

Peter Bannenberg (1959)

1995	Diploma in architecture, Technical University, Delft.

Walter van Dijk (1962)

1991	Diploma in architecture, Technical University, Delft.

Kamiel Klaasse (1967)

1995	Diploma in architecture, Technical University, Delft.

Mark Linnemann (1962)

1991	Diploma in architecture, Technical University, Delft.
1998	Sofa Prize, 'Furniture of the Future' (with Eibert Draisma).
1993	2nd Prize, Urban Villa Hilversum (with Matthijs Bouw, Michiel Snelder).
1996	3rd Prize, Archiprix (for Parkhouse/Carstadt).
1999	Rietveld Prize (for 'WOS 8')
	Rotterdam Design Award.
	Prize, Bauwelt-Sonderpreis.
	Teaching, TU, Delft /TU, Eindhoven /Rotterdam Academy /Amsterdam Academy /TU, Vienna /Bartlett School, London /Berlage Institute, Amsterdam /ETH, Zurich /SCI-Arc, Los Angeles.

NMDA (USA)

(Neil Denari Architects, Incorporated)

Founded in Los Angeles in 1988.

Neil M. Denari (1957)

1980	B. Arch., University of Houston.
1982	M. Arch., Graduate School of Design, Harvard University, Cambridge, MA.
	Collaboration, Aerospatiale, Paris.
1983-88	Collaboration, James Stewart Polshek & Partners, New York.
1986-88	Teaching, Columbia University, New York.
1988-97	Teaching, Southern California Institute of Architecture, Los Angeles.
1990-92	Teaching, Shibaura Institute of Technology, Tokyo.
1993-95	Teaching, University of Texas, Arlington.
1994	Teaching, Bartlett School, London.
1995	Teaching, Columbia University, New York.
1996	Author, Interrupted Projections, Toto Publications, Tokyo.
	Prize, ID Magazine /Architectural Foundation of Los Angeles (for Galerie MA).
1997>	Director, Southern California Institute of Architecture, Los Angeles.
1999	Author, Gyroscopic Horizons, Princeton University Press, New York.

www.archined.nl/news/9803/denari_eng.html

NO.MAD Arquitectura (Spain)

Founded in Amsterdam in 1989, also in Madrid.

Eduardo Arroyo (1964)

Has travelled in 66 countries.

Has dived 372 times in different oceans.

Has lived in a 16th-century hotel in Paris, on a barge on a canal in Amsterdam, in a Tibetan monastery, on a volcano in eastern Iceland.

Author, Al otro lado del espejo.

Author, Territory (in preparation).

1988	Diploma in architecture, Escuela Técnica Superior de Madrid, specializing in town planning and construction.
1989-90	Collaboration, OMA Rem Koolhaas.
1996 >	Professor, Escuela Técnica Superior de Madrid.
1999	1st Prize for Architecture, CEOE, Spain.
	1st Prize for Construction, COAVN, Spain.
	Selected for the Spanish Architecture Biennale.
2000	Selected for the International Exhibition, Hanover.
	Selected for the Venice Architecture Biennale.
2000	Teaching, UBA, Buenos Aires /Universidad de Barcelona /University of Ferrara /Palermo /Alcalá.

NOX (Netherlands)

Founded in Rotterdam.

Lars Spuybroek (1959)

	B. Arch. (Honours), Technical University, Delft.
1989	1st Prize, Archiprix.
1991	Mart Stam Incentive Prize.
1991-95	Teaching, Technical University, Delft.
1992-95	Teaching, Tilburg Academy.
1993-95	Teaching, Amsterdam Academy.
1993-96	Teaching, Arnhem Academy.
1996	Teaching, Technical University, Eindhoven.
1997	Iakov Chernikov Prize.
	Teaching, master class on 'the media and architecture', Berlage Institute, Amsterdam (with Bert Mulder).
1998	Zeeuwse Architectuurprijs.
	Teaching, Columbia University, New York.
1999	Selected for the Mies van der Rohe Award.
	Teaching, summer master class, Netherlands Architecture Institute (with Robert Lang, ARUP).
2000	Selected for the Venice Architecture Biennale.
	Member of the jury, Prix de Rome.
2000-01	Teaching, Gesamthochschule, Kassel.
2000-02	Teaching, University of Westminster, London.
2001	Teaching, Columbia University, New York.